1985

The
Romantic
Impulse
in Victorian
Fiction

The
Romantic
Impulse
in Victorian
Fiction

DONALD D. STONE

Harvard University Press

Cambridge, Massachusetts

London, England

1980

Copyright © 1980 by the President and Fellows of Harvard College
All rights reserved
Printed in the United States of America
Publication of this book has been aided
by a grant from
the Andrew W. Mellon Foundation

Library of Congress Cataloging in Publication Data

Stone, Donald David.
The romantic impulse in Victorian fiction.

Includes bibliographical references and index.
1. English fiction—19th century—History and
criticism. 2. Romanticism—England. I. Title.
PR878.R73S7   823'.809   79-27736
ISBN 0-674-77932-0

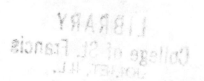

For Jerome H. and Elizabeth Buckley

Preface

    The extent and variety of the Romantic legacy to Victorian fiction are matters that have received surprisingly little attention; yet the young Charles Dickens, George Eliot, Anthony Trollope, Charlotte Brontë, George Meredith, Elizabeth Gaskell, and Benjamin Disraeli attained a sense both of their creative potential and of their artistic selfhood through the works and biographical examples of Byron and Wordsworth, Scott and Shelley, Coleridge and Carlyle, and Rousseau and Schiller—to name some of the more prominent sources of influence and inspiration. In George Eliot's work in particular the richness of the Romantic heritage can be seen; but even in a presumed anti-Romantic like Trollope an underlying Romantic sensibility can be detected. It was through my work on Trollope that I became aware of the importance of the Romantic impulse in Victorian fiction; and, puzzled that no one had treated this theme at book length before, I decided to examine the effect of that impulse on six additional novelists, whom I selected for the diversity and splendor of their achievements.

An earlier version of chapter 2 appeared in *The Worlds of Victorian Fiction*, Harvard English Studies, 6 (Cambridge, Mass.: Harvard University Press, 1975). I am grateful to the Department of English and American Language and Literature, Harvard University, for permission to reprint this article in its revised and expanded form.

There are many people and institutions to whom I owe considerable gratitude: first of all, to Gordon N. Ray and the John Simon Guggenheim Memorial Foundation for generously providing me with the time and confidence to see this study through; second, to Ruth apRoberts for her thorough and vigorous reading of the manuscript. To Robert and Vineta Colby, Robert Ginsberg, Wendy Martin, David Richter, and Michael Timko I am indebted for constructive readings and suggestions. To the staffs of the New York Public Library, the British Library, and the libraries of Queens College, Princeton University, Oxford University, and the University of California at Los Angeles, I acknowledge my continuing gratitude. And I wish to thank Frances LaVista and Thelma Silver, who, along with Rebecca Amann and Ida Pizzo of the Queens College Word Processing Center, typed the manuscript, and Camille Smith, who did the judicious editing.

Contents

The
Romantic
Impulse
in Victorian
Fiction

Introduction

---

*. . . the peculiar strength evolved by such writers as
Byron and Shelley, who, however mistaken they may be,
did yet give the world another heart and new pulses,
and so are we kept going. Blessed be those that
grease the wheels of the old world, insomuch as to
move on is better than to stand still.*

Tennyson

The extraordinary richness of the Victorian novel can be attributed in large part to the various literary traditions that converged just as the young George Eliot, Dickens, Trollope, the Brontës, and Meredith were commencing their reading careers. This legacy included the great eighteenth-century works of Fielding and Smollett, Richardson and Sterne, Defoe and Goldsmith, with their epic and mock-epic structures, their meticulous analyses of character as seen from tragic or ironical perspectives, their studies of man as an isolated or domesticated creature; the Gothic novel and the German romance with their extravagant appeals to nonrational modes of perception; and the importation of Rousseau's Romanticism in the form of the Jacobin novels of Godwin, Holcroft, and Bage, in which the idea of the natural goodness of man was made the basis for reformist principles. In addition, there was the impetus provided by the Romantic reinterpretation of Shakespeare as the apostle of Nature, defier of the rules of classicism, and pioneer diagnostician of the modern disease of self-consciousness; and there was the flourishing of interest in the old, "romantic" forms of literature—folk ballads, tales of chivalry, and variants of the *Arabian Nights* adventures. And above all, there was that native "burst of creative activity in our literature," in Matthew Arnold's phrase, which had taken place during "the first quarter of our century": Romantic poetry with its abundance of "energy" and "creative force." Individual Victorian novelists drew upon many or all of these literary sources, and upon nonliterary sources, too, which interacted with the literary influences. George Eliot's Evangelical training, for example, allowed for modes of thought and feeling that later gave her a sense of kinship with Schiller and Rousseau, and Elizabeth Gaskell's Unitarian upbringing contributed to the affinity she later felt with Wordsworth and Carlyle. For the great Victorian novelists, the literary past was a blessing rather than a burden, and Romanticism was the part of that past that perhaps affected them most strongly. Whether they accepted or reacted against the Romanticism of their early years, their attitudes toward those Romantic values enriched and intensified the individual and social dilemmas described in the novels.[1]

In speaking of a "Romantic impulse" in Victorian fiction, I wish to draw attention to two obvious, if not always sufficiently appreciated, facts: first, the great Victorian writers grew up during the period in which Romantic poetry and Scott's transformation of romance were being created and widely circulated; and second, whether the future novelists were bewitched or appalled by the new themes and styles, their sense of themselves as writers, as creators, was largely defined in terms of the Romantic images of Byron and Wordsworth, Shelley and Scott. That the Romantic poets provided the novelists with new subject matter—characters from humble or pastoral life, inspired by Crabbe and Wordsworth, for example, or willful heroes and submissive heroines drawn in the Byronic manner—and with new attitudes toward those subjects is of obvious importance; but perhaps even more significant was the new Romantic sense of the author as sage, as hero, as inspired genius, as magician imaginatively competing with reality rather than merely reflecting it in his works. George Henry Lewes's conception of the "true artist" draws upon this Romantic sense of the creative self: "He works according to the impulse from within, not according to the demand from without." The literary artist could thus be seen as a human deity, able to summon a new world into existence through the power of imagination. "This world was never meant for genius!" contended Edward Bulwer Lytton. "To exist, it must create another." But there was also the fearful sense of a Charlotte Brontë that the possessor of "the creative gift owns something of which he is not always master—something that at times strangely wills and works for itself."[2]

The Romantic impulse released the creative energies in many future Victorian novelists: it provided the impetus for Charlotte Brontë and her sisters to transform their childhood reading materials into a kingdom of fantasy, as well as for a presumed arch-realist like Anthony Trollope to fabricate a domain of forty-six novels whose characters (as he admitted in his *Autobiography*) he lived with night and day. By way of contrast, the realistic impulse of a Fielding, a Jane Austen, or a Thackeray dictated a different means of operation and a less exalted manner of regarding the creative act: for them it was essential to expose the false or "romantic" modes of perception encouraged by other novelists, and to replace the unrealistic conventions of the updated Cinderella, the Gothic, or the silver-fork novel with a clear-sighted sense of the limited possibilities of real life. To express this theme did not require the production of more than a half-dozen novels in all; no inner compulsion decreed that the realistic novelists should write to express their creative genius—let alone to "create another" world superior to that in which they found themselves. But Charlotte Brontë and Trollope sought to create characters as real as life, whom they recognized, nonetheless, to have been conjured up by a process of creative magic. One recalls that Trollope found "a touch of romance" in the "productiveness" of a novelist otherwise less fortunate than he; and he admitted to an enduring "power" within him that enabled him to feel "intimacy" with each of his invented characters.[3] While Brontë admired Thackeray for being in control of his creative impulse, she herself—like Trollope and Dickens—was at the mercy of energies that she felt could not, and ought not to, be resisted.

Although the term "Romantic" was not applied to the poets

as a group until late in the nineteenth century, the awareness that "a revolution in English literature" (as Charles Kingsley called it in 1853) had taken place was apparent as early as 1831 when Macaulay, reviewing Thomas Moore's biography of Byron, recognized that for all their differences and mutual antipathies Wordsworth and Byron were part of the same new literary current, characterized by imaginative reverence toward nature and a preoccupation with the singularities of self. "What Mr. Wordsworth had said like a recluse," said Macaulay, "Lord Byron said like a man of the world, with less profound feeling, but with more perspicuity, energy, and conciseness." In identifying Wordsworth and Byron as the two great modern English poets, Arnold singled out the figures whose achievements and personalities had drawn the strongest response from the young Victorian generation. "Wordsworth's poetry is great," Arnold affirmed, "because of the extraordinary power with which Wordsworth feels the joy offered to us in nature, the joy offered to us in the simple primary affections and duties; and because of the extraordinary power with which, in case after case, he shows us this joy, and renders it so as to make us share it." This transmission of the value of "joy," "nature," and "primary affections and duties" may account for what Arnold (in "Memorial Verses") deemed Wordsworth's "healing power," but the Romantic sense of the "power" wielded by the poet also stimulated Arnold's critical imagination. In this respect, Byron had the advantage over Wordsworth: where the older poet instilled a sense of reverential calm and passive wonder, Byron produced a more active and passionate response in his readers. While deploring Byron's insufficiency of "ideas" and "culture," Arnold nevertheless warmed to the thought of Byron as "the greatest natural force, the greatest elementary power, . . . which has appeared in our literature since Shakespeare."[4]

Of only slightly lesser potency than Wordsworth and Byron were the examples offered by Shelley and Scott. (Keats's appeal depended less on his personality than on his language and imagery, while Coleridge's influence was of a more philosophical than creative nature.) While Arnold, judging writers in terms of their power, wrote off Shelley as "ineffectual," and while Kingsley blamed him for inspiring "a spasmodic, vague, extravagant, effeminate, school of poetry," other Victorians saw Shelley as the incarnation of Carlyle's hero as poet: he alone among the English Romantics, according to Lewes, was a "seer" offering the "Gospel" of "Love and Hope" to the nineteenth century. For Browning, Shelley typified the subjective poet, as praised by the German Romantics, who looked within for guidance, not reflecting in his works the commonplace objective reality that everyone can see for himself, but instead apprehending "what God sees—the *Ideas* of Plato, seeds of creation lying burningly on the Divine hand."[5] For the Victorian critic and would-be creator, the Romantic revolution was embodied in those figures, Byron, Wordsworth, and Shelley, who bore the visible marks of power and genius.[6] That such superbly endowed poets had also come to appear the incarnations of egoism and diabolical willfulness, of violently heterodox or repellently reactionary views, may in part explain why Sir Walter Scott sustained a reputation throughout the nineteenth century as the one Romantic whose biography was as exemplary and "healthy" as his novels. Refusing to think of himself as a "genius," Scott was the decisive model for those Victorian writers raised in a religious atmosphere in which imaginative stimulation (such as one found in fiction or poetry) was deplored. As the creator of the "passive hero" who is contrasted with the defiant and antisocial heroes of romance, Scott was also the popularizer of the image of the artist as dutiful citizen, obedient inhabitant of a world of law and order whose values he shared with his protagonists. Yet, paradoxically, Scott also probably did more than any other Englishman to establish the validity of the "romantic" point of view for Victorian readers. In 1874 Robert Louis Stevenson claimed that "with Scott the Romantic movement, the movement of an extended curiosity and an enfranchised imagination has begun."[7]

Was there, then, such a thing as a "Romantic movement"? The great English Romantics were sufficiently individualistic to dislike being grouped with even one or two other poets; and the Victorians accordingly regarded them as individuals of varying power and achievement who happened to have written at a time when revolutions of an industrial, philosophical, and political nature were taking place.[8] To Carlyle in 1832, despairing over the absence from the scene of a poet-hero who would transcend and reverse the destructive and materialistic principles of the age, the Romantic poets seemed less like allies than like egoistic members of "Lake Schools, and Border-Thief Schools, and Cockney and Satanic Schools" who had now largely "burnt or smouldered themselves out, and left nothing but a wide-spread wreck of ashes, dust and cinders." Poets like Browning and Tennyson at about this time, however, found the Romantic poets inspiring role models. Sir Charles Tennyson tells us that after Byron's "death at Missolonghi, the fourteen-year-old Tennyson, who felt almost as though the world had come to an end, ran out to his beloved brook, threw himself down on the ground and carved upon the sandstone the words, 'BYRON IS DEAD' "; and six decades later the Poet-Laureate, who by then judged Keats and Wordsworth the finest of modern poets, still acknowledged in Byron "a genius superior to his own." Byron provided the original fiery stimulus to poetic ambition for Tennyson and Browning and was succeeded by the more salubrious examples of Wordsworth, the poet-healer, Shelley, the poet-sage, and Keats, the poet-craftsman.[9]

One is obliged to use labels like "Romantic" and "Victorian" in comparing the aims and achievements of Shelley and Browning, Keats and Tennyson, or Byron and Arnold, not only because the Victorian poets were aware of the influences on them, but because the manner in which they reacted to or resisted their predecessors' examples determined their own abilities to continue and develop as poets. It has often been suggested that Arnold's repudiation of Romantic themes and vision in his critical writings necessitated the virtual abandonment of his own creative instinct, which he recognized to be hopelessly Romantic.[10] In "The Scholar Gypsy," for example, Arnold found himself emotionally aligned with that Romantic tradition, with its defense of the powers of the imagination, which his intellect found wholly untenable; while in *Empedocles on Etna*, to his chagrin, he realized that he had come closer to Byron's *Manfred* than to the classic models he had hoped to emulate. The argument that Tennyson, in renouncing his Keatsian preoccupation with beautiful and sensuous effects of sound and imagery in favor of a more socially responsible position, renounced his own creative birthright and became a lesser poet seems far less convincing today than it did thirty years ago. It might, in fact, be contended that Tennyson's strength as a poet depends on the combination of his Romantic and his Victorian sympathies, that his later position as poet-sage arguing from his own instinctive feelings and speaking for mankind derives from the Romantic glorification of the poetic role. Where Keats had been on the brink of renouncing aesthetic in favor of humanistic and societal goals, Tennyson made that transition in his own career. An ironical distinction between Tennyson and his predecessors is that he was self-consciously Romantic in a way in which they were not; but the mature Romantics' "effort to create order out of experience individually acquired" was undertaken no less deliberately in *In Memoriam* than in *The Prelude*.[11] Browning's gradual repudiation of Shelley did not mean a cessation of Romantic currents in his life and work; he continued to trust firmly to instinct, for example, and to abhor all forms of tyranny, political or paternal; and he never disavowed the Shelleyan view of the artist as true diviner of the age. Browning did turn away from what he discerned to be Shelley's limitless faith in the potential of will to effect change on earth; but this was as much a rebuke of his own optimistic, and mildly blasphemous, youth as it was a critique of Shelley. The poet of *Pauline* recognized very early the need for a more cautious appraisal of the will, as well as for more objective poetic forms, than that provided by the author of *Epipsychidion:*

> I'll look within no more.
> I have too trusted my own lawless wants,
> Too trusted my vain self, vague intuition—
> Draining soul's wine alone in the still night . . .
> *(Pauline*, ll. 937–940)[12]

Yet, even as he rejected Shelley's ideas, Browning commanded, at the conclusion of *Pauline*, that the "sun-treader" "be to all what thou hast been to me!" (l. 1028). Certainly, the premise that a "Romantic" temptation, or danger, or "movement," existed must be accepted if the genesis and evolution of Victorian poetry are to be understood.

In approaching the Victorian novel, however, one should be guarded in the use of the term "Romantic"—or at least conscious of its slippery meaning.[13] Drawing upon so many literary traditions, the Victorian novelist was affected by the themes of chivalric and Eastern romance as well as by those of Romantic poetry; and the resultant combination of romance and Romanticism is often so tangled as to make it difficult to dissociate one from the other. If the basic premise of romance is that individual wish-fulfillment may be achieved in defiance of the laws of probability and reality, the prerogative of the Romantic imagination is similarly to deny reality, or any material strictures, in favor of an individual intuition of some higher truth. (One can see the Romantic sensibility of Coleridge and Newman already active in their youthful willingness to see in the *Arabian Nights* a realm of wonder more vast and real than the world grasped by mere sense experience.) The labeling of the poets as "Romantic" is an acknowledgment not only of their kinship with the German and French Romantic schools but of their connection with the native English romance and ballad traditions as well. The role of the imagination, like the conception of the poet-seer, may have been formulated from German sources, yet the object of the imagination remained mostly British. But where the Victorian poets were influenced by the Romantic poets as fellow craftsmen, the Victorian novelists were not so much influenced as inspired by the Romantic poets' creative examples. And here one must stress the fact that Romanticism entailed a variety of competing and contradictory images. The Romantic poets differed from each other in crucial respects; and each individual poet presented a different face to different admirers. Hence, to speak of Byronic affinities in Charlotte Brontë is not the same as to speak of a Byronic strain in Trollope. The histrionic fabricator of *Childe Harold's Pilgrimage* and *Lara* differs from the ironist of *Don Juan* who mocks self and society alike; the same poet who inspired a score of romantic love plots on the Corsair-and-devoted-slave-maiden pattern also encouraged the development of the anti-hero. The Wordsworth of the Victorian novelists, for that matter, was more likely to be the author of *The Excursion* and the poems of humble life, which they read in their youth, than the creator of *The Prelude*, which was not published until 1850.

As far as the Victorians were concerned, no such thing as a homogeneous Romantic impulse existed. Just as there were varieties of Romantic narrative modes to choose among—from the homely realism and measured heroic couplets of Crabbe's verse to the extravagant mixture of hyperbole and allusiveness of Carlyle's seriocomic *Sartor Resartus*—so too was there within each Romantic author a choice of styles and personas. One might speak of the pre-Victorian strain in some Romantics as well as of the Romantic impulse in the Victorians; whereas Browning endeavored in good faith, for a time, to recreate Shelley in his own earnestly Victorian image, Wordsworth and Coleridge, conversely, often gave signs of being Victorian in their support for the authoritarian and domestic structures despised by Shelley. Browning's and Lewes's Shelley (together with the Byron of Disraeli and John Morley) was the model of progressive radicalism, while Wordsworth and Coleridge were claimed as apostles of political and religious conservatism; the spirit of progress and the quest for permanence, which John Stuart Mill identified as the dominant countertendencies of the age, can both be legitimately defined as Romantic. The tendency of Romanticism to diverge in opposite directions was apparent from the start. The self-willed Byronic hero and the self-made industrialist were both indebted to the revolutionary spirit that liberated the individual from those moribund rules and dictates of the past which constrained his attempt at self-realization. Jeremy Bentham no less than Byron (or Wordsworth in the Preface to *Lyrical Ballads*, for that matter) expressed dissatisfaction with outworn conventions and provided a philosophical rationale for the release of individualist energies.[14] The historical release of individual energy in a manner unsuspected by the young Wordsworth and Coleridge—into the destructive forces of the French Revolution or the competitive spirit of the Industrial Revolution —horrified the two poets and served to push them toward a political position that seemed like apostasy to many of their contemporaries. From another point of view, however, Wordsworth and Coleridge affirmed faith in the invisible but permanent structures that inspire human reverence—church, nation, nature —hence pointing the way to the Oxford Movement; and in the process they turned their criticisms against the ravages of the Industrial Revolution at home, provoking a Romantic reaction against the misapplication of individual initiative.[15]

That the Romantics may be seen as both the liberators of the individual imagination and the first to warn against the excesses of individualism is an inescapable paradox. Romanticism can be said to embody rebelliousness and reverence, a principle of dynamic growth and the spirit of conservation, Prometheanism and Stoicism, the will to create and that fear of the will which paralyzes creativity. Modern students of Romanticism have tended to rally behind one or the other Romantic poles: the Byronic refusal to serve anything other than the dictates of the ego or the Wordsworthian withdrawal into an inner world of Vision. For those who regard Wordsworth as the key Romantic —the "Evangelist" of a religion of internalized apocalypse— Byron is clearly an embarrassment, a Satanic proponent of "negative romanticism," the spirit of defiance that has not accepted or will not accept the Romantic principle of integration.[16] But for those who find in Byron a modern existential hero, affirming his free will and refusing to lose his ego in nature or in some mystic vision of society or the universe, Wordsworth seems a sorry case of compromise and self-negation. (Shelley's dual status as visionary and political radical, seeking the transformation of society through the expansion of the sympathizing powers of the imagination, explains why he seemed so attractive to Lewes and other Victorian liberals, who otherwise associated Romanticism with forms of social irresponsibility.) For the budding Victorian writer, both Romantic poles offered incentives toward their own future creativity. Whereas Trollope and Charlotte Brontë associated Byron's rebellious energies with the Promethean will to create,[17] a novelist like Elizabeth Gaskell needed a more reverential model, such as Wordsworth provided, to allow her to overcome her guilt about heeding the clamoring of her artistic instinct.

Whereas Romanticism often posed a threat to the Victorian poets by allowing them to view themselves in an inflated manner —exalted above or alienated from their fellow men, it provided a magnificent opportunity to the Victorian novelists, who created a literary form large and supple enough to absorb Romanticism without becoming totally Romantic. In directing the individual away from egoistic or false heroic aims and toward communal and domestic goals—the great subject of Victorian fiction—the Victorian novelists continued a tendency that was already implicit in one aspect of Romanticism.[18] However, in weighing the rights of the individual against the claims of society, in permitting the visionary aims of its protagonists to carry some weight, the Victorian novel allowed for that richness of texture, that strength of ethical and imaginative concern, which informs the masterpieces of Dickens, Eliot, Trollope, and the others. Despite, or because of, its emphasis on being true to life, the Victorian novel allowed a presentation of reality wide enough to include Romantic values and romantic fancies as part of the total picture; the novel form made it possible to portray men and women in the context of their social and domestic spheres, while at the same time it permitted the reader to enter the minds of the characters and share their occasional desires to transcend that context. One should not forget that the Victorian novelists were, in the main, outsiders, cut off from the communal and domestic ties they celebrated; and they were outsiders as much because they were artists as because they had been born or lived outside the pale of Victorian respectability.[19]

All seven of the novelists I consider in this book retained a lifelong ambivalence toward Romanticism and the Romantic idols of their childhood: I have selected them for examination because of the vigor and variety of means by which they redefined, reworked, and reacted against Romantic values. In their creative evolution, they were immeasurably aided by the examples of two Scotsmen in transmuting Romanticism into Victorian themes and values. It was Scott and Carlyle, above all others, who conditioned the Victorian attitude, positively and negatively, toward Romanticism and romance. (The novelists' varying attitudes toward Byron, Wordsworth, and Shelley will be spotlighted in the individual chapters.) Following the section devoted to Scott and Carlyle, I have chosen briefly to discuss three important Victorian novelists, not treated later in the book for reasons of space, whose differing attitudes toward Romanticism are echoed in many of the figures considered at length. Much of what holds true for Thackeray, a dedicated realist, Bulwer Lytton, a second-hand Romantic, and Emily Brontë, a thoroughgoing Romantic, applies to Trollope, Disraeli, and Charlotte Brontë. In their contrasting views and novels may be seen the strengths and weaknesses of the Romantic impulse.

SCOTT AND CARLYLE

Scott's pivotal position in the development of the Victorian novel derives from his search for a literary form that would accommodate the opposing Romantic poles of rebellion and reverence. As the poet of *Marmion* and *The Lady of the Lake,* he admitted to a sympathy for his rogue-heroes and defiant Scottish Clansmen (the products of what Carlyle contemptuously called the "Border-Thief School" of Romantic poetry): "a robber or Captain of Banditti never comes across me," he declared, "but he becomes my hero."[20] Yet for all his immersion in the folk ballads of his native land, for all his delight with the chivalric romances of Ariosto and the German supernatural romances, Scott was equally a descendent of eighteenth-century empiricist and rationalist traditions that affirmed trust in common sense and respected the machinery set up to maintain law and security within society. Scott's sensibility contained a credulous and imaginative streak, which directed him to be first a collector of romantic ballads, then a creator of romantic poetry, and finally the supreme romantic novelist of the age; but it also contained a dutiful and self-denying streak, which found expression in his life as lawyer, magistrate, and honorable citizen. Robert Kiely has argued that in the contrast between the Highlanders' dangerous individualism and the Lowlanders' law-abiding attitudes that we find in the Waverley novels Scott presents "two versions of reality, one of which is ultimately repudiated in favor of the other. In the end, what seems most stimulating to his creative imagination is almost invariably that which is unacceptable to his reason."[21] I suggest that Scott may instead be offering two versions of Romanticism: a Burke-derived loyalty to the structures of political and religious restraint, and an almost Byronic fascination with the disruptive energies of the individual.

Coleridge acknowledged this "contest between the two great

moving principles of social humanity" in Scott's novels, although he mistook the proponents of one cause for the defenders of the other: for him it was the Clansmen—plus the Saxons in *Ivanhoe* and the supporters of the Stuart cause in *Waverley*—who represented "religious adherence to the past and the ancient, the desire and the admiration of permanence," while their opponents, Normans or English Whigs, represented "the passion for increase of knowledge, for truth, as the offspring of reason—in short, the mighty instincts of *progression* and *free agency*."[22] It is a typically Romantic confusion on Coleridge's part that the individualists should seem the defenders of "permanence" while their law-abiding antagonists should be the agents of "progression and free agency," but it is a confusion that Scott himself occasionally shared and helped perpetuate. For so long as his Romantic imagination was tempted to side with the rebellious individual even though his reason supported the claims of society, Scott was obliged to associate the feudal loyalties of the Clansmen with Burkean Toryism. Conversely, however, his tendency to turn his fictional heroes away from their "romantic" delusions was accompanied by the countergesture—which the Victorian novelists were to emulate—of allowing Edward Waverley, Frank Osbaldistone, and company to settle for a new form of romance, rooted in domestic affections and civil responsibilities. William Hazlitt said of Scott what later commentators observed of Dickens and George Eliot: "Sir Walter has found out (oh, rare discovery) that facts are better than fiction; that there is no romance like the romance of real life."[23]

Reviewing his own novels under the cover of anonymity, Scott proudly drew attention to their "air of distinct reality": although they contain heroes who are invariably passive, as he admitted, the "Historical Romances" allow the novelist to treat subjects "in a spirit of delineation at once faithful and striking."[24] Given his dual nature, Scott was always attracted by true stories that seemed preposterously romantic ("romantic" in the old sense of the word, as defined in the *OED*, meaning "of a fabulous or fictitious nature; having no foundation in fact"). *Guy Mannering*, *The Heart of Midlothian*, and *The Bride of Lammermoor*, for example, were based on unlikely but actual events. Planning his biography of Napoleon, Scott exulted in a "wonderful" project

"in which every incident shall be incredible and yet strictly true
—a work recalling recollections with which the ears of this
generation once tingled, and which shall be read by our children
with an admiration approaching to incredulity." Scott's relish for
"wonderful" subjects extended to his enthusiasm for the Romantic poets' excursions into romance, such as Coleridge's
"Christabel" or Wordsworth's "Rob Roy's Grave" (which preceded by twelve years Scott's fictional treatment of Rob Roy),
and it affected his celebration of his Romantic contemporaries.
Scott eulogized Byron in particular as if the poet had been a
bandit-hero in one of his own novels: "That mighty Genius,
which walked among men as something superior to ordinary
mortality, and whose powers we beheld with wonder, and something approaching to terror, as if we knew not whether they were
of good or evil."[25]

Much as Scott admired Byron, his own life, as chronicled in
J. G. Lockhart's biography, was markedly different from Byron's,
as related by Thomas Moore. Where Byron had been the incarnation of the man of "genius," prone to rebellious and heterodox views and actions, defiant of social norms and laws, Scott
appeared to the Victorians as the quintessential artist as gentleman and good citizen, loyal to the Hanoverian monarchy (despite
his Stuart sympathies) and conspicuously honorable in the payment of his financial debts. Scott's example did much to neutralize
the image of the artist as popularized in Moore's biography: just
as he did more than any novelist before him to make the novel a
respectable genre that could be read in even the most religious of
households, so in his life he did much to counter the popular prejudice against the artist-figure and the dangerous implications of
the imagination. Scott's attainment of self-mastery has been elo-
quently praised by his most recent biographer, Edgar Johnson:
"By nature strongly emotional, even obstinately willful, Scott
molded himself into a man of reason amenable to logical judgment and control. Ultimately he proved able to say of himself,
and with truth, 'My feelings are rather guided by reflection than
impulse.' "[26] Scott's lack of egoism (which Hazlitt especially
praised) set him apart from Byron and Wordsworth; he would
never have considered himself superior to the age he lived in,
and rather than reject the conventions and literary traditions of

the past, he repeatedly paid homage to them—even as he respected the new literary realism of a Jane Austen or a Maria Edgeworth. In *Redgauntlet* (1824), perhaps the most autobiographical of his novels, Scott hinted at his sense of the therapeutic nature of the literary process: "The exercise of the pen [Darsie Latimer confesses to his Journal] seems to act as a sedative upon my own agitated thoughts and tumultuous passions." Although Romantic themes and figures may inspire one to want to create, the actual writing process serves to exorcise those "vague fears, wild expectations, and undigested schemes": "by arresting them as they flit across the mind, by throwing them on paper, and even by that mechanical act compelling ourselves to consider them with scrupulous and minute attention, we may perhaps escape becoming the dupes of our own excited imagination; just as a young horse is cured of the vice of starting, by being made to stand still and look for some time without any interruption at the cause of its terror."[27] Latimer's discovery is an acknowledgment of the underlying thesis of Scott's novels— the tendency of romance to dissolve once it is examined up close —just as his adventures up to the moment of that discovery form part of the legacy of romantic realism that Scott bestowed on the Victorian novel.

Redgauntlet contains a later version of the basic pattern of *Waverley* (1814) and *Rob Roy* (1817): a hero of imaginative cast of mind, nourished by the romantic fancies of the literature of chivalry (Frank Osbaldistone in *Rob Roy*, having translated Ariosto into English, hopes to translate Ariosto's themes into practice), learns through experience to reject those fancies in favor of adult responsibilities. All three novels deal with attempts to restore the Stuarts to the throne, but what initially appears to be a "romantic" cause fit for the pages of Ariosto as well as Ann Radcliffe—the attempt to crown a "hero of romance" with the help of Highlanders who resemble "banditti" —turns into a futile expenditure of energy and a cause of human misery. On close examination, the romantic leaders seem to be rash, ambitious men, while many of their followers appear suspiciously like plunderers for whom the Stuart cause is a pretext for self-aggrandizement. Scott pursued the flawed nature of chivalric heroism in *A Legend of Montrose* (1819), in which support for the Stuarts serves as a cover for personal ambition and as an outlet for clan vendettas. In *Waverley* the young protagonist awakens from what Scott calls "the romance of his life" to face "its real history"; and his enlightenment is demonstrated in his turning away from the adventurous heroine Flora MacIvor, "precisely the character to fascinate a youth of romantic imagination," to the more domestic-minded Rose Bradwardine, whose "very soul [as Flora observes] is in home."[28] Waverley's allegiance shifts from feudal to domestic ties; and while the Highlander phase of his life allows him to give way to his "poetic" and "impulsive" nature, his later career is imbued with a new, securer version of romance. Scott developed this emergent theme in the novel that succeeded *Waverley: Guy Mannering* (1815) is a hymn to domesticity, in which truth is proven stranger than romantic fiction.

Scott's later novels reveal his dual impulse to search for new sources of romantic material even while determining, in the end, to deflate or disavow the excesses and implications of romanticism. The quest for romantic subjects led him to exotic places (Zetland in *The Pirate*, 1822; Palestine in *The Talisman*, 1825) and adventurous periods (twelfth-century England in *Ivanhoe*, 1820; fifteenth-century France in *Quentin Durward*, 1823), and it led him to create romantic Amazons in the spirit of Ariosto in Flora MacIvor and Diana Vernon (in *Rob Roy*) as well as tragic heroines in the manner of Richardson's Clarissa in Lucy Ashton (*The Bride of Lammermoor*, 1819) and Clara Mowbray (*St. Ronan's Well*, 1824).[29] The repeated discovery of the insubstantiality of romantic fancies when exposed to the light of experience did not deter Scott from looking for more and more romantic-seeming topics—or from writing increasingly disenchanted novels. *A Legend of Montrose*, which exposed the flimsiness of chivalric pretensions in his native Scotland, was followed by *Ivanhoe*, where, despite all the fine speeches and colorful adventures that represent chivalric "glory" in action, the reader is liable to side with the outsider Rebecca, who deems the career of the knights "a life spent miserably that ye may make others miserable." While Richard the Lion-Hearted and his followers pursue a life of glory, the respect for law and domestic security at home are undermined. *The Talisman* may be read as a vale-

dictory attempt to celebrate chivalric honor in its most appropriate setting—the Palestine of the Crusaders—but here, ironically,
it is the Moslem Saladin whose prudence and generosity and
healing ability are more admirable than the frenzied ambitions
of most of Richard's disputatious knights.[30] A number of late
Scott novels also seem like more explicitly disillusioned variations on early works. The romantically doomed lovers of *The
Bride of Lammermoor* are echoed in Clara Mowbray and Francis
Tyrrel of *St. Ronan's Well,* but the pathos of their forbidden
love is made to seem grotesque by being set against the comic
world of the nonromantic figures who throng to the spa where
the novel takes place. Scott admitted in his Preface to having
attempted a work in the style of Jane Austen, but the result is
an uncomfortable (although sometimes dramatically affecting)
linking of the plot of *Clarissa* with the setting of the Bath scenes
in Smollett's *Humphry Clinker.* In *Redgauntlet* the Stuart cause
of *Waverley* is revived as travesty—the desperate measures of
madmen on behalf of a Pretender (who as a young man had
answered Waverley's "ideas of a hero of romance") now pre-
maturely aged as a result of a life of self-indulgence and self-
will. Perhaps the saddest example of the deflation of romantic
idealism in Scott is Minna Troil in *The Pirate.* Her loss of illusions means not an awakening to adult responsibilities and
domestic happiness, as in Waverley's case, but a blasting of her
very nature: "gifted with such depth of feeling and enthusiasm,
yet doomed to see both blighted in early youth, because, with
the inexperience of a disposition equally romantic and ignorant,
she had built the fabric of her happiness on a quicksand instead
of a rock."[31]

Scott's hold on the Victorians was as contradictory as his own
nature: they could abandon themselves to the romantic adventures and characters of his books; they could interpret his works
as reactions against the sort of romanticism that might otherwise
offend their sensibilities; and they could see in the novels a
transmutation of Romantic values into the realm of everyday
experience. It was Scott, of all his contemporaries, who did most
to neutralize the negative implications of the Romantic imagination, yet it was also Scott who was hailed by Robert Louis
Stevenson and William Ernest Henley as the key figure in the

Romantic movement, the liberator of the imagination. Scott was surely instrumental in transforming the meaning of the word "romantic" (a term of abuse, as Ian Jack notes, which in 1805 referred to "the dangerous ascendancy of the imagination over the judgment")[32] from a negative to a positive value among nineteenth-century readers. "Romantic" may refer to doomed causes in his novels and poems, but it also applies to Edinburgh ("mine own romantic town!" he calls her in *Marmion*) and the Lake Country (in *Guy Mannering*), to youthful feelings and generous ideals, and to the desire to dignify experience wherever possible.

Scott's legacy to the Victorian novelists was enormous.[33] He opened up the realm of the imagination to future novelists who, out of commonsensical or religious motives, might otherwise have scorned or feared the medium of fiction; and he made the craft of fiction respectable on financial as well as social grounds. Moreover, he provided a structural model for the novel in which the demands of the individual are made subservient to the needs of society, to the rule of law, to the prerogative of property, and to the context of history. Walter Bagehot astutely drew attention in 1858 to Scott's combination of "matter-of-fact sagacity," his eye for concrete detail, and his "romantic imagination," which colors his presentation of characters and story.[34] Scott brought romance down to earth, brought his individuals out of the clouds of romantic myth, dispelling in the process illusions of human potentiality such as the Romantics had favored. But he also allowed for the depiction of romantic themes and characters such as, for example, Trollope's chivalric-minded elder gentlemen or Dickens's and Elizabeth Gaskell's feudal-minded loyal servants. One finds Scott's traces both in the inflated romantic Toryism of Disraeli's political novels and in the deflation of a romantic Pretender in Meredith's *Harry Richmond;* and when Dickens or Eliot, Thackeray or Pater turned to the writing of historical fiction, each followed the same pattern of focusing on the conflicting loyalties and the inevitable (and often sorrowful) changes that accompany the transition from past to present. R. H. Hutton's view that Scott's works "are pivoted on public rather than mere private interests and passions," and that his main characters are intentionally passive so that we can see the contending forces of history as they affect the characters, rather than the way the characters affect history, can be applied to the aim of much Victorian fiction in which hero and heroine are made subservient to the world they live in. One remembers Henry James's complaint about *Middlemarch* that Dorothea Brooke is subordinated to the community rather than made the cause for the other characters' existence (as would happen in a James novel); but Eliot's masterpiece is the ultimate and happiest product of Scott's search for a form that would accommodate individual Romantic ideals to a microcosmic world threatened by change.[35]

Not all Victorians, however, regarded Scott's example as salutary. In 1828 Frederick Denison Maurice sounded a protest that Carlyle was to repeat ten years later: "he knows what is, but not how or why it is so. He has seen the outward, but he has not connected it with that which is within." From a religious point of view, Maurice considered Scott's novels deficient in the "moral" qualities he found in the poetry of Shelley and Wordsworth: the moral author's works, contends Maurice, oblige his readers to disregard the objective world and "have the effect of flinging men back upon themselves; of forcing them to look within for the higher principles of their existence; of teaching them that the only happiness, and the only virtue, are to be found by submitting themselves uniformly to the dictates of duty, and by aiming and struggling always towards a better state of being than that which ourselves, or those around us, have hitherto attained." Because he dwells on man's external qualities—and denies him the power of will—Scott lacks the ability to "influence" readers that Shelley and Wordsworth possess. Maurice betrays his Romantic bias by quoting the famous lines from *Julian and Maddalo* beginning "It is our will / which thus enchains us to permitted ill." Carlyle's important attack on Scott picks up on Maurice's charge that the novelist lacked a Shelleyan religious dimension. Responding to Lockhart's recently published biography, Carlyle bemoaned the fact that Scott's "life was worldly; his ambitions were worldly. There is nothing spiritual in him; all is economical, material, of the earth earthy." That which three years later George Henry Lewes was to claim as Shelley's achievement, Carlyle found nonexistent in Scott: the possession of a "doctrine," a grasp of life's great mystery. The "highest literary man" of the nineteenth century had "no message whatever to deliver to the world," was content merely to amuse his readers with picturesque descriptions and lively adventures.[36]

Carlyle's tribute to the "veneration of great men," which opens his Scott essay, is symptomatic of the difference between himself and his great Scottish countryman. The two writers shared a love for Goethe and for German literature—Scott translated *Götz von Berlichingen* and German ballads; Carlyle, *Wilhelm Meister's Apprenticeship* and German romances—and received similar training in eighteenth-century precepts of common sense and rationalism. Nonetheless, Carlyle's Calvinist heritage and Romantic worship of genius combined to form a sensibility that was the antithesis of Scott's. Where the novelist was generous, tolerant, and free of egoism to the point of virtual self-effacement in his literary creations, Carlyle was impatient, dogmatic, and obsessed with the sort of heroic ideal that Scott felt to be a charming attribute of youth but a handicap to one's growth toward maturity. Where Scott's protagonists learn to resign their will and submit to an ethic of civil responsibility, Carlyle's heroes are superior to circumstances: their mission is to overcome disorder, to triumph over chance and chaos. For Scott history demonstrates how men are the products of changing times, while for Carlyle "History is the essence of innumerable biographies."[37] In the early essay "Signs of the Times" (1829), Carlyle condemned the decline of belief in "individual endeavour" and "wonder," blaming the mechanistic theory that subordinated man to a world in which his will is of no avail: "For it is the 'force of circumstances' that does everything [in this false view]; the force of one man can do nothing." Scott's characters submit to a context of objective reality that for Carlyle has no validity; his fictional world, thus, reflects the despair of modern men who "have lost their belief in the Invisible, and believe, and hope, and work only in the Visible." In recognizing that his was "not a Religious age," Carlyle did not intend to deceive himself and his readers into believing that extinct deities could be restored to life: what he wanted, as he affirmed in *Sartor Resartus* (1830–31), was "a new Mythus."[38] But in order for new, genuine values to be revered, the old and present-day allegiance to shams had to be swept away. Scott had erred in acquiescing to a fiction of reality; what Carlyle's readers and heroes alike had to do was to follow his own example of first tearing down and then rebuilding reality in conformance with his own, Carlyle's, divinely inspired needs. In this respect, Scott's culpability, in Carlyle's eyes, was exceeded by that of another and greater Romantic figure, Byron.

For all their preoccupation with self, the Romantics by and large nourished the happy illusion that they were representative (if also inspired) men whose perceptions had been granted them so that, having transformed their own nature, they could preach the message of self-transformation to others. Scott's unwillingness to glorify his ego and Byron's refusal to see himself without a sense of ironical self-deflation not only set them apart from the authors of *The Prelude* and *Sartor Resartus* but also exposed them to attack from their fellow Romantics. Carlyle's attitude toward Byron is of crucial importance in the evolution of both his message and his self-image: before Carlyle could reject Byron he had to reject the rebellious and self-mocking Byronic aspect of his own nature. One of Carlyle's discarded ambitions was to be a novelist: as early as 1822 he was thinking of writing a novel with an autobiographical hero of a Byronic (and Wertherian) cast of mind who repudiates the world but is saved by a loving heroine.[39] The theme of a sensitive, despairing protagonist hoping to be redeemed by love—which Carlyle returned to in the unfinished *Wotton Reinfred*—was a staple of both Romantic and early Victorian fiction; but it is of biographical significance that whereas the young Carlyle identified with Byron, the mature Carlyle expressed contempt for both the novel form that he had been unable to master and the Byronic characteristics that he had overcome. "Carlyle read and criticized Byron as a contemporary," as Charles R. Sanders reminds us, "and in many important respects, as one Romantic speaking of a fellow Romantic."[40] But where Byron was justified, in Carlyle's view, in rebelling against the false values of the age (the values that Scott, to his discredit, accepted), he erred in two instances: in allowing himself to become a self-indulgent artist and in dying before he could pass through his defiant phase.

Carlyle's expressions of grief at Byron's death are sincere indications of his sense that the most highly endowed of the English Romantics—"the noblest spirit in Europe," whose loss affected him as if they had been brothers—had died before he could become the English Goethe, the very hero-poet England needed. Byron had memorably uttered the "Everlasting No," but was cut off before having the chance to say the "Everlasting Yea"; he had embodied Romantic Prometheanism but had not matured sufficiently to accept, or to help create, the principle of Romantic quiescence.[41] Had Byron lived on, however, he would have had to shed more than his rebelliousness to satisfy Carlyle: he would have had to take himself more seriously as an artist, so seriously, perhaps, that he might have been obliged to abandon his artistic calling. A year after Byron's death, Carlyle warned his fiancée Jane Welsh "against narrowing the basis of her life by making 'Literature' written large her all-in-all. He himself had had to learn this lesson at a high cost." The pursuit of "Literature" meant a neglect of duty, women writers, Carlyle charged, forsake their "household and social duties," while "Byron and all strong souls" cut themselves off from "life" and "become discontented and despicable, or wretched and dangerous."[42] Carlyle's Puritanical mistrust of the artist's life, his deep-seated suspicion that it implied a surrender to egoism and a repudiation of duty, contended with his youthful conviction of the superiority of literary genius; and the gradual change in his choice of heroes, from Goethe to Frederick the Great, indicates something of his complex combination of Puritanism and Romanticism.

There is little point in denying Carlyle's basic Romanticism—despite the embarrassment of those who would prefer to see his good qualities defined as Romantic and his bad ones as Victorian or Calvinist. M. H. Abrams, who recently selected Carlyle's phrase "Natural Supernaturalism" as the title for his stimulating book on Romantic theodicy, sees in *Past and Present* the attempt to transfer to the historical sphere the basic Romantic pattern of "alienation and reintegration." Carlyle's quintessentially Romantic attempt "to reconstitute the grounds of hope" led to a call for "strenuous economic activism" of a rather different nature from Wordsworth's "visionary quietism"; but even Carlyle's emphasis on socially productive action rather than contemplation may be seen as an outgrowth of Romantic ambitions toward participation in life that were already evident in Shelley and Byron. Carlyle's specifically Romantic characteristics include his reaction against the eighteenth-century mechanistic view of man and the universe, his faith in instinct and the will and the right of genius to fashion rules out of its own divinely ordained needs, and his sense that the external world is less substantial than the Invisible realm of wonder.[43] However, Carlyle's Romanticism includes negative aspects too. His anti-intellectualism and his reliance upon instinct are aligned, as John Morley noted, with Rousseau's similar demonstration of that "cruelty inherent in sentimentalism, when circumstances draw away the mask": "We begin with introspection and the Eternities, and end in blood and iron." The apostle of "reverence" and work and common sense, Morley admits, has spoken to convictions deep-seated in the average Englishman; but as the apologist for the heroic will, he has also become the spokesman for "those whom steady self-reliance and thrifty self-securing and a firm eye to the main chance have got successfully on in the world." The connection between the Romantic imagination and the "language of power," so brilliantly established by Hazlitt in his study of *Coriolanus,* applies to Carlyle's obsession with hero-worship. The imagination is an "aristocratic" faculty, and hence the poetic principle is "anti-levelling": "Poetry is right-royal. It puts the individual for the species, the one above the infinite many, might before right." The imagination ultimately leads us to side rather with "oppressor than oppressed."[44] The process, in other words, by which the humane young Carlyle turned into the reactionary Chelsea sage perhaps reflects a fundamental contradiction in Romanticism itself.

Carlyle's first heroes were poets, above all Goethe, whose Olympian self-mastery Carlyle was to hold up as model for future writers. "This man rules, and is not ruled," he proclaimed in 1827; "his faculties and feelings are not fettered or prostrated under the iron sway of Passion, but led and guided in kindly union under the mild sway of Reason." This respect for energies kept under control would later inform Carlyle's sense of the hero as leader or king; but one should also note at this stage his Romantic fascination with those same disruptive energies, as illustrated in his admiration for Byron and for Schiller's Karl

Moor. Of the hero of *The Robbers*, Carlyle declared, "there is a towering grandeur about him, a whirlwind force of passion and of will, which catches our hearts, and puts the scruples of criticism to silence."[45] For the young Carlyle the poet's life was his message: Goethe's outgrowing of his Wertherian phase was the pattern for other writers, like Carlyle himself, to follow; and thus the protagonist of *Sartor Resartus* must similarly pass through a Romantic phase—complete with Wertherian sorrows and Childe Haroldean wanderings—before he can arrive at that mastery of self which leads to oracular wisdom. In the later version of the hero as poet, Carlyle turned from biography to message, from preoccupation with the poet's life to consideration of what his writings would inspire. As long as the young Carlyle sympathized with Byron the man, he could overlook the flawed nature of Byron's writings; however, in the essay on the poet Ebenezer Elliot ("Corn-Law Rhymes," 1832), written in place of a projected review of Moore's biography of Byron, Carlyle dismissed the self-indulgence of the Romantic poets in favor of the "earnest truth-speaking man" whose subject was not the martial force celebrated in ancient epic but a theme worthy of modern times: "Tools and the Man." The poet-hero characterized in Carlyle's lectures *On Heroes, Hero-Worship, and the Heroic in History* (1841) is a prophet who has "penetrated . . . into the sacred mystery of the Universe; what Goethe calls 'the open secret.' "[46] But where Shelley's poet-hero spoke in behalf of love and sympathy, Carlyle's poet has become one who inspires a proper reverence and sense of obedience, one who encourages others to bend the knee to the unalterable prohibitions and the acknowledged legislators of the world—the Cromwells and Fredericks. Scott's refusal to be a "great man" may have encouraged Carlyle to look elsewhere for his exemplars, yet Carlyle's increasing preoccupation with history—the substitution of fact for poetry or fiction as his primary interest—was also based on his grasp of the dangerous tendencies at work in the modern world, dangers that only a hero very different from Byron could subdue.

Carlyle's "Victorian" phase officially began in 1837 with the publication of *The French Revolution*, his stunning reminder to his countrymen of how a nation undermined by lack of faith and lack of leadership succumbed to the discharge of violent energies. (Carlyle's description of the Frenchman who "has no God in the world" was echoed in Thackeray's description of the characters of *Vanity Fair*, "a set of people living without God in the world.") Carlyle's Romantic bias found expression in his sense of the inevitability of the French Revolution as a force of Nature sweeping away "shams" and "corrupt worn-out Authority." The tragedy of the Revolution, however, was that it lacked a hero to control those energies: Louis XVI was destitute of will and hence was unworthy to govern, while Mirabeau died before he could assume his destined role. The radical aspect of Carlyle's view of history can be seen in his sympathy for the suffering French, as well as in his sympathy for the vast numbers of unemployed workers at home. But his answer to the "Condition-of-England Question," in *Chartism* (1839), is a call for leaders by whom it is the supreme "right of man" to be guided, whether obediently or forcibly. The right of the leader, as he affirms in the lectures on hero-worship, is to defy anarchy and restore order: what the mightiest, the "Noblest Man . . . *tells us to do* must be precisely the wisest, fittest."[47] In *Past and Present* (1843) Carlyle discovered just such a model from the past in Abbot Samson, whose self-discipline seemed a far cry from the Romantic egoism expressed in the form of Byronic Dilettantism or Bentham-inspired Mammonism. The poet, like the laissez-faire manufacturer, was now little more than an egoist to Carlyle; and where Carlyle had once celebrated a poet who towered over Weimar, dwarfing its official leader, Karl August, he now turned to praise the Pussian ruler who had snubbed Voltaire.

Carlyle's shift from poetry to history may be said to parallel Scott's movement from romance to realism. Both writers allowed enough Romanticism in their work, enough outlet for imaginative and religious wonder, to arouse the sensibilities of Dickens and Stevenson, Newman and Ruskin; but both also directed attention to what Dickens called the "poetry of fact." Carlyle's contention in *The Diamond Necklace* (1837) that the nineteenth century is a veritable "Age of Romance," that reality if examined closely enough is filled with wonder, was a source of inspiration to realists and romancers alike: "Romance exists," he affirmed, and "it exists, strictly speaking, in Reality alone." Scott provided the impetus for many a young Victorian's decision to become a novelist, while Carlyle influenced the choice of themes in Victorian fiction as surely as he directed attention to the decisive issues in Victorian life. The combined influence of Scott and Carlyle is most obviously evident in Dickens's and Elizabeth Gaskell's industrial and historical fiction; but their traces can be found in unexpected places too. Carlyle's conception of the "captain of industry," which Gaskell drew upon for her portrait of the industrialist John Thornton in *North and South*, is an updated version of Scott's feudal captains of old. One recalls that in *Past and Present* Carlyle cited *Ivanhoe* in defense of his "historical" account of the feudal ties between masters and subjects; and the celebration of feudal loyalties and responsibilities in Scott and Carlyle was to have both salutary and negative effects throughout the century. Carlyle's view that modern workers have a "right" to be protected endeared him to Victorian radicals, even as his hymn to leadership was taken as a justification for the economic policies of a W. R. Greg. (Greg's famous critique of *Mary Barton* may be seen as one form of Carlyleanism opposing another.) Perhaps the most singular Victorian tributes to Carlyle occur in two novels in which he turns up as a character: as Sandy Mackaye in Charles Kingsley's *Alton Locke* and as Dr. Shrapnel in Meredith's *Beauchamp's Career*. For Meredith's idealistic protagonist, Nevil Beauchamp, Carlyle's "fire-and-smoke" writings are the occasion for his recognition of social inequities and his discovery of the culpability of England's aristocrats in refusing to assume their ancient role as responsible leaders. After Carlyle's works have inspired him, Dr. Shrapnel's subsequent appearance enables Beauchamp to focus his energies on the areas in need of help—even though, with characteristic irony, Meredith demonstrates that England resists all efforts to face reality and make needed change. Sandy Mackaye's Carlylean effect upon the proletarian poet Alton Locke, by contrast, is of a more genial nature. Mackaye persuades Locke to put away his Byronic and Shelleyan discontent in favor of "self-restraint and method" and honorable labor. "Ay, Shelley's gran'; always gran'," he observes, "but Fact is grander."[48] Carlyle's part in the transition from Romantic to Victorian sensibility cannot, perhaps, be described more succinctly than that.

ROMANTIC AND ANTI-ROMANTIC NOVELISTS

The polarizing effects of Romanticism upon the Victorian novel can be seen in the differing positions assumed by three novelists: Thackeray, an unregenerate realist; Edward Bulwer Lytton, a Romantic-turned-realist; and Emily Brontë, an unregenerate Romantic. The eldest, Bulwer Lytton, who was born in 1803, had probably the highest reputation of the three during his lifetime, being termed by the 1859 *Encyclopaedia Britannica* "unquestionably the greatest living novelist of England."[49] The youngest, Emily Brontë, born in 1818, remained for much of the century in the shadow of her older sister: Elizabeth Gaskell's biography of Charlotte Brontë passes over the author of *Wuthering Heights* as an unlikable and uncultivated individual ("all that I . . . have been able to learn about her has not tended to give either me, or my readers, a pleasant impression of her"),[50] and Charlotte herself, in the 1850 Preface to her sister's novel, hints that perhaps its Byronic hero should never have been created. Thackeray, born just midway between Bulwer Lytton and Brontë in 1811, found his path crossing Bulwer's and the Brontë family's on a number of occasions: as Charlotte Brontë's most admired novelist, to whom *Jane Eyre* was dedicated, he appears in *Villette* as one side of the hero Paul Emanuel; as Bulwer Lytton's chief critic during the 1840s, he may be given credit for Bulwer's transformation into the author of the realistic *The Caxtons.* As the continuator of Carlyle's and Scott's efforts in this direction, Thackeray became, to his Victorian contemporaries, the living standard of literary realism. His was a more reticent version than Flaubert's or Zola's, to be sure; but, like theirs, his sense of realism was formulated in opposition to the Romantic themes and figures popular in his youth.

To a certain degree, Thackeray's anti-Romantic posture may

be seen as a reaction against one aspect of his nature. As a boy, he was apparently as fond of chivalric romances and the *Arabian Nights* as young William Dobbin in *Vanity Fair*; and as a Cambridge student, he fell, for a time, under the spell of Shelley, regarding him as virtuous in spite of his "absurd creed," and intending to write an essay on him. (Later, traveling in Germany, he yielded to Schiller's spell.) Thackeray's "romantic" turn of mind, at this stage, can be seen in his eulogy of Napoleon (Becky Sharp's hero) at a college debate, and in his positions, at the Debating Society, in support of dueling and feudal government and in favor of the propositions that fiction works to the betterment of the "moral character" and that the poetry of "passion" surpasses in "moral influence" the "poetry of intellect."[51] Although many of his tender feelings and sentimental fancies were forced underground as he assumed the role of a man of the world, Thackeray's divided sensibility was reflected throughout his career: as a youthful member of Bohemian artist circles with a conservative sense of a fixed social hierarchy; as a soft-hearted cynic with an unromantic sense of man's depraved inner nature and a chivalric feeling toward all the victims of life; as an independent-minded novelist, proud of his influence and yet ashamed, in part, of his artistic calling. An unsympathetic commentator has blamed Thackeray's ironic and sentimental-melancholy disposition on his "repressed romanticism," which led, in the end, to the extinction of his "creative impulse"; but even Thackeray's admirers have called attention to the blight caused by his anti-Romanticism. "His emphasis on common sense as an antidote to cant," notes Gordon Ray, "blinded him to the ways in which life can be enriched by the imagination."[52]

Thackeray's early literary burlesques were a form of self-criticism turned outward, attacking the debased romanticism in vogue in the 1830s and 1840s in which Byronic Corsairs rematerialized as noble highwaymen and tender-hearted murderers, and "Spasmodic" poets saw themselves as Shelleyan geniuses set loftily apart from their insensitive fellow men. A contemporary reviewer, accounting for the cathartic aspect of reality found in Thackeray's novels, recalled that when the novelist started writing, "Things had ceased to be called by their right names; the principles of right and wrong were becoming more and more confounded; sham sentiment, sham morality, sham heroism, were everywhere rampant; and romance-writers every day wandering farther and farther from nature and truth."[53] Following Carlyle's lead, Thackeray declared himself opposed to all forms of humbug and cant; and, like Scott, he endeavored to show in his writings that life consists of limitations and frustrations rather than of opportunities for human freedom and potentiality. In his travel book, *Notes of a Journey from Cornhill to Grand Cairo* (1845), Thackeray not only denied the romantic quality of the fabled cities of the "East"—Athens, Cairo, Jerusalem—but derided the false "rapture and enthusiasm" that Byron in particular, "with an eye to the public," had manufactured on his voyages. "Wherever the steamboat touches the shore adventure retreats into the interior, and what is called romance vanishes." In such a setting, "Byronism becomes absurd instead of sublime, and is only a foolish expression of Cockney wonder." The Crusaders' stronghold, Jaffa, inspired Thackeray with a sense of the falsity conjured up in *The Talisman*: "When shall we have a real account of those times and heroes—no good-humoured pageant, like those of the Scott romances—but a real authentic story to instruct and frighten honest people of the present day, and make them thankful that the grocer governs the world now in place of the baron?"[54] Thackeray's remorselessness toward romance is vividly illustrated in his burlesque of Scott, *Rebecca and Rowena: A Romance upon Romance* (1850): here, despite his avowed attempt to assert the very spirit of romantic wish-fulfillment that Scott had shrunk from by not allowing Ivanhoe and Rebecca to be united, Thackeray ends by transforming his heroine into a "faultless" and dutiful replica of Rebecca's original foil, Rowena (having been duly converted, "a better Christian than Rebecca now was never said her catechism"). The children to whom the tale was in large part addressed may have found disheartening the author's moral: "It is only hope which is real, and reality is a bitterness and a deceit."[55]

Thackeray went considerably further in the direction of realism than Carlyle and Scott had thought necessary; and he even satirized his two predecessors on occasion. Carlyle's celebration of heroes especially nettled him; and in his novels and burlesques Thackeray repeatedly debunked the glories of the military hero or the pretensions of the poet-hero. Warfare, in *The Luck of Barry Lyndon* (1844), is seen as "murderous work," and the prowess of Carlyle's future hero-extraordinary, "Great Frederick," is undermined when the narratory considers "What a number of items of human crime, misery, slavery, go to form that sum-total of glory!" In the subtitle to *Vanity Fair*, "A Novel without a Hero," Thackeray made clear his disbelief in the existence of such figures in real life; and, as Gordon Ray suggests, in the lectures on *The English Humourists* (1855), he was "pointedly anti-Carlylean" in choosing to celebrate an unromantic century that lacked heroic dimensions.[56] Thackeray's favorite target, Bulwer Lytton, offended not only in his choice of robber- and murderer-heroes, like Paul Clifford and Eugene Aram, whom Bulwer deemed exempt from the dictates of ordinary morality, but in his Romantic sense that as an artist he was not subject to the dictates of mere reality. In his brilliant burlesque of *Eugene Aram*, "George de Barnwell" (1847), Thackeray made it clear that villainy was villainy and reality reality despite Bulwer's efforts to disguise both in superfine language. Comparing Thackeray to Bulwer's ally Dickens, David Masson in 1851 tipped the balance in Dickens's favor by speaking of his romantic "idealism" as opposed to his rival's merely photographic methods: "Art is called Art, says Goethe, precisely because it is *not* Nature; and even such a department of art as the modern novel is entitled to the benefit of this maxim." Thackeray responded to Masson with the insistence "that the Art of Novels *is* to represent Nature: to convey as strongly as possible the sentiment of reality."[57] The novelist, hence, must be the servant of reality and not seek to transcend or tamper with it. His only mission, Thackeray felt, is to reproduce "morals and manners," not to attempt (as Bulwer and Dickens and Disraeli were doing) to use the novel as a platform for social change or for discussions of "algebra, religion, political economy, or other abstract science. We doubt the fitness of the occasion, and often (it must be confessed) the competency of the teacher." Such sentiments, along with Thackeray's unShelleyan refusal to take himself seriously as an artist, moved Dickens in his obituary tribute to charge his great rival with feigning "a want of earnestness" and making "a pretence of undervaluing his art, which was not good for the art that he held in trust."[58]

But for Thackeray a writer was only a writer, not a divinely inspired seer with knowledge of the "sacred mystery of the universe," just as in his early novels a rogue was set down as a rogue and not made (as he was by Bulwer) the Shakespearean occasion for the author's reaching "the highest province of fiction." Complaining of the "eloquent clap-trap" of *Eugene Aram*, the twenty-one-year-old Thackeray vowed, "when my novel is written it will be something better."[59] The intensity of his animus against Bulwer's idealization of criminals was such, however, that before Thackeray could write the masterpieces of his maturity, *Vanity Fair* (1847–48), *Henry Esmond* (1852), and *The Newcomes* (1853–55), he had to vent his spleen in the form of the burlesques and the novels about rogues, *Catherine* (1840) and *The Luck of Barry Lyndon*. The explicit purpose of *Catherine* may be to show villains for what "they are: not dandy, poetical, rose-water thieves; but real downright scoundrels, leading scoundrelly lives" (the case was taken from the Newgate Calendar); but the drift of the novel is toward an unCarlylean, as well as anti-Bulwer, sense of life in which purpose and free will are nonexistent. Man is shown to be by no means innately good, as the Romantics believed: where Dickens had allowed Oliver Twist's innocence of heart to exempt him from environmental contamination, Thackeray implies that all men have a touch of the rogue which surfaces or not according to the circumstances in which they find themselves. Professing to find consolation in this "doctrine of destiny," Thackeray sardonically notes that it is a blessing for men to be able to blame forces beyond their control: better "to deem oneself in the hands of Fate than to think—with our fierce passions and weak repentances; with our resolves so loud, so vain, so ludicrously, despicably weak and frail; with our dim, wavering, wretched conceits about virtue, and our irresistible propensity to wrong—that we are the workers of our future sorrow or happiness. If we depend on our strength, what is it against mighty circumstances? If we look to ourselves, what hope have we?" Success, hence, becomes a matter of luck, and villainy is the potential fate of every man. "I look into my heart," Thackeray writes in the Prelude to *Henry Esmond*, "and think that I am as good as my Lord Mayor, and know I am as bad as Tyburn Jack."[60]

Yet Thackeray's selection of rogues as his first fictional protagonists also revealed, for all his moral protestations to the contrary, a "sneaking kindness" toward them, as he admitted in the case of his feelings for Catherine,[61] and a lurking sense of identification with enterprising rascals as surrogate *artists*. This link is explicit in his portrait of Becky Sharp, which glows or dims in proportion to the extent with which Thackeray sees her energies and satiric spirit as reflecting his own novelistic prerogative. Becky's career as a Byronic rebel, an outcast trying to create a position for herself in the world, is linked, in the course of *Vanity Fair*, with that of other Romantic self-made heroes—with Satan and Napoleon—and in various ways she is seen as a female Byron. Of her Byronic misanthropy, Thackeray comments: "All the world used her ill, said this young misanthropist, and we may be pretty certain that persons whom all the world treats ill, deserve entirely the treatment they get. The world is a looking-glass, and gives back to every man the reflection of his own face."[62] Yet Becky's Byronic, mocking deflation of the inhabitants of Vanity Fair is uncomfortably close to Thackeray's own tendency toward burlesque. While George Osborne plays the stereotyped role of the Don Juan figure, a Corsair without even the one redeeming Byronic virtue of tenderness toward women, it is Becky whose married life contains the suggestion of a scandalously Byronic "guilt." Becky's major "crime" in the novel is usurping a masculine posture, presuming to act in a world where action almost inevitably involves a harmful reaction upon others; her husband Rawdon's "virtue," conversely, is his assumption of the feminine attribute of passivity and forbearance, which Thackeray holds up for praise in his later novels. Both in his semiconscious identification with his rogue-heroine and in his semicontemptuous celebration of his passive characters, Thackeray reveals, for all his reiterated repugnance toward romance and Romanticism, more than a hint of the coexistence in the Romantics of Promethean assertiveness and stoical quiescence.

Thackeray's tendency to divide his characters into rogues and innocents, those who act and those who forbear, reflects a latent Romanticism that harkens back to Scott and Byron. Even as he criticized the male Byronic role—misanthropic, rebellious, cynical—as a histrionic posture, Thackeray adopted for his Amelia Sedleys and Lady Castlewoods the Byronic pattern (to quote Macaulay) of "woman all softness and gentleness, loving to caress and to be caressed, but capable of being transformed by passion into a tigress." Hence, Amelia is happy to play the Byronic "slave" to George's "Sultan." And from Scott, Thackeray borrowed more than the plot idea (for *Henry Esmond*) of an attempt to restore the Stuarts to the throne: he made Scott's "passive hero" the prototype for his own chivalric-minded, self-effacing Dobbins and Esmonds; and he repeated Scott's contrasting feminine heroines, the ambitious Diana Vernons and Flora MacIvors versus the home-oriented Rose Bradwardines and Brenda Troils, in his own Beatrix and Rachel Castlewood, the one a frustrated romantic adventuress and the other a heroine of domestic romance. The ingrained sense of human culpability and the excessive regard for those (like Amelia) whose nature it is "to sacrifice [themselves] and to fling all . . . at the feet of the beloved object"[63] encouraged Thackeray to develop simultaneously into a fatalist and a sentimentalist. It is ironic that the pioneering "realist" among Victorian novelists, who created delectable burlesques of the debased Romantic spirit of the age, was himself, in certain respects, an embodiment of the Romantic polarities carried to their extremes.

In Edward Bulwer Lytton, Thackeray's chief target for satire in the 1840s, second-hand Romanticism found its Dunciad-laureate. Bulwer has many admirable qualities: his Carlylean assault on the forces of materialism, his immersion in Continental literature and ideas, his ambitious views concerning the nature of fiction. And his novels have much to recommend them: cleverly constructed plots and a variety of styles and subject matter extending from the satire of the dandies in *Pelham* to the marvelous hokum of *Zanoni*. But much of his work is sabotaged by defects of character—the delusions of grandeur that intermingled with his paranoia, the humorlessness that prevented his seeing the negative side of his nature, and the credulous streak that made him an easy mark for spiritualism and occultism. ("Shakespeare has come to me," he informed his son after one of his seances, "and gave me most thrilling advice as to the future and other predictions.")[64] Confident from his early childhood that he had been born for greatness, Bulwer could never grasp why his wife, his mother, and hostile critics were unable to take him at his own estimation. Lacking "sympathy with mankind," as his grandson admitted, Bulwer nevertheless expected others to accept his lofty image of himself, whether projected in his life or his books, as a "tragic hero, maligned, misunderstood, but ever ready to forgive." In the early years of this century, it could be suggested that Bulwer's flaws were owing to that "romantic vein, so much in vogue in the early nineteenth century"; while in recent years Allan Christensen has claimed that Bulwer's merit was that "he made of the art of fiction a vehicle to carry on the idealist tradition of Romantic poetry and so helped not only to save the soul of man but also to save fiction to serve visions other than that of mimetic realism."[65] As the self-conscious heir to the Romantic traditions of his youth, Bulwer is a crucial link between the generation of Byron and that of Dickens, but he is also a testimony to the fact that Romanticism by itself could not account for the Victorian novel's particular strength.

One is tempted to think of Bulwer as the supreme "Spasmodic" novelist of his time, as wildly overrated in some quarters (by such notables as Matthew Arnold, Harriet Martineau, and even Carlyle after an initial revulsion against him) as the Spasmodic poets were in their day—and, like them, combining in his autobiographical heroes the qualities of Byronic egoism and Shelleyan persecuted divinity. Bulwer drew upon the Continental Romantics for inspiration: upon Rousseau's habit of "self-study" which gave him "a knowledge of the more hidden recesses of the heart" and which encouraged subsequent writers to exhibit the "record and history" of the "Within . . . as well as the Without";[66] upon Goethe's and Schiller's examples in overcoming the torments and waywardness of their youthful, subjective egos; and upon the German Hegelians for pointing to a higher reality, that which the genius finds in his own creative mind, than the delusive material reality of the external world. Rousseau's sense of himself as a persecuted genius finds disturbing echoes in the

Bulwer heroes; Bulwer's partiality for Schiller resulted in a novel with a robber-hero (*Paul Clifford*), a biography of the German poet, and a number of translations; while his admiration for Goethe found expression in the creation of several imitation Werthers (like Falkland, the hero of his first novel), imitation Wilhelm Meisters (most notably Ernest Maltrevers), and imitation Fausts (Eugene Aram and Zanoni). Applying to the novel what he had learned from the German idealists, Bulwer repeatedly insisted on the author's right to present the lofty images implanted in his mind, rather than reproduce the insignificant—and invalid—reality of everyday experience. Opposing the move toward Dutch realism, he allied himself with those artists and critics of the past who had decreed "that Nature is not to be copied, but *exalted*; that the loftiest order of art, selecting only the loftiest combinations, is the perpetual struggle of Humanity to approach the Gods";[67] and he immodestly linked himself with such great creators as Sophocles, Raphael, and Shakespeare, who had asserted what in another context he called the "Normal Clairvoyance of the Imagination" and who had chosen to create figures of larger and nobler proportions than ordinary mankind.

Mary Shelley's allegory about the Promethean ambitions of the Romantic ego, *Frankenstein*, might be taken as a comment on much of Bulwer's achievement. Bulwer's delusions of grandeur concerning his own genius led him to create the sort of heroes he deemed worthy of a Sophocles or a Shakespeare: criminals. Like Schiller in *The Robbers* or Shelley in *The Cenci*, Bulwer invested his individual malefactors with the virtues lacking in their oppressors, thus making their crimes often seem like acts of justice. Crime, he alleged, was the proper subject of "genius," the highest expression of human passion. "The element of the highest genius," he wrote John Forster, "is not among the village gossips of Miss Austen; it is in crime and passion, for the two are linked together. It is the art of that genius to make you distinguish between the crime and the criminal, and in proportion as your soul shudders at the one, to let your heart beat with the heart of the other."[68] Bulwer's attempts to create new Iagos and Macbeths, however, resulted only in the production of melodramatic villains, who lack verisimilitude and who speak or soliloquize in language of an absurdly unnatural staginess. For Bulwer, life *was* melodrama, with noble heroes (like their creator) beset by worldly individuals oblivious to Truth and Beauty, with heroes forced into a life of crime or heterodox behavior because of the greater wickedness of the world. In the 1840s Bulwer gave up politics to devote himself to his literary career; and one sometimes wishes that Shakespeare, on one of his spiritualist visitations, had advised Bulwer to remain in the political arena, where rhetoric very often does pass for reality and where questions of morality seldom intrude. Thackeray's criticism of Bulwer's novels—for example, of "How Eugene Aram, though a thief, a liar, and a murderer, yet being intellectual was amongst the noblest of mankind"[69]—seems, in retrospect, no more than Bulwer deserved: the bulk of his fiction offers a false morality, a fake reality, and a distorted sense of the prerogatives of artistic genius and willful individuals.

Bulwer's early heroes are not all criminals, but they are invariably set apart from and above the standards of others. The world and the genius are incompatible; and as a result the typical Bulwer hero is either rebellious or idle, a Eugene Aram or a Godolphin. (Godolphin's idleness is intended to be seen as a Hamlet-like indecisiveness under similarly trying circumstances.) Even *Pelham* (1828), the one mildly amusing novel among the early works, relies on a comic perspective that is largely the product of authorial disdain. Its hero determines to rise in the world by pretending to sympathize with the fashionable foibles of those he mocks; but while Pelham in the end decides to shed his dandyism and "be useful to [his] friends and to mankind,"[70] the later spokesmen for worldly values in Bulwer, like Lumley Ferrers in *Ernest Maltrevers* (1837), combine scornfulness with downright malevolence. More typical of Bulwer's Romantic spokesmen is the hero of his first novel, *Falkland* (1827), whose superiority to his fellow men is seen in his self-preoccupation and his Byronic misanthropy: the latter quality leads him to flee from the false allure of the "bel mondo," while the former inclines him to accept as his right the homage of female admirers. Despite an initial hesitation on his part when the married Lady Emily Mandeville flings herself at his feet ("All who had loved [this imitation Manfred], he had repaid with ruin; and *one*—the first—the fairest—and the most loved—with death"), he nevertheless accepts her proposal, in effect disclaiming all responsibility for what may ensue. "No one," he tells her, "much less one whom I love so intensely, so truly as I do you, shall ever receive disgrace at my hands, unless she can feel that that disgrace would be dearer to her than glory elsewhere." Their love is consummated, accompanied by a roll of thunder and a row of asterisks; but the wickedly virtuous world intrudes, and Lady Emily, worshipful to the end, dies of a broken blood vessel. Proud of her son's first novel, Bulwer's mother also expressed dismay at his choice of hero: "what does his superiority consist of?" she asked. "And what does it all come to? Presumptuous egotism! selfish vanity in attachments that do no good to their possessor, and do harm to others . . . Why write as if you thought that power could exist without purpose, or purpose without belief?" Bulwer subsequently dismissed the novel as a Goethean effort at self-therapy: like the author of *Werther,* "I had rid my bosom of its 'perilous stuff,' I had confessed my sins, and was absolved—I could return to real life and its wholesome objects."[71] In *Pelham,* however, Bulwer introduced another Byronic malcontent, Reginald Glanville—with whose portrait he claimed credit for ending the "Satanic mania"—and in novel after novel, he presented additional variations on this prototype.

In *Paul Clifford* (1830) the Bulwer hero masquerades as a highwayman, ostensibly so that the author can attack the injustices of a prison system that turns innocents into criminals, but more fundamentally so that he can attack the values of the noncriminal world as more venal than those of his good-hearted rogues. "The older I grow," claims the hero, "the more I see of men and of the callings of social life—the more I, an open knave, sicken at the glossed and covert dishonesties around." As a combination of Schiller's Karl Moor and Byron's Corsair, Clifford is "one of those accomplished and elegant highwaymen of whom we yet read wonders, and by whom it would have been delightful to have been robbed"; yet Bulwer lays all his vices to "circumstances," while Clifford's virtues, his generosity and "natural and inborn gentility," are the result of his innate goodness. The botched morality of *Paul Clifford,* wherein a hero may prey on others and still be superior to them in the end, is repeated in

Eugene Aram (1832), Bulwer's muddled retelling of the story of an actual murderer, whose crime is given quasi-religious sanction. As an impoverished scientist with Faustian ambitions, Aram is tempted to rob and kill a thoroughly worthless individual: "Was it not an ordination," he reflects after the event, "that called upon men to take fortune in their own hands, when Fate lavished her rewards on this low and creeping thing?" In response to Thackeray's criticism, Bulwer removed passages from the first edition of *Eugene Aram* in which the murderer sees himself, while he commits his crime, as a "Priest" before an altar, making "a great and solemn sacrifice to knowledge," and he also exonerated Aram from the murder charge, contrary to historical fact. Even with the revisions, however, he retained the identification between his hero and the "genius," implying that such exalted individuals inhabit a world of values beyond good and evil and that their only nemesis is "Fate."[72]

Perhaps the key Romantic works in Bulwer's oeuvre are the companion novels *Ernest Maltrevers* and *Alice; or, the Mysteries*, both published in 1837, the first year of Victoria's reign. His hero, an admitted copy of Wilhelm Meister, is intended to represent "the Man of Genius," with "a desire for the Good, a passion for the Honest, a yearning after the True." In short, he is Edward Bulwer Lytton, surrounded by a cast of characters who exist only to praise him or to conspire against him. Virtually every Romantic cliché finds its way into Bulwer's *Bildungsroman*, and when the characters are not acting out Byronic or Goethean charades, they often pause to discuss the currents of Romanticism from Ariosto to Shelley. Although Bulwer criticizes the Byronic mode in the figure of the narcissistic poet Castruccio Cesarini (the book deserves a place in the annals of camp if only for the scene in which the hero comforts the crazed poet, wiping "the froth from the white lips"), Maltrevers undergoes a Byronic pilgrimage to the East, in *Alice*, so that he can oppose the savage Arab life to the hypocrisies and vanities of the Western world. In the end, however, he settles for the "Mysteries of Life," which turn out to be a union of the "Actual and the Visionary"; and he is allowed to marry his long-lost love Alice, after the two have been kept apart for nearly twenty years by what Bulwer calls "fate" but what to the reader will seem like the machinations of soap opera.[73] Bulwer's determination to produce a Shakespearean masterpiece, with Sophoclean overtones (he eventually translated *Oedipus*), results in the presentation of Iago-inspired plots, lurid mad-scenes, melodramatic deathbed tableaux, and the hint of incestuous love. Virtually everything the author had felt or experienced or read as a Romantic found its way into the Maltrevers novels, and the result is an unintentional parody of the Romantic ethos, a work much admired by many Victorian readers but an instructive reminder of what George Eliot, Trollope, and Meredith had to overcome or qualify before they could achieve their own distinctive visions.

Bulwer's treatment of women in his novels illustrates in particular how a Romantic preconception filtered into Victorian fiction. The adoring Byronic slave-maidens (Gulnare in *The Corsair*, Kaled in *Lara*, for example) are reincarnated as Bulwer's worshipful heroines, content to die at their idols' feet. Seduction by a Bulwer hero is tantamount to a visitation by Jove: Alice's "fall" only raises her high, since (as the author assures us) "If a woman has once really loved, the beloved object makes an impenetrable barrier between her and other men; their advances terrify and revolt,—she would rather die than be unfaithful even to a memory." Alice is an extreme case of feminine patience and devotion—when an emotionally exhausted Maltrevers finally returns to her, she tells him, "I ask not if you have loved others since we parted—man's faith is so different from ours"—but she suggests the legions of Agnes Wickfields and Mary Garths whose womanliness their authors equate with angelic fortitude and self-denial. An aggressive woman, by contrast, is someone to inspire fear or repugnance, like the mistakenly worldly Lady Constance in *Godolphin*, or like Lady Ellinor in *The Caxtons* who embodies "that moral contradiction—*an ambitious woman*." The Romantic genius thrived on a supportive woman, or, like Wordsworth and Shelley, on a cluster of women; and even as the Victorian novelists rejected the male egoism of their predecessors, they held on to the figure of the good angel, ever ready (as Thackeray says of his Amelia) to provide "a kind soft shoulder" on which the hardened male can "lean, and a gentle hand to soothe our gouty old pillows," yet one who never presumes to stand by herself. Bulwer's version of this Romantic stereotype is identical to Thackeray's: "A thing to protect, to soothe, to shelter,—oh, how dear it is to the pride of man! The haughty woman who can stand alone and requires no leaning-place in our heart, loses the spell of her sex."[74]

The ease with which Bulwer adapted himself to Victorian forms and attitudes does not reflect an insincerity of either his Romantic or his Victorian views. Instead, it reflects something of the continuity between Romanticism and Victorianism, not to mention the pre-Victorian concern with social problems showed by many Romantics. At the end of *Alice* the hero has resolved "to mix in the living World, and to minister usefully to the great objects that refine and elevate our race"; and in the 1850s Bulwer himself returned to parliamentary life. In his 1848 Preface to *Pelham* he noted with approval "an extraordinary improvement in the intellectual and moral features of the English world, since I first entered it as an observer. There is a far greater earnestness of purpose, a higher culture, more generous and genial views" than had been customary in the more individualistic ethos of the Regency period.[75] (*Pelham* itself, as Bulwer reminds us, pointed to this change of attitude, for even as the novel rebuked the Byronism of the 1820s its hero was seen transferring his allegiance to the constructive views of Bentham and Mill.) The high point of Bulwer's Victorianism is *The Caxtons* (1849), published about the same time as *Vanity Fair* (1847–48) and *David Copperfield* (1849–50), and like those novels a hymn to domestic values and fictional realism. Probably the most popular of his books during his lifetime, and the most rapturously received by the critics, *The Caxtons* is fascinating, for all its lifelessness, as a compendium of Victorian clichés, a remarkable contrast to the debased Romanticism of *Falkland*, *Eugene Aram*, or *Ernest Maltrevers*. With its tribute to the Victorian belief in self-help and home values, the novel sets out to attack the false Romanticism of the past and to invest the domestic hearth with a new form of romance. Bulwer's twin protagonists are Pisistratus Caxton and his cousin Vivian, the former self-denying (Bulwer makes it clear that he is no "genius") and home-oriented, the latter a Byronic individualist, rebelling against all forms of "paternal authority" and orthodox behavior.[76] In the end, the life of self-sacrifice is richly rewarded—Pisistratus takes his industrious work habits to Australia and returns home an Aeneas turned Rothschild—while the life of self-indulgence leads to crime (a villainous attempt to abduct Lady Ellinor) and repentance. With its endorsement of the values of prudence and Podsnappery, *The Caxtons* amounts to a romance of Philistinism. An admiring Thackeray now apologized to Bulwer for his former antagonism; while Dickens made use of Bulwer's presentation of Australia as the materialist kingdom of heaven in the dénouement to *David Copperfield*.

If one disregards Bulwer Lytton's actual accomplishments and thinks only of his ambitions and critical principles, he seems an impressive figure: adept in a wide variety of literary forms— novels, plays, historical romances, Arthurian poetry, translations —and a leading spokesman for Romantic values. In his dissatisfaction with material reality, he experimented with the new approaches of supernaturalism, occultism, and science fiction. And in his concern with Romantic subjects in an age more suited to realism, he handled themes that later writers were to treat with finer art and greater psychological intensity—such as the *Eugene Aram* plot of a poor student who feels superior to conventional notions of good and evil and who murders a seemingly useless individual, which was used to better effect in *Crime and Punishment*. Dickens was surely indebted to Bulwer when, reversing his accustomed view that villains are born rather than conditioned by social forces, he created his sympathetic "warmint," Abel Magwitch, in *Great Expectations*. (The final courtroom scene in that novel is reminiscent of the similar scene in *Paul Clifford*: Pip, noting how a "broad shaft of light" links judge and doomed prisoner, is reminded of the "absolute equality" whereby all men are subjected "to the greater Judgment that knoweth all things and cannot err.") And Emily Brontë made memorable use of the Bulwer-Byronic hero who rejects the ordinary forms of morality in her portrait of Heathcliff. The Brontës read Bulwer, along with his master Byron, in their youth; and if Branwell Brontë perhaps saw himself as something of a Eugene Aram or a Falkland, at least two of his sisters, Charlotte and Anne, adopted a critical and moral attitude toward such figures in their novels. (Charlotte Brontë was especially determined, for example, not to give her protagonists the noble exteriors of Bulwer's characters.)

Whether Emily Brontë intended her hero to be judged from the moral point of view that her sister applied to Rochester in *Jane Eyre* has never been resolved satisfactorily. Charlotte Brontë had no doubt about Heathcliff's "unredeemed" nature, but she suggested in her Preface to *Wuthering Heights* that Emily "did not know what she had done" when she created him, that her sister had acted under the force of a creative inspiration that had rendered her passive during the act of writing. No English novel has inspired such a diversity of interpretations as *Wuthering Heights*; and Heathcliff in particular has been viewed as an anarchic force of nature, a mythic figure thrust into the real world, a Byronic-derived Satanic outcast, a Marxist proletarian-rebel, a representation of the Freudian Id, and a reflection of the heroine's adolescent narcissism.[77] One is tempted to suggest that the novel's popularity is in large part the result of its oblique allusions and its unwritten passages, those dealing, for example, with Heathcliff's origins or motivations, which later readers have interpreted or supplied themselves to suit their own interests. There is much to pity in Heathcliff's youthful deprivation; but as is the case with Bulwer's similarly bereft heroes, there is also something childish about his diabolical antics (such as hanging his wife Isabella's pet dog), something of the smell of Byronic greasepaint about his physiognomy ("A half-civilized ferocity lurked yet in the depressed brows and eyes, full of black fire"). A number of Victorian critics, in consequence, judged Heathcliff and his companions in the novel as representatives of "the brutalizing influence of unchecked passion . . . [,] a commentary on the truth that there is no tyranny in the world like that which thoughts of evil exercise in the daring and reckless breast."[78] In this reading, Heathcliff is analogous to Bertha in *Jane Eyre:* not a hero, but a warning example of the self-destructiveness of the unregulated will. But where Charlotte Brontë deliberately put her characters into a moral context, her sister seems to have thought less in terms of conventional morality than of aesthetic logic—of the relations of her characters to literature rather than to life.

One is tempted to say that *Wuthering Heights* is the Bulwer

Lytton novel that Bulwer himself lacked the genius to write. It has many of Bulwer's stocks in trade: self-willed characters, supernatural occurrences, charged romantic landscapes, a love that transcends death. Within a Bulwer novel the description of Heathcliff's rage following Cathy's death would seem appropriate and properly absurd: "He dashed his head against the knotted trunk; and, lifting his eyes, howled, not like a man, but like a savage beast getting goaded to death with knives and spears." (One recalls the similarly thwarted Castruccio Cesarini's mad fits, in *Ernest Maltrevers*, or the desolation of Falkland after Lady Mandeville's death.) Emily Brontë's triumph was that she went over the same Byronic terrain—"a perfect misanthropist's heaven," as Lockwood describes it—as that followed by Bulwer, and yet avoided making her story seem like the stuff of parody.[79] Bulwer's fiction proves that *Wuthering Heights* is not the great romantic exception among English novels, as was once thought to be the case; yet Emily Brontë had a sense of humor and a conviction that were denied Bulwer. However literary her characters may be in their origins, she believed in them sufficiently to make later readers accept their melodramatic rantings as the echoes of some primal force of reality.

On the basis of *Wuthering Heights*, Emily Brontë may be called the Romantic novelist par excellence, shunning, like Shelley or Byron, "the common paths that others run" (as she writes in one of her poems), and casting "the world away" for a "God of visions." She was far more uncompromisingly Romantic than her sisters; her credo might be taken from her poem "To Imagination":

So hopeless is the world without
The world within I doubly prize.

Wuthering Heights might be cited in justification of the Romantic faith in the artist's ability to create reality out of imagination (the view of Bulwer), although it should be added that Emily Brontë learned from Scott how to set off Romantic rebels against a romantically colored landscape and how at the same time to bind them to the real world with the help of social circumstances (laws of entail, marital rites) and loyal retainers (Nelly Dean).

The double plot of the novel embodies the polarity within Romanticism: the rebellious passion of Heathcliff for Cathy versus the quiescent devotion of Hareton to the younger Cathy. It is possible that in a second novel Emily Brontë might have provided a more persuasive treatment of the second plot; perhaps if Emily had lived longer, as Charlotte suggested, her work would have grown "mellower" and "sunnier" and more Victorian. Because she died with only *Wuthering Heights* completed, however, her life took on a mythic cast of its own—enabling later readers, including the frustrated Romantic Matthew Arnold, to praise her "soul," which

> Knew no fellow for might,
> Passion, vehemence, grief,
> Daring, since Byron died.[80]

The richness of Victorian fiction derives from a variety of literary sources, but the Victorian novel was especially enriched by the diversity of themes and values provided by Romanticism. The importance granted to the faculty of sympathy, for example, and the emphasis placed on the redeeming qualities of nature and the imagination, which we find in many of the great Victorian novels, attest in large part to the Romantic impulse of their creators. The Victorian novelists, while rejecting the claims for the autonomy of will made by some Romantics, nevertheless based their consciousness of themselves as creators on the images of the Romantic authors that circulated during the early part of the nineteenth century. While Victorian writers in general inherited from the Romantic poets the linkage of creative impulse with artistic responsibility, the Victorian novelists in particular saw in their calling the opportunity to combine those roles of magician and seer, Promethean creator and Miltonic sage, which the Romantics, in moments of self-exaltation, had seen as their birthright. From Scott and Carlyle, the Victorian novelists learned to avoid some of the less beneficial aspects of Romanticism and to transform some of the features of romance and Romanticism into Victorian virtues. They learned, for example, to place their fictional characters within a wide social and historical context while also allowing due credit to individual ideals and aspirations; and they discovered that reality provided plenty of romance if examined closely enough. Perhaps the greatest achievement of Victorian fiction was the creation of a form large enough to include Romantic values within a realistic context, to allow for the coexistence of the competing claims of society and the individual, authority and the imagination, urban and rural ways of life.

The seven novelists I discuss in this book demonstrate a variety of responses to the Romantic tradition and a diversity of reactions to the same Romantic figures. Byron, for example, was an important influence on Trollope, Disraeli, and Charlotte Brontë, yet each of these novelists was attracted to a different side of Byron. The Promethean Byronic energies that awakened Trollope and Disraeli to a sense of their potential power as creators and leaders frightened Brontë into the eventual abandonment of her creative gifts. Wordsworth's appeal to Elizabeth Gaskell and George Eliot allowed for the release of the creative spirit in a less rebellious, more reverential, spirit; however, whereas Gaskell found solace in the Wordsworthian themes of fortitude and quiescence (noting, as she developed as an artist, the less salutary aspect of those themes), Eliot responded to the ambitious strain in Romanticism, which extolled the artist as seer and legislator of mankind. In Dickens and Meredith, the Romantic and romance traditions proved capable of uniting, although Dickens's version of Romanticism was perhaps less liberating, in the end, than Meredith's. In the following chapters I dwell on the novelists' absorption of the Romantic view of women to illustrate that some aspects of Romanticism were less desirable than others; but I place Meredith last in the sequence of novelists because this highly gifted and intelligent Romantic Victorian was able to demonstrate the vitality of his Romantic background while yet discarding the Romantic devaluation of women.

TWO

Trollope, Byron, and the Conventionalities

*I don't mind a little Byron now and again,
so there is no nonsense.*

Ayala's Angel

The likeliest way to substantiate the existence of a Romantic impulse in Victorian fiction is to look at the unlikeliest of Victorians to whom the term "Romantic" might be applied: Anthony Trollope. As Thackeray's and Jane Austen's chief disciple among nineteenth-century novelists, Trollope seems the most soberly and solidly realistic of writers, as little likely to favor the Romantic leanings of his fictional characters as to adopt for himself the role of a Romantic artist. Whether presenting the marvelously comic scene in which Lizzie Eustace, reading *Queen Mab*, is hypnotized into thinking herself a Shelleyan heroine ("What a tawdry world was this in which clothes and food and houses are necessary! How perfectly that boy poet had understood it all"), or relating the tragic account of Julius Mackenzie's Shelleyan rebellion against the conventionalities of the world, Trollope generally appears remorseless toward those who stray beyond accustomed social boundaries, who incline toward Romantic willfulness and self-expression or even toward a romantically colored view of life.[1] George Eliot's praise of his "presentation of even, average life and character," George Meredith's assertion that "Trollope seems wanting in certain of the higher elements that make a great novelist," and Thomas Carlyle's dismissal of the novelist for being "irredeemably imbedded in commonplace" are all testimonies to his contemporaries' impression of Trollope as an anti-Romantic. The posthumous publication of his *Autobiography*, which revealed his refusal to consider himself a Romantic "genius" relying upon "inspiration" to guide his hand ("To me it would not be more absurd if the shoemaker were to wait for inspiration, or the tallow-chandler for the divine moment of melting"), confirmed this image of a no-nonsense, doggedly industrious literary craftsman, an image that has persisted until recently.[2]

That Trollope belongs in the company of George Eliot, Charlotte Brontë, and Charles Dickens, all of whom grew up in an age of Romantic poetry and romance fiction and retained a good deal of their childhood fondness for these works throughout their lives, is readily apparent. Echoes of, and allusions to, Byron, Shelley, Scott, and Ann Radcliffe, among others, abound in his fiction, essays, and letters. Although Byron is certainly the most unexpectedly significant of Trollope's formative influences, two other key Romantic figures, Carlyle and Scott, were instrumental in conditioning the young Trollope's attitude toward his future career. The one provided him with a work ethic, the other with a vocation. If Carlyle was Trollope's "dear old English Homer," from whom he claimed to have "perhaps . . . learned more than from any other English writer," Scott was equally important for having, as Trollope maintained, "inaugurated altogether a new era in Prose Fiction." With Scott the writings of novels was established for the first time not only as a respectable calling but as a lucrative one as well.[3]

Scott, the "Great Unknown," was for Trollope, as for probably the majority of Victorian novelists, the great exemplar; and there were many points of personal correspondence between Trollope and Scott. A passage from Scott's Diary reads uncannily like a capsule version of Trollope's *Autobiography*: "What a life mine has been!—half-educated, almost wholly neglected, or left to myself; stuffing my head with most nonsensical trash, and undervalued by most of my companions for a time; getting forward, and held a bold and a clever fellow, contrary to the opinion of all who thought me a mere dreamer." Both Scott and Trollope pursued joint careers as civil servants and authors; both were dutiful, honorable, self-deprecating men, amazingly prolific as writers (Scott's reference to himself as a creative "machine" is paralleled by Trollope's reference to his own "mechanical mind"), and both were candid—to the horror of Carlyle and others—about their weakness for "worldly things."[4] Scott's notation, expressed near the end of his life, that he had "been perhaps the most voluminous author of the day; and it *is* a comfort to me to think that I have tried to unsettle no man's faith, to corrupt no man's principle," is reflected in Trollope's proud claim, made in the *Autobiography*: "I have ever thought of myself as a preacher of sermons, and my pulpit as one which I could make both salutary and agreeable to my audience. I do believe that no girl has risen from the reading of my pages less modest than she was before, and that some may have learned from them that modesty is a charm well worth preserving."[5]

As late as 1879 Trollope hailed Scott, "who still towers among us as the first of novelists," for the "salutary" lessons to be learned in his works. As an artist, Scott was animated by his "duty as a teacher," and (despite his love of the old romances) by a pioneering interest in literary realism. "If he was not always life-like himself," Trollope affirmed, "he produced a love for such likeness which has imposed an obligation on all English novelists coming after him."[6] Scott's fascination with feudal times and values is affectionately mocked in Trollope's description of the Thornes of Ullathorne—for example, in Miss Thorne's reconstruction of a medieval quintain, and in her belief "that a purity had existed which was now gone; that a piety had adorned our pastors and a simple docility our people, for which it may be feared history gave her but little true warrant" (*Barchester Towers*, chap. 22). Nevertheless, the creator of *Doctor Thorne* romantically insisted that his native land "might surely . . . be called feudal England, or chivalrous England," rather than a "commercial country" in which "buying and selling" is mistakenly deemed "the noblest work of man" (chap. 1). Trollope's indebtedness to Scott can be seen in his various depictions of chivalric-minded elderly gentlemen and of determined ugly-duckling heroes and heroines who fit the pattern of Jeanie Deans.[7] And Scott's idealization of the "gentleman," that quintessentially honorable and "passive hero," no doubt influenced the conception of Plantagenet Palliser. Although the early novel that is most obviously modeled after Scott, *La Vendée*, is not one of Trollope's successes, it reveals to us an apprentice novelist turning instinctively to a subject—the abortive royalist counter-rebellion that took place in France during the Revolution—that Scott himself had deemed (perhaps unbeknown to Trollope) a parallel to "the war conducted by Montrose and the Scottish Highlanders."[8] Perhaps even Trollope's curious wish to publish two of his novels anonymously (*Nina Balatka* and *Linda Tressel*) reflects an inclination to copy Scott.

If Scott supplied Trollope with the model of a successful and prolific novelist, Carlyle provided him with a needed moral incentive: "Know thy work and do it." Numbering himself among the young (and, in his case, undirected) men who "sat at [Carlyle's] feet believing, trusting, and learning,"[9] Trollope was impressed by the Carlylean eulogy of labor and gospel of honesty in word and deed, as well as by the vivid narrative style of the historical works; but he was also put off by the shrillness and onesidedness of Carlyle's philosophical solutions, and repelled by the repeated attacks on novels and novelists.[10] Carlyle's famous criticism of Scott's worldliness, of his alleged lack of spiritual values, is reflected indirectly in *Barchester Towers*, where worldly values are seen to be part of human nature. (There is a direct, and ironic, echo of Carlyle's query in *Past and Present*—"Who shall be Abbot?"—in the opening chapter of *Barchester Towers*, "Who Will Be the New Bishop?" But where Carlyle exhibits a well-disciplined Abbot Samson triumphing over earthly concerns, Trollope shows us Archdeacon Grantly in the act of succumbing to "worldly" and "ambitious" and all-too-human weaknesses.)[11] Trollope's most important allusion of Carlyle, of course, is the figure of Dr. Pessimist Anticant in *The Warden*, the doctrinaire "censor of things in general" who compares "ancient and modern times, very little to the credit of the latter" (chap. 15). If Trollope's "program for the novel," as Ruth apRoberts notes, "is formulated in reaction to Carlyle," this involves both a fictional defense of mid-Victorian England—a demonstration "that we are [not] all going to the—Mischief!" as Carlylean "doctrine" decrees—and a defense of the novelist's role in sustaining the moral integrity of his readers.[12]

Rejecting a potential Carlylean role of the Hero as Novelist, Trollope nevertheless defined the novelist's task as showing his readers the attractiveness of honest conduct. "The preaching of the day is done by the novelist," he avowed in the first issue of his journal, *Saint Pauls*, "and the lessons which he teaches are those to which men and women will listen." It should be observed, however, that Trollope was describing here what the novelist does as a matter of course, not necessarily intentionally. With something of a nod to Keats's famous outburst against "poetry that has a palpable design upon us"—was it not one of Carlyle's faults that, like Dr. Pessimist Anticant, he had taken undisguisedly to "reprobating everything and everyone"?— Trollope warned his friend Kate Field, an aspiring author, against making her readers "think that *you* are trying to teach, or to preach, or to convince. Teach, and preach, and convince if you can;—but first learn the art of doing so without seeming to do it. We are very jealous of preachers. We admit them at certain hours and places for certain reasons."[13] This modification of Keats and Carlyle indicates an adaptation of varying Romantic attitudes for the benefit of the novelist; but the most significant of Trollope's pronouncements on the novel suggests a mingling of Carlyle and Wordsworth. "Both sympathy and imagination must be at work," he advised Kate Field, "—and must work in unison—before you can attract." In the *Autobiography* Trollope united the Wordsworthian emphasis on sympathy, whereby the writer seeks to expand and educate his readers' feelings, with the Carlylean dogma of truth of expression:

> No novel is anything, for purposes either of comedy or tragedy, unless the reader can sympathise with the characters whose names he finds upon the page. Let an author so tell his tale as to touch his reader's heart and draw his tears, and he has, so far, done his work well. Truth let there be,—truth of description, truth of character, human truth as to men and women. If there be such truth, I do not know that a novel can be too sensational.

His prior assertion that a "good novel should be both [realistic and sensational], and both in the highest degree" should remind us that Trollope was aiming not at Romantic or anti-Romantic dogma, but rather at "human truth"—a truth that encompassed both attitudes.[14] The Carlylean sense of "Natural Supernaturalism," of the mystery and wonder of human life, was translated by Trollope (as Ruth apRoberts brilliantly demonstrates) into the presentation of "the sensationalism of reality"—into the romance of real life. That Trollope felt that he had not disobeyed all of Carlyle's precepts—that he had retained something of the young acolyte "believing, trusting, and learning"—is seen in the closing pages of the *Autobiography*, where he shows that he has followed the call to "Produce! Produce!" with a vengeance: "I have published," he archly confesses, "much more than twice as much as Carlyle."[15]

Far more potent, however, than the good advice of Carlyle and the creditable example of Scott was the "bad," brilliant example of Lord Byron. The specter of Byron haunts Trollope's characters with such frequency as to remind us of the great Romantic poet's enormous appeal to the youth of Trollope's generation, some of whom, in becoming spokesmen for the Victorian values of their adult generation, had to turn upon their childhood idol with savage force. The standard of reality and the redefinition of the hero and heroic conduct that many Victorian novelists developed in their writings are often veiled critiques of their own youthful predilections. For example, when Johnny Eames, who strongly resembles the young Anthony Trollope, is described as knowing "much,—by far too much,—of Byron's poetry by heart" (*The Small House at Allington*, chap. 14), the author is pointing up that flaw of Johnny's character which will cause him grief in *The Small House at Allington* and *The Last Chronicle of Barset*. When Phineas Finn charges Byron with falsity (*Phineas Finn*, chap. 14), he is speaking for Carlyle, who condemned Byron for lacking sincerity and for being "a dandy of sorrows" and "a sham strong man."[16] For disoriented young men like Johnny Eames and Charley Tudor (in *The Three Clerks*), however, Byron offers a histrionic role, "the character of a Don Juan" (*Small House*, chap. 4), scoffing at social conventions and playing at being in love. Johnny defends his posturing with pseudo-Byronic self-justification: " 'Love is one thing and amusement is another,' he said to himself as he puffed the cigar-smoke out of his mouth; and in his heart he was proud of his own capacity for enjoyment" (*Last Chronicle*, chap. 46).

The lure and danger of Byron, both in his personal life and in the imaginative appeal of his poetry, were connected in the minds of novelists like Charlotte Brontë with the lure and danger of the creative imagination itself. That the power of the imaginative faculty, which called a new world into being, could be linked with heterodox standards of personal behavior frightened the author of *Jane Eyre* into continual acts of penance for the possession of such powers. It became necessary for her heroines, therefore, to suppress their imaginative natures in favor of the restraints of reality, even though it was their author's own intense imagination that called them into being in the first place. Trollope was born in 1815, Charlotte Brontë in 1816. They were in their teens, therefore, when Thomas Moore's biography of Byron, containing extracts from his journals and letters, appeared in 1830. (Was it coincidental that Trollope "commenced the dangerous habit of keeping a journal" in that year?) This work, more than anything else written about Byron, created the image of the poet-genius that Victorian writers grew up with— and, in many cases, reacted against. "There is something divine in the thought that genius preserves from degradation, were it but true," Charlotte Brontë once wrote; "but Savage tells us it was not true for him; Sheridan confirms the avowal, and Byron seals it with terrible proof."[17]

Like Brontë, Trollope considered his "dangerous mental practice," while a lonely and insecure youth, of imaginary "castle-building" the source of his later ability to write novels. Even so, he insisted, his boyhood fantasies were bound "down to certain laws, to certain proportions, and proprieties, and unities. Nothing impossible was ever introduced,—nor even anything which, from outward circumstances, would seem to be violently improbable." Unlike Charlotte Brontë, whose fantasies at times controlled her, Trollope was always able, he claimed, to impose order on his imagination. "I learned in this way," he asserts, "to maintain an interest in a fictitious story, to dwell on a work created by my own imagination, and to live in a world altogether outside the world of my own material life." Trollope described his novels as "shorn . . . of all romance" and noted that in *Rachel Ray*, for example, he had "attempted to confine [himself] absolutely to the commonest details of commonplace life among the most ordinary people, allowing myself no incident that would be even remarkable in every day life."[18] But the artistry that conceals imaginative intensity may be as powerful as the artistic impulse that exposes what Arnold called in Byron's case "the pageant of his bleeding heart." Despite the modesty about his artistic gifts expressed in the *Autobiography*, the insistence that he was no "genius," Trollope's "amazing ability" (as a recent biographer notes with regard to his writing *Doctor Thorne* while on a postal service mission to Egypt) "to abstract himself from his surroundings and be lifted by his imagination back into Barsetshire" is proof of the artist's imaginative power. The world of *Doctor Thorne*, moreover, was enhanced by romantic values that Trollope refused to see in those Middle Eastern lands which afforded such possibilities for Byronic description.[19]

Trollope's definition of the artist is far more Romantic than the *Autobiography* suggests, although some of the evidence can be found in it. While he ranked the novelist lower than the poet, Trollope acknowledged that "the lessons inculcated by the novelists at present go deeper than most others." The novelist would not "dream that the poet's honour is within his reach;— but his teaching is of the same nature, and his lessons all tend to the same end. By either, false sentiment may be fostered; false notions of humanity may be engendered; false honour, false love, false worship may be created; by either, vice instead of virtue may be taught. But by each, equally, may true honour, true love, true worship, and true humanity be inculcated; and that will be the greatest teacher who will spread such truth the widest." Trollope's belief in the instructive capabilities of the novelist represents a sublimated expression of the Romantic will to power. In *The New Zealander* (1855) he describes the writer as one to whom it "is given in a certain degree to guide mankind," either for good or ill. The writer who preaches truthful conduct, "be he poet, historian, romancer or what not, is the true leader of the people," and the one person capable of delaying, for a time, the decline that Trollope felt must befall England.[20]

This expression of faith in the power of literature is an admission of Trollope's own susceptibilities as a reader. In his lecture in defense of fiction "as a Rational Amusement," Trollope recalls the impact of Ann Radcliffe's novels on him and doubts "whether in these practical and unpoetic days there is left, even among the young, enough of the true spirit of romance to comprehend even what was once the effect of these wonderful compositions." "To be too romantic is not the fault of our time," he acknowledges, almost regretfully, and he credits the Victorian novelists with having replaced the romantic attitude prevalent in his youth with a "manner of looking at life . . . [that] is realistic, practical, and, though upon the whole serviceable, upon the whole also unpoetical rather than romantic." But the novel itself, he observes, evolved out of the desire for "unreal romance"; and while Trollope's fiction evolved out of a childhood hunger for the ordinary pleasures denied him, a deprivation that enabled him to poeticize domestic bliss as the greatest of human pleasures, his literary career was also determined by the ambition to attain the sort of artistic power, without the artistic license, that Byron more than anyone else had displayed earlier in the century. "To be known as somebody," he declares in the *Autobiography*, "—to be Anthony Trollope if it be no more,—is to me much." In a famous passage he admits to a lifelong Promethean desire to " 'hew out some lump of the earth,' and to make men and women walk upon it just as they do walk here among us,—with not more of excellence, nor with exaggerated baseness,—so that my readers might recognize human beings like to themselves, and not feel themselves to be carried away among gods or demons."[21]

The story of Trollope's childhood suffering, his awareness of being cut off from his parents and despised by boys his age, is well known, and his biographers have seen in the contrast "between the outward assurance [of his manner] and the inward uncertainty; between the seeming asperity and the actual tenderheartedness; between the rough insensibility of gesture and the delicate transparency of mind," the effects of his "tormented childhood." His friend T. H. Escott laid special stress on Trollope's "recurrent moods of indefinable dejection and gloom," the underlying melancholy that Trollope attributed to his pessimistic nature.[22] One thinks of the traumatic effects of Byron's unhappy childhood, his sense of being scorned because of his physical infirmity, and how he too had a dual capacity for high spirits and melancholy, which found expression in his writings in sparkling satire and morbid self-analysis. Trollope's recommendations to aspiring writers that they avoid intruding their personality into their work and that they resist the temptation to satire are reminders of his Victorian determination to escape the demands of the ego. Byron's satire was morally blunted, Trollope claimed, because he could not help giving the impression that he was avenging "himself upon a world that had injured him" rather than aiming to correct the abuses of his age. Trollope also warned himself against indulging in the excesses of satire and romance, which had led his mother to "the pitfalls of exaggeration." Frances Trollope possessed humor and compassion in abundance, gifts that her son inherited and learned to express in a more restrained manner than she had in her writings. In contrast to his morbidly self-indulgent and intellectually wasted father, Trollope's mother overflowed with romantic emotions and energies. "She raved . . . of him of whom all such ladies were raving then," her son recalled, "and rejoiced in the popularity and wept over the persecution of Lord Byron."[23] Trollope's portraits of romantically inclined women, such as Lady Glencora Palliser, and of men who inflict great suffering upon themselves, such as Louis Trevelyan (in *He Knew He Was Right*), contain more than a hint of his parents.

Byron's family background was far more disorganized than Trollope's, but the novelist may well have compared himself to the poet, who had also been a student at Harrow, where some of Trollope's unhappiest childhood experiences occurred, and had apparently had the same tutor, Henry Drury. Trollope's sporadic periods of study at Harrow and Winchester took place at the time when, as Henry Taylor noted, "enthusiasm for Lord Byron's impassioned but often rather empty moroseness and despair . . . had passed away from some of the more cultivated classes, and found, perhaps, its surest retreat in the schoolboy's study and in the back shop." To the disoriented, the dependent, and the dispossessed, Byron provided fantasies of power and escape and love. "The very wildness and remoteness" of *The Corsair* and *Lara*, for example, appeal, according to William Hale White, "not to the prosperous man, a dweller in beautiful scenery, well married to an intelligent wife, . . . but to the poor wretch, say some City clerk, with an aspiration beyond his desk, who has two rooms in Camberwell, . . . but who is able to turn to that island in the summer sea where dwells Kaled, his mistress—Kaled, the Dark Page disguised as a man, who watches her beloved dying."[24] As a mildly dissolute young postal clerk in London, Trollope was proud of his acquaintance with Shakespeare, Scott, and Byron. Like Johnny Eames, he considered himself then "a deep critic, often writing down his criticisms in a lengthy journal which he kept" (*Small House*, chap. 14), and perhaps even writing quires of romantic verse, poor in expression but rich in poetic feeling, like those of his seemingly prosaic heroine, Miss Mackenzie.

The immediate cause of Trollope's change from an unhappy clerk, uncertain of his future, to a respected and self-regarding official and novelist was his reassignment to Ireland. There he received the fellowship he had craved and a pleasant taste of power as a postal official. There, too, his imagination was stirred by the sight of so much decay and wasted energy—reminders of his own past life. The result was a novel, *The Macdermots of Ballycloran* (1845), which powerfully describes the collapse of an Irish family, partly as a result of their uncontrollable passions. ("The Irish character is peculiarly well fitted for romance," he writes in the *Autobiography*;[25] and Ireland offered him the chance in several novels to warn against the excesses of romantic feeling.) His mother's *Domestic Manners of the Americans* had been a monumental demonstration of how one could salvage a frustrated adventure by writing it up, and *Childe Harold's Pilgrimage* had provided the evidence that one's personal sufferings and wanderings could be transmuted into art. The Byronic danger, faced by Browning as a young poet as surely as by Trollope as an aspiring novelist, was that one might not be able to put a sufficient distance between oneself and one's subject matter. To achieve an illusion of authorial neutrality became

Trollope's and Browning's goal; and while the poet's magnificent use of the point of view of his characters has always inspired praise, Trollope's own adroit use of the differing angles of vision of his characters to achieve comic or tragic effects has only recently come to be appreciated. The various characters who adopt Byronic attitudes or perform Byronic actions, for example, are generally the victims of their own highly colored self-projections, not projections of Trollope's own views as he wrote. But there were sufficient similarities between Byron and Trollope in outlook and writing habits to force the novelist to chastise the Byronic streak in himself, at times with vindictive energy. Susceptible as he was to the influence of his reading, Trollope was distressed, even as a young man, by the ability of "the Corsair & Jack Shepherd" and Bulwer Lytton's Byronic hero-villains, characters mingling "Cupids morality with general atrocities," to cause "extensive injury" by exciting "admiration & emulation" in others. Unlike his mother, who idealized Byron, Trollope had no illusions about him: "certainly a clever man," he wrote in rebuke to Frances Trollope's poetic tribute, "—but as selfish a bon vivant as ever lived and no more worthy of the etherial character so often given him than I am."[26]

The points of similarity between the two men are noteworthy. They were both compulsive travelers who preferred cosmopolitan values to the insular prejudices of their native land. Trollope's remark that "one is patriotic only because one is too small & too weak to be cosmopolitan," his attack on enforced conscription ("a man should die rather than be made a soldier against his will"), and his dislike of martial glory are expressions of an independent spirit that, like Byron's, refused on occasion to bend to the dictates of convention.[27] At least three of his works were refused or criticized on the grounds of impropriety. (One of them, "A Ride across Palestine," involves a woman who disguises herself as a man, like the page Kaled in *Lara*.) Both writers spoke against cant wherever they saw it, and both indulged in self-deprecation as if to chastise their own weaknesses. The mood of ironical self-deflation in Trollope's *Autobiography* is reminiscent of the self-criticism indulged in by Byron in his journals. Byron's notorious speed as a writer was more than matched by Trollope's; and both men defended their haste on the grounds of being more truthful as well as more inspired as a result. In *The Bertrams* Trollope extols Byron's letters as the finest models of the genre. Keats criticized Byron's work for being a description of what he observed rather than what he imagined, the very charge that reviewers often used against Trollope. Byron's declared aim in *Don Juan*, "to show things really as they are," might also serve to characterize Trollope's goals in early works like *The Three Clerks* (1857) and *The Bertrams* (1858) or in later novels like *The Eustace Diamonds* (1870) and *The Way We Live Now* (1873):

> for I avow,
> That till we see what's what in fact, we're far
> From much improvement with that virtuous plough
> Which skims the surface, leaving scarce a scar
> Upon the black loam long manured by Vice,
> Only to keep its corn at the old price.
>
> (12.40)[28]

Byron's attacks on the materialistic values and hypocritical attitudes in his society enabled Victorian writers to see him as their ally in behalf of noble and truthful conduct: Ruskin, for example, admired his devotion to justice, Arnold his assault on the fortress of Philistinism, Meredith his refusal to "pander to the depraved sentimentalism of our drawing rooms."[29] Trollope, while respectful of the aim, was mistrustful of the results. Like Byron, Trollope saw in man's essential frailty, his inability to "hear the devil plead, and resist the charm of his eloquence" (*The Three Clerks*, chap. 9), the cause of the sorry state of his society. But where Byron and his heroes stand aloof from the world, refusing to "yield dominion of his mind / To spirits against whom his own rebell'd" (*Childe Harold*, 3.12), Trollope and his protagonists often reconcile themselves to the faulty ways of the world. "His novels," Michael Sadleir observes, "are almost without exception novels of a conflict between individual decencies and social disingenuities," and often enough the protagonist "yields to the pressure or to the temptations of convention."[30] This makes for tragic effect, on occasion, but the concession to social values is also sometimes necessary. In *The*

Last Chronicle of Barset, for example, Trollope, instead of using the almost Byronically proud and antiworldly figure Josiah Crawley as a moral standard by which to measure the world of Barsetshire, uses the world as a means of putting this noble but flawed figure into perspective. Trollope allows his comfortable, worldly pastor Mark Robarts the right to "question whether the man was not served rightly by the extremities to which he was reduced. There was something radically wrong within him, which had put him into antagonism with all the world, and which produced these never-dying grievances" (chap. 21). In a Trollope novel a figure resembling Manfred or Childe Harold becomes a lesson in self-destructive pride and can be saved only by the enjoyment of worldly goods, as in Crawley's case, or by marriage, as in the case of Lord Chiltern in *Can You Forgive Her?*

The area of human concern where Trollope unequivocally calls for truthful conduct is that of love relations; and here one must disagree with the critic of Trollope who, noting correctly enough that "no one has ever confused Trollope with Byron," maintains that he was "not a romantic figure, and . . . idyllic love did not affect him profoundly."[31] The love stories in his novels are not, in the main, concessions to popular taste. They are exhibitions, most of the time, of lovers' capacity for integrity, which establish a necessary contrast to the demonstrations of frailty and culpability in the other figures in the novels. (The integrity of the lovers in *Lady Anna* was such as to outrage public taste.) Here Trollope shows the influence of Byron sublimated into the Victorian myth of domestic happiness. (The credit, however, belongs to Charlotte Brontë, Dickens, and Bulwer Lytton—not Trollope—for having transformed the proud and dedicated slave-maidens of Byron's romantic tales into loyal Victorian housewives.) Henry James paid special tribute to the "clinging tenderness" and "passive sweetness" of Trollope heroines like Lucy Robarts and Mary Thorne, whose one function in life is to cling to the men they love.[32] They cling very prettily, for the most part, and show a becoming Jane Eyre-like pride of spirit on occasion, although their devotion, as Trollope indicates in the cases of Emily Hotspur and Lily Dale, can harden into obstinacy or self-destructiveness. The heroine frequently rejects a more qualified suitor because she cannot bow to him as a god, and she often admits (as does Mary Masters in *The American Senator*) that she "would sooner marry a man I loved, though I knew he would ill-use me" (chap. 59). There are instances when a woman like Lady Glencora abandons the "romance of her life" —her devotion to a man she knows "to be a scapegrace, and . . . [likes] . . . the better on that account" (*Can You Forgive Her?*, chap. 69)—in favor of the "rich reality" of a life with Plantagenet Palliser.[33] But the tenacity with which women like Gertrude Woodward or Hetta Carbury or Emily Hotspur cling to inferior men proves the cynical admission Trollope made to Escott that "in love affairs women are generally without discrimination." (Gertrude's devotion to her criminal husband, Alaric Tudor, suggests the similar case of Mrs. Bulstrode's loyalty to her husband in *Middlemarch*.) One remembers the words of one of Byron's slave heroines, who muses that women can "love whom we esteem not."[34]

Examples of such devotion among Trollope's male characters are less frequent, although there is the wonderful exception of Ontario Moggs in *Ralph the Heir*. The bootmaker's romantic son is devoted to Polly Neefit with a fervor that his sister, who reads him "the story of Juan and Haidee" and implores him to "be true to her;—if it's for twenty years" (chap. 48), obviously approves. (The most theatrical examples, and the truest, of romantic passion sometimes occur among such lower-class or vulgar characters in Trollope as Aunt Greenow in *Can You Forgive Her?* and Tom and Gertrude Tringle in *Ayala's Angel*.) The chivalric devotion of Trollope's older male figures to the women they love frequently goes unrewarded, although Plantagenet Palliser is a conspicuous exception whose gentlemanly virtues prove more potent in the end than Byronic impetuosity and good looks. Another sublimated version of Byronic devotion involves the intense dedication of sisters to brothers in Trollope. Kate Vavasor's devotion to her vicious brother George (*Can You Forgive Her?*), Charlotte Stanhope's machinations in behalf of idle Bertie Stanhope (*Barchester Towers*), and Mrs. Harold Smith's efforts to save her brother Sowerby from ruin (*Framley Parsonage*) are examples of sisters' loyalty to worthless brothers. On occasion, however, Trollope satirizes the aspirations to Byronic devotion, as in the case of Mrs. Dobbs Broughton, who imagines herself "with suicidal hands, destroy[ing] the romance of her own life," yet fears lest "some poet did not immortalize her friendship in Byronic verse" (*Last Chronicle*, chap. 51).

Trollope's younger male figures have a tendency to be weak under pressure, especially in matters of love; and Trollope admits the impossibility of heroic action among men in novels like *Ralph the Heir* and *The Eustace Diamonds*. Because men must act in the world, their capacity for integrity becomes dulled, while women, whose duty in life is to *be* rather than to do anything, can maintain disproportionately high standards of moral purity. As Lady Fawn reasons in *The Eustace Diamonds*, "a man out in the world had so many things to think of, and was so very important, that he could hardly be expected to act at all times with truth and sincerity" (chap. 46). Men may play at being Don Juans and then repent, as in the case of Harry Clavering (*The Claverings*) or Paul Montague (*The Way We Live Now*) or John Caldigate; but their tyranny over women is such that even the exaggerated double standard that the bigoted Madame Staubach upholds in *Linda Tressel*, and which Trollope here deplores, is not so very far from the Byronic (and Thackerayan) male-female distinction that one often finds in the novels:

> Such women seem to think that Heaven will pardon that hardness of heart which it has created in man, and which the affairs of the world seem almost to require; but that it will extend no such forgiveness to the feminine creation. It may be necessary that a man should be stiff-necked, self-willed, eager on the world, perhaps even covetous and given to worldly lusts. But for a woman, it behoves her to crush herself, so that she may be at all points submissive, self-denying, and much-suffering. (Chap. 1)[35]

Remove the religious sanction from this account of men and women and we are back in the realm of Byron's Don Juans and Corsairs, whose names are "link'd with one virtue, and a thousand crimes." In Trollope, however, that "one virtue"—fidelity in love—is sometimes missing too.

Trollope frequently inserts into his realistic narratives a male protagonist with Byronic tendencies and features who compels attention from others in the manner of one of Byron's "Fatal Men." Sometimes the man must be expelled, as in the case of George Vavasor or Ferdinand Lopez (*The Prime Minister*), while on other occasions he is allowed to prosper, as in the case of Daniel Thwaite ((*Lady Anna*). The imperious Luke Rowan in *Rachel Ray* (1863), for example (the novel Trollope claimed to have "shorn of all romance"), is described as "conceited, prone to sarcasm, sometimes cynical, and perhaps sometimes affected. It may be that he was not altogether devoid of that Byronic weakness which was so much more prevalent among young men twenty years since than it is now" (chap. 4). Walter Marrable, the dark, swarthy young man (in *The Vicar of Bulhampton*, 1868) who has "received much injury" in his life and whom Mary Lowther prefers to the gentlemanly Harry Gilmore, is distinguished by "a certain ferocity" of expression (chap. 13). The most ferocious and tyrannical of these Byronic figures is George Vavasor (of *Can You Forgive Her?*, 1864), who sports in addition to the requisite dark hair and glowering eyes a Byronic wound—in his case an ugly facial scar. Trollope's ability to put a Byronic convention to new and interesting use is exhibited in the tailor hero of *Lady Anna* (1871): "Daniel Thwaite was swarthy, hard-handed, black-bearded,—with a noble fire in his eyes, but with an innate coarseness about his mouth which betokened roughness as well as strength" (chap. 10). Thwaite has the dilated nostrils, slightly parted lips, and commanding expression that typify the physiognomy of a Lara; but by transposing the Byronic model to the lower classes, Trollope anticipates D. H. Lawrence's attempt to make romantic supermen out of working-class men.[36]

Byronic males whose energy is seen as a necessary component of the society they marry into appear less frequently in Trollope, however, than Byronic figures whose individualist values, or lack of any values, pose threats to their well-being and, in extreme cases, to the society they prey upon. There are at least four categories into which such males fit, although a character often has characteristics of more than one Byronic type. (In Byron the protagonist often exhibits all four traits.) These are the Don Juan figure, the romantic adventurer, the man of destiny, and the defier of convention; and Trollope's feelings toward each of the types are as ambivalent as his attitude toward Byron himself. The Don Juan posture is an affectation adopted by displaced clerks like Charley Tudor and Johnny Eames to give a semblance of poetic meaning and entertainment to their lives, or by bored young men with time on their hands like Bertie Stanhope in *Barchester Towers* or Jack De Baron in *Is He Popenjoy?* Trollope treats such posing with comic indulgence, even when, as in Bertie's case, his genial Lothario is described as being "above, or rather below, all prejudices. No virtue could charm him, no vice shock him . . . He had no principle, no regard for others, no self-respect, no desire to be other than a drone in the hive, if only he could, as a drone, get what honey was sufficient for him" (chap. 9). A more complicated case is that of Eames's successful rival for Lily Dale's hand, Adolphus Crosbie, who tries to disguise his shabby, and ultimately self-punishing, conduct by telling himself that the "world" has ever treated its Don Juans like "curled darlings" (*Small House*, chap. 25). Trollope underscores the passive nature of his would-be Don Juans by showing that they are sometimes manipulated by the women they think they are winning and that, moreover, they crave punishment for their offenses. (Crosbie, for example, wishes that Lily had "a dozen brothers" who would avenge her.)

In his important attack on Byron in 1834, Henry Taylor described Byronic heroes as "creatures abandoned to their passions, and therefore weak of mind. Strip them of the veil of mystery and the trappings of poetry, resolve them into their plain realities, and they are such beings as, in the eyes of a man of masculine judgment, would certainly excite no sentiment of admiration, even if they do not provoke contempt."[37] Taylor might have been describing Trollope's aim in *An Eye for an Eye* (1870), the anti-Byronic tragic novel he wrote immediately after his great anti-Byronic comic novel, *The Eustace Diamonds*. Fred Neville is no "villain," Trollope protests, "simply a self-indulgent spoiled young man who had realized to himself no idea of duty in life" (chap. 12). Neville repeatedly disguises his selfish actions as romantic "adventures"; and he deludes himself into thinking that, after he has seduced the Irish girl who is passionately devoted to him, the Irish priest Father Marty "might be persuaded to do for him something romantic, something marvelous, perhaps something almost lawless" (chap. 14).

Other versions of the adventurer in Trollope appear as commercial pirates. The Corsair is transformed into Ferdinand Lopez (in *The Prime Minister*, 1874), "a self-seeking, intriguing adventurer, who did not know honesty from dishonesty" (chap. 24), but who, like Byron's pirate, is capable of love. Augustus Melmotte, in *The Way We Live Now* (1873), is the apotheosis of the adventurer, a swindler whom everyone respects because he is so successful at his game.[38] "There's nothing like being a robber," one of his admirers declares, "if you can only rob enough" (chap. 32). Trollope had already shown how commercial fraud is disguised by romantic rhetoric in an early novel, *The Struggles of Brown, Jones, and Robinson* (1861), illustrating "the way in which we all live" (chap. 1). "The groundwork of advertising is romance," observes the central figure in that book. "It is poetry in its very essence. Is *Hamlet* true? . . . Advertisements are profitable, not because they are believed, but because they are attractive" (chap. 10). Melmotte wins the admiration of the reader, at times, for his mixture of romantic persiflage and self-awareness. Knowing that his days as a swindler are numbered, he looks "up at the bright stars" (as if contemplating a Childe Haroldean interplanetary pilgrimage) in a passage of comic brilliance tinged with Byronic wistfulness:

> If he could be there, in one of those unknown distant worlds, with all his present intellect and none of his present burdens, he would, he thought, do better than he had done here on earth. If he could even now put himself down nameless, fameless, and without possessions in some distant corner of the world, he could, he thought, do better. But he was Augustus Melmotte, and he must bear his burdens, whatever they were, to the end. He could reach no place so distant but that he would be known and traced. (Chap. 62)

Trollope's variation on the Byronic figure ostensibly manipulated by fate is best seen in Louis Trevelyan in *He Knew He Was Right*, which I will discuss separately. Byron's most vivid case of the individual who feels "a power upon me which withholds,

/ And makes it my fatality to live" is Manfred (1.2.23–24), whose manifestation of self-will leads to a desire for self-oblivion. The most extreme case in Trollope of a man driven by a "Fury" and "conscious of being so driven" is that of George Vavasor (*Can You Forgive Her?*, chap. 56). Trollope is more sympathetic to other figures who lack self-control, such as Owen Fitzgerald in *Castle Richmond*, Burgo Fitzgerald in *Can You Forgive Her?*, and Mountjoy Scarborough in *Mr. Scarborough's Family*. Such characters genuinely cannot control their self-destructive impulses. In most instances, however, Trollope shows that a figure like Trevelyan, who blames fate for his misfortunes, has only himself to blame. "Fate is a good excuse for our own will," as Byron pungently observes in *Don Juan* (13.12), deflating the very notion of the "Fatal Man."

It is as the defier of convention that the Byronic character exerts perhaps its most suggestive and dangerous influence on Trollope and his characters. The description of Johnny Eames's boyish desire for license gives way to accounts of individuals living in such violation of convention that they cut themselves off from the human community, where, in Trollope, true happiness flows. The path of exile taken by Childe Harold is followed by such diverse figures as the Stanhope family in *Barchester Towers*, Lord Lovel in *Lady Anna*, and the Marquis of Brotherton in *Is He Popenjoy?*, all of whom prefer the relaxed moral climate in Italy.[39] The lure of bohemianism is best expressed by Madame Goesler in *Phineas Finn* (1867): "it is so pleasant to feel oneself to be naughty!" she tells Phineas; "there is a Bohemian flavour of picnic about it which, though it does not come up to the rich gusto of real wickedness, makes one fancy that one is on the border of that delightful region in which there is none of the constraint of custom,—where men and women say what they like." "It is pleasant enough to be on the borders," Phineas replies (chap. 72)—and Trollope's sympathies are of a borderline nature. He could show the need to defy conventions in a late novel like *Dr. Wortle's School* (1879): "It is not often that one comes across events like these, so altogether out of the ordinary course that the common rules of life seem to be insufficient for guidance," says Dr. Wortle. "To most of us it never happens; and it is better for us that it should not happen. But when it does, one is forced to go beyond common rules" (chap. 7). But he worries about the effects of flouting convention on persons like Crawley or Trevelyan or Julius Mackenzie (in "The Spotted Dog," 1870). Mackenzie's desire to assert himself in contempt of the "conventional thraldom of so-called 'gentlemen' " results in a life of perpetual self-degradation. The Editor who narrates this moving tale observes at the end, after Mackenzie has been driven to suicide: "This was the upshot of his loud claims for liberty from his youth upwards;—liberty as against his father and family; liberty as against his college tutor; liberty as against all pastors, masters, and instructors; liberty as against the conventional thraldom of the world!" Trollope's individualistic streak was no doubt the reason that he told Kate Field that "nature intended me for an American rather than an Englishman." Yet he preferred "to be a bad Englishman . . . than a good American," perhaps because of the security from the threats of unconventionality and excessive self-reliance that his more orderly society provided.[40]

The destructive potential of the human will, self-alienated from human ties and social conventions, is the main subject of *He Knew He Was Right* (1868).[41] This brilliant novel and *The Eustace Diamonds* (1870) are the key masterworks in which Trollope shows the dangerous effects of Byronic defiance when translated out of the world of Corsairs and Laras and into the real world. But where Trollope treats Byronic attitudes with devastating satire in *The Eustace Diamonds*, he shows the tragic results of stiff-necked pride in the account of Louis Trevelyan's pursuit of humiliation and self-destruction in *He Knew He Was Right*. The initial cause of Trevelyan's decline into madness is the attention paid to his wife by an elderly acquaintance who enjoys being mistaken for a Don Juan by her husband. Both husband and wife feel that the other should apologize—he for being suspicious, she for refusing to obey his orders—and the unwillingness of either to give way reinforces each one's opinion that he or she alone is right. The desire to be proved right drives Trevelyan to wish that the adultery he has feared might happen in fact. "They who do not understand that a man may be brought to hope that which of all things is most grievous to him," Trollope remarks, "have not observed with sufficient closeness the perversity of the human mind" (chap. 38). From refusing to believe in his wife, Trevelyan grows to disbelieve in everyone and everything. Self-exiled to Italy, he gloats to his former best friend that it has been his "study to untie all the ties; and, by Jove, I have succeeded. Look at me here. I have got rid of the trammels pretty well,—haven't I?—have unshackled myself, and thrown off the paddings, and the wrappings, and the swaddling clothes. I have got rid of the conventionalities, and can look Nature straight in the face" (chap. 92).[42]

But what can Trevelyan see other than that he has caused his own ruin? Mad as he is, believing himself "to have been the victim of so cruel a conspiracy among those who ought to have been his friends" as well as the victim of "the terrible hand of irresistible Fate," Trevelyan still has glimmers of the truth. He half suspects "that he had brought his misery upon himself by being unlike to other men" (chap. 84). Even so, he relishes the sense of his tragic role: "He almost revelled in the idea of the tragedy he would make" (chap. 45). Once again Trollope uses a character's point of view to great effect. It is Trevelyan, not Trollope, who conceals the real ignominiousness of his position by investing himself with the trappings of Othello and Lear. Trollope had seen in his father an example of self-inflicted suffering, and he had presented a related kind of suffering in Josiah Crawley, who is deluded into considering himself a latter-day St. Paul. Perhaps the best precedent in Byron for this kind of destructive pride is Lara, "a stranger in this breathing world" and a "thing of dark imaginings," who has been the instrument of his own moral degradation:

> But haughty still, and loth himself to blame,
> He called on Nature's self to share the shame,
> And charged all faults upon the fleshly form
> She gave to clog the soul, and feast the worm;
> Till he at last confounded good and ill,
> And half mistook for fate the acts of will.

Trollope expunges the criminal element from Byron's self-doomed figures but retains the

> . . . strange perversity of thought,
> That swayed him onward with a secret pride
> To do what few or none would do beside.
>
> *(Lara,* 1.18)

The pursuit of a tragic role in life is a self-defeating enterprise in Trollope, an expense of spirit in a waste of shame. To offset the gloomy aspect of the Trevelyan sections of *He Knew He Was Right,* Trollope employs three romantic counterplots, plus a comic subplot, to show the advantages of "self-abnegation" in a love relationship. The bohemian journalist Hugh Stanbury, for example, learns to find in domestic life the romantic dreams of his youth. Charles Glascock's gentlemanly conduct in behalf of others prompts his American fiancée, who abandons her countrymen's ethic of self-reliance, to note that "the heroes of life are so much better than the heroes of romance" (chap. 85). Dorothy Stanbury's love for Brooke Burgess, on the other hand, enables her to mature from an overly passive maiden into a young lady with a newly won sense of self-importance. Even the comical-pathetic clergyman Gibson provides a parody of Byronic attitudes. Wavering between the desire to play Don Juan to both of the French sisters and the wish to escape their matrimonial nets, Gibson ascribes his weakness to "some mysterious agency [that] interferes with the affairs of a man and drives him on,—and on,—and on,—almost,—till he doesn't know where it drives him" (chap. 65).

It is this comical-pathetic side of the imitation of Byron that Trollope stresses so successfully in *The Eustace Diamonds.* Lizzie Eustace is the comic counterpart of Louis Trevelyan: obstinate, self-willed, defiant of conventions. She, too, by her perverse refusal to understand and act on the truth, cuts herself off from the respectable world. But Lizzie is so shallow a creature, so lacking in identity, that hers may be called the comedy of a lack of will, just as Trevelyan's is the tragedy of an abundance of will. Trollope frequently shows how a character's overresponsiveness to Byronic or Shakespearean description of behavior colors his own personality. "Half at least of the noble deeds done in the world are due to emulation, rather than to the native nobility of the actors," he declares in *The Last Chronicle of*

Barset (chap. 31). Lizzie's defect is that she is all performance: half of her life consists of the absorption of lies and the other half of the mangled transmission of them. "She liked lies," Trollope says of her, "thinking them to be more beautiful than truth. To lie readily and cleverly, recklessly and yet successfully, was, according to the lessons which she had learned, a necessity in woman and an added grace in man" (chap. 79).

From a novelist who can provide sympathy even for his worst villains, the vitriol lavished on so comparatively harmless a being seems odd at first glance. Lady Eustace is compared at various points in the novel to "a witch whistling for a wind, and ready to take the first blast that would carry her and her broomstick somewhere into the sky" (chap. 35); to Tennyson's Vivien, the seductress of Merlin; and to Spenser's Duessa, who finally appears "soiled, haggard, dishevelled, and unclean" (chap. 76) to the young man she has hoped to entrap. Part of the reason for his hostile attitude undoubtedly lies in the fact that in this, the third volume of the series of political novels he was working on, Trollope wished to show that just as romantic feeling is debased by Lizzie into Byronic posturing, so too has politics been turned into a rhetorical game by mountebank politicians like Daubeny-Disraeli. *The Eustace Diamonds* enabled Trollope to mount an indirect attack on Disraeli, whose novel *Lothair* had recently appeared (and was rumored to have received the highest advance payment for a Victorian novel). Trollope's description of Disraeli's fiction in the *Autobiography* sounds very much like an account of Lizzie's romantic fantasies: it contains the "flavour of paint and unreality," "the glory of pasteboard," "a wealth of tinsel," "the wit of hairdressers," "the enterprise of mountebanks," "a feeling of stage properties, a smell of hair-oil, an aspect of buhl, a remembrance of tailors, and that pricking of the conscience which must be the general accompaniment of paste diamonds."[43] When Trollope observes of Lizzie that "there was no reality about her" (chap. 61), he is comparing her to one of Disraeli's characters—a point that is underscored when he doubts "whether paste diamonds [instead of her famous necklace] might not better suit her character" (chap. 17). It is "poetic" justice that she ultimately is captivated by the rhetorical audacity of the Jewish adventurer Emilius: the incarnation of Disraeli himself. "Presuming, as she naturally did, that something of what he said was false," Trollope remarks, "she liked the lies. There was a dash of poetry about him; and poetry, as she thought, was not compatible with humdrum truth" (chap. 73).

The connection between lies and poetry is at the center of Trollope's satire—a satire directed against himself and his readers, as well as against Lizzie Eustace. The plot involving a stolen necklace allowed Trollope to poke fun at the popularity in the mid-Victorian period of mystery novels with romantic villains and elaborately contrived plots.[44] Trollope's determination to keep no secrets from his readers is a violation of the code of the genre, as is his reminder to us that he is presenting reality instead of fiction. Trollope's insistence that the novel must be "truthful" if its readers are to learn lessons in realistic conduct is perhaps his central article of artistic faith, his reply to Carlyle's charge that fictions are worthless because they are a form of lying. But even the most realistic of fictions remains a fiction. It was Trollope's goal, as he noted in the *Autobiography*, to pass off the creations of his imagination as human beings like his readers. It was the sense of the writer's power, and the forcibleness of his susceptibilities as a reader, that prodded Trollope into becoming a writer; and the satire in *The Eustace Diamonds* is directed at the creative and the absorptive processes alike. This is the novel, after all, in which Trollope stages a performance of his own unproduced play, *The Noble Jilt*, so that it can be attacked on the grounds of improbability.

Lizzie Eustace's believing in the existence of Corsairs because she has read Byron is a naive and eloquent testimony to the powers of art. For Lizzie, every man she meets is a potential Conrad, possessing "that utter indifference to all conventions and laws which is the great prerogative of Corsairs" (chap. 44). When her necklace is stolen, she admires the most eligible candidate for the role of Corsair and thief, Lord George de Bruce Carruthers; and she considers that his disposal of his accomplice, Patience Crabstick, by dropping "the girl overboard, tied up in a bag, . . . would [be] a proper Corsair arrangement" (chap. 62). (Lord George, to her disappointment, turns out to be innocent and brutally honest.) She feels that there would "be a certain charm in being . . . mastered" by such a man (chap.

51); and she imagines that being "hurried about the world" with him, "treated sometimes with crushing severity, and at others with the tenderest love, not to be spoken to for one fortnight, and then to be embraced perpetually for another, to be cast every now and then into some abyss of despair by his rashness, and then raised to a pinnacle of human joy by his courage—that . . . would be the kind of life which would suit her poetical temperament" (chap. 44). Even Lizzie's romantically derived masochism is a sham masochism. She lacks real emotional feeling. Poetry for her, whether Byron or the Bible, is a matter of intoxicating words only; and when Emilius makes his floridly worded proposal to her, she finds in it "a taste of the Bible" mixed with the flavor of the "Juan and Haidee" episode (chap. 79). Lady Eustace reappears, somewhat subdued in character, in *Phineas Redux* and *The Prime Minister*. In the latter book her Corsair finally materializes in the shape of the adventurer Ferdinand Lopez, who dares her "to escape with [him and her fortune] from the cold conventionalities, from the miserable thraldom of this country bound in swaddling clothes." "Mr. Lopez," she replies, "I think you must be a fool" (chap. 54).

One should keep in mind that it is the response to Byron, rather than Byron himself, that is satirized in *The Eustace Diamonds*. And one should not forget that Trollope's master in the deprecation of Byronism was Byron himself, who was able in *Don Juan* to mock the sort of "Poeshie" (as he once called it) that had achieved such popularity. Trollope's descriptions of fashionable life in his novels contain echoes from the English cantos of *Don Juan*. (Lady Dumbello, née Griselda Grantly, might have stepped out of Byron's satire; and there is even a suggestive description of a fox hunt in *Don Juan*.) Trollope's personal respect for Byron at this period is evident in a letter, written two months before he began *The Eustace Diamonds*, in which he dismissed Harriet Beecher Stowe's famous attack on the poet as the most "outrageous piece of calumny—in the real sense of the word— . . . ever published."[45]

In three late novels, *Is He Popenjoy?* (1875), *Ayala's Angel* (1878), and *Mr. Scarborough's Family* (1881), Trollope again employs Byronic figures and attitudes for part of his subject matter, but his treatment of them is mellower than in the past. The would-be Don Juan, Jack De Baron, and the dissolute Marquis of Brotherton are both allowed an element of poignancy. Like Trollope's other Byronic defiers of convention, the Marquis exiles himself to Italy; but he must eventually face the meaninglessness of his existence: "It had been the resolution of his life to live without control, and now, at four-and-forty, he found that the life he had chosen was utterly without attraction" (*Popenjoy*, chap. 53). In *Ayala's Angel* Trollope describes an elderly artist living in defiance of all conventions in Rome ("Conventions are apt to go very quickly, one after another, when the first has been thrown aside"; chap. 17), who threatens to cast off his son for wanting to live in conventional domestic bliss in England. The central figure of this charming book is a bohemian artist's daughter, who dreams of an "Angel of light" whom she can adore in the manner of one of Byron's slave-maidens. Her angel materializes in the figure of a satirically minded, red-haired "Angel of the earth." Reality is invested with romance; and Colonel Stubbs, Ayala's high-spirited angel, speaks in favor of both values: "I don't mind a little Byron now and again," he concedes, "so there is no nonsense" (chap. 18).[46]

It is in one of Trollope's last novels, *Mr. Scarborough's Family*, however, that he paid the fullest tribute to the power of Byronic romance and at last acknowledged publicly his own relish of authorial power. Old Scarborough's defiance of justice and truth would be a self-punishing moral offense in *Orley Farm* or *The Eustace Diamonds*; yet Scarborough gets his way again and again without feeling remorse. Like a romantic plot-maker, he creates alternate versions of the truth in order to mystify and fool the world. He has two legally valid marriage certificates, one made before and one after his elder son's birth, so that he can apply the laws of primogeniture to whichever son is worthier of inheriting his large estate. Each son seems an expression of the Byronic polarities of romance and satire: Mountjoy, who has the features of a Corsair, is extravagantly self-destructive, while Augustus is cynical and vindictive. In a sense, they are his literary creations as well as his sons. Scarborough's doctor sees a decidedly "romantic" quality in him: "he has within him a capacity for love, and an unselfishness, which almost atones for his dishonesty," he declares. "And there is about him a strange dislike to conventionality and to law which is so interesting as to make up the balance" (chap. 53). Scarborough makes a Byronic defense of his actions to his principled lawyer: "You don't understand the inner man which rules me,—how it has struggled to free itself from conventionalities. Nor do I quite understand how your inner man has succumbed to them and encouraged them." "I have encouraged an obedience to the laws of my country," the lawyer replies. "Men generally find it safer to do so." "Exactly; and men like to be safe. Perhaps a condition of danger has had its attractions for me" (chap. 19).

"One cannot make an apology for him," the doctor admits after Scarborough's death, "without being ready to throw all truth and morality to the dogs. But if you can imagine for yourself a state of things in which neither truth nor morality shall be thought essential, then old Mr. Scarborough would be your hero" (chap. 58). The key word here is "imagine": put into the real world, Scarborough and his excessively individualistic standards would subvert social harmony, but set within the realm of romance, where all things are permissible, he becomes a romantic hero. A Romantic demon existed in most of the major Victorian novelists; that in the thirty-five years of his writing career so obviously "realistic" a writer as Trollope devoted so much attention to the exposure of romantic illusions proves that in his own case the demon was never fully exorcised. In old Scarborough Trollope allows his romantic sensibilities full rein at last. At the end, it is true, Scarborough chooses to revert to the truth with regard to the inheritance of his estate before, like Prospero, breaking his wand forever. But in the meantime, he enables Anthony Trollope to exhibit his fascination with Byronic romance and, in so doing, to assert his own artistic power. The novel allowed Trollope, within sight of his own death, to dare the conventionalities.

THREE

Benjamin Disraeli
and the
Romance of the Will

*The power of the passions, the force of the
will, the creative energy of the imagination,
these make life, and reveal to us a world of
which the million are entirely ignorant.*

Lothair

Historians have long recognized the Romantic element in Disraeli's political beliefs, and their view of his place in history has been considerably influenced by their attitudes toward those Romantic traits.[1] Disraeli viewed a political career as a Romantic mission, as a vehicle for his Romantic artistry: in public service a Shelleyan devotion to the welfare of others could be united to a Byronic display of will and a Keatsian display of imagination. As one of the earliest English statesmen to capitalize on what Walter Bagehot called the public readiness to be governed by appeals to their imagination, Disraeli had many detractors who were disturbed by the ways in which he, in creating a myth of his own role and person for public consumption, occasionally disregarded humble matters of truth.[2] The hero of Trollope's series of political novels, Plantagenet Palliser, was conceived, in large part, in protest against the manner in which Disraeli had risen to eminence. Everything about Palliser's political ideals and performance is at variance with Disraeli's:

He was not a brilliant man, and understood well that such was the case. He was now listened to in the House, as the phrase goes; but he was listened to as a laborious man, who was in earnest in what he did, who got up his facts with accuracy, and who, dull though he be, was worthy of confidence. And he was very dull. He rather prided himself on being dull, and on conquering in spite of his dulness. He never allowed himself a joke in his speeches, nor attempted even the smallest flourish of rhetoric. He was very careful in his language, labouring night and day to learn to express himself with accuracy, with no needless repetition of words, perspicuously with regard to the special object he might have in view. He had taught himself to believe that oratory, as oratory, was a sin against that honesty in politics by which he strove to guide himself.[3]

Palliser's dullness and honesty lead him to only a limited success, as head of the sort of coalition government that, Disraeli noted, England did not love. Disraeli, by contrast, took advantage of his resources of imagination and language to become one of the most popular, if also one of the most mistrusted, of Victorian British leaders. The Romantic state of mind that he brought to politics is candidly and often engagingly revealed in his novels, and the connection between Disraeli's Romantic politics and his literary endeavors provides an intriguing perspective on the allure and dangers of the Romantic impulse.

Where Trollope sought to conceal or discipline his Romantic sensibility, Disraeli delighted in exposing and making use of his. Although he was, like his friend Edward Bulwer Lytton, a second-generation Romantic, Disraeli gave his assent to many of the cardinal Romantic tenets, such as faith in the supremacy of the will as controller of one's destiny and in the primacy of the imagination as arbiter of reality and redeemer of mankind. However, he also gave the impression, on occasion, that he was taking advantage of these beliefs and of the credulity of his audience in order to create an effect. In this respect, his championing of the rights of the imagination, for example, might be compared with the claims of his predecessors. The Romantic poets' refusal "to submit the poetic spirit" to what Wordsworth called "the chains of fact and real circumstance" is well known: in Blake's case, for example, "the things imagination saw were as much realities as were gross and tangible facts." One of the most extreme instances involving a Romantic poet's disregard for historical accuracy occurs in Keats's "On First Looking into Chapman's Homer," where Cortez is substituted for Balboa as the discoverer of the Pacific Ocean. However accidental the original slip may have been, once Keats's imagination had conjured up Cortez he was obliged to leave the line as it stood: "Or like stout Cortez when with eagle eyes / He star'd at the Pacific." Keats's claim for the "truth of the imagination" is well known. "What the imagination seizes as Beauty must be truth—whether it existed before or not," he says in a famous letter. The imagination, as far as a Romantic poet is concerned, *creates* truth, rather than reflects something that for a scientist or explorer is merely real. "The Imagination may be compared to Adam's dream—he awoke and found it truth."[4]

Keats's words help to clarify a major theme in Disraeli's political life and in his fiction: the supreme importance of the imagination as an instrument of redemptive power and the consequent irrelevance of facts. It is this faith in the imagination (and in what Keats calls "the holiness of the Heart's affections") that prompts the words of Sidonia in Disraeli's best-known novel, *Coningsby*: "Man is only truly great when he acts from the passions; never irresistible but when he appeals to the imagination. Even Mormon counts more votaries than Bentham."[5] The heroes of Disraeli's novels aspire to be leaders in a thoroughly Romantic fashion: by influencing their constituents through the magnetic force of their brilliantly endowed imaginations. Disraeli's popularity as a statesman was based on this realization; he claimed that his motive in writing the trilogy of *Coningsby, Sybil,* and *Tancred* was to recognize "imagination in the government of nations as a quality not less important than reason."[6] But it was his resultant lack of interest in the factual details so dear to Utilitarian philosophers and realistic novelists that won him so many enemies as a statesman and a writer. "The intellectuals detested him almost to a man," as Robert Blake notes. Trollope's denunciation of the novels as having only the "flavour of paint and unreality" is the classic statement showing why the then Prime Minister and his novels should both be consigned to the dust bin:

> In whatever he has written he has affected something which has been intended to strike his readers as uncommon and therefore grand. Because he has been bright and a man of genius, he has carried his object as regards the young. He has struck them with astonishment and aroused in their imagination ideas of a world more glorious, more rich, more witty, more enterprising than their own. But the glory has ever been the glory of pasteboard, and the wealth has been a wealth of tinsel. The wit has been the wit of hairdressers and the enterprise has been the enterprise of mountebanks.[7]

An answer to this line of attack (though not made in response to Disraeli) is to be found in Oscar Wilde's "The Decay of Lying," a defense of the creative power of the imagination and the need to divert from reality in the name of something better—which brings us back to Keats's premise quoted earlier. What to a Romantic-minded author is poetic license, to a realist is lying. When a Tory member of Parliament chooses to embellish the truth or discard it altogether, as Disraeli did on a number of occasions, he faces the resistance of opponents who are uninterested in whether he is speaking on behalf of what to him appears a larger and grander objective. "I like a lie sometimes," one of his fictional characters admits, "but then it must be a good one."[8]

The second major component of Disraeli's Romanticism was his faith in the transforming power of the human will. If his associates in the Young England group "sought to revive a Toryism not the less potent for having never existed outside their imagination,"[9] Disraeli, with a mixture of idealism, ambition, and pragmatism, was uniquely able to transform some of their political fancies into concrete policy and action. The key Romantic personality for Disraeli (as for George Smythe, the leading figure in Young England and the model for Coningsby) was Byron, whose assertion of will in his life and whose celebration of will in much of his work were seen by repentant first-generation Romantics like Coleridge and Southey as a Satanic predilection: the liberated imagination and will finding expression in egoistic fantasies and questionable behavior. The Romantics were willing to admire heroes, as Carl Woodring notes, because "they lived in an atmosphere where will was ascendant . . . In the actuality around them, reason subsided under the growing supremacy of will. The old Renaissance belief in man's freedom, immortality, and reason became less prudently belief in man's freedom, creative imagination, and illimitable power of will."[10] In Disraeli's case, however, the dangerous potential of the will was neutralized by his boyish faith in romance. No setback encountered by the future Prime Minister and his literary protagonists could make them abandon their sense of being ordained to occupy a dominating position. Thackeray spoke with admiration and mockery of Disraeli's "strong faith" in his heroes' ambitious fantasies: the reader "can't help fancying (we speak for ourselves), after perusing the volumes, that he too is a regenerator of the world, and that he has we don't know how many thousands a year."[11] But if an individual has sufficient faith in his willpower, Disraeli repeatedly proclaimed, he will not go unrewarded: the prerogative of the romance hero—to come into good fortune "without any effort or exertion of your own"[12]—accompanies the ambition of the Byronic hero.

Disraeli's huge political success—achieved in spite of the handicaps of his non-Christian birth and his nonaristocratic background—is a tribute to the possibilities of romance as well as to the hold that romance and Romantic values had on the Victorians. A reaction against the excesses of Romanticism is characteristic of what we think of as Victorianism: Victorian writers replaced the Romantic glorification of the individual will with an emphasis on communal and domestic values. "Close thy Byron, open thy Goethe" was Carlyle's shorthand way of arguing that English society would collapse if men and women saw themselves as superior to the world they lived in. The call for self-renunciation and a redirection of one's individual energies into social causes is the theme of that great work to which all Victorian fiction aspires, *Middlemarch*. But while Disraeli did open his Carlyle he never closed his Byron, and it was with reference to George Eliot that he tartly observed that when he wanted to read a novel, he wrote one.[13] Unlike many of his contemporaries who worshipped Byron in the early nineteenth century but regarded him as one of the sins of their youth when they and the century reached middle age, Disraeli never lost his enthusiasm for the figure whom he once claimed to be "greater even as a man than a writer."[14] There is a suggestion in Disraeli's first novel, *Vivian Grey* (1827), that if Byron had only lived longer and returned to England he might have become a political force to reckon with. (Byron himself had toyed with the idea of achieving fame in a political and military, as well as literary, capacity. After his eloquent speech in the House of Lords defending the rights of the people during the Frame-Work Bill debate, Byron noted that "Ld. H[olland] tells me I shall beat them all if I persevere." In later years, however, he denied being "made for what you call a politician, and should never have adhered to any party." The "intrigues" and "contests for power" that Disraeli delighted in Byron professed disgust for.)[15] The hero of Disraeli's second novel, *The Young Duke* (1831), distinguishes himself politically by speaking in the House of Lords in favor of Catholic Emancipation, the subject of Byron's own speech in the same House in 1812. Disraeli's efforts on behalf of Jewish rights were an extension of Byron's pro-Catholic efforts, just as Disraeli's continuing and deliberately provoking references to "the sacred and romantic people from whom I derive my blood and name" were in line with Byron's great pride in his own ancestry.[16]

Byron's hold on the public resembled Napoleon's: theirs seemed the triumph of men of destiny whose egotism was bold and splendid enough to speak for and direct the hidden wishes of the multitude. Disraeli associated himself with the assertive Byron, although in times of dejection he also identified with the thwarted Byron, the melancholy figure bumping his head against social convention and cosmic fate. Unlike Bulwer Lytton, however, and greatly to his own advantage as novelist and statesman, Disraeli was able to adopt the role of the self-mocking Byron as well. Disraeli was later to identify himself with another Romantic statesman, Napoleon III, and just as Byron's rise to literary power provides the plot for his early novel *Venetia* (1837), Louis Napoleon's rise to political eminence is celebrated in his last novel, *Endymion* (1880). In both cases, Disraeli was fascinated by the spectacle of a man of strong will attaining influence over others.[17] Louis Napoleon's determination to link "the rights of the people and the principles of authority" is similar to Disraeli's romantic Tory conviction that the aristocracy is the natural ally of the people; and where Louis Napoleon confidently invoked his uncle's name and his own "Star" as proof that he was "fated" to lead France, Disraeli interpreted his ambitions in a similarly romantic manner. Both leaders were hugely popular with multitudes hungry for a grand myth, and both were assailed as charlatans.[18]

Disraeli gained greater prominence as a statesman than as a writer, but as a young man he hoped to win for himself the literary power that Byron had wielded and also to wield political power over others as a result of following the Byronic formula. To know oneself thoroughly, as Byron had known himself, meant to be aware of the passions that animate mankind. "Self-knowledge," as he notes of successful orators in *The Young Duke*, "is the property of that man whose passions have their play, but who ponders over their results. Such a man sympathises by inspiration with his kind. He has a key to every heart. He can divine, in the flash of a single thought, all that they require, all that they wish" (p. 307). "It is the personal that interests mankind," he writes in *Coningsby*, "that fires their imagination, and wins their hearts. A cause is a great abstraction, and fit only for students; embodied in a party, it stirs men to action; but place at the head of that party a leader who can inspire enthusiasm, he commands the world" (p. 112). It was Disraeli's fantasy to become the acknowledged and the unacknowledged legislator of the world: Shelley's famous line from "A Defence of Poetry" is quoted in the novel *Venetia*, which appeared just as Disraeli was finally preparing to enter Parliament. The Shelleyan echo should remind us that Disraeli's Romanticism was ultimately directed toward a goal of public service, not selfish gratification.[19] In recent years the Byronic clinging to a position of "self-assertion in an alien universe" has been interpreted as an existential triumph, a heroic model of "humanistic self-reliance";[20] but the Byronic conquest of self-will, as displayed in his campaign for Greek independence, was hailed by many Victorians as an example of humanistic self-denial. By linking the Byronic will with the Shelleyan sympathetic imagination, Disraeli attempted to show that Romantic convictions could be made to serve the public interest. In his political speeches and his novels alike, Disraeli increasingly held up Romantic values as bulwarks against the anti-Romantic, socially corrosive forces of materialism, Utilitarianism, and nihilism.

In a diary entry for 1833, Disraeli, who had recently been twice defeated in bids for a Parliamentary seat, noted how difficult it would be to overcome the obstacles and prejudices lying in the way of the political success he craved. For the moment, he acknowledged, writing was "the safety-valve of [his] passions," but he panted "to act what" he wrote about. He then described three of his novels as "the secret history of [his] feelings." "In *Vivian Grey* I have portrayed my active and real ambition. In *Alroy* my ideal ambition. *The Psychological Romance* [*Contarini Fleming*] is a development of my poetic character."[21] Despite differences in the books' backgrounds and subject matter, the theme in the trilogy is the same: the determination to achieve power in one form or another. There is a passage or two in each book in which the hero thinks of exerting power for humanitarian or libertarian ends, but this is only incidental to the grand ambition itself.

"Superior power, exercised by a superior mind" (*VG*, p. 12), is the professed goal of Vivian Grey while yet a schoolboy; but this Byronic audacity gives way to Byronic melancholy when Vivian's schemes for political power are thwarted. In the second part of the novel, Vivian switches from an active to a passive role: he looks on while, in a memorable episode, a German minister, Beckendorff, achieves the very sort of power he has desired. Beckendorff himself sounds for the first time in Disraeli's writings the belief in the power of the will to achieve what it wishes. "If, in fact, you wish to succeed," he tells Vivian, "success . . . is at your command" (p. 395). In *The Wondrous Tale of Alroy* (1833), which was inspired partly by Disraeli's trip to the Middle East in 1831, partly by his fascination with a minor Jewish prince of the twelfth century who had declared himself the Messiah and achieved a brief success,[22] Disraeli advanced the claim that his Jewish ancestry entitled him to be considered as worthy a claimant for English office as any nobleman. His hero, Alroy, describes himself as "the descendant of sacred kings, and with a soul that pants for empire" (p. 9); and the escapades of the original princeling are blown up into the heroics of one who is a cross between Napoleon and Moses. Although the heroism comes to nothing, Disraeli protests that "a great career, although baulked of its end, is still a landmark of human energy" (p. 255).

Whether fantasying himself as a Metternichian minister of state in *Vivian Grey*, a Jewish Napoleon in *Alroy*, or a great writer in *Contarini Fleming* (1832), Disraeli's obsession in the trilogy is with power. Like Vivian Grey, Contarini Fleming spends his childhood dreaming that "life must be intolerable unless I were the greatest of men. It seemed that I felt within me the power that could influence my kind" (*CF*, pp. 28–29). In the course of the novel, Contarini indulges in a number of power games: in his schoolmates he sees "only beings whom I was determined to control" (p. 23) through the force of his eloquence; the creatures his youthful poetic imagination invents he sees as an army which will "go forth to the world to delight and to conquer" (p. 39); even his beloved he regards with a possessive eye, and despite an operatic flourish of grief after her death, he consoles himself with the thought "that at the moment of departure her last thought was for me" (p. 254). By his father, who has achieved a political prominence not unlike that of Beckendorff in Disraeli's first novel, Contarini is advised to model himself upon "really great men; that is to say, men of great energies and violent volition, who look upon their fellow-creatures as mere tools, with which they can build up a pedestal for their solitary statue" (p. 111). An admirer of Napoleon, the elder Fleming represents the cynical extreme to which Disraeli's Byronic fancies might have led him. Looking upon people as brutes who can easily be manipulated, Fleming believes "all to depend upon the influence of individual character" (p. 95). The son rejects the political career his father has directed him toward, but he uses the same methods when he becomes a Shelleyan poet, determined to "exercise an illimitable power over the passions of his kind" (p. 255).

In no other Disraeli novel are the author's ambitions and self-conceit so profusely illustrated as in *Contarini Fleming*. It might be said that if Narcissus had been a novelist, this is the book he would have written. Everyone Contarini meets he longs to dominate, and everything he sees becomes a subjective correlative of his own feelings. Having crossed the Swiss Alps and visually absorbed the geographical and meteorological props so dear to a Romantic poet, he exults in the new images he can use to overwhelm his readers. Creativity is reduced to the status of a martial art. Contarini's exploits form a pattern-book of romantic behavior—a boyish version of Bulwer Lytton's Maltrevers novels. At one point, for example, he persuades his schoolmates to follow in the footsteps of Schiller's robbers. (They balk, however, at his proposal that they become Byronic pirates.) Contarini defends his egotistical adventures as sentimental heroics in an "age of reality" (p. 141). The fictionalized Byron in Disraeli's novel *Venetia* similarly sees himself as having a "chivalric genius" in a "mechanical age" (*V*, 201). But while Contarini lusts after power, Disraeli has neglected to grant him conspicuous talents other than the audacity that demands to have whatever it wishes. When the young hero confesses his desire to be a poet to a successful artist whom he has just met, he is told, "when a mind like yours thinks often of a thing, it will happen" (*CF*, 56). This artist figure, Peter Winter, is presented as a foil to Contarini's father; but while Contarini chooses the poet's career over the politician's, he still honors the advice his father has given him: "with words we govern men" (p. 99).

Disraeli's own dazzling career was established at the fortuitous moment when the protectionist wing of the Tory party lacked an articulate spokesman to argue its cause. Disraeli's desire to achieve success as a poet is evidenced in the poem he began about this time, *The Revolutionary Epick* (1834), which aimed at presenting Shelleyan principles in Miltonic form, and in the verse play *The Tragedy of Count Alarcos* (1839), which he undertook, as he claimed, in competition with Shakespeare. (The subject of both works is the attainment of power. In the poem the spirits of Burkean "Feudalism" and Shelleyan "Federalism" contend, but the narrative breaks off just as "that predestined Man [Napoleon], / Upon whose crest the fortunes of the world / Shall hover," arises—with perhaps the aim, like

Disraeli's, of reconciling the claims of tradition and liberty. The protagonist of *Alarcos*, on the other hand, discovers that the price of political power is murder.) No reader of these turgid outpourings would wish that Disraeli had pursued a poetical career at the expense of his political goals; but perhaps the fairest way to interpret *Contarini Fleming* is in light of the political and personal frustrations its author was experiencing at the time. The colossal egotism of Contarini is a mask for Disraeli's insecurity. At one point dejectedly believing himself "the object of an omnipotent Destiny, over which I had no control," Contarini later consoles himself with the thought that "Destiny is our will, and our will is our nature" (pp. 203, 318). The boyish romance of an outsider who triumphs over everyone and everything was indeed a "safety-valve" for the energies of one who saw himself as an innately gifted individual in an age that lacked heroic grandeur. "I am only truly great in action," he confided to his diary in an effort at self-hypnotism. "If ever I am placed in a truly eminent position I shall prove this," he added prophetically; "I could rule the House of Commons, although there would be a great prejudice against me at first."[23]

During the same decade in which Disraeli composed his autobiographical trilogy, he wrote three other novels with no higher aim in mind than making money to pay off his debts. But although *The Young Duke, Henrietta Temple*, and *Venetia* were initiated as hack works, they are a good deal more fun to read than Disraeli's serious novels of the period. They also express aspects of his active, ideal, and poetic ambition, but without the egotistical bombast and with a certain amount of mockery directed at his own high pretensions. The willingness to satirize his ambitions and posings is one of the most endearing of Disraeli's Byronic traits. In each of the books a young woman is the moral agent who converts a selfish young man to a sense of domestic or social responsibility. One might almost say that under the romantic trappings of these books a Victorian conscience is struggling to be heard. (*Henrietta Temple* and *Venetia* were published in 1837, the year Victoria ascended the throne.)[24]

The hero of *The Young Duke* is an immensely wealthy young lord who spends his money lavishly and then converts to a serious sense of his duties as an aristocrat. The novel contains marvelous and witty set pieces of fashionable life—no less effective for being almost entirely the concoctions of Disraeli's imagination—and a description of a gambling den in which all the aristocratic forms are thrown off to reveal "hideous demons" lurking underneath (*YD*, 264). In the Romantic tradition, Disraeli saw Utilitarians rather than aristocrats as major threats to the moral and social well-being of the age. His animus against Utilitarian philosophers is humorously expressed in the description of the Benthamite writer whose hatred of aristocrats extends to a hatred of mountains: "Rivers he rather patronised; but flowers he quite pulled to pieces, and proved them to be the most useless of existences. Duncan Macmorrogh informed us that we were quite wrong in supposing ourselves to be the miracle of Creation. On the contrary, he avowed that already there were various pieces of machinery of far more importance than man; and he had no doubt, in time, that a superior race would arise, got by a steam-engine on a spinning-jenny" (p. 321). Disraeli's answer to the Utilitarian theories is the figure of the young duke at the end of the novel, whose feudal determination to take care of a people imaginatively enthralled by him is seen to be more effective in the long run than any Benthamite legislation.[25]

Whether Disraeli himself could achieve political prominence is a matter for doubt in these books. Despite the will to be great, the heroes of Disraeli's early novels do not always achieve their objective or enjoy it for long. Those who do succeed, moreover, do so with the help, or at the will, of others. Disraeli interrupts the narrative of *The Young Duke* at one point to express his anguish that the most "supernatural" of energies—such as those of Byron or Napoleon—have been known to "die away without creating their miracles" (p. 88). A sense of personal insecurity is especially evident in *Henrietta Temple*. His hero, Ferdinand Armine, possesses "the power and the will" (*HT*, p. 45) of his chivalric ancestors: as the "near descendant of that bold man who passed his whole life in the voluptuous indulgence of his unrestrained volition," Armine decides that he need only be willful himself for all to yield "to determination" (p. 128). Moreover, Armine possesses the requisite Romantic imagination: "His imagination created fantasies and his impetuous passions struggled to realise them" (p. 290). In the end, however, he attains his desires in large part because of Disraeli's own strong need for a fantasy of "acceptance" at this stage in his career.[26] Armine achieves his goal because others are eager and determined to thrust greatness on him: "The most gifted individuals in the land emulated each other in proving which entertained for him the most sincere affection" (p. 436). The Romantic faith in will is overshadowed by the romancer's reliance on wish-fulfillment.

The twin heroes of *Venetia* are no less than Byron and Shelley, whom Disraeli renames Plantagenet Cadurcis and Marmion Herbert. Disraeli's defense of his Romantic idols is tempered, however, by his recognition that the same imaginative energies that produce great poetry can also find expression in questionable conduct. As a young radical poet and philosopher, Herbert has "celebrated that fond world of his imagination, which he wished to teach men to love" (p. 225). But despite intense idealism, Herbert's disbelief in conventional morality, his atheism, and his revolutionary politics wreck his marriage and exile him from England. It is intriguing to contemplate Matthew Arnold's "beautiful and ineffectual angel" becoming a general and fighting in the American Revolution against his native land; Disraeli sets his novel far enough in the past that his Shelley-figure can achieve that fate. However, the sight of his daughter Venetia and his wife Lady Annabel, from whom he has separated under conditions that echo Byron's separation from Lady Byron (Herbert's defense of American freedom is similarly reminiscent of Byron's crusade for Greek independence), is enough to make him cast off his past beliefs and sigh instead for "domestic repose" and "domestic bliss."[27] "The age of his illusions had long passed" (pp. 380–382); in middle age Herbert cautions his poetic and political disciple Cadurcis that it is more important for a poet to "sympathise" with his fellowmen than to express his scorn for or exert his will upon them: "It is sympathy that makes you a poet. It is your desire that the airy children of your brain should be born anew within another's, that makes you create; therefore, a misanthropical poet is a contradiction in terms" (p. 448). Disraeli illustrates in Herbert's career the waste of an idealistic imagination and in Cadurcis's case the misuse of imaginative energies.

Despite his Romantic sympathies, Disraeli by 1837 had come to see, as Coleridge had earlier, that imagination and will have negative possibilities: by stressing Ferdinand Armine's passivity in *Henrietta Temple*, Disraeli disengaged his hero from any mis-expenditure of will. (Scott had employed a similar strategy in the Waverley novels.) In Cadurcis, Disraeli embodies what to young Victorians appeared to be the quintessentially Byronic man of imagination and will. "If ever there existed a being who was his own master, who might mould his destiny at his will, it seemed to be Cadurcis" (p. 175). Yet Venetia's mother, quite rightly from a Victorian point of view, rejects Cadurcis's appeal for her daughter's hand on the basis of his "genius." "Spirits like him," Lady Annabel says, are swayed by a dangerous impulse: "It is imagination; it is vanity; it is self, disguised with glittering qualities that dazzle our weak senses, but selfishness, the most entire, the most concentrated" (p. 311). When Cadurcis insists to his friend Masham (modeled after Bishop Wilberforce) that he must have Venetia, the Bishop replies that Cadurcis only really wants what his imagination has seized upon for momentary gratification. Once he had married Venetia, he "would probably part from her in a year, as her father parted from Lady Anna-bel." "Impossible!" replies Cadurcis, "for my imagination could not conceive of anything more exquisite than she is." "Then it would conceive something less exquisite," says the Bishop. "It is a restless quality, and is ever creative, either of good or of evil" (p. 250). The portrait of Cadurcis is the culmination of Disraeli's lifelong Byron-mania: we see Cadurcis evolve from a moody and willful child, whose mother is every bit as eccentric as Lady Gordon, to a young man of strange habits (including the famous diet of biscuits and soda water), misanthropic moods, and extraordinary literary success.[28]

Disraeli collected information about Byron and Shelley from a variety of published and unpublished sources: among others, Thomas Moore's *Life of Byron*, Thomas Medwin's remembrances of Byron and Shelley, and anecdotes related by Edward Tre-lawny, Lady Blessington, and Byron's former manservant, Tita, whom Disraeli had acquired as a human souvenir during his trip to the East in 1831. But a recognition of Byron's genius did not prevent Disraeli from seeing an incompatibility between

imaginative ambition and domestic virtues: if Medwin, Tre-
lawny, and Moore were not sufficient witnesses to the improprie-
ties of genius, his father Isaac D'Israeli's *The Literary Character, or The History of Men of Genius* was a treasure-trove of
biographical episodes proving that men like Byron could not be
"tamed" to fit the hopes of a character like Venetia.[29] In the end,
Disraeli was obliged to drown both his Byron and Shelley figures, despite their abrupt conversion away from their willful
early lives, their Shelleyan unorthodoxy and Byronic "selfism."
Although Disraeli himself was now in the process of toning
down his Romantic rhetoric and posture in the hope of attaining
recognition in the House of Commons, he was not about to show
his poetic idols selling out. *Venetia* seems intended, as Disraeli's
biographer observes, as a "last tribute to the Byronic myth . . .
a final protest against the respectable world with which he now
had to come to terms."[30] But if Romantic flamboyance was no
longer serviceable to Disraeli, the Romantic tradition of humanitarianism could now be turned to account.

The great trilogy of the 1830s represent Disraeli's major claim
to be taken seriously as a novelist. In these works, for the first
time, his heroes have a mission; they want not only power, like
the early heroes, but something to direct that power toward.
They want to see England governed by a real aristocracy, composed of talented and earnest young men who inspire others by
their creative abilities. Noting a debt to Carlyle's idea of "Hero
Worship" in *Coningsby*, Thackeray smiled at the "pining" of
"Young England . . . for the restoration of the heroic sentiment,
and the appearance of the heroic man."[31] Indeed, the spirit of
Carlyle and Scott had been joined to the spirit of Byron and Shelley, and the result—in *Coningsby* and *Sybil* at least—is the sort
of work to please novel-readers who would perhaps rather be
reading political tracts. Yet a Romantic quality permeates even
these books. The appeal is to the imagination, but the imagination speaks not only the "language of power" (in Hazlitt's
phrase) but the language of sympathy. A Byronic magnetic figure
is still required to fire the passions of the public, but this figure
also needs Shelley's humanitarian imagination. In defending the
moral force of poetry, Shelley maintains, "A man, to be greatly

good, must imagine intensely and comprehensively; he must put himself in the place of another and of many others; the pains and pleasures of his species must become his own. The great instrument of moral good is the imagination; and poetry administers to the effect by acting upon the cause."[32] In *Coningsby, or The New Generation* (1844), Disraeli treats the political hero as Shelley regarded the poet: a great man, like a great book, produces "a magnetic influence blending with our sympathising intelligence, that directs and inspires it" (p. 129).

Coningsby himself exerts over his schoolmates "the ascendant power, which is the destiny of genius" (p. 109); and he is granted a heroic will so that he and his friends can satisfy the English people's craving for great leaders to lead them in a time of crisis. "Surely of all 'rights of man,' " as Carlyle declares, somewhat less attractively, in *Chartism*, "this right of the ignorant man to be guided by the wiser, to be, gently or forcibly, held in the true course by him, is the indisputablest."[33] For leadership, according to Carlyle and Disraeli, not only satisfies an instinctive need of the multitude—it also keeps the multitude from satisfying their passions in socially destructive ways. When Coningsby asks Sidonia, Disraeli's portrait of a wealthy Jewish Tiresias-figure who knows everything and everyone, whether "Imagination," which "once subdued the state . . . may not save it," Sidonia replies, "Man is made to adore and to obey: but if you will not command him, if you give him nothing to worship, he will fashion his own divinities and find a chieftain in his own passions" (p. 253).

In *Sybil, or The Two Nations* (1845), Disraeli shows to what a state the abdication of leadership by the aristocracy and the church has brought modern England. In that novel "a spirit of rapacious covetousness, desecrating all the humanities of life," has been spread by the newly powerful middle class. Their goal, as Disraeli sees it, is "to acquire, to accumulate, to plunder each other by virtue of philosophic [that is, Utilitarian, laissez-faire] phrases, to propose a Utopia to consist only of WEALTH and TOIL" (p. 36). Deserted by their natural allies, the upper classes, and exploited by the middle classes, the workers have been left totally degraded and at the mercy of Chartist slogans, which promise relief but lead only to destructive acts. It is precisely at such a time, as Sidonia urges, that great men are called for—not to follow the spirit of the age but to change it, to advocate reverence for heroic values in place of materialism, and to protect the poor who cannot defend themselves. Ten years earlier Disraeli had contended that "The Monarchy of the Tories is more democratic than the Republic of the Whigs. It appeals with a keener sympathy to the passions of the millions; it studies their interests with a more comprehensive solicitude."[34] A political career for Harry Coningsby or Charles Egrement (the hero of *Sybil*) is seen as a romantic crusade, a chivalric adventure in which the successful hero slays Whig (or factitious Tory) dragons and ends up in Parliament making speeches in favor of the "rights of labour" (*S*, p. 339). The creator of these heroes draws at least as much from *Arabian Nights* fantasies of wish-fulfillment as from his observations of the actual political process. "Life was a pantomime," as Coningsby discovers; "the wand was waved, and it seemed that the schoolfellows had of a sudden become elements of power, springs of the great machine" (*C*, p. 498).

Tancred, or The New Crusade (1847) brings Disraeli's political trilogy to a brilliant, if also perplexing, climax. It is much less earnest in tone, though no less serious in purpose, than *Coningsby* and *Sybil*, and the seriousness is not deflected by Disraeli's many witty, and sometimes perverse, digressions.[35] Tancred himself is an extremely earnest young nobleman, the descendant of crusaders, who wants "to see an angel at Manchester" (*T*, p. 76) and who does in fact see an angel on Mount Sinai. For Tancred, another Disraeli hero possessed of "indomitable will and an iron resolution" (p. 43), the achievement of political power is meaningless without a secure national religious faith to prop it up. "It is time to restore and renovate our communications with the Most High," he tells his astonished father. "What ought I to DO, and what ought I to BELIEVE?" (p. 56). To Coningsby and his friends, Tancred complains that without a magnetic religious influence directing human behavior, "Individuality is dead; there is a want of inward and personal energy in man; and that is what people feel and mean when they go about complaining there is no faith" (p. 152). Luckily for Tancred, Sidonia appears in time to encourage him to find the answer to his dilemma by penetrating "the great Asian mystery" (p. 128)—that is, by traveling to Palestine to discover why God chose to speak to mankind from there and not from Manchester.

Tancred's adventures in the Middle East are an odd sort of reverie to be coming from a member of Parliament who was about to assume the mantle of Tory leader Robert Peel.[36] Yet the brilliant political invective Disraeli was using in his campaign against Peel and against the repeal of the Corn Laws at about this time was a product of the same imagination that created Tancred's "new crusade" to bring back religious principles to England and, at the same time, created the intrigues of the Arab prince Fakredeen to attain power for himself by any means possible. (Fakredeen's alliance of Arab princes, for example, may be a parody of Disraeli's own Young England Party.) Disraeli's gift for romantic image-making was matched by his brilliant ability to expose the sham underneath. If principle and opportunism appear almost inextricably connected in Disraeli's personality— as do the polar Romantic attitudes of reverential obeisance and heroic self-assertion—the novelist personifies and travesties this dualism in the contrasting characters of Tancred and Fakredeen.

Tancred's pilgrimage seems serious enough until he meets Fakredeen—this "Syrian Vivian Grey," as Leslie Stephen calls him[37]—who parodies Tancred's earnestness and utters many of Disraeli's sentiments. Fakredeen is ambitious, vain, and unscrupulous; but he is given many of the author's favorite ideas, including the maxim "everything comes if a man will only wait" (p. 303). While Tancred seeks to convert the world—as soon as he can find a principle of religious certainty for himself—Fakredeen wants only to conquer it. The two men join forces for a time in a preposterous plan to "conquer the world, with angels at our head," as Tancred explains, "in order that we may establish the happiness of man by a divine dominion" (p. 434). He settles in the end for domestic bliss, an angel in the house taking the place of the Angel of Arabia. (There is possibly an allusion to Keats's *Endymion* here: Tancred's beloved supplants the angel he has sought, while Endymion's Indian maid is the physical incarnation of Cynthia, goddess of the Moon.) Eva, his Jewish bride-to-be, comforts Tancred for the loss of some of his illusions. "Perhaps," she suggests, "all this time we have been dreaming over an unattainable end, and the only source of deception is our own imagination" (p. 499). The novel ends in confusion with Tancred still wanting to believe—and Disraeli wanting Tancred to want to believe—but with what to believe in still a matter for doubt.

What ultimately redeems the book is not its message (although Disraeli considered this his most important book) but its wit, seen in the political intrigues of Fakredeen, which mock the pretensions of many a Disraeli hero and the young Disraeli himself; in the epigrams, such as "Christianity is Judaism for the multitude" (p. 439); and above all in the mockery directed against an English society that has lost all reverence for spiritual values. The parody of Robert Chambers's *Vestiges of the Natural History of Creation*, which had recently appeared and which offered in popular form an evolutionist's theory of history, is one of the great set pieces of Disraeli's comic spirit. Lady Constance hands Tancred a copy of " 'The Revelations of Chaos,' a startling book just published, and of which a rumour had reached him." "It is one of those books one must read," Lady Constance blithely declares. "It explains everything, and is written in a very agreeable style."

> "It explains everything!" said Tancred; "it must, indeed, be a very remarkable book!"
> "I think it will just suit you," said Lady Constance. "Do you know, I thought so several times while I was reading it."
> "To judge from the title, the subject is rather obscure," said Tancred.
> "No longer so," said Lady Constance. "It is treated scientifically; everything is explained by geology and astronomy, and in that way. It shows you exactly how a star is formed; nothing can be so pretty! A cluster of vapour, the cream of the milky way, a sort of celestial cheese, churned into light, you must read it, 'tis charming."
> "Nobody ever saw a star formed," said Tancred.
> "Perhaps not. You must read the 'Revelations;' it is all explained. But what is most interesting, is the way in which man has been developed. You know, all is development. The principle is perpetually going on. First, there was nothing, then there was something; then, I forget the next, I

think there were shells, then fishes; then we came, let me
see, did we come next? Never mind that; we came at last.
And the next change there will be something very superior
to us, something with wings. Ah! that's it: we were fishes,
and I believe we shall be crows. But you must read it."

"I do not believe I ever was a fish," said Tancred. (Pp.
112–113)

This famous passage should remind us that Disraeli was perfectly serious when, speaking at Oxford in 1864, he declared
himself on the side of the angels, protesting that "instead of
believing that the age of faith has passed, I hold that the characteristic of the present age is a craving credulity."[38] Evolution,
like Utilitarianism, deprived man of his power of volition; yet
for Disraeli, as for Newman and Tennyson, the will to believe
was a proof that there was something to believe in, something
that affirmed the power of the will after all.

Like Keats in his substitution of Cortez for Balboa, Disraeli
knew that the scientists' discoveries could not be discounted;
in terms of the requirements of the imagination and the will to
believe, however, such facts were irrelevant. "Craving credulity"
is both the theme of and the danger in two of Disraeli's last three
fictional works: *Lothair* (1870) and the unfinished "Falconet."
The doubts and fears of the 1870s and 1880s find vivid expression in these books. Lothair, a young nobleman who like Tancred
is searching for religious certitude, is characterized in terms of
passivity rather than willfulness. "I often think . . . that I have
neither powers nor talents," he laments at one point, "but am
drifting without an orbit" (*L*, p. 289). He finds himself at the
mercy of several opposing religious and political doctrines, all
of which Disraeli treats with a certain amount of sympathy.
The most troublesome temptation comes from Cardinal Grandi-
son, whose endorsement of Roman Catholicism is an invitation
for Lothair to resign his will altogether. The cardinal expresses
Disraeli's fear that the rise of science has aided materialism and
atheism. "The world is devoted to physical science," he charges,
"because it believes these discoveries will increase its capacity
of luxury and self-indulgence. But the pursuit of science leads
only to the insoluble." For the cardinal, as for Sidonia, "all the

poetry and passion and sentiment of human nature are taking refuge in religion" (p. 67).[39] "Religion is civilisation," he argues later in the novel; "the highest: it is the reclamation of man from savageness by the Almighty. What the world calls civilisation, as distinguished from religion, is a retrograde movement, and will ultimately lead us back to the barbarism from which we have escaped" (p. 249). Like Dostoevsky, at about the same time, Disraeli is warning that when God is not believed to exist all things become permissible.

Lothair's susceptibility to Roman Catholicism does not lead to conversion only because he is even more susceptible to a strong-minded woman, Theodora, who wins him over to the cause of Italian freedom, and because Disraeli sees Jerusalem, not Rome, as the real fountainhead of religious truth. Action becomes the antidote for Lothair's morbid introspection; his romantic activity as a soldier in the cause of Italian unification is described as an "easy distraction from self-criticism" (p. 271). He is not the first troubled Romantic to come to that conclusion. "A region of Doubt . . . hovers forever in the background," Carlyle declared in 1831; "in Action alone can we have certainty."[40] "The only tolerable thing in life is action," especially youthful action, as Theodora's friend the Princess of Tivoli says to Lothair. "You have many, many scrapes awaiting you . . . You may look forward to at least ten years of blunders: that is, illusions; that is, happiness. Fortunate young man!" (pp. 150–151). It is the princess who later sounds the theme of the romance of the will in opposition to the cardinal's doctrine of renunciation. "The power of the passions, the force of the will, the creative energy of the imagination," she proclaims, "these make life, and reveal to us a world of which the million are entirely ignorant" (p. 289). In the opposition between the romance of the will and the need for obedience and reverence, Lothair takes one side and then another, settling finally, like Tancred, for domestic bliss in a world of unresolved and unresolvable questionings.

There is no way of knowing what the outcome of "Falconet" would have been: before his death Disraeli had completed fewer than ten chapters of this novel, in which all values seem to be dissolving and only self-righteous hypocrites like Falconet (modeled after the Liberal leader Gladstone, whom Disraeli regarded as the "Arch Villain") or nihilistic philosophies seem to be thriving. England seems exhausted of her energies, and no youthful heroes have yet appeared when the manuscript breaks off to indicate how the visitors from the East and Germany, who turn up in the novel to preach a doctrine of "Destruction in every form," are to be thwarted—if they are to be thwarted. In one of the last scenes we are shown one of the invaders recommending a book by "a friend of Schopenhauer," a book that presumably offers Schopenhauer's message of the sublimation of the will.[41]

Yet despite the sense that his was "an age of dissolving creeds" ("Falconet," p. 475) and threats to civil order—or perhaps because of the realization that he himself had risen to power by seizing the initiative in a time of social instability—Disraeli's last completed novel, *Endymion* (1880), is the most romantic and optimistic of all his works. "It is a privilege to live in this age of rapid and brilliant events," he had exulted in 1864. "What an error to consider it an utilitarian age! It is one of infinite romance. Thrones tumble down and are offered, like a fairy tale, and the most powerful people in the world, male and female, a few years back were adventurers, exiles and demireps."[42] Disraeli may have been describing the rise to power of men like Louis Napoleon, but he was also contemplating his own success, the fulfillment of the unrealistic ambition stated in the 1833 diary. By 1875 he was not only prime minister but Lord Beaconsfield. There is no mention of dissolving creeds in *Endymion*: indeed, Nigel Penruddock's rise to the position of Roman Catholic cardinal is celebrated here—though it would have been deplored in *Lothair*—because it is an assumption of power.[43] All ways to eminence are to be admired, whether in the figure of Endymion, who becomes prime minister of the Whig, not the Tory, party; Vigo, who as a railway magnate is linked with what to the Victorians was the most visible symbol of material progress; or Prince Florestan, who is Disraeli's version of Napoleon III with touches added from the wondrous career of Alroy. "All you have got to do is to make up your mind that you will be in the next parliament, and you will succeed," Lady Montfort tells Endymion; "for everything in this world depends upon will." "I think everything in this world depends upon women," replies

Endymion; to which Lady Montfort retorts, "It is the same thing" (*E*, p. 290).

Endymion expresses Disraeli's Romantic view of history, in which heroes triumph by the force of their will, buttressed by the spirit of romance, in which wishing for something to happen is enough to make it happen. Endymion rises from poverty to political power without having to engage in any of the intrigues and subterfuges necessary for climbing the "greasy pole." His only conspicuous qualities are youth, tact, and "the power and melody of his voice" (p. 385). Yet he is awarded the highest honors partly because of his intense desire for them and largely through the agency of a set of fairy godsisters. "If we cannot shape your destiny," his sister Myra contends of the power of women, "there is no such thing as witchcraft" (p. 249). Myra devotes her will, which Endymion recognizes to be "more powerful than his" (p. 421), to the great aim of making her brother prime minister. "I have brought myself, by long meditation, to the conviction that a human being with a settled purpose must accomplish it," she claims, "and that nothing can resist a will that will stake even existence for its fulfillment" (p. 113). In the end, all men and women of indomitable will have assumed power: Myra herself becomes the Queen of France, the bride of King Florestan. How little Disraeli decided to rely on reality in concocting *Endymion*—how much he chose to present a Keatsian set of imaginative values instead—can be seen in the way he used as prototype for Florestan's hugely successful career an emperor who in historical fact had been driven from power a decade earlier.

One might be tempted to dismiss *Endymion* as an exuberant piece of wish-fulfillment if not for the disconcerting links between the improbabilities of its plot and the historical improbabilities that saw the rise of so many self-proclaimed men of destiny in the nineteenth century. Despite the revulsion of Victorian intellectuals—many of them searching for an authentic principle of authority to replace the fallen gods of their ancestors, and in no mood to hail the exploits of a survivor from the Romantic period—Disraeli had discovered that his Romantic views were shared by many of his countrymen. By no means an original thinker, as Bagehot recognized, he was able to rise to power by demonstrating a force of personality and by *"applying* a literary genius, in itself limited, to the practical purpose of public life."[44] His success indicates that in an age of disbelief people will follow a leader who believes in his own star and who is able to exert power over others with the right image and rhetoric. The power of words and images was a central Disraelian concern, as both a fictional and a national theme: "He thought in symbols," as Louis Cazamian noted, "and was acutely alive to the power of images over human thought and conduct, for he recognized it in himself." When Gladstone defeated Disraeli in 1880, he exulted that "the downfall of Beaconsfieldism is like the vanishing of some vast magnificent castle of Italian romance";[45] yet there occurred in the 1880s a revival of the romantic spirit, whether in the form of the fiction of Robert Louis Stevenson and H. Rider Haggard or in the form of imperial adventurism, which the Victorians had never really exorcised.

The adventurist and merely rhetorical aspects of Disraeli's Romanticism—the qualities that Trollope, for example, found so offensive—cannot be defended; but a more positive strain of Romanticism dominates his mature views. The negative aspect of his Romantic impulse is readily seen in the early novels, where his youthful narcissism and Byronic egoism are ingenuously revealed. In subsequent novels, however, he exhibited the humanitarian and reverential side of Romanticism; and in this respect, his development from self-preoccupation to concern for society may be said to parallel the development within Romanticism itself. The Romantic celebration of the powers of heroic will and sovereign imagination was transformed into a recognition of the need for responsible leadership and a sympathetic, morally attuned imagination. In the end, the country's political, economic, and spiritual interests and the imaginative desires of Coningsby, Egrement, and Tancred—and Disraeli himself—are seen to be synonymous. To Disraeli's credit, while he translated into political and fictional terms the romance of the will, his Byronic sense of self-mockery forbade his ever taking himself and the idea of leadership unduly seriously, and thereby insulated him from Carlylean delusions of grandeur.

A perennially boyish element in Disraeli accounted for his

persistence in regarding life as a romance in which, like Aladdin, he had only to will things for them to happen. But this sense of wonder was related for Disraeli, as it was for Coleridge and Newman, to a belief in spiritual forces in the universe with which modern man seemed increasingly to be losing touch. Coleridge's Biblical reminder that "WHERE NO VISION IS, THE PEOPLE PER-ISHETH" is close to Disraeli's insistence on the role of imagination in the nation's life.[46] Against the Utilitarian appeal to a self-interested populace in a materialistic universe, he offered a Romantic dream of human potentiality in a world of mutual respect. In the unfinished "Falconet," moreover, he seemed to be warning of a triumph of nihilism in a world that has lost faith in the Romantic values that sustain spiritual belief and that produce altruistic heroes. Uncharacteristic though it appears in theme and tone when compared with his other novels, "Falconet" betrays the sense of anxiety that underlies the euphoric fantasy of *Endymion*. Far more fearsome, as Disraeli realized, than the famous "leap in the dark" by which he had acted in 1867 to enfranchise members of the English working class, was the leap into darkness that might result from modern man's disenfranchisement from the visionary imagination.

FOUR

Charlotte Brontë
and the
Perils of Romance

*This hag, this Reason, would not let me look up,
or smile, or hope: she could not rest unless I
were altogether crushed, cowed, broken-in, and
broken-down. According to her, I was born only to
work for a piece of bread, to await the pains of
death, and steadily through all life to despond.
Reason might be right; yet no wonder we are glad
at times to defy her, to rush from under her rod
and give a truant hour to Imagination—her soft,
bright foe, our sweet Help, our divine Hope. We
shall and must break bounds at intervals, despite
the terrible revenge that awaits our return.*

Villette

Although she is often considered a Romantic writer, whose best-known novel records the triumph of self and the imagination over reality and the constraints of the world, Charlotte Brontë regarded herself as a realist, bound, like her favorite novelist Thackeray, to the disconcerting fact of human limitations and frustrations. Her novels pledge allegiance to what is "plain and homely" (Preface, *The Professor*), to "real knowledge of life amidst its perils" (*Jane Eyre*, p. 100), to the "shores of Reality" (*Shirley*, I, 105), and to the "homely web of truth" (*Villette*, II, 274). Her claims for the realism of her narratives make surprisingly good sense if we compare her works to those of an unregenerate Romantic like Disraeli. Disraeli's youthful heroes live in a world where wishes have only to be made to be fulfilled; Brontë's protagonists have to fight for every meager scrap of the sustenance that their world delights in withholding from them. Both authors were nourished by *Arabian Nights* fairy tales and enthralled by Byron in childhood, but where

Disraeli sought to apply the Byronic formula to political affairs, Brontë struggled to reject her infatuation with Byron in her mature works. If Disraeli hoped to remake the world to fit his Romantic standards, which included faith in the transforming power of will and the recognition of imagination as the guiding star of political life, Brontë tried to bring her Romantic dreams and ideals within the compass of reality. Where he had prescribed romance as a panacea, she endorsed reality as a purgative. Trollope, who loathed Disraeli for his politics and his novels, applauded *Jane Eyre* for its realism: it would last, he predicted, "because the men and women depicted are human in their aspirations, human in their sympathies, and human in their actions."[1]

Like Trollope and Disraeli, Brontë was torn by conflicting ambitions: a Romantic will to power and a proto-Victorian desire for acceptance and accommodation, a longing to dominate by the force of her artistic genius and a craving to belong to a secure social and domestic establishment.[2] Unlike her sister Emily, for whom the "world within" was sufficient to blot out the social context, Charlotte Brontë tried repeatedly to participate in the world outside the Haworth parsonage, even if this ultimately meant suppressing the Romantic impulse which had made her a writer in the first place. Brontë's utilization of Romantic values and the paraphernalia of romance within a realistic framework accounts for the distinctive nature of her work and vision. She is not quite a Victorian novelist in that her focus is invariably on the individual existing in a largely hostile world and her standards are those of the individual and not society. (In *Jane Eyre* the standards of society and the individual seem to be the same in the end, which is why the book is her most "Victorian" and her most popular work.) Yet she is not fully a Romantic either because of her gloomy sense of human nature and her religious doubts concerning the unaided individual's ability to achieve truth or happiness or salvation. In *Shirley*, her one novel that touches on social problems, she criticizes the egoism and lack of sympathy of the Yorkshire millowners in the face of their workers' widespread misery, but she is unable to consider the possibility of meaningful reforms or changes because of her Romantic image of a world of masterly leaders and devoted followers and because of her Protestant sense of the value of fortitude amid suffering. (The suffering of women as well as workers constitutes the theme of *Shirley*, but tenaciously held Romantic biases, combined with a mixture of religious and fatalistic beliefs, make it impossible for her to see an end to their dilemma in this world.) In one sense, Brontë's Romantic sensibility was sustained by her Protestant beliefs: the "total reliance of the individual upon himself," as a recent commentator observes, "accounts for the fact that the crisis of each of Charlotte's novels comes when the protagonist reaches a crucial decision which introspection rather than the advice or teaching of others reveals to him as right."[3] However, Brontë also adhered to the neo-Calvinist view that saw in the human will the source of evil—the view that gradually persuaded Coleridge to mistrust even the creative will as a form of Satanism.

While Brontë's sternly Protestant upbringing deepened her dread of the human will, it also heightened her sensitivity toward the one Romantic poet with a "sense of inward discord and the reality of evil," Byron.[4] But where Disraeli had revered Byron as a humanitarian and satirist and Trollope had been fascinated by his defiance of the conventionalities, Brontë was drawn to his embodiment of imperious and masculine will. That "genius" was not necessarily immune from "degradation" in personal life Byron had made readily clear to Brontë's generation; yet, as an adolescent, she recommended his work (apart from *Don Juan* and "perhaps" the "magnificent Poem" *Cain*) to her austere, and closest, friend Ellen Nussey with the insistence that greatness in one's work implies greatness in one's life. One cannot overstate the importance of Byron in determining Charlotte Brontë's sense of herself as an artist; but it would be a mistake to overlook the influence of non-Romantic writers and books in shaping her themes and language—the *Bible* and the *Arabian Nights*, Cowper and Isaac Watts, Bunyan and Balzac.[5] Even among the Romantics, Brontë looked to authors other than Byron for guidance. She sent Wordsworth a copy of one of her Angrian tales, and she sought advice from Byron's archenemy Southey in determining whether or not to continue as a writer. (Fortunately, she did not follow his advice.) Reading a biography of Southey in later years, she was reassured to note that the

Poet Laureate's life disproved the contention of "some people" (notably Moore in his life of Byron) "that Genius is inconsistent with domestic happiness." No Romantic writer, however, led so salutary a life as Scott, or was so readily allowed into the households of religious families who otherwise banned works of the imagination. "For fiction—read Scott alone," Brontë advised Ellen in 1834; "all novels after his are worthless"; while "Scott's sweet, wild, romantic Poetry can do you no harm nor can Wordsworth nor Campbell's nor Southey's." Scott's considerable achievement as a novelist in fusing the aims of a romantic-minded protagonist with the rules of his society would be emulated by Brontë in *Jane Eyre* and, even more successfully, by another of Scott's admirers, George Eliot, in *Middlemarch*. But the young Brontë also marveled at Scott's "wonderful knowledge of human nature" as revealed in the portrait of the evil Varney in *Kenilworth*, and this provoked her biographer, Unitarian-bred Elizabeth Gaskell, to remark on how readily an isolated young woman was willing to identify "human nature" with "intense and artful villainy."[6]

Scott's benign temperament allowed him to envisage the possibility, in novels and in life, of an accommodation between the claims of self and society, passion and duty, romance and reality. The efforts of the Brontë protagonists to find a middle position between passionate rebellion and rigid self-control (the polarities that Jane Eyre sees in herself), between what one critic calls "Romantic *panache* and realist prudence," are not usually so successful.[7] The movement of a Brontë novel is from a Romantic starting point which is never quite lost sight of to a Victorian destination which is never quite reached. The result, in all her novels except *Jane Eyre,* is a confusion of realms, an uncomfortable combination of romantic wish-fulfillment for some characters and obstructive realism for others. The Brontë heroes and heroines are typically orphans, castaways in a world where their few surviving relatives are generally hostile or indifferent, in search of a home that they must construct for themselves in idea if not in fact. In her first three novels (*The Professor, Jane Eyre,* and *Shirley*) a home is created, sometimes through the aid of supernatural machinery, while in her last completed book, *Villette,* the chance for a home is snatched from the protagonist's hands by the action of supernatural machinery. The lack of a humanly happy ending has been cited by recent admirers of *Villette* as proof of its mature sense of "reality," but my own view, which I will develop later, is that the forces of fantasy are forced to regroup in *Villette* but are still very much in possession of the field.

The precarious situations of the Brontë protagonists reflect the anxieties of their creator, for whom life was indeed a battle in which she was constantly on guard against enemies external and internal. The oscillation in Brontë's girlhood between contending needs and inner voices formed the habit of mind in which she and all her protagonists see themselves as the central figures in a Bunyanesque allegorical struggle: lacking relations and friends, they have instead such allies as Imagination, Observation, Duty, Tact, and Conscience, and such antagonists as Fate, Reality, Hypochondria, and Suffering. Deploring the "unhappy discord which runs through Miss Brontë's conceptions of life," Leslie Stephen observed that Brontë "seems to be under a desire which makes her restless and unhappy, because her best impulses are continually warring against each other. She is between the opposite poles of duty and happiness and cannot see how to reconcile their claims, or even . . . how distinctly to state the question at issue." "If life be a war," as Lucy Snowe assumes, "it seemed my destiny to conduct it single-handed" (*Villette*, II, 58). To Ellen Nussey, Brontë stoically recommended "Submission—courage—exertion when practicable —these seem to be the weapons with which we must face life's long battle."[8]

The facts of life, as they appeared to the sickly, motherless child growing up at the Haworth parsonage, were ones of need and deprivation. In concert with her surviving sisters and brother, she sought refuge in an imaginary world where foundlings turned out to be aristocrats, where irresistible Byronic males pursued or were pursued by passionately devoted maidens, and where the dead could be revived at the children's will. The creating and writing of these fantasies represented a romance of will in contrast to the powerlessness the children felt in their everyday lives. (With their father growing old and nearly blind, and with their very home tied to his tenure as minister, the inevitability of the children having to make their way in the world in one subservient role or another was uncomfortably apparent.) The children pretended to be genii, possessed of unlimited powers: in one of Charlotte Brontë's earliest surviving writings, the narrator muses that he, his companions, and their world do not really exist, but are "the mere idea of some other creature's brain." But along with the euphoria that such creativity generated in her mind—the enjoyment, as she admitted to Wordsworth, of creating "a world out of your own brains" whose inhabitants "have no father nor mother but your own imagination"—came a sense of the unnaturalness and dangerousness of her habits. For writing meant an escape from reality, and as the need for that escape intensified so too did the opposing spirit of conscience and reason to warn her away from the lures of the imagination and to direct her toward a realistic goal in life. "If you knew my thoughts," she wrote despairingly to Ellen Nussey; "the dreams that absorb me; and the fiery imagination that at times eats me up and makes me feel Society as it is, wretchedly insipid, you would pity and I dare say despise me."[9]

In her great biography of Charlotte Brontë, Elizabeth Gaskell makes much of her subject's self-discipline, the habit of masking her feelings and repressing her fancies. "I carefully avoid any appearance of preoccupation and eccentricity, which might lead those I live amongst to suspect the nature of my pursuits," she proudly (and not quite accurately) replied to Robert Southey, who had cautioned the young would-be writer that "Literature cannot be the business of a woman's life, and it ought not to be." Feelings thus camouflaged, however, did not disappear. The fantasy world was initially the one in which she was master of circumstances, the reality that which required submission from her. At twenty-five, while serving as governess (a position she hated, though she made it and teaching the occupations of most of her protagonists), she complained to Ellen of the painfulness of "living in other people's houses—the estrangement from one's real character—the adoption of a cold frigid apathetic exterior." Learning to wear a mask through life was the object of many women in the nineteenth century; the Brontë biography clarifies in vivid detail the differences between what was allowable to men and what to women, differences that shaped the novelist's conception of reality. Men might challenge reality if they chose; women must submit to it. The single male among the Brontë children, Branwell, was brought up with the prospect of having (in Gaskell's trenchant words) "his fate in his own hands." He was "expected to act a part in life; to *do*," while his sisters were "only to *be*."[10]

If the fantasies that she set in the imaginary world of Angria initially allowed her a mastery otherwise denied her, before long she had been mastered by the fantasy apparatus: the Angrian characters were more compelling, more real to her than the people whom it was her duty to serve as teacher or governess. In her journal she complained that students ("oafs," "dolts," and "swinish multitude" are various Brontë epithets for her protagonists' pupils) interrupted her enjoyment of Angria's "vivid light of reality," that "mighty phantasm . . . conjured from nothing,—from nothing to a system strange as some religious creed." Even during her stay in Brussels, where she had gone to acquire language skills in preparation for her future teaching career, she still recurred, as she wrote Branwell, "as fanatically as ever to the old ideas, the old faces, and the old scenes in the world below."[11] (By then she was twenty-seven.) Like Lucy Snowe, the protagonist of *Villette* who confesses to inhabiting a world of dreams as well as the real world but who is sometimes unsure which world is which, Brontë became so accustomed to the habits and coloring of the "world below" that she viewed the external world, at times, as a materialization of Angria. Extremely shortsighted, and with a strong visual imagination, she also tended to find many odd correspondences between her dead relations and people she later met. (George Henry Lewes, for example, reminded her of Emily.) Brussels and London, when she finally visited them, seemed reincarnations of the cities of Angria. As for her Belgian schoolmaster, Constantin Heger, for whom she felt an intense passion despite the refusal of her conscience to recognize anything of the kind, she had created him in her imagination long before she met him.[12]

Heger was one of several father-figures to whom Brontë felt a lifelong need to devote herself. Describing her feelings as a twenty-six-year-old schoolgirl in his establishment, she confided, "It is natural to me to submit, and very unnatural to command."[13] The Brontë heroines characteristically fall in love with men who, like Rochester in *Jane Eyre*, are old enough, or else seem old enough, to be their fathers. The most distant of father-figures, and ultimately the most compelling, is "Fate"—that "great abstraction," as Lucy Snowe calls him, "on whose wide shoulders I like to lay the mountains of blame they were sculpted to bear" (I, 233). Closer to home, the Reverend Patrick Brontë, almost as aloof as Fate but rather less fearsome, in addition to supplying Charlotte with Tory principles to which she subscribed more dogmatically than he had, provided his children with the precedent for a writing career. (One of his moralistic tales, "The Cottage in the Wood," contains the basis for *Jane Eyre*.)[14] The two greatest idols of Charlotte Brontë's life, however, were Lord Byron and the Duke of Wellington. The imperfect man of destiny and the duty-minded Iron Duke mingled in her fantasy world: Wellington—Irish-born, like her father—provided military models from his Peninsular campaign for her fictive hero Zamorna's triumphant exploits in the African world of Angria. More important, Wellington's real-life sons figured as leading male characters in Angria. Arthur Wellesley, Marquis of Douro, eventually metamorphosed into the Duke of Zamorna, the most commanding presence in Angria; while his brother, Charles Wellesley (later renamed Charles Townshend), became Brontë's inveterate narrator.

Zamorna, Charlotte Brontë's most audacious creation, is a Byronic inspired genius—he writes Byronic poetry at intervals—and an imperious lover whose creed it is "that all things bright and fair live for him." He is also, in one instance, the disgraced Byron, condemned by society and pursued by fate. Although there is evidence that she knew some Byron at the age of ten, Byron's decisive influence on Brontë began in 1833, the year her father purchased Thomas Moore's edition of the *Complete Works* and the nearest library bought Moore's absorbing biography of Byron.[15] A year later she described Zamorna in terms reminiscent of one of Byron's masterly outlaw-heroes and of Byron himself: "O Zamorna! what eyes those are glancing under the deep shadow of that raven crest! They bode no good . . .

All here is passion and fire unquenchable. Impetuous sin, stormy pride, diving and soaring enthusiasm, war and poetry, are kindling their fires in all his veins, and his wild blood boils from his heart and back again like a torrent of new-sprung lava. Young duke? Young demon!" Zamorna's brother Charles is the satirical commentator on other men's follies, especially his brother's; he is the literary observer in a world where other men act, the detached man "burdened neither by domestic ties, religious scruples nor political predilections."[16] Brontë's use of Charles as her narrator allowed her to describe the exploits of his aggressive brother at an often amused but still admiring distance—but it also enabled her to express Byron's (and her own) satirical spirit in addition to his more flamboyant side, and perhaps it permitted her to feel through her identification with Charles a relationship with Wellington. Even in fantasy, however, it was necessary for her to assume a male persona: it was males, after all, who acted, and writing meant doing, meant fathering creations of her own imagination.

As if to compensate for this usurpation of a male prerogative, Brontë developed and came to identify with a succession of devoted Angrian females whose role it is to submit wholly to the dictates of the masterly Zamorna. Byron had created such submissive maidens in the first place, as Francis Jeffrey noted in his 1814 review of *The Corsair* and *The Bride of Abydos*, as foils to "the lordly pride and martial ferocity of the men." (Byron's women all follow the same pattern, Macaulay complained: "all softness and gentleness, loving to caress and to be caressed, but capable of being transformed by passion into a tigress.")[17] Among Zamorna's devotees are his doomed wife, Marian Hume, who was to provide the model, as well as part of the name, for the gentle Paulina Mary Home de Bassompierre in *Villette*;[18] his Celtic, self-appointed slave, Mina Laury; and his ward, the willful Caroline Vernon, the first example in Brontë of a pupil falling in love with her "master" but also a reflection of Caroline Lamb in the manner in which she pursues Zamorna. (We are told that Byron, Wellington, and Napoleon are among Caroline Vernon's heroes.) Mina admits that her "Master" rarely thinks of her and cannot "appreciate the unusual feelings of subservience, the total self-sacrifice I offer at his shrine." Her relations with Zamorna are apparently asexual, unlike those between him and the passionate Caroline, but both women are described as losing their identity in the duke: Mina's "very life was swallowed up"; and Caroline's one wish, while yet a girl, is "to give up heart, soul, and sensations to one loved hero, to lose independent existence in the perfect adoption of her lover's being." Whether overtly or subliminally erotic, the passion that both women endure became the basis for Charlotte Brontë's conception of love. In the same year that she wrote "Mina Laury," she refused a proposal of marriage from Ellen Nussey's brother on the grounds that she did not feel disposed to die for him, "and, if ever I marry, it must be in that light of adoration that I will regard my husband." (Her masculine-named and male-seeming heroine Shirley Keeldar later reverts to the same romantic impulse.)[19] Submission on the part of women meant being realistic—even the unfeminine act of creativity could be sanctioned as long as Brontë felt herself to be mastered by creative impulses while she wrote—but the habit of making her Angrian heroines give way in all things gives them the air of being "inevitable victims."[20]

The Angrian fantasies always contained a certain element of realism, references to parliamentary debates and military expeditions and fashionable London gatherings, gleaned from the family copy of *Blackwood's*, or even allusions to domestic details of the Brontë household;[21] but what may have begun as an attempt not to lose sight of the real world blurred into an inability to distinguish between fantasy and reality. Consequently, as Angria's hold on her increased in the later narratives, so too did her censorship of the Angrian exploits. A sense of psychological realism developed, which enabled her to see the once splendid Zamorna as an object lesson of the destructiveness of a life of uncontrollable passion. Charles's withdrawal from an active role in life, on the other hand, became linked with her own lonely position. "One cannot live always in solitude," he complains in one of the last Angrian tales. "One cannot continually keep one's feelings wound up to the pitch of romance and reverie." Meanwhile, the dazzling kingdom of Angria, a tribute to the high ambitions of noble men (and, as such, a world with similarities to Disraeli's fictional depictions of Regency splendor), degenerates into the seat of "ambition—tyranny—licentiousness—insolence—avarice—blood-thirstyness—bad faith."[22]

But even though a realistic focus was imposed upon the realm of romance—with Yorkshire locations eventually replacing Angrian sites—Brontë persisted in clinging to the original dreams of wish-fulfillment that had summoned Angria into existence. A comparison of the comparatively early Angrian tale "The Foundling" (1833) with one of the last, and the most realistic, of the stories, "Captain Henry Hastings" (1839), reveals the same hunger on the author's part for an ennobling career, an ennobled identity, and a place to belong. Edward Sidney, the adolescent author's orphan-hero, feels convinced that "some superhuman power must be watching over me and directing events for my good. I feel that I spring from no common root—my own mind tells me so." Unable to rise to a position of power in England, he sails to Angria in search of adventure and, as it turns out, his noble identity. Six years later Brontë chose for her protagonist a lonely governess, an "insignificant—unattractive young woman wholly without the bloom—majesty or fullness of beauty." However, her intellectual gifts and her ability to exert "considerable influence over her scholars" enable Elizabeth Hastings to achieve the power of an Edward Sidney: "She quickly gained a large circle of friends—had constant invitations to the most stylish houses of Zamorna [the city named for Brontë's hero]—acquired a most impeccable character —for ability—accomplishment—obliging disposition—& most correct & elegant manners—of course her class enlarged, & she was as prosperous as any little woman of five feet high & not twenty years old need wish to be."[23] The foundling and the governess merged into the protagonists of Brontë's four novels, and the romantic search for adventure and identity was adapted to fit a pattern that Brontë pointedly regarded as corresponding to the real world. Northrop Frye has defined the dreamlike "quest-romance" as "the search of the libido or desiring self for a fulfillment that will deliver it from the anxieties of reality but will still contain that reality."[24] Brontë's goal was the opposite of this: for her protagonists she sought a realistic fulfillment that would deliver them from the lures of romance but would still contain that romance. Other vestiges of Angria survived—

willful heroes, self-abasing heroines, wonder-working genii, implacable forces of evil—but Brontë, when she was in control of her materials, domesticated Angria even if she did not positively exorcise it.

Elizabeth Gaskell described Charlotte Brontë's first novel as a reaction "against the exaggerated idealisms [that is, the Angrian tales] of her early girlhood"; in *The Professor* (1846) she "went to the extreme of reality." Brontë herself insisted to George Henry Lewes that she had taken "Nature and Truth" as her "sole guides" and had "restrained imagination, eschewed romance, repressed excitement," and avoided "over-bright colouring."[25] Compared to *Vivian Grey* or *Wuthering Heights*, *The Professor* seems unromantic indeed, lacking the combination of Disraelian audacity and Byronic melancholy of the one book or the passionate ardor and pagan intensity of the other. But Brontë's version of reality remains a personal vision. The situation in which her foundling-hero William Crimsworth finds himself seems like something imagined by someone with a persecution-complex. Crimsworth is orphaned and friendless; his closest relation, his brother, hates him for no other reason than to substantiate Brontë's belief that men would rather follow Cain's example than Abel's. (In this respect, her familiarity with fairy-tale accounts of sibling rivalry—which Dickens also drew upon for the relationship between Oliver Twist and Monks— combined with her Protestant belief in the survival of the Old Adam. The fact that she and her siblings loved each other was beside the point; *they* were exceptions.) Reality for her hero means work—degradingly servile work, in the beginning, as clerk to his tradesman brother—and it means an allegorical voyage through life with associates like Duty, Liberty, Reason, Resentment, Grief, and (for relief) his "darling, [his] cherished-in-secret, Imagination" (p. 26), to replace the relatives who have washed their hands of him.

Like the hero of "The Foundling," Crimsworth is a displaced aristocrat: "What a nobleman you would have made," a perverse acquaintance jeers at him, adding, "as it is, you've no power; you can do nothing; you're wrecked and stranded on the shores of commerce; forced into collision with practical men, with whom you cannot cope" (p. 34). Crimsworth's decision to abandon the prospect of a tradesman's life and to seek adventurous work away from England echoes the choice of Edward Sidney. Brontë explained Sidney's leaving England for Angria as follows:

> The peaceful tranquil character of the times in which he lived was unfavorable to rising talent. England was still almost stagnant; his ardent spirit longed to be tossing on the stormy ocean of political or martial contention . . . Active exercise of his corporeal, as well as intellectual powers, seemed necessary for the complete gratification of his desires . . . He determined to quit England for ever and pursue Glory in regions more likely to be blessed by her presence.[26]

Crimsworth's soberer pilgrimage to Belgium is restated in religious as well as romantic rhetoric:

> Liberty I clasped in my arms for the first time, and the influence of her smile and embrace revived my life like the sun and the west wind . . . Difficulty and toil were to be my lot, but sustained by energy, drawn on by hopes as bright as vague, I deemed such a lot no hardship . . . [T]here were pebbles, inequalities, briars in my path, but my eyes were fixed on the crimson peak above; my imagination was with the refulgent firmament beyond, and I thought nothing of the stones turning under my feet, or of the thorns scratching my face and hands. (P. 54)

(When such imagery is evoked by Lucy Snowe, who repeats Crimsworth's pilgrimage in *Villette*, the language is joyless and the goal bleak. "I know not that I was of a self-reliant or active nature," Lucy declares; "but self-reliance and exertion were forced upon me by circumstances"; I, 40.) Fate is kind to Crimsworth, as it had been to Sidney. Soon after his arrival in Brussells, he is appointed to be an English teacher, and his success in subduing mutinous students is reminiscent of the martial exploits of an Angrian commander. With such self-control, and with the aid of the father of a student he has fortuitously saved from drowning, Crimsworth rises in his profession. Like Elizabeth

Hastings, he becomes a wealthy schoolmaster, selecting students from "the best families." Best of all, he is able to trade in his "darling Imagination" for the real thing, Frances Henri, a former pupil who has hitherto followed a regimen similar to his own: "fortitude" laced, in private, with "poetry" (p. 228).

Brontë's defiance of romantic conventions is seen in the relative plainness of her hero and heroine. To set off their unassuming natures and features, she characterizes Crimsworth's tyrannical brother in terms of Byronic quivering nostrils and eyes that shoot "a spark of sinister fire" (p. 39), and she allows the schoolmaster a student very different from Frances, a sensual, noble-born copy of Caroline Lamb (her name is Caroline too) of whom it is said "Byron would have worshipped her" (p. 96). But for all their plain exteriors and their need to work for a living, Crimsworth and Frances are latent Romantics. Refusing to be beholden to any man unless it "suits" him, determined to "follow [his] own devices" come what may (p. 49), Crimsworth is aptly described by his bride-to-be as "un peu entêté, exigeant, volontaire" (p. 236). Frances, moreover, is as devoted to her "maître" as any Byronic maiden, although she has a spirited nature of her own, and she is excited by Byron's poetry. Her flashes of caprice are such, Crimsworth says, that he "frequently dosed her with Wordsworth . . . and Wordsworth steadied her soon" (p. 268).[27] Both characters are parentless and homeless. "If ever I possess a home," Crimsworth tells Frances, "it must be of my own making" (p. 182). After ten years of work as schoolmasters, the Crimsworths are able to achieve that ideal: having become economically independent from teaching, they retire to a home in England cozily named Daisy Lane. Crimsworth can even afford to be sociable now—he had "left no friends" behind in England, as he is reminded, "for you made none" (p. 214)—while Frances can afford to indulge her feelings at long last. Such luxuries come dearly in the Brontë universe. As if to qualify her otherwise happy ending, Brontë notes that Crimsworth's sadistic brother is prospering more than ever (the same will be true of Lucy Snowe's enemies in *Villette*) and that the Crimsworths' son Victor is showing signs of imitating his uncle, if not Byron himself: his mother sees in his fits of temper "a kind of electrical ardour and power—which emits, now and then, ominous sparks" (p. 281).

Although she did not entirely eschew romance in *The Professor*, Brontë controlled her visionary bent in that book as best she could: she was as determined as her main characters not to resort to the dictates of impulse. One result of this holding back is that when romantic feeling breaks free in the novel it generally does so in an unpleasant and vindictive manner—taking the form of Crimsworth's hypochondria, or his son's tantrums, or his brother's savagery. However, in the scene where Crimsworth declares his love for Frances, Brontë differentiates between "impulses we can control" and "others which control us, because they attain us with a tiger-leap, and are our masters ere we have seen them." Perhaps, she muses, these exceptional and irresistible yieldings to "Instinct" are permissible because "Reason" considers them sane (p. 230). (Immoral impulses, one would presume, can be controlled.) At any rate, feeling and the imagination must have their way too; and in her next novel, *Jane Eyre*, Brontë endeavored more successfully than she ever would again to accommodate the conflicting claims of reason and feeling. Reality would be achieved by showing the dangers of yielding to impulse, but wish-fulfillment could be attained too once temptations were overcome. A Victorianized romance celebrating the virtues of home and duty is the reward for the rejection of the excesses of romance and Romanticism.

The Victorian element in *Jane Eyre* (1847) stands in marked relief to the unyielding Romanticism of *Wuthering Heights*. Charlotte Brontë's 1850 preface to the reissue of her sister's novel indicates a somewhat distant admiration for its powerful account of "harshly manifested passions," of untrammeled egoism inflicting harm upon itself and others. (In contrast, the heroine of *Jane Eyre* is allowed a "social heart"; p. 401.) But if she is reluctant to praise the romantic theme of the novel, she concedes Emily Brontë's rightness in having yielded to the demands of creative impulse. While "scarcely" thinking it "right or advisable to create beings like Heathcliff," she argues that her sister, in possessing "the creative gift," owned "something of which [she was] not always master—something that strangely wills and works for itself." After the publication of *Jane Eyre*, Brontë protested to Lewes, on these very grounds, her inability, or unwillingness, to withstand the cry of "imagination": "When she shows us bright pictures, are we never to look at them, and try to reproduce them? And when she is eloquent, and speaks rapidly and urgently in our ear, are we not to write to her dictation?" In any case, impulse cannot be resisted if a writer is to be at her "best" or most fluent; it "becomes [one's] master" and "will have its own way—putting out of view all behests but its own." (Her idol Thackeray, however, she admiringly observed, was "never borne away by his own ardour—he has it under control. His genius obeys him—it is his servant, it works no fantastic changes at its own wild will, it must still achieve the task which reason and sense assign it, and none other." Male writers, it seems, might control their impulses—not so the Brontë sisters.)[28]

The realism of *Jane Eyre* paradoxically depends on its author's acknowledgment of the need for romance in real life. Moreover, the sense of reality in the book is abetted by Brontë's wonderful control over her materials from start to finish: though the characters may give way to impulse, may waver between opposing compulsions, the author knows exactly what she is doing. All the conflicting forces in the book are resolved in her most emotionally and structurally satisfying conclusion.[29] As in *The Professor*, a homeless orphan searches for a fixed abode in the world, and her quest takes the form of a pilgrimage from one potentially desirable resting place to another until she can at last assume the role (as Jane describes it) of a "messenger-pigeon flying home" (p. 540). At every state of her pilgrimage, she incurs temptations and witnesses warning examples of good and bad behavior. As a child, Jane is thrust into a world of unloving and malicious relations. The fate of John Reed, her pampered cousin whose lack of early training in self-control results in his moral collapse and eventual suicide, is clearly intended as a warning of what Rochester might have become (and what Branwell did become) without the intercession of Jane, his "good angel." "I was like nobody there," Jane admits, rather proudly, of her status at Gateshead Hall (p. 13). Like Crimsworth, she refuses to be beholden to her relatives—"a benefactress is a disagreeable

thing," she reflects of her Aunt Reed (p. 34)—and her relations
are not given any qualities that might inspire gratitude. Jane's
only source of consolation is her imagination, which is drawn to
descriptions of shipwreck as well as to the *Arabian Nights*, and
which further exacerbates her lonely position by conjuring up
ghostly visions.

The second stage of Jane's pilgrimage is Lowood School, where
she finds in her fellow pupil Helen Burns an example of fortitude
in the face of misfortunes, an attitude very different from her
own rebelliousness. Helen's copy of *Rasselas* seems dull to Jane
because of its absence of "fairies" and "genii" (p. 55), and perhaps too because of its stoical theme; but Jane presumably re-
ceives the necessary "dose" of realism through her acquaintance
with Helen—the dose that Crimsworth administered to Frances
Henri by reading to her from Wordsworth. For Helen, the only
resting-place of consequence is "Eternity," her "mighty home"
(p. 67). Although in time Jane becomes a teacher at Lowood, the
lack of loved acquaintances (with the death of Helen and the
departure of Miss Temple) removes the associations "that had
made [Lowood] in some degree a home to me." Like Crimsworth
—and Edward Sidney before him—Jane craves adventure, even
in the form of "a new servitude," so long as it will take her into
"the real world" (pp. 99–101). This turns out to be Thornfield
Hall, aptly named from a religious-allegorical point of view,
where the prospect of romantic fulfillment is dangled before her,
but a fulfillment that she must reject on moral grounds. Rochester, the master of Thornfield Hall, correctly reads Jane's control
over her dual nature in her face: "My fine visions are all very
well," she seems to say, "but I must not forget they are absolutely unreal. I have a rosy sky, and a green flowery Eden in my
brain; but without, I am perfectly aware, lies at my feet a rough
track to travel, and around me gather black tempests to en-
counter" (pp. 399–400). The reification of Jane's pleasanter
dreams—the establishment of a domestic Eden—is possible only
when her rough pilgrimage over the domain of reality, with
conscience as her guide, is completed.

Although one thinks of the Thornfield section of *Jane Eyre* as
the romantic center of the book, Brontë is insistent here in her
determination to keep a distance from romance. The district in

which Thornfield is located is "less picturesque" and "less romantic" than the region about Lowood (p. 114); and when the servant Grace Poole's addiction to alcohol is broached (a matter of some importance for the plot), the narrator apologizes, "oh romantic reader, forgive me for telling the plain truth!" (p. 133). Jane is described as plain, Rochester even as ugly: they are by no means the "handsome" figures that Brontë noted "Bulwer and Byron heroes and heroines" to be.[30] When romantic fancies or figures appear in this section, they are invariably disclaimed or mocked. Just before Rochester shows up in the novel, Jane is bemused by romantic visions of the "Gytrash"; when Rochester suddenly appears, he "broke the spell at once" (p. 136). Jane's saving of his life at this point is dismissed as "an incident of no moment, no romance, no interest" (p. 140). He himself is haunted by no "Vampyre," as a romantic reader might expect; instead he is plagued by an insane wife. In this novel that became the model for so many subsequent romances, Brontë was overturning the conventions of Gothic romance.

The contrasting figures of Blanche Ingram and Bertha Rochester point up the excesses of the moribund romanticism from which Brontë's and Jane's natures shrink. Blanche fits the image of a beautiful romance heroine, one of the ladies of Angria whose features the author copied from engravings of fashionable Regency women. Tall and dark-skinned, resembling a "Spaniard," she professes, in the manner of Trollope's fatuous Lizzie Eustace (in *The Eustace Diamonds*) to "doat on Corsairs" and banditti (p. 225). It is obvious that a "realistic"-minded man like Rochester would not marry her even if he were free to do so. (Lizzie Eustace's stale romanticism does, in fact, drive her into the arms of a bigamist.) Bertha's role in the novel has been linked to Brontë's readings in Gothic romance; but here as elsewhere Brontë subverts her reader's romantic expectations. In a Radcliffe novel Rochester would have been a Bluebeard, locking up his innocent, defenseless wives. (Jane, soon after arriving at Thornfield, fantasizes that she is in Bluebeard's castle.) Instead, he is at Bertha's mercy; romantic despotism has given way to marital incompatibility. Bertha represents, to be sure, Romantic energy at its most willful and uncontrolled, *la bête humaine* personified: "What it was," Jane says of Rochester's wife, "whether beast or human being, one could not, at first sight, tell: it grovelled, seemingly, on all fours; it snatched and growled like some strange wild animal; but it was covered with clothing; and a quantity of dark, grizzled hair, wild as a mane, hid its head and face" (p. 370).[31]

Rochester has an obvious resemblance to Byron in character and features: for example, his comparison of his life to a "crater-crust which may crack and spue fire any day" (p. 271) recalls Byron's famous description of his creative energies as a pouring forth of lava to prevent an earthquake. But Rochester is a Byron moralized and made fit for Victorian consumption. Unlike Heath-cliff (or Huntingdon in Anne Brontë's *The Tenant of Wildfell Hall*), Rochester is salvageable and hence capable of life in the Victorian world. Brontë defended her character on the grounds of his having "a thoughtful nature and a very feeling heart; he is neither selfish nor self-indulgent; he is ill-educated, misguided; errs, when he does err, through rashness and inexperience: he lives for a time as too many other men live, but being radically better than most men, he does not like that degraded life, and is never happy in it. He is taught the severe lessons of experience and has sense to learn wisdom from them."[32] It is perhaps unfortunate that we do not see Rochester learning from experience in the novel: his bad habits are blamed on his upbringing—"a wild boy, indulged from childhood upwards" (p. 273)—just as his disastrous marriage to Bertha is blamed on hostile relations. As usual in Brontë, the cruelty of one's relatives is one of the commonplaces of reality. When Jane returns to him, Rochester acknowledges "the hand of God" in his chastisement (p. 571); but it is the hand of Charlotte Brontë that releases him from Bertha. It is a tribute to Brontë's imagination that, seeing Rochester as clearly as she does, she is able to convince the reader of his existence too—despite the evasions in matters of past history and the absurdities in matters of dialogue. In spite of the many references to Providence in the novel, it is love that causes Rochester to reform, and it is the democracy of lovers that puts Jane and Rochester on an equal footing at the end of the novel.

All the while that Brontë is setting up romantic expectations for the reader—and then deflating them—Jane Eyre is learning to allow for some romance within her realistic sense of life's limitations. Jane's pilgrimage, although described with a combination of religious and Romantic rhetoric, is toward a home neither in Heaven (as in the case of Helen Burns and St. John Rivers and Bunyan's Christian) nor in her imagination (as it would be for a Keatsian Romantic) but on earth—in a domestic context. Toward this realistic aim she is aided by a supernatural machinery that Brontë at various points links with Providence and Nature: religion and romance conspire, in this way, to secure Jane's real happiness.[33] A "kind fairy" (p. 102) advises Jane to place the advertisement that leads to her position at Thornfield; she trusts herself to her "mother, Nature" (p. 412) when she flees Thornfield, having learned about Rochester's wife and refusing to be his mistress; and Nature and Providence lead her to the Moor House, where she learns that she has kind-hearted relations and an unexpected inheritance. Finally, it is "the work of nature" (p. 536) that allows her to hear Rochester's voice, across many miles, in time to resist accepting her cousin St. John Rivers's marriage proposal. Jane's development, which is the real subject of the book, is away from the emotional violence of her nature, which causes her, when confronted with "positive, hard characters, antagonistic to my own," to know no middle position "between absolute submission and determined revolt" (p. 511).[34] The excesses of feeling and conscience must be avoided so that Jane can reach a position equally distant from the barbarism and lack of self-control of a Bertha Rochester and the barren self-discipline of an Eliza Reed. The compromise Brontë reaches is one that is Victorian in purging the protagonists' egoism and in integrating them into a domestic and societal sphere of action and ethics, but one that is Romantic as well in refusing to denigrate the claims of the imagination and of individual integrity.

Jane's rejection of St. John Rivers is more important, in some respects, than her repudiation of Rochester's unlawful pleas. For Rochester's claim on her is of a human nature. Rivers has the Romantic features of a Shelley—the good looks that Rochester lacks—and his marriage proposal has a Shelleyan abstract quality to it that ignores her human identity. Rivers is a compendium of Romantic characteristics: it is he, not Rochester, who resembles the heroic and domineering Zamorna. His features are classi-

cally perfect, but a quivering of his nostrils indicates inner discontent. Like Byron, he believes in his predestination, and "he
hides a fever in his vitals" (p. 455). When he describes his past
ambition to Jane—"I burnt for the more active life of the world"
(p. 462)—he echoes the Angrian foundling Edward Sidney; and
while Rivers's destination is farther off than Angria or the
Byronic East, he is in effect transforming into a religious mission
the Romantic wanderlust. Brontë's description of Rivers is itself
a transmutation into religious form of Thomas Moore's portrait
of the restless, unmarriageable Byronic genius:

> The humanities and amenities of life had no attraction for
> him—its peaceful enjoyments no charm. Literally, he lived
> only to aspire—after what was good and great, certainly:
> but still he would never rest; nor approve of others resting
> round him. As I looked at his lofty forehead, still and pale
> as a white stone—at his fine lineaments fixed in study—I
> comprehended all at once that he would hardly make a
> good husband: that it would be a trying thing to be his
> wife . . . I saw he was of the material from which nature
> hews her heroes—Christian and Pagan—her lawgivers, her
> statesmen, her conquerors. (Pp. 501–502)

Jane's feeling for Rivers recalls Mina Laury's for Zamorna: "I
could not resist him," Jane admits (p. 510); and later, "I was
tempted to cease struggling with him—to rush down the torrent
of his will into the gulf of his existence, and there to lose my
own" (p. 534).[35]
    It is Rivers who mocks Jane's hunger for "domestic endear-
ments and household joys" (p. 499) ("The best things the world
has!" she replies); and with his focus on Heaven, he is right. But
Jane's destination, like Rochester's, or like Adam's and Eve's at
the end of *Paradise Lost*, is "homeward." By resisting Rivers,
Jane withstands the ultimate Romantic threat to her individuality: the temptation to become a Byronic slave-maiden like one of
her Angrian heroines. With Rochester, she maintains a sense of
integrity and interdependence. The domestic hearth became, for
the Victorian generation, the meeting place of sublimated romantic passion and civil morality; and the brief but climactic Fern-
dean section of *Jane Eyre* represents one of the earliest and most

satisfying of Victorian fictional attempts to balance the opposing claims of the individual and society. In her greatest novel Charlotte Brontë acknowledges the reality of romance, and in her account of the domestication of two of the rebellious individuals who people the earth she allows for a romance of reality as well.[36]

In writing her next novel, *Shirley* (1849), Brontë determined to prove that she could handle a public theme, despite the paucity of her personal experience, and that she could avoid her fondness for "melodrama" (which George Henry Lewes had warned her against). *Shirley* would contain "something real, cool, and solid," she promised her readers at the outset (I, i). Like Caroline Helstone, one of the two heroines of the book, Brontë earnestly wished "to see things as they were, and not to be romantic" (I, 191). From stories told her by her father and by other contemporary witnesses, and from old newspaper reports, she learned about the Luddite riots in the early part of the century; and from recent exposure to Jane Austen, whom Lewes had recommended as a model of realism, she took the example of an ironical point of view—for a few chapters.[37] There are several admirable qualities to the novel: vivid characterization and a shrewd psychological grasp of some of the causes of social discontent in her own time as well as thirty years earlier. Her linking of the grim situation of workers with the unhappy position of women enabled her to criticize both the organization of industrial society and the submissive role of women. "Invention may be all right," the deferential, unemployed worker William Ferren says, "but I know it isn't right for us poor folks to starve. Them that governs mun find a way to help us: they mun mak' fresh orderations" (I, 151). Similarly, Caroline complains to the "Fathers" of England with regard to the degraded status of and the lack of occupations for single women: "God surely did not create us, and cause us to live, with the sole end of wishing always to die . . . Existence never was originally meant to be that useless, blank, pale, slow-trailing thing it often becomes to many" (II, 81). The fear of poverty makes workers obey autocratic millowners, but when they see their jobs taken from them as a result of the new machines, "Misery generates hate" (I, 30).

Loneliness and poverty may drive women into unhappy marriages, but the role of the old maid is worse. "Is there not a terrible hollowness, mockery, want, craving, in that existence," Caroline movingly protests, "which is given away to others, for want of something of your own to bestow it on? . . . Does virtue lie in abnegation of self? I do not believe it. Undue humility makes tyranny; weak concession creates selfishness . . . Each human being has his share of rights" (I, 193–194).

This is well-argued; but *Shirley* works toward a conclusion in which realistic questioning is met with fantasy solutions. So long as Charlotte Brontë was true to her Romantic impulse, as in *Jane Eyre,* she could contain it within a realistic framework. In *Shirley,* where she vows that the "shores of Reality" shall be her and her characters' only goal, regressive Romantic compulsions raise their ugly heads. Her concern for the "condition of women" was based on sad personal experience; and in her letters to W. S. Williams (who read her manuscripts for Smith, Elder and Company, her publishers, and who worried about the prospects open to his unmarried daughters), she repeatedly sounded the theme that the woman whom "destiny" denies the "vocation" of marriage must discipline herself to "do what she can, live as she can, complain as little, bear as much, work as well as possible." That the social system was unjust to women she admitted; yet she insisted that the role for "women or operatives" alike was patience—and the only source of relief was Heaven. (Having rejected Helen Burns's and Rivers's views in *Jane Eyre,* she reversed herself with a vengeance in *Shirley* and *Villette.*) With Elizabeth Gaskell, Brontë agreed that "the amelioration of our condition depends on ourselves"; but while she thought some changes could be made, there remained "other evils—deep-rooted in the foundations of the social system—which no efforts of ours can touch; of which we cannot complain; of which it is advisable not too often to think."[38] In *Shirley* protest against the harsh realities of life is stifled by a sense of personal frustration and a romantically colored version of fortitude. Women and workers alike are sacrificed to the quiescent strain in Romanticism in which masters (in both the sexual and economic senses of the word) must be obeyed. In *Sybil* Disraeli foresaw a romantic alliance between workers and ruling classes in which aristocrats like Charles Egrement would work chivalrically on behalf of the people and against the selfish interests of the middle classes. In *Shirley* Brontë sees the millowners as the real masters; and when Caroline proposes coming to the aid of Robert Moore, the millowner whom she loves in secret and whose mill is about to be attacked, she is rebuked by her friend Shirley: "How? By inspiring him with heroism? Pooh! These are not the days of chivalry: it is not a tilt at a tournament we are going to behold, but a struggle about money, and food, and life" (II, 26).

A world of struggle, hunger, and deprivation was indeed Brontë's idea of reality, but while her sympathies were with the sufferers, her imagination went out to the conquerors. Not inappropriately, Napoleon and Wellington are at war at the same time the millowners and workers clash; battles rage among nations and among individuals, and no satisfactory resolution seems possible. Social problems, Brontë felt, stem from the will to power—whether of millowners over workers or of men over women—yet she accepted this as a necessary, if tragic, aspect of life. "All men, taken singly, are more or less selfish," she says of the actions of the mercantile interests; "and taken in bodies they are intensely so." A sense of chivalry or sympathy is foreign to them. "A land ruled by them alone," she warns, "would too often make ignominious submission—not at all from the motives Christ teaches, but rather from those Mammon instils" (I, 185). That said, however, she chooses for her hero a millowner, Robert Moore, who demands absolute submission on the part of his workers, and who refuses to consider the plight of those whom his new machinery will make destitute. "I will have my own way," he says to Ferren. "*I'll never give in*" (I, 151). (This is the rhetoric and position of Zamorna in the Angrian tales.) Although his attitude softens somewhat in the course of the book, Robert does not undergo a change of heart comparable to Thornton's in Elizabeth Gaskell's *North and South*. Brontë compares his pride to that of Coriolanus and treats his military success in squashing the riot at his mill as if it were a victory by her idol, the Duke of Wellington (whom she had linked with Coriolanus in a student paper written for her Belgian schoolmaster, Heger).[39] Where Gaskell prefers the altered Thornton, who is made to realize that workers and masters, women and men are dependent on each other, Brontë prefers her hero to be as indomitable as Wellington, gracious only in victory.

Men may play the conquering hero with women too, because of their ability to rescue single women from lives of loneliness and destitution. The comic use of the presumptuous curates in *Shirley*—charmless egoists dangling the possibility of marriage before unmarried Yorkshire women—only underscores the bitterness of the women's prospects in the novel. Even the obstinate and cruelly unperceptive Reverend Helstone, Caroline's uncle, whose lack of feeling toward his wife hastened her early death, is considered an eligible male to whom parents would gratefully sacrifice their daughters. The late Mrs. Helstone had selected her husband over a more devoted suitor because, being indifferent toward her, "he was, consequently, more master of her and himself" (I, 54); while a future "Mrs. Helstone, inversing the natural order of insect existence, would have fluttered through the honeymoon a bright, admired butterfly, and crawled the rest of her days a sordid, trampled worm" (I, 128). With such selfishness, perversity, and lack of understanding among individuals, "It is good for women, especially," Brontë caustically and frustratedly writes, "to be endowed with a soft blindness: to have mild, dim eyes, that never penetrate below the surface of things —that take all for what it seems" (I, 300).

Unfortunately, Brontë's sensitive heroine, Caroline Helstone, is too astute to be able to feign blindness. She has no role in life to relieve her anxieties and loneliness, nor does she have internal consolation: although "her imagination was full of pictures" (I, 192), the images—of Robert, who will not marry her because of her poverty—cause her added grief. Wishing to see things as they are in a realistic Brontë universe, Caroline understandably sickens and nearly dies on two occasions. She is rescued the first time by the appearance of a wealthy new neighbor, Shirley Keeldar, who is as romantic-minded as Caroline would dare to be if she had the money; and she is raised from her deathbed the second time when Shirley's companion, Mrs. Pryor, announces that she is Caroline's long-lost mother. Given the desolate prospect open to her in the first part of the novel, Caroline may well have been intended for a consolation attainable only in Heaven. Yet the death of Anne Brontë (whom Caroline resembles in her modesty and her view of women's right), which occurred while Charlotte was writing this novel, may have persuaded Charlotte to find an alternative to her heroine's original fate.[40] Robert's eleventh-hour proposal of marriage presumably saves Caroline from further anxieties. But given Robert's obstinate nature, and the fact that he has recently proposed to Shirley for the sake of her money, and given the harrowing view of marriage expressed in the book—"Millions of marriages are unhappy," says Caroline's uncle; "if everybody confessed the truth, perhaps all are more or less so" (I. 109)—the reader may suspect that Caroline's future will turn out to be only marginally more satisfying than the dread alternative. The resolution of Brontë's last two novels betray a refusal to be logical: marriage may provide an unhappy fate for women in general, but it means a happy ending for Brontë's heroines; teaching is treated as a degrading ordeal in *Villette*, but Lucy Snowe's contentment is made to rest on her having a school to run. If Jane Eyre's happiness rests solidly on her having taken the examples of other people to heart, the happiness of Caroline and Shirley depends on their ignoring all such warning signs. Caroline's love for Robert's masterly disposition ominously resembles the misplaced devotion of her late aunt for the Reverend Helstone.

The greatest disappointment of *Shirley*, however, is Brontë's inability to think of any fate for her independent-minded co-heroine, with her masculine name and magisterial ways, other than to be consigned to the arms of the least interesting of all the Brontë heroes. Louis Moore, Robert's brother, is Shirley's former tutor; and it is his pedagogic capacity as "master" that makes Shirley look up to him as precisely the man of her (or Brontë's) dreams. Despite her sentiments concerning women's capabilities, Shirley says from the beginning that nothing charms her "more than when I meet my superior—one who makes me sincerely feel that he is my superior . . . [I]t is glorious to look up" (I, 238). This is not the sort of hero-worship Carlyle had in mind; it addresses neither the needs of women nor the condition of England. Shirley craves a "master," a hand that will hold her "in check," a man she will "find it impossible not to love, and very possible to fear" (II, 255–256). Just before he proposes,

Louis tells Shirley (with only a touch of irony) that his ideal mate is a helpless orphan, "Something to tame first, and teach afterwards: to break in, and then to fondle," who will eventually turn out "the exemplary and patient mother of about a dozen children" (II, 333)

Finishing the novel under the pressure of grief caused by the successive deaths of Branwell, Emily, and Anne, Charlotte Brontë emotionally regressed to the time when she had lived in her Angrian dreamworld, and she bestowed on her heroines a fate that resembles that of the devoted Angrian maidens Mina Laury and Caroline Vernon. (Robert calls his Caroline "Lina," heightening the similarity in name as well as role.) "Better to be without logic than without feeling," as Frances Henri insists in *The Professor* (p. 253). Brontë's reaction to Harriet Taylor's essay on "The Emancipation of Women" was to castigate the author for forgetting that "there is such a thing as self-sacrificing love and disinterested devotion"; she suspected the author to be "a woman who longed for power, and had never felt affection."[41] Such romantic views may apply to a limited Romantic context: for example, it hardly matters that Keats endows Madeline in "The Eve of St. Agnes" with no other emotion than an erotic devotion to Porphyro; the lovers in that poem dissolve into a dreamworld, in any case. In *Shirley*, however, Brontë was attempting a novel with social as well as personal implications; and *The Corsair* makes a poor model for an industrial novel.[42] Submission to dominating males is her solution to the condition of women, and as for the condition of England, Mrs. Pryor has the following advice: "Implicit submission to authorities, scrupulous deference to our betters (under which term I, of course, include the higher classes of society) are, in my opinion, indispensable to the well-being of every community" (II, 66–67). One might guess that such a passage had been written by Lady Eastlake, who had assailed *Jane Eyre* for showing "the mind and thought which has overthrown authority and violated every code human and divine abroad, and fostered Chartism and rebellion at home,"[43] rather than by the creator of Jane Eyre, who had sought a position midway between self-assertiveness and self-abasement. But the fate of women is paralleled by the fate of England. *Shirley* ends with the triumph of industrialism: "a mighty mill, and a chimney, ambitious as the tower of Babel," rise ominously over lands that were "once green, and lone, and wild" (II, 361).

Villette (1853) is Brontë's climactic though not quite her best work, her fullest if scarcely her most satisfying achievement. Where the romantic element in *Jane Eyre* is universal—the fact that nearly everyone shares Jane's dream, in one way or other, makes it a realistic book—the sufferings of Lucy Snowe are personal and exclusive. The more one knows about Charlotte Brontë the likelier one is to respond to *Villette*, which is not the case with *Jane Eyre* for all its autobiographical allusions. Brontë's last book is realistic in the sense that in her own life reality was synonymous with suffering and loss: after binding the heroines of *Shirley* to masterly males, she declared herself bound in *Villette* to the ultimate master and father-figure, "Fate." In one of her most (justifiably) paranoid moods, Lucy Snowe gives this explanation for Heaven's apparent neglect of her pleas for "consolation and support": "With what dread force the conviction would grasp me that Fate was my permanent foe, never to be conciliated. I did not, in my heart, arraign the mercy or justice of God for this; I concluded it to be a part of his great plan that some must deeply suffer while they live, and I thrilled in the certainty that of this number, I was one" (I, 198). The intensity of suffering that Brontë conveys through her heroine is a considerable achievement: one must go to Dostoevsky's Underground Man for a comparable effort. But theirs is the suffering of a persecution complex, a misery that rejoices and finds identity in a sense of election to doom. Lucy clings to "Truth" as a form of crucifixion: "I invoked Conviction to nail upon me the certainty, abhorred while embraced, to fix it with the strongest spikes her strongest strokes could drive; and when the iron had entered well my soul, I stood up, as I thought renovated" (II, 278). What may be overlooked in a reading of this passage is the fact that Lucy is mistaken in what she has assumed to be true. (She has deduced on the basis of misleading appearances that Paul Emanuel, the schoolmaster she loves, is engaged to another woman.) Lucy's fate is fixed from the beginning of the book: her identity is as unchanged and unchanging as the little countess Paulina's or Graham Bretton's—she admits as much (II, 33, 39)—and therefore it is inexact to speak, as recent admirers of the book have done, of Lucy's growth, her development toward a stoical acceptance of a "tragic sense of life."[44] What is extraordinary is the extent to which Lucy suffers while everyone else in the novel prospers.

The claim of *Villette* to be called Brontë's most objective book rests on the assumption that what a morbid vision conjures up is therefore real: to the degree that the possessor of that vision is Lucy, Brontë's character, and not Brontë herself, one may find much to praise in the author's use of point of view. The structural weakness of the book, however, is that the novelist uses a morbid point of view to define a morbid character, but she relies on that character's vision to express objectively what is happening to the other (very different) characters in the novel. Lucy is the last of the author's foundling-protagonists, but the dictates of romance are not so much banished as inverted in her case. Unlike Edward Sidney or William Crimsworth or Jane Eyre, orphans who seek adventure and a home in the world, and who find relations or make relationships that bind them to that world, Lucy's goal is unadventurous and she is, by the end of the novel, the only character without a home or relations. When Paul asks if she is homesick, she sighs, "To be home-sick, one must have a home; which I have not" (II, 142). And "Fate" decrees that she and Paul, unlike Frances and Crimsworth, will not be able to make a home together.

"Life is so constructed, that the event does not, cannot, will not, match the expectation," Lucy says (II, 204); yet this grim maxim holds true only for her. Even Miss Marchmount, the old woman to whom at the beginning of the book Lucy serves as paid companion after all her own relations have mysteriously died or disowned her (Brontë provides the vaguest of clues to suggest that Lucy comes from a human background at all), has a second cousin to inherit her wealth—and to withhold for a long time the modest legacy bequeathed to Lucy. Brontë's main character inhabits a wasteland while everyone else is refreshed: "When I had full leisure to look on life as life must be looked on by such as me," she admits, fairly early in the book, "I found it but a hopeless desert: tawny sands, with no green field, no palm-tree, no well in view. The hopes which are dear to youth, which bear it up and lead it on, I knew not and dared not know" (I, 197). In *Villette* Brontë shifts her heroine's goal from a home on earth to rest in Heaven. Along with Helen Burns in *Jane Eyre* and the suffering workers in *Shirley*, Lucy intones, "His will be done," and resigns herself to a dark pilgrimage "through the wilderness of this world" (II, 240).

But if fate is a "dread foe" to Lucy, if "reality" impersonates an "evil, grovelling, and repellent hag" (I, 136) for her sake, another order of reality and a kinder fortune are applied to the secondary figures in the novel. Traveling to Villette (Brussels) at the dictate of "Fate" in order to find work there, Lucy meets old acquaintances from England: Graham Bretton, who has become a successful doctor, and Paulina Home, last seen as a sensitive child infatuated with Graham and now a sensitive young countess in love with him. Paulina's character is strikingly like Caroline Helstone's, but she is blessed with sufficient money, as well as high rank, to be able to indulge her devoted, romantic nature. (Foundlings no longer *become* aristocrats, as in the Angrian fantasies; the two are split into two disparate characters, Lucy and Paulina.) Brontë's publisher George Smith was surprised that she had not reserved Graham for Lucy; but Brontë protested, "he is far too youthful, handsome, bright-spirited and sweet-tempered; he is a 'curled darling' of Nature and of Fortune, and must draw a prize in life's lottery." Despite her insistence that she was avoiding "the spirit of romance" in *Villette*,[45] Brontë had, in fact, written a novel with a split focus, romantic where Graham and Paulina are concerned, "realistic" in Lucy's case. Graham is plainly the hero of romance: even as a youth he is treated like the "Grand Turk" in the *Arabian Nights* (I, 25), and with his perfect, Grecian features, his quivering upper lip and dilated nostrils, he fits the romantic stereotype. Paulina resembles "an airy, fairy thing" (II, 29); and her devotion to Graham, firm but undemanding of return, is modeled after that of Zamorna's first wife, Marian Hume. The chapter in which Graham and Paulina, "nature's elect," become engaged is fittingly titled "Sunshine," while the next chapter, devoted to Lucy's sufferings, is titled "Cloud." But then Graham "was born victor," Lucy explains, while "some are born vanquished" (II, 234).

The necessity for Lucy's suffering is mandated not so much by the logic of the novel's structure—or the desire to conform to an objective sense of reality, for that matter—as by the depressed spirits with which Brontë composed *Villette*. Left completely to herself, except for her duties to her father, Brontë found herself after the completion of *Shirley* retreating to early memories: to recollections of her sisters, to the experiences in Brussels that had been reshaped by wish-fulfillment into the form of *The Professor*, to the Angrian fantasies themselves. In her last novel all the important events and griefs and books (ranging from the Bible and Bunyan to the *Arabian Nights*) that had shaped her life converge, but they are seen through an Angrian telescope. *Villette* has rightly been called "the most Angrian" of her novels,[46] but not only because characters like Graham and Paulina have counterparts in the early tales. Brontë's imaginative nature—strengthened by her short-sightedness—had also colored Brussels and the Belgian schoolmaster Heger to fit Angrian dimensions. She saw the work of Angrian genii wherever she turned: in 1851 the sight of the Crystal Palace, for example— "such a bazaar or fair as Eastern genii might have created"— suggested the exotic palaces of Angria; the acting of Rachel, also in 1851, in which Brontë saw expressed "the feelings and fury of a fiend," revived memories of the wildest forces of evil that had once been let loose in Angria.[47]

In *Villette* these Eastern trappings and evil presences abound. The chandelier at a concert suggests "the work of eastern genii," and Lucy "almost looked to see if a huge, dark cloudy hand— that of the Slave of the Lamp—were not hovering in the lustrous and perfumed atmosphere of the cupola, guarding its wondrous treasure" (I, 264). The great passage describing Lucy at the midnight fete in Villette is the climactic Angrian spectacle in the novel—and Lucy enjoys the splendors despite her awareness that this "land of enchantment" is the result of paint and pasteboard (II, 259). The scene at the theater where Lucy sees Vashti resembles the performance by Rachel that Brontë had seen only to the extent that the French actress had brought to life Angrian passions: "Hate and Murder and Madness incarnate, she stood" (II, 7), a diabolical force reminiscent of the Angrian archvillain Alexander Percy or of Zamorna in one of his Satanic fits. The most outrageously retrogressive, most evil personage in the novel, however, is Madame Walravens. It is at this woman's instigation, with the aid of the wily priest Père Silas and the heartless headmistress Madame Beck, that Lucy's beloved Paul Emanuel is sent on the mission to the West Indies from which he never returns. Brontë, whose portraits of Madame Beck and Père Silas are remarkable without being unrealistic, must needs make of this nemesis-figure a hunchbacked dwarf, "Malevola, the evil fairy," dressed "like a barbarian queen":

> She might be three feet high, but she had no shape; her skinny hands rested upon each other, and pressed the gold knob of a wand-like ivory staff. Her face was large, set, not upon her shoulders, but before her breast; she seemed to have no neck; I should have said there were a hundred years in her features, and more perhaps in her eyes—her malign, unfriendly eyes, with thick gray brows above, and livid lids all round. How severely they viewed me [notes Lucy], with a sort of dull displeasure!

"Hoar enchantment here prevailed," Lucy says of Madame Walravens's den; "a spell had opened for me elf-land" (II 176).

Lurid description of this sort can be laid to Lucy's deranged imagination, but it is Charlotte Brontë's childhood imagination that is being tapped. For a moment, in *Villette*, it looks as if Lucy herself may be aided by the same good fairies who have watched over Graham and Paulina. When she suffers a physical and nervous collapse and is rescued by Père Silas and Graham (now Doctor Bretton), Lucy compares herself to one under the protection of *Arabian Nights* deities, and she describes her medication as "Genii-elixir or Magi-distillation" (I, 210–211). But Graham's reappearance is calculated, in the end, to show how distant he and his good fortune are from Lucy and her fate. And Père Silas's watchfulness is ultimately that of a spy who later acknowledges that he has not "for a day lost sight of you, nor for an hour failed to take in you a rooted interest" (II, 183). Angrian romance is inverted in Lucy's case: she is watched over by bad spirits, and Paul Emanuel is *not* revived as he would have been in the Angrian world.

Lucy's beloved "Master" is perhaps the finest piece of por-
traiture in Brontë's novels. Ugly, obstinate, imperious, childish,
caustic, yet also modest, chivalric and loving, Paul brings the
novel to life whenever he appears. Amid the abstractions and
personifications that seem to be Lucy's only close companions—
Hope, Fate, Reason, Feeling, and all the rest—he is her only
link with humanity. However, as Elizabeth Gaskell explained,
"the idea of M. Paul Emanuel's death at sea was stamped on
her imagination till it assumed the distinct force of reality; and
she could no more alter her fictitious ending than if they had
been facts which she was relating." Brontë's depressed spirits
during the writing of *Villette*—her suffering under "the canker
of constant solitude" and her "intolerably poignant" memories
of her sisters and their fates—negated the chance for a novel
with a humanly satisfying resolution. Her description of Lucy
to her publishers as "morbid and weak at times" was an admission of her own feelings at the time: "anybody living her life
would necessarily become morbid."[48] The marvel, one must add,
is that she could write *Villette* at all.

For writing all along had been the greatest Romantic temptation. Each of her novels had been composed as an escape from
the gloomy facts of her life. Writing *Shirley*, she explained to
Williams, "took me out of dark and desolate reality into an unreal but happier region."[49] Hence, the scourging of Lucy Snowe's
imagination was a prelude to Brontë's abandoning of her creative
gifts. Before she knows the worst that life has in store for her,
Lucy is sustained by "the strange necromantic joys of fancy"
(I, 93). As her misery intensifies, however, the consolation offered
by Imagination, her "good angel," is offset by the tyrannical
dictates of the "hag" Reason, who "could not rest unless I were
altogether crushed, cowed, broken-in, and broken-down" (I,
290). As Reality and Reason extend their giants' hold over her,
Lucy's once-consoling "Creative Impulse" is transformed into
a commanding "deity, . . . a dark Baal with carven lips and
blank eye-balls, and breast like the stone face of the tomb." The
fancy cannot cheat at all, it seems: romantic reverie becomes for
Lucy, as it had been for Charlotte Brontë, a "tyrant" as fearsome as Reality, and one which compels a "sacrifice" from its

votary (II, 134). By attempting to banish Imagination, she has turned romance into yet another enemy: Lucy can no more live with romance than she can without it.

Villette ends with the protagonist accepting rest rather than fulfillment; and despite Brontë's sporadic efforts toward writing two more works of fiction,[50] the opportunity to stop writing and accept the stultification offered by "real life," as she termed her marriage to Arthur Nicholls, was irresistible. Fate, that ultimate father figure, was inexorable to her, she deduced, and the wisest course was "absolute submission" (as Jane Eyre had described her near-engagement to St. John Rivers). A romance of will was no longer possible in earthly terms, yet romance was necessary to her too. If "reality" was to be her lot on earth, she would sacrifice her creative impulse and look ahead to an afterlife in which all would be well. "I often think that this World would be the most terrible of enigmas," she had once declared, "were it not for the firm belief that there is a World to come where conscientious effort and patient pain will meet their reward."[51]

FIVE

Elizabeth Gaskell, Wordsworth,
and the
Burden of Reality

---

*It is the woes that cannot in any earthly way be escaped
that admit least earthly comforting. Of all trite, worn-out,
hollow mockeries of comfort that were ever uttered by people
who will not take the trouble of sympathising with others,
the one I dislike the most is the exhortation not to grieve
over an event, "for it cannot be helped." Do you think if
I could help it, I would sit still with folded hands, content
to mourn? Do you not believe that as long as hope remained I
would be up and doing? I mourn because what has occurred
cannot be helped.*

Mary Barton

In the creative imaginations of Trollope, Disraeli, and Charlotte Brontë, Romanticism was largely identified with the dangerous and alluring figure of Byron—and, to a lesser extent,
with Shelley. However, another Romantic poet played a prominent and notably unByronic role in the shaping of the Victorian
literary conscience: Wordsworth. The intoxicating effect of
Byron on many an adolescent Victorian is tellingly described
by Charles Kingsley's tailor-poet Alton Locke. The world of
Childe Harold, The Corsair, and *Lara,* recalls Locke, "chimed in
with all my discontent, my melancholy, my thirst after any life
of action and excitement, however frivolous, insane, or even
worse." As a stimulus to action (if also to discontent), the
Byronic will to power had a tonic effect on many great Victorians, whether translated into the sphere of political liberalism as
in Disraeli's case or into the realm of creative assertiveness as in
Trollope's. Charlotte Brontë's association of the Byronic with
the artistic impulse was not so fortunate: while activating her

youthful imagination, the Byronic impulse also served to retard her continuation as a mature novelist. Wordsworth's influence, by contrast, was seen as quietly restorative. That Brontë recognized as much can be seen in the episode of *The Professor* where the heroine shows signs of Byronic willfulness: Crimsworth exorcises the "white demon" by "dosing" Frances "with Wordsworth . . . and Wordsworth steadied her soon."[1]

Only a few years after the great Romantic rebel's death, Byron's fame was already being eclipsed by the poet whom in 1833 Bulwer Lytton dubbed "the apostle, the spiritualizer of those who cling to the most idealized part of things that are— Religion and her houses, Loyalty and her monuments—the tokens of the Sanctity which overshadows the Past." Thackeray's Colonel Newcome, on his return to England, is astonished to hear "that Byron was no great poet . . . And that reverence for Mr. Wordsworth, what did it mean?"[2] It was in Wordsworth's "healing power" (in Matthew Arnold's phrase), his prescribing of the therapeutic charms of Nature and the cultivation of feelings, that troubled Victorians like Mill, Newman, Thomas and Matthew Arnold, Frederick Denison Maurice, Kingsley, George Eliot, and Elizabeth Gaskell found a source of calm and renewed inspiration. As the poet of humble life who celebrated fortitude and resignation and who preached "the religion of gratitude," Wordsworth was the one major Romantic poet congenial to the tastes even of Evangelically minded Victorians, brought up to a life of duty and self-denial and suspicious of imaginative literature.[3] If the ego-centered imagination of a Rousseau or a Byron posed a threat, in many minds, to the very foundations of society, Wordsworth's mood of reverence for and acquiescence to the eternal forms and powers, be they natural or religious or national, seemed safe enough. And while Browning might bemoan the desertion from liberalism of the "lost leader" ("Deeds will be done,—while he boasts his quiescence," avowed the young disciple of Shelley), Wordsworth's humanitarian strain was not lost on Carlyle and on two of the founders of Christian Socialism, Kingsley and Maurice, nor on their admirer, the creator of *Mary Barton*. Modern preference for *The Prelude* over *The Excursion*, though justifiable on aesthetic grounds, has obscured the fact that Wordsworth's Victorian admirers knew him in

terms of the latter poem—that "poetic charter," as his biographer Mary Moorman calls *The Excursion*, "of the poor, the
ignorant, and the underprivileged." The growth of the poet's
imagination, the subject of the first poem, was intended as a
prelude to the expression of his humanitarian sympathies in the
second work.[4]

For gifted women of Charlotte Brontë's and Elizabeth Gaskell's
generation, the creative imagination was often seen as a threat to
religious beliefs and domestic responsibilities. The "will to
write," Elaine Showalter argues, occasioned considerable guilt
in many Victorian women: "Work, in the sense of self-development, was in direct conflict with the subordination and repression
inherent in the feminine ideal. The self-centeredness implicit
in the act of writing made this career an especially threatening
one; it required an engagement with feeling and a cultivation
of ego rather than its negation." If the very compulsion to
write could seem a form of Byronic willfulness, Wordsworth's
demonstration of the didactic function of literature had an encouraging effect on a writer like Gaskell who, according to Edgar
Wright, needed a "cloak" of "moral duty" in order to allow her
"creative urge [to] assert itself."[5] Growing up in an atmosphere
where "self-development" for its own sake was considered the
height of wickedness, and contentedly adapting herself early on
to the life of a busy and dedicated wife and mother, she nevertheless found relief in the sort of imaginative reverie that has
persuaded one biographer that in an earlier generation Elizabeth
Gaskell might have been "another Mrs. Radcliffe."[6] Her fondness for ghost stories, her tales of murder and revenge, and her
idealized memories of the rural community of Knutsford where
she had been raised following her mother's death all attest to a
decidedly romantic literary imagination; but if she could let her
imagination roam free, on occasion, in her stories, the novels
were subject to intermittent bursts of self-censorship. Gaskell's
fictional characters (especially those from her early works) must
often atone for even minimal acts of willfulness, partly in order
to expiate the novelist's will, which had been compelled to
create them. Their rebelliousness invariably gives way to self-
discipline. This endorsement of submissiveness in her characters,
in addition to the compensatory consolation they receive from

nature and the fact that many of them are humbly born, has led a number of Gaskell's critics to link her with Wordsworth. Echoes of Lucy Gray, the Old Cumberland Beggar, and Michael, for example, abound in her fiction; and if, like many Victorians, she seems oblivious to the Wordsworthian "burthen of the mystery," she shares the Wordsworthian sense of the burden of reality, a profound sympathy toward all who suffer and mourn and a realization of the tragic bounds of life.[7]

Wordsworth's centrality in English literature in part comes from his embodiment of the antithetical nature of English Romanticism, which is to say the antithetical nature of England herself. Like his great predecessor Milton, Wordsworth is a poet of both heroic will and reverent submission. Continental observers of England in the Romantic and post-Romantic periods have pointed up what seems to be a discrepancy between the individualistic bias of the English national character and the Protestant heritage which stresses subordination of the will. Byron and Wordsworth accordingly appear as the opposing representatives of English Romanticism, with partisans of Byron stressing his native, radical humanitarianism and deploring Wordsworth's conservatism, and with partisans of Wordsworth emphasizing their poet's altruism and sympathy for the oppressed at home and relegating Byron to the company of Continental Romantic egoists. In truth, Byron and Wordsworth were alike altruistic and individualistic, humanitarian and narcissistic: the very intensity of their self-absorption made them aware of man's helpless state, his inner frailty, and his mistreatment at the hands of others. Wordsworth too was capable of creating rebellious figures whom he identified with or linked to his radical youth. Even in his "Ode to Duty," which seems to have been written for the Victorians rather than for his own generation, the poet, tired of "unchartered freedom" and longing "for a repose that ever is the same," insisted (in a subsequently canceled stanza) that "submissiveness was choice" on his part. Byron in his last phase fought for some of the same ideals that Wordsworth as a lapsed radical had seemingly abandoned; but Wordsworth, along with his fellow apostates Coleridge and Southey, raged against the industrialists who were destroying, as he lamented in *The Excursion*, the heritage of British native independence. For Victorians distressed by the principles of industrialism and Utilitarianism, which treated man as a tool or a statistic, Wordsworth's "use of human beings as ethical symbols had a particular appeal . . . Wordsworth countered the broad generalisation of economic man with a broad generalisation of moral and sentient man."[8]

But while Romantic individualism could be diverted to humanitarian causes and transformed into quiescence, it could also, as Crane Brinton observes, lead to the sort of economic individualism that was alternately deplored and celebrated by the Victorians.[9] Hence, Gaskell's Wordsworthian sympathy for the victims of industrialism, expressed in *Mary Barton*, is complicated by her Unitarian-fostered admiration for such "captains of industry" as Thornton in *North and South*. The tendency of Romantic dualism to turn into Victorian self-division is best seen in Gaskell's philosophical mentor, Carlyle, who repeatedly preached the necessity of the "Annihilation of Self" in tones so idiosyncratic as virtually to undercut his message. Carlyle's critique of Byronic egoism is related to his attack on the selfishly materialistic advocates of laissez-faire, but Carlyle looks to heroes to make things come right again. Individualism is both the evil and its cure, provided that industrialists transform themselves by donning the chivalric trappings of the presumably selfless knights of old. The Manchester millowner W. R. Greg was to see himself and his class in precisely this exalted Romantic role, although it did not stop him from opposing legislative attempts to reform the factory system or from criticizing *Mary Barton* as a misguided effort to preach discontent rather than submissiveness to the workers. The brilliance of Carlyle's diagnosis of England's ills and the impracticality (or worse) of his proposed cure served to divide the aims of his reform-minded admirers, Maurice, Kingsley, and Gaskell. They finally split over the issue of selfless individualism, with Maurice placing increasing stress on the Carlylean theme of self-suppression, Kingsley stressing the heroic tendency, and Gaskell seeking a means of combining the two.

The desire to effect a compromise between selflessness and individualism is of marked importance in the great nineteenth-century women's novels. It is an interesting fact of literary history that while Victorian England saw the flourishing of such distinguished poets as Emily Brontë, Christina Rossetti, and Elizabeth Barrett, no major English Romantic woman poet preceded them. The individualistic energies that found expression in Byron and Shelley seemed exclusively masculine in nature: the male imagination was the burning coal or lamp or Eolian Harp, while the female was seen in a subservient light as inspirer, adoring onlooker, or auditor. "Women must want [that is, lack] Imagination," Keats surmised, "and they may thank God for it."[10] There were important "romantic" women novelists of the period, such as Ann Radcliffe and Mary Shelley; yet they were concerned not with primacy of imaginative vision—the great theme of Romantic poetry—but rather with the horrors occasioned when willful males seek to translate their visions into deeds. The typical strategy of nineteenth-century women writers, whether of romantic or realistic disposition, was to draw a realistic critique of Romantic male presumptions. Where men hankered after heroism, women customarily craved reality. Yet their presuming to write at all was a Romantic temptation. Aspiring to the representation of reality, which alone (as Evangelically trained or Utilitarian-minded critics allowed) could be the subject matter of fiction, women romanticized the reality of the public life that was closed to them even as they also idealized the reality of the domestic sphere that remained open.[11] The Victorian novel may be seen, accordingly, as the reserve and refuge of women like Charlotte Brontë, Elizabeth Gaskell, and George Eliot, whose determination to make themselves heard in spite of the prohibitions laid on their sex found expression in the powerful subject of much Victorian fiction: the struggle between realistic possibilities and romantic aspirations, between societal or domestic values and the needs of the individual, between Wordsworthian quiescence and Byronic rebelliousness.

The view that women have a monopoly on sympathy and self-denying behavior on behalf of others was prevalent throughout the century and was encouraged by male as well as female writers. Women writers crusaded against the willful energies of the male ego that found expression in the bloody aftermath of the French Revolution, as well as in the Napoleonic career, and in the competitive spirit unleashed by the Industrial Revolution

at home. Expressed in fictional terms, this mission is best illustrated in *Jane Eyre*, the greatest of the Victorian allegories in
which an enlightened woman educates the undisciplined Romantic male into a sense of Victorian responsibility. If potency
of imagination was allowed only to Romantic men, the sympathetic imagination, which Wordsworth and Shelley had endorsed as the aim of literature, seemed a feminine characteristic.
"The poetry and pathos which [George Eliot] seeks to reveal
under commonplace surroundings," Leslie Stephen declared late
in the century, "is found chiefly in feminine hearts." Hence, a
humanitarian-minded man, such as the minister Thurstan Benson
in Gaskell's *Ruth*, is usually described as being feminine in
nature. Similarly, without apparent irony, Trollope says of his
self-denying clergyman, the Reverend Septimus Harding in *The
Warden*, "He had that nice appreciation of the feelings of others
which belongs of right exclusively to women." George Eliot's
fictional Evangelical curate, the Reverend Edgar Tryan, in "Janet's
Repentance," and Frederick Denison Maurice in real life showed
that masculinity and sympathy were not incompatible; but
Maurice's assault upon the great enemy "self-will and selfishness" was largely an attack on a male bastion because men had
the greater opportunity to make mischief in the world. Wordsworth, Coleridge, and Southey all offered precedents in their
sympathy for the victims of the Industrial Revolution, in their
reaction against the radicalism and willfulness of their youth,
and in their development of religious and political views that
stressed fortitude and submissiveness; but it was Carlyle, above
all, who expanded this Romantic turn upon Romantic unruliness
into the doctrine of renunciation and selfless labor.[12]

Elizabeth Gaskell's Unitarian background stimulated a lifelong
struggle between her creative and her self-denying instincts.
Fiercely individualistic for all their vaunted reasonableness,
Unitarians were constantly warned against the presumptuousness of the will. Maurice, raised as a Unitarian, accordingly
identified evil with the self-will of the individual refusing to
submit himself to Christ; hell, for Maurice, consisted of the will
having its own way.[13] Unitarian ideals of service to society
played a prominent role in nineteenth-century England: themselves persecuted for so long, Unitarians became champions of

the oppressed and influential propagandists for education, religious tolerance, and women's rights. But accompanying the reformist strain in Unitarianism was an impulse that favored economic individualism, that saw in the industrialists—many of whom were Unitarians—a power and right deriving from natural law that was not to be interfered with.[14] A habit of combining assertiveness and "enlightened self-discipline" was to mark the career of Gaskell's greatest predecessor among Unitarian women authors, Harriet Martineau, whose reformist instincts were joined to a dislike of any governmental meddling in the prerogatives of the industrialists.[15] Martineau's distinctly Unitarian sense of belonging to an elite of martyrs who have been called on to perform self-denying heroic action is apparent in the Gaskell heroines and in Gaskell herself: the rescue-work that her heroines (and, on rare occasions, heroes) nobly perform in behalf of others was copied by the author herself when she set out to write *Mary Barton* and *Ruth* or when she determined, in her biography of Charlotte Brontë, to defend her friend against the malicious personal charges raised against her.

Brontë's attempt to conquer her Romantic demon is more than matched by Gaskell's desire, in her *Life of Charlotte Brontë*, to eliminate virtually every scrap of romanticism from Brontë's character. The "coarseness" and wildness that appear in Brontë's character and work are attributed to outside factors: the primitive Yorkshire community in which she grew up and Brussels where she was educated into French ways, her father's "eccentricity," her brother's unmanageableness. Brontë herself, Gaskell assured her publisher, George Smith, was invariably womanly and submissive, "as opposed to the common ideas of her being a 'strong-minded emancipated' woman." Gaskell was not blind to Brontë's Romantic side—the Angrian tales, she nervously wrote Smith, give "one the idea of creative power carried to the verge of insanity"—but she chose to honor the woman at the expense of the writer. Or rather, she chose to honor an icon of Charlotte Brontë as dutiful, self-denying saint, which was patterned in part after her own image. Gaskell's minimal treatment of the Brontë novels (which are the reason, one might logically assume, for making Brontë the subject of a book) was not untypical of Victorian literary biographies; but it suggests an unspoken feeling in the biographer that writing novels was wrong, was less commendable, in any case, than Brontë's performance of her womanly duties.[16]

Offering kindly discouragement to a young mother and would-be novelist, Gaskell warned that a woman must needs neglect her real children in order to live with her fictional creations. "When you are forty," she added by way of consolation, "and if you have a gift for being an authoress [and have *"lived* an active and sympathetic life"] you will write ten times as good a novel as you could do now, just because you will have gone through so much more of the interests of a wife and mother." Gaskell's own earliest literary effort, aside from her letters, was the diary she began in her mid-twenties to chronicle the early years of her daughter Marianne. In the diary we find some of the themes of the later fiction: the danger of willfulness in a woman (Marianne at six months was showing alarming signs) and the need for the habit of "self-restraint"; the sense that a woman's life is directed toward her maternal responsibilities; a fear lest one be contaminated by worldly values, such as might be picked up even in an infant school; and an abiding belief in the "fragility of life." In later years, when Marianne herself had ambitions of becoming a novelist, Gaskell did not seek to dissuade her, insisting only on the importance of being as objective as possible in narration and description, of observing "what is *out* of you, instead of examining what is *in* you." If a woman must become a novelist, the illusion should be maintained that her book is writing itself, that no self-seeking author is involved in the creative process.[17]

To an admirer of *Mary Barton*, Gaskell confessed that the writing of the book had been a source of "great pleasure," and that she had become so "deeply, sometimes painfully" involved with her story and characters "that parting with them was like parting with friends." In the letters to her friend Eliza Fox, herself a painter and feminist, Gaskell admitted the consolation she derived from writing, a consolation otherwise denied her in Manchester, since "here we have no great external beauty either of nature or art the contemplation of which can put calm into one; and take one out of one's little self—and shame the demon . . . Conscience away." "One thing is pretty clear," she declared; "*Women*, must give up living an artist's life, if home duties are to be paramount." Nonetheless, since "it is healthy for [women] to have the refuge of the hidden world of Art," and since the practice of art affords one "peace," one might aspire to a "blending" of "Home duties and the development of the Individual." The instinctive association of individualism with the artist's life bothered her, however, and she insisted in a follow-up letter to Eliza that self-satisfaction must never be one's goal. Artistic creation as a form of pleasure is replaced by the idea of creation as a duty to which God has appointed one, a task in which one can forget oneself, such as Gaskell recommended to her daughter. In the biography of Charlotte Brontë she articulated this solution to her anxiety as a writer: faced with the separate duties of a woman and an author, one must perform the household tasks ("a woman's principal work in life is hardly left to her own choice"), "and yet she must not shrink from the extra responsibility implied by the very fact of her possessing such talents."[18]

The need to conceal one's literary impulse beneath a moral cloak was widespread among nineteenth-century women writers, very few of whom would have disagreed with Gaskell's view that "If Self is to be the end of exertions, these exertions are unholy."[19] It is partly because of this self-mistrust that so many of the women's novels were addressed to issues of social reform, as well as themes of domestic quiescence: the writing of moral tales and "novels with a purpose" alleviated some of the guilt the women might have had at writing in the first place. Three years before Thomas Hood's "Song of the Shirt" and Elizabeth Barrett's "Cry of the Children" were to popularize the theme of the abuse of modern workers, Frances Trollope (Anthony Trollope's mother) turned her attention to the young victims of the Industrial Revolution in *The Life and Adventures of Michael Armstrong, the Factory Boy* (1840). Melodramatic to a fault and often relying on characters and plot situations lifted from Dickens and Radcliffe, Frances Trollope's work was nonetheless a forerunner of the novel of social concern with which women of the 1840s were to find a special identification as outsiders sympathizing with the plight of the neglected and mistreated.[20] By contrast, Disraeli's social novels of this period were more concerned with aristocrats discovering a romantically colored sense of their feudal responsibilities; while even Dickens at this point of his career, despite his sympathy for the poor, was close in temperament and manner to eighteenth-century novelists like Smollett for whom the role of the poor in fiction was to provide comic relief.

Wordsworth's crucial example, in the *Lyrical Ballads* as well as *The Excursion*, in showing the potential for nobility and tragedy in the lives of the poor and in celebrating their fortitude under the pressure of intense grief was elaborated in Charlotte Tonna's influential *Helen Fleetwood* (1841), which directed the attention of the Evangelicals who had suppressed the slave trade abroad to the plight of England's internal slave market in children as factory workers. It is within this tradition that Gaskell's *Mary Barton* (1848) belongs. In 1849 Charlotte Brontë's *Shirley* made explicit for the first time the link between suffering workers and women denied an active role in life; but Brontë's fondness for masterly Byronic males was strong enough to quash any reformist instincts. Gaskell's superiority to Frances Trollope and Charlotte Tonna is evident in the greater verisimilitude of her characters and in the wider context in which she places her action and makes her appeal to the reader. Her aim in *Mary Barton* is more than the correction of specific abuses: it is a Wordsworthian expansion of the reader's sympathy. Moreover, in Gaskell's declaration, "It is the woes that cannot in any earthly way be escaped that admit least earthly comforting"— in her admission, "I mourn because what has occurred cannot be helped"—she moves beyond the use of the novel for reformist purposes to that more generalized Wordsworthian mood in *The Excursion* when the poet, having heard the story of Margaret, movingly and helplessly says, "I blessed her in the impotence of grief."[21] Gaskell's ultimate object of sympathy is the human condition: John Barton's tragedy is that he is a helpless human being even more than he is a mistreated workman. Already in her first novel we have a hint of that Chekhovian awareness of the frailty of human life and aspirations, though as yet without the compensating comic vision, which informs her masterpiece, *Wives and Daughters*. The evolution from *Mary Barton* to *Wives and Daughters* involves a growth in scale as well as in artistic subtlety, but without the experience of writing the first novel—without the commitment to the writer's life that she half-feared and for which she needed the didactic impetus—Gaskell could not have gained the confidence in self and the expansion in vision that permeate her last novel.

Elizabeth Gaskell deliberately placed herself in a Wordsworthian frame of reference in order to justify her debut as a writer. Her letters, and numerous quotations in her fiction, show familiarity with all the Romantic poets, but Wordsworth was her favorite: "my heart feels so full of him," she declared in 1836. Gaskell's Wordsworth was the Victorian Wordsworth, the poet of humble life and unlimited powers of empathy, whose message in "The Old Cumberland Beggar"—"We have all of us one human heart"—she was fond of quoting.[22] This is the Wordsworth whom Kingsley celebrated as illustrating, along with Burns, Crabbe, Hood, and Dickens, the tradition of "democratic art—the revelation of the poetry which lies in common things." As a young wife, Gaskell herself observed, apropos of Wordsworth, "The beauty and poetry of many of the common things and daily events of life in its humblest aspect does not seem to me sufficiently appreciated." Her earliest published work, the first of a projected series of "sketches among the poor" undertaken in collaboration with her husband, was written, as she admitted, "in the manner of Crabbe . . . but in a more seeing-beauty spirit" that obviously derives from Wordsworth.[23] The main figure in this poem became the heroine of Gaskell's first published work of fiction ("Libbie Marsh's Three Eras," 1847) and the "germ," as she told Eliza Fox, of Alice Wilson in her first novel, *Mary Barton*. We are told of this dutiful, unmarried woman that "Without the natural ties, she sought to bind / Hearts to hers, with gentle, useful love."[24]

There is obviously a touch of Elizabeth Gaskell herself in this portrait of the Cumberland Beggar turned self-denying heroine: deprived of parental ties at an early age, and hoping to find security and love in an alien world (Manchester, in Gaskell's case) by being generous and self-effacing. However, there is also a morbid and self-revealing strain in the portrayals of Libbie Marsh and Alice Wilson, which is evidenced in the fact that happiness to Alice, haunted by memories of her childhood home, comes only with a senility that restores her childhood to her. Alice escapes her renunciatory life (which is held up as the feminine model for Mary Barton to follow) by withdrawing into "that happy world of dreams" (I, 268) in which she is tended to by mother and old friends; and one is not sure whether this is to be taken as confirmation or unconscious mockery of Wordsworth's faith in the consolation of memory.[25] Alice's lifelong hope of revisiting her childhood home is thus accomplished in a manner that prevents her from discovering "how changed from the fond anticipation of what it was to have been" (p. 179) the world of her childhood has become. A desire to rediscover, or to recreate in one's mind, the lost home of one's childhood is typical of the Romantic imagination. That Gaskell realized the dream of "home" to be a danger to her heroines' moral health is seen in the decision of such women as Margaret Hale in *North and South* and Molly Gibson in *Wives and Daughters* to renounce such a regressive fantasy of returning to the past and instead to face realistically the world of change. The Wordsworthian model of this realization is "The Brothers" in which the returning sailor-brother must leave the home he has long dreamed of because it is haunted by memories of the dead past. In Gaskell's novel *Ruth*, the heroine's sad fate results, ironically enough, from her desire to return to her childhood home in the company of Bellingham, who uses the occasion to take advantage of her.

In the best of her early stories, "The Moorland Cottage" (1850), Gaskell introduces in Maggie Browne the first of her heroines to be linked with Lucy Gray, finding in nature a consolation often lacking in their closest relations. "But there was a danger of the child becoming dreamy," the narrator warns, "and finding her pleasure in life in reverie, not in action, or endurance, or the holy rest which comes after both, and prepares for further striving or bearing" (II, 293). The desire to escape one's responsibilities takes many forms in Gaskell's work and life, in dreams of home, in evocations of the past, in exertions of romantic obstinacy, or in the refuge of art itself. Maggie is shaken from her reverie by hearing the Wordsworthian "still, sad music of humanity"—the intimations of mortality and human distress—

and is thus enabled to find real comfort by providing comfort to others. In other stories of this period like "Half a Life-time Ago" and "The Well of Pen-Morfa" (1850), the Wordsworthian themes of fortitude and family-feeling in the face of adversity are used to morbid effect.[26] But it is in her first novel, *Mary Barton*, that Gaskell's Wordsworthian sensibility is most fully aroused, both for better and for worse.

The unsatisfactory Wordsworthian aspect of *Mary Barton* is seen in the character of Alice Wilson, whose display of fortitude under pressure is intended to serve as a lesson to the novel's heroine (when Mary expresses relief at not having become a domestic servant, Alice replies that she "little knows the pleasure o' helping others"; p. 34), but whose attainment of bliss in the form of a second childhood functions as a warning instead. Alice epitomizes all those self-denying Victorian women, providing sympathy in an otherwise hostile world. In stark contrast to Alice is the brilliantly conceived figure of Mary's father, John Barton; and if Alice is Gaskell's model of resignation, the rebellious Barton draws forth her deeper sympathy. In her letters Gaskell repeatedly refers to him as a Wordsworthian tragic "hero." Barton is a generous-hearted Manchester workman whose distress at the hunger and poverty around him (the novel is set in the industrial depression years of the late 1830s and early 1840s) impels him to become a Chartist and eventually drives him to murder the millowner Carson's contemptible son. (One Wordsworthian source for Barton is the sailor in "Guilt and Sorrow," whom the sympathetic poet depicts as the victim of an oppressive social system: returning home from the sea robbed of the means of provision for his family, he becomes a murderer.) Replying to charges of having set workers against masters and ignored the principles of political economy, Gaskell protested that her purpose had not been incendiary. "I had so long felt," she explained, "that the bewildered life of an ignorant thoughtful man of strong power of sympathy, dwelling in a town so full of striking contrasts as this is, was a tragic poem."[27]

She might have subtitled her novel "A Study in Contrasts," since she stresses the gap between the lives of rich and poor inhabitants of Manchester, the former having the means but lacking sympathy and the latter having the sympathy but lacking means. For a Methodist like Alice, the clinging to a dream of redress in heaven, one's ultimate "home," negates any desire for earthly consolation, but Barton's frustration reminds us that Unitarians and Christian Socialists alike stressed the need to improve man's lot on earth: to show, in Kingsley's phrase, "how the will of God may at last be done on earth, even as it is done in heaven."[28] Having pawned his coat in order to purchase medicine for a woman who is dying of starvation, Barton notices the contrast between the glitter of the druggist's shop and the squalor he has just witnessed:

> It is a pretty sight to walk through a street with lighted shops; the gas is so brilliant, the display of goods so much more vividly shown than by day, and of all shops a druggist's looks the most like the tales of our childhood, from Aladdin's garden of enchanted fruits to the charming Rosamond with her purple jar. No such associations had Barton; yet he felt the contrast between the well-filled, well-lighted shops and the dim gloomy cellar, and it made him moody that such contrasts should exist. (P. 69)[29]

In her preface to *Mary Barton*, Gaskell traced the origin of her tale to her thoughts of "how deep might be the romance in the lives of some of those who elbowed me daily in the busy streets of the town in which I resided" (I, lxxix). The crowd passing Barton in the street "looked joyous" and therefore alien to him; but Gaskell hoped that by revealing the feelings of a man of the crowd to her more fortunate readers she might bring the classes closer together, as Wordsworth had decreed, by the power of sympathy. She took for her epigraph lines from Carlyle that reflected the seriousness of her purpose, but she might have chosen instead Carlyle's words in praise of the Corn-Law rhymer, Ebenezer Elliot: "if all parties are to love and help one another, the first step towards that is, that all thoroughly understand one another!"[30]

Gaskell's lack of self-confidence results in flaws in the handling of Barton. She makes the mistake, for example, of attributing his frustration to a lack of instruction in the sacred texts of David Ricardo and Adam Smith. When Barton is baffled by the discrepancy between the misery of the workmen and their families in times of economic distress and the comfort of the factory owners, she interjects that she knows "that this is not really the case" (p. 24), but that she is attempting to show Barton's mistaken views. And she strains to create a reconciliation scene between him and Carson when Barton, now contrite, is on his deathbed. Gaskell's predilection for such reconciliation scenes in her novels, scenes that do not work in strictly realistic terms, results from her Christian beliefs, but it also shows something of her desire to emulate Wordsworth, reconciling and binding "together by passion and knowledge the vast empire of human society." In the end, for all his weaknesses and Gaskell's timidities, John Barton is a commandingly tragic figure; and his evolution from generosity to criminality is portrayed with such power and authenticity that judicial as well as economic qualms are waived: "Your heart would have ached to have seen the man, however hardly you might have judged his crime" (p. 411). When, at the end of the book, Carson intones the dicta of political economy, he is answered by the till then quiescent voice of the artisan Job Legh, who reminds us that Barton's dilemma arose from his inability "to make great riches and great poverty square with Christ's Gospel" (p. 446), and who adds, in echo of Carlyle, "to my thinking, them that is strong in any of God's gifts is meant to help the weak,—be hanged to the facts!" (p. 448).[31]

It is no wonder that, with her ability to see more than one side, Elizabeth Gaskell was unable to reconcile the various conflicting elements in her first novel: her reiterated agreement with the political economists versus her sympathy for Barton's dilemma, which undermines that acquiescent attitude; her presentation of Alice Wilson as a model of fortitude versus her devastating description of Alice's happiness as a state of senility. The conflict between what Gaskell half-mockingly referred to as her various "warring members"—the religious self that preached universal brotherhood, the domestic self that saw to the house and family, and the private self that found release in artistic creation and self-delight[32]—is echoed in the discord within Mary Barton and the Gaskell heroines who follow her. Mary's role in the novel is to develop in the manner of one of Scott's protagonists, away from a fondness for the sort of romance that inflates one's self-image and toward a subordination of the individual to society. But what is hardly an orderly progression in the case of Scott's heroes often becomes a confusing zigzag in Gaskell's work. The determination both to avoid escapist romance and to transform reality into something as good as romance is evident in Gaskell's preface to *Mary Barton* and in the depiction of her heroine's progress. We initially see Mary as a good-natured but vain and headstrong girl, whose reading of romances has fueled her ambition to become a "lady" and her fantasy of marrying Carson's son, who has been pursuing her. The archrealist Trollope may be fond of such King Cophetua and beggar maiden alliances, but Elizabeth Gaskell never suggests the possibility or desirability of such a uniting of the worlds of the rich and the poor as Disraeli presents in *Sybil*. (In any case, Trollope's heroines are always innately noble, and Disraeli's Sybil turns out to be highborn.) However, just when Mary abandons her romantic illusions Gaskell transforms her into a romantic heroine. Abandoning all thought for herself and hoping to save her beloved Jem Wilson from the charge she knows her father to be guilty of, she gains in "dignity, self-reliance, and purpose" (p. 302). Her search for the witness who can provide Jem with an alibi is a genuine feat of heroism. Finally, in the courtroom scene where she comes to deliver Jem, she takes on the appearance of Beatrice Cenci (p. 376) and the character of a Jeanie Deans. Mary must reject the willful trait she shares with her father (and with her aunt Esther, whose romantic delusions have led to a life of prostitution) in favor of the submissive ethic of Alice Wilson; but Gaskell wants the path of duty to radiate with glory too.[33]

The suspicion that the three most significant characters in *Mary Barton*, Alice Wilson, John Barton, and Mary, represent aspects of Elizabeth Gaskell's conflicting tendencies toward self-expression and self-repression is heightened in her second novel with a purpose, *Ruth* (1853). The assurance she received from writing *Mary Barton*, confirmed by expressions of admiration from Carlyle and other notable Victorians, is reflected in the calm mood of *Cranford*. But a revulsion against that very self-confidence is implicit in the confused direction *Ruth* takes. The writing of *Ruth* was occasioned by an assertive need to speak out against the neglectfulness of society in failing to protect such innocents as her heroine Ruth Hilton and in persecuting them after their "fall"; but Gaskell also admitted that she had "tried to make both the story and the writing [of a book "very close to my heart"] as quiet as I could, in order that 'people' (my great bugbear) might not say that they could not see what the writer felt to be a very plain and earnest truth, for romantic incidents or exaggerated writing." She was distressed by the charge that the book was "unfit for family reading," and to Eliza Fox she mused, self-mockingly, "I must be an improper woman without knowing it."[34] The Unitarian stress on consideration for and tolerance toward the victims of society is evident in Gaskell's crusading spirit, which shows itself in the choice of topic and in various flashes of insight throughout the novel; but a defensive attitude toward her readers and a fear of self-will turned the crusade into a campaign of persecution against the very person she was seeking to redeem. Ruth, the fallen woman, suffers for Elizabeth Gaskell's own presumptuousness in writing; and the attack on lying, an important motif in Gaskell's work, can be seen as a veiled critique of fiction itself.

Ruth is descended from the abandoned heroines of the old English ballads, whom more recent poets like Wordsworth and Crabbe had treated in a realistic and sympathetic manner.[35] It was typical of the Romantic writers, beginning with Rousseau, to place the blame for such a victimization on the male or society or both. In the Evangelical climate of the first half of the nineteenth century, however, the stricken woman was held to account, the self being considered not intrinsically innocent but innately wicked. Gaskell's dilemma in *Ruth* is that while she draws on the Romantic and Unitarian defense of the individual as against society, she is also highly suspicious of the will. The novel begins with a description of the stifling atmosphere in which her youthful heroine first finds herself, lacking relations and guidance in the ways of the world. Gaskell invokes her Unitarian heritage when she declares, "The daily life into which people are born, and into which they are absorbed before they are well aware, forms chains which only one in a hundred has moral strength enough to despise, and to break when the right time comes—when an inward necessity for independent individual action arises, which is superior to all outward conventionalities" (III, 2).[36] However, the suggestion that she will be defying the conventionalities in the name of "independent individual action" is frustrated as the novel proceeds. Ruth, who is entirely lacking in will at the time of her seduction, must gain a sense of identity precisely so that she can repudiate and atone for the presumed willfulness of her youth. The result is that Gaskell's cardboard repentant Magdalene in the second part of the book bears no relation to the figure in the early sections, "obedient and docile by nature, and unsuspicious and innocent of any harmful consequences" (p. 60).[37]

As one of the most romantic in nature of her characters, Ruth must pay a penalty for qualities that Gaskell shared and felt obliged to abhor. Living (like Gaskell) in a world alien to her feelings, Ruth finds consolation only in nature and in romantic reveries. When commanded by her employer to attend a ball, in her capacity of seamstress, so that she can repair any torn dresses, Ruth catches her first glimpse of a world for which poverty and distress never exist: "inside it was warm, and glowing, and vivid; flowers scented the air, and wreathed the head, and rested on the bosom, as if it were midsummer" (p. 14). The happy dancers seem to Ruth "without any semblance of care or woe as if they belonged to another race of beings! Had they ever to deny themselves a wish, much less a want? . . . Here was cold, biting, mid-winter for her, and such as her . . . What was winter to them?" (p. 17). The sense of distance between the worlds of rich and poor harkens back to the scene of John Barton looking into the druggist's window, but where Barton regards the contrast with anger, Ruth is awed. Gaskell's sympathetic treatment of Ruth's feelings at this point is an indication of the novelist's instinctive romantic sympathies; she refuses to mock Ruth's fancies, as Flaubert in the similar scene in *Madame Bovary* mocks Emma when she has her first taste of romantic delights at the ball at La Vaubyessard. Unlike Emma Bovary, Ruth has no need of artificial stimulation; her happiest moments are in the presence of nature—"Even rain was a pleasure to her" (p. 64)—where she reveals her kinship to those other "pure" women in English literature, Wordsworth's Lucy Gray

and Hardy's Tess. But where Wordsworth performs a mercy-
killing on his heroine lest she should ever see beyond the comforts of nature to "what man has made of man," and where
Hardy subjects Tess to the cruelties of a malign universe, Gaskell
wants her heroine to pass out of the realm of romance so that
she may bear up under the burden of reality. In her innocence
she seems "meek and gentle . . . , so patient, and so grateful"
(p. 123) to the Unitarian minister and his sister, Thurstan and
Faith Benson, who rescue her after her lover has abandoned her.
But her abandonment has taught Ruth that there are no romantic
sources of consolation she can trust: "Now she knew the truth,
that earth has no barrier which avails against agony" (p. 83).

Once her heroine has been taken up by the Bensons, and
properly and lovingly domesticated, Gaskell's attention shifts to
this selfless pair. When Benson begins to tell his sister about
Ruth, whom he has just prevented from committing suicide,
Faith is on her guard: "Nothing very romantic, I hope, Thurstan.
Remember, I cannot stand much romance; I always distrust it."
"I don't know what you mean by romance," he replies. "The
story is real enough, and not out of the common way, I'm afraid"
(p. 111). Yet something of Ruth's romantic quality rubs off on
them; and Faith soon defends the necessity of lying about Ruth's
situation (about to become a mother, she is passed off as a
widow and a distant relation of the Bensons), admitting that she
has discovered in herself "a talent for fiction, [since] it is so
pleasant to invent, and make the incidents dovetail together"
(p. 149). It is the implication that to protect Ruth necessitates
lying about her that makes Gaskell abandon her original intention of stressing Ruth's innocence; her vocation as novelist suddenly seems open to question. When Ruth's son Leonard begins
to tell fanciful stories, this is accordingly interpreted by the
Bensons and Ruth as a dangerous habit which must be whipped
out of him. "Story-telling," in their eyes, represents "a strange,
odd disregard of truth" (p. 200); and while Gaskell smiles at
their earnestness, she is also engaged, in the second part of the
book, in scourging romantic willfulness from her main characters. It is essential, thus, that Leonard be told of his illegitimacy
as early as possible (a cruelty that some contemporary reviewers

deplored) because he must learn to adapt himself to a world that forbids illusions.

When the self-righteous businessman, Bradshaw, discovers the facts of Ruth's previous history, he reacts with typical Philistine brutality: "The world has decided how such women are to be treated," and the "world" is so far right "that no one can fly in its face with impunity, unless, indeed, they stoop to deceit and imposition" (p. 347). But Bradshaw seems to be correct in the latter respect: what indeed would have become of Ruth if the Bensons had not lied? "Our telling a lie has been the saving of her," as Faith Benson protests (p. 358), long after the lie has been discovered. Thurstan Benson replies to Bradshaw in the spirit of Maurice and Kingsley: "I take my stand with Christ against the world . . . What have the world's ways ended in? Can we be much worse than we are?" (p. 347).[38] Still, Ruth must expiate her sin to the world's satisfaction before Bradshaw can relent to the extent even of attending her funeral. In contriving the means for Ruth to become (in the words of one of the last chapter titles) "A Mother to Be Proud of," Gaskell occasions a typhoid epidemic to hit the town so that Ruth, serving as a nurse, can eventually save the life of the man who had deserted her. That done, she ascends to heaven, having atoned not only for her sin but for Gaskell's romantic predilection for story-telling.

If *Mary Barton* and *Ruth* reflect and are disfigured by Elizabeth Gaskell's fear of self-will, which she associates not only with John Barton and Ruth Hilton but with her own creative drive, the book written between these novels, *Cranford* (1851–53), reflects a sense of self-assurance that allows for at least a myth of self-reliance, and the work that followed *Ruth*, *North and South* (1855), finds a positive virtue in the energies released by the will. *Cranford* is a remarkable book: it allows us to share the illusions of the innocent ladies who live in a village seemingly remote from the dangerously worldly values of Drumble (Manchester); but Gaskell also enables us to see how fragile these illusions are. Much of the comedy and poignance of *Cranford*, so beautifully intermingled, results from this very confidence of the ladies that they are safe—safe from men, from violence, from the "vulgarity" of facts and money worries, from mortality itself. The news of Lady Glenmire's engagement to Dr. Hoggins is met by Miss Matty Jenkyns, the heroine of the novel, with a shudder of "gentle pity": "One does not know whose turn may come next. Here, in Cranford, poor Lady Glenmire might have thought herself safe."[39]

When Miss Matty reads over the love letters of her long-dead parents, we see in the response of the narrator, Mary Smith, a reminder of the precariousness of it all: "There was in them [the family letters] a vivid and intense sense of the present time, which seemed so strong and full, as if it could never pass away, and as if the warm, living hearts that so expressed themselves could never die, and be as nothing to the sunny earth. I should have felt less melancholy, I believe, if the letters had been more so" (pp. 42–43). Gaskell's sense of the desperately fragile nature of life was apparent in her first literary expression, the diary written in her twenties; and perhaps it is the view that the world does not offer any enduring comfort that makes her come down so hard on Ruth's youthful illusions and, a bit less hard, on John Barton's notion that the misery of the poor should be relieved by the rich in defiance of laws of political economy. In *Cranford*, on the other hand, illusions of Providential protection are allowed to flourish to such a degree that the reader is likely to forget, when thinking back on the novel, the facts to the contrary: the deaths of so many of the characters (three by the end of the first serial installment alone); the collapse of the Drumble bank, which momentarily reduces Miss Matty to penury; the installation of the railroad, which here, as in "Cousin Phillis" and *Wives and Daughters*, symbolizes the triumph of that industrial progress which will soon reduce the values of Cranford to as distant a memory as the sentiments expressed in Miss Matty's parents' letters.[40]

Cranford is allowed to exist in the first place because of Gaskell's desire to preserve in art the memory of the town of Knutsford where she had spent her childhood; but its survival depends on an element of wish-fulfillment on her part. At the moment when Cranford's euphemistic "elegant economy" is to be replaced by genuine poverty in Miss Matty's case, help arrives, first in the generosity of her friends, and second in the arrival of her long-lost brother Peter. The narrator's father assures Mary that Miss Matty's rescue by her friends shows "how a good innocent life makes friends all around" (p. 141)—a reminder of the Alice Wilson-Cumberland Beggar ethic, perhaps, but a defiance of the logic of *Ruth* in which innocence is resourceless before the onslaught of the world. He also notes, however, with reference to Miss Matty's brief, unbusinesslike career in trade, that such generosity and "simplicity might be very well in Cranford, but would never do in the world" (p. 145). Miss Matty's brother's providential return, relatively prosperous and conveying in the stories of his past adventures the spirit of the *Arabian Nights*, is the purest example of wish-fulfillment that Gaskell had yet permitted herself. One remembers that her own mariner-brother had disappeared when she was in her teens. It is typical of Gaskell's "realistic" sense of life to regard death as "the only reality" (*Wives and Daughters*, VIII, 239), but in the relaxed mood in which she wrote *Cranford* romance and humor are allowed their due, all the more needful because of life's precariousness.[41]

It was to *Cranford*, curiously, that Charlotte Brontë referred when she asked Gaskell, in an often quoted letter, whether she was always, when writing, "quite *your own woman*, uninfluenced unswayed by the consciousness of how your work may affect other minds; what blame, what sympathy it may call forth?" Yet it is precisely in *Cranford* rather than her other early novels that we find duplicated the personal tone of Gaskell's letters.[42] Brontë's difficulty in connecting the author of the self-assured, genial *Cranford* with the author of the more tortuously didactic *Mary Barton* and *Ruth* is a striking indication of how Elizabeth Gaskell sometimes succeeded in passing off a saintly icon of herself for the real woman. The moral crusader aspect of her personality was genuine enough, but so too was the side capable of romantic reveries and wonderful humor with which Brontë was unfamiliar. Gaskell's acquaintance with Charlotte Brontë at this point in her life served to bolster her romantic and assertive side. Miss Matty gives way to more aggressive heroines, who bear a resemblance to the Brontë protagonists. A reviewer in *Blackwood's* was quick to see the Brontë influence in *North and South* (1855), although he was not particularly pleased with Gaskell's substitution of a "fair gladiator" for the more passive heroines in her previous work.[43]

With *North and South* the Wordsworthian quiescence gives way to the other pole of Romanticism, affirmation of the power of individual energy. If the reaction against the individualist impulse in *Ruth* had turned into a revulsion against her artistic self, with *North and South* Gaskell learned how to integrate the expenditure of romantic impulses into a modern setting, without having to seek vicarious release in Gothic horror stories or tales set in the safely distant past. The advantage of selecting Manchester as the setting for her novel is that there, as compared to a town like Middlemarch, there need be no conflict between individual energies and the needs of the community. In Manchester, as Asa Briggs has noted, "all depended on individual enterprise"; the city was a monument to initiative rather than self-denial, a living proof that, in the words of a Manchester editor, "trade has now a chivalry of its own." Carlyle, in *Past and Present*, was not alone in seeing in the captains of industry potential successors to the chivalric knights of old. Even Disraeli, despite his repugnance toward scientific-utilitarian opposition to the realm of imaginative wonder, could direct his hero Coningsby's attention away from "the Age of Ruins" to the living reality of Manchester. Here, observes Disraeli, is the proof of the triumph of science in the modern world. And he acknowledges that "rightly understood, Manchester is as great a human exploit as Athens," although he claims that its inhabitants are unable to "conceive [its] grandeur . . . and the immensity of its future."[44]

The millowner W. R. Greg, Gaskell's friend despite his criticism of *Mary Barton*, was fully aware of the implications Disraeli alludes to. For him Manchester was the glory of modern England, and the "genius" responsible for that glory was the scientific spirit; scientists and engineers he hailed as "the real poets . . . and wonder-workers of our day." Greg's animus against *Mary Barton* and Kingsley's *Alton Locke* was based on his view that the novelists had ignored the factory owners' side of the question. The workers' virtue, according to Greg, lies in their submissiveness and self-discipline, which, if continuously maintained, offer them the means to rise from the ranks and become captains of industry themselves. Gaskell's portrait of John Thornton in *North and South* is an act of partial homage to Greg and his views. A self-made man, Thornton seems to Margaret Hale, the novel's heroine, "a man ready to do and dare everything"; his very face conveys the look of "resolution and power" which she, like Elizabeth Gaskell, finds both attractive and problematic. For Margaret's father, the steam-hammers of the mills evoke "the wonderful stories of subservient genii in the Arabian Nights"; and when Thornton boasts that the creation and utilization of such inventions, which reflect the "imagination of power," prove that "man has it within him to mount, step by step, on each wonder he achieves to higher marvels still," Mr. Hale is reminded of the heroes of the old ballad "Chevy Chase."[45]

But such achievements, for Thornton as for Greg, depend on the masters being left to do whatever they wish, uninfluenced by the desires and needs of the workers. Complaint by the workers amounts to "rebellion" against that class of men who, having achieved a deserved prominence by their own efforts, are "ordained by nature to rule over the non-privileged. The few ought to direct and teach, the many to learn."[46] Gaskell does not disagree with the millowners' paternalistic ethic. What she shows in *North and South*, however, is that the application of the laissez-faire philosophy—the argument of Thornton and Greg that no restrictions should be imposed on the factory owner's independence, and that he in turn will not meddle with his workers' freedom—is both lacking in Christian morality and untrue to the facts of life. For the belief that anyone can rise to the top by sheer, unimpeded force of will, however she and her heroine may be awed by the romantic implications, inevitably conflicts with Gaskell's sense of the circumstances in life that oppose this illusion of self-sufficiency.

The fragility of human supports forms the countertheme of *North and South*, in contrast to the romance of the will represented in the careers of Thornton and Margaret. The first evidence of this precariousness is seen when Margaret's father, an Anglican minister, loses his faith in the authority of the church. Having been raised away from home by her aunt, but maintaining faith in the virtues of her Cranford-like home (here called Helstone) and the natural authority of her father, Margaret returns to find the "staid foundation . . . reeling and rocking" (p. 34). Her father's abandonment of his clerical post and the family's consequent move to Manchester (renamed Milton-Northern in the novel) gives Margaret her first profound awareness of the instability of life. Later, when she returns for a brief visit to Helstone, which she has earlier cherished in her memory as resembling "a village in a poem—in one of Tennyson's poems" (p. 12), she is appalled to find everything there transformed, much of it for the worse. "A sense of change," writes Gaskell, "of individual nothingness, of perplexity and disappointment over-powered Margaret" (p. 400). Wordsworthian quiescence loses significance in such a "stagnant" setting (p. 301). But Thornton's myth of self-reliance is similarly disproved when circumstances beyond his control threaten the loss of his hard-earned position.

Gaskell's moral impulse dictates that Thornton be made to learn that he is not as independent as he fancied, that he is as subject to assaults of passionate impulse from within (as seen in his violent love for Margaret) as he is to assaults from passionate mobs of unemployed workers from without, and that there are economic forces that he cannot control either. He must learn, in Margaret's echo of Carlyle's message in *Past and Present*, that "God has made us so that we must be mutually dependent" (p. 112). Near the end of *North and South,* a chastened Thornton refuses partnership with a brutalized, selfish worshiper of the "Gospel of Mammonism," as Carlyle would call it, and he proves both in his friendlier relations with his workers and in his marital alliance with the new owner of his mills, Margaret, that he recognizes his responsibility as well as his interdependence. Even at the end, however, Thornton conveys the author's mixed conception of his character: a "good" man, "large and strong and tender, and *yet a master*."[47]

In Margaret's development in the novel, too, we see a subjugation of the powers of will under the twin disciplines of suffering and increased self-insight. Her father's misfortune and her mother's illness oblige her to suppress her own feelings and bear the family's responsibilities; and Thornton's passionate declaration of his feelings for her fills her with momentary revulsion toward him and self-revulsion at the thought of his "having mastered her inner will" (p. 235). In both instances, however, Margaret finds herself expanding as a human being rather than shrinking into the self-abasing posture of one of Gaskell's earlier heroines. Looking back on her life, Margaret recalls her youthful romantic illusions:

> On some such night as this she remembered promising to herself to live as brave and noble a life as any heroine she had ever read or heard of in romance, a life sans peur et sans reproche; it had seemed to her then that she had only to will, and such would be accomplished. And now she had learnt that not only to will, but also to pray, was a necessary condition in the truly heroic. Trusting to herself, she had fallen. (Pp. 411–412)

But while such a passage might logically fit, in slightly revised form, a description of Mary Barton or Ruth, it seems out of place here; and the fact that Gaskell wrote these words so near the end of the book makes one suspect that she was conscience-stricken for having in fact permitted her heroine to live up to the romantic ideal Margaret assumes she has forfeited.

Margaret's "fall" is owing to the lie she has told in order to protect her brother, a naval officer who supported a mutiny at sea, from possible arrest; but Gaskell has allowed no alternative to lying (one remembers the Bensons' inability to do otherwise in *Ruth*) and has indeed demonstrated in Mr. Hale's religious self-righteousness, however worthy its motive, the impossibility of the individual doing what he believes "right without sacrificing others" (p. 104). The purely moral impulse can be tainted by selfishness too. It is typical of Gaskell, in this most open-minded of her novels, to argue that "Loyalty and obedience to wisdom and justice are fine; but it is still finer to defy arbitrary power, unjustly and cruelly used—not on behalf of ourselves, but on behalf of others more helpless" (p. 109). Byron and Shelley could scarcely have said it better than that. Margaret's lie is uttered on behalf of her brother—whose offense is justified in the passage just quoted—and her self-reproaches to the contrary, she seems only the more heroic for her action. Margaret's bravery and nobility are evidenced in her various chivalric adventures and services in the book, which include watching over her parents like a "Roman daughter" (p. 243), protecting her brother, and preserving Thornton first from an angry mob and later from financial distress. In a reverse of the ending to *Cranford*, it is the woman who rescues the man; and Gaskell ensures Margaret's independence by making her an heiress. Margaret's very acceptance of Thornton over her other suitor, Henry Lennox, and her preference for Manchester over London are based on the fact that Thornton and Manchester romantically embody the passion and energy and self-assurance that seem lacking elsewhere.

Having acknowledged the claims of passion and energy and paid homage to the force of will in *North and South*, Elizabeth Gaskell spent much of the next decade atoning for this romantic lapse. While holding up Charlotte Brontë as a model heroine for her suppression of Romantic impulses in favor of a life of self-denial, Gaskell also devoted her attention during this period to didactic horror stories in which innocent women are victimized by the possessive or murderous passion of those close to them. In "The Poor Clare" (1856), written while she was working on the Brontë biography, she considered the possibility of one of her self-denying heroines being possessed, for a time, by a demonic double. Gaskell had dealt with the adventures of an individual leading a double life as early as "The Squire's Story" (1853), in which, possibly under the influence of Bulwer's *Paul Clifford* and *Eugene Aram*, she amusingly described how a highwayman and murderer passed himself off for a while as a respected gentleman. The theme is picked up in "The Grey Woman" (1861), whose very title, as well as the "sensational" details of the plot, shows its indebtedness to Wilkie Collins, whose *The Woman in White* had been published the preceding year. But there is a disturbing note in this tale of a woman being pursued by her vengeful husband—a nobleman whom she discovers to be the leader of a band of murderers—which suggests a sense of anxiety on the author's part. Increasingly, the stories of this period deal with typical Gaskell heroines persecuted by fathers, husbands, and lovers. The ethic of "bearing up" under pressure, praised and rewarded in the case of Margaret Hale, becomes an invitation to emotional vampirism, such as is demonstrated in the "sensationalism" of *A Dark Night's Work* (1863). Here, a weak father's dependency on his daughter (a theme that runs through Gaskell's work from *Mary Barton* on, and which sugests that unconsciously she may have seen herself as the victim of her good self) becomes an intolerable burden.

In an early story like "Hand and Heart" (1849), it was assumed that innocence is infectious, that a self-denying protagonist would influence for good the willful beings who surrounded him or her. However, in stories like "Lois the Witch" (1859) and "Crowley Castle" (1863) goodness is unavailing against the forces of evil unleashed by undisciplined wills. In the best of these tales of victimization, "Lois the Witch," the author produces a considerable amount of dramatic tension by the ingenious device of transporting one of her typical heroines from England to Salem in the late seventeenth century; there her good qualities are misinterpreted and abused by the warped passions and "diseases of imagination" (VII, 164) of the Puritans. Lois Barclay's martyrdom in an alien world was depicted at a time when Gaskell's letters were filled with personal misgivings about living in a city as uncongenial to her health and feelings as Manchester. Another woeful tale published the same year, "The Crooked Branch," reverts to the theme of Wordsworth's "Michael." In it a rural couple are robbed and beaten by the beloved son of their old age, who has been corrupted by worldly values.

In *Sylvia's Lovers* (1863) Elizabeth Gaskell's crusade against passion and romance reaches its climax; but the book is also her most romantically colored and passionately conceived work. The problem with this brilliant but deeply flawed novel is that half its main characters belong (as did Lois Barclay) in another, more domesticated world, while the others would be at home in the willful world of *Wuthering Heights*. Her one historical novel, *Sylvia's Lovers* is set on the northeast coast of England during the time of the war with France in the late eighteenth century, a place and time that afford a release to Gaskell's Romantic instincts; but Gaskell's Victorian conscience forces her, at the same time, to look askance at such "a primitive set of country-folk, who recognise the wildest passion in love, as it exists untamed by the trammels of reason and self-restraint (VI, 407–408). Scott might have been able to resolve the tension between romantic and antiromantic impulses, but Gaskell's self-divided nature ensures that her romantic and realistic tendencies are not reconciled by the novel's end. It may be that when she considered calling her book "The Specksioneer"—after the romantic "hero" of the book, the harpoonist Charley Kinraid—Gaskell had in mind a romantic outcome; but in considering as alternative title "Philip's Idol" (to point up the nonromantic Philip Hepburn's misplaced love for the book's heroine), she harkened back to the self-mistrustful nature of her work, which had found expression in her fear, as articulated in the diary, of making an "idol" out of her daughter Marianne. In Sylvia Robson's contrasting "lovers," the romantic sailor Kinraid and the dutiful shopkeeper Philip Hepburn, Gaskell had two potentially admirable protagonists—but for different kinds of fiction.

The "Romantic" nature of the romantic novel, as Robert Kiely has suggested, lies in the depiction of the supremacy of the individual and in the presentation of society as inconsequential "except in a negative and secondary sense."[48] In the Victorian novel, by contrast, a communal set of values is celebrated to which the individual must give allegiance, although he or she can attain heroism in the act of self-renunciation. In *Sylvia's Lovers*, Gaskell is beset by conflicting loyalties, one responding to the spontaneity and willfulness of her romantic characters, the other showing both the self-destructiveness and the illusory nature of a life of will. To a Romantic novelist like Disraeli the will is capable of attaining whatever it wishes; to a writer like Elizabeth Gaskell, painfully aware of the burden of reality, the individual counts for very little in the end. Philip senses the truth of this—"He had meant to shape his life," Gaskell says apropos of his business life, "and now it was, as it were, being shaped for him" (p. 217)—yet he persists in his tragic course of trying to will Sylvia's love away from Kinraid and toward himself. Deluding himself into thinking that what he desires must be the will of God, "he yearned in that terrible way after a blessing which, when granted under such circumstances, too often turns out to be equivalent to a curse" (p. 187). The ineffectuality of the will is underscored in Gaskell's choice of epigraph for the novel:

> O for thy voice to soothe and bless!
>   What hope of answer, or redress?
> Behind the veil, behind the veil.

However, it is the omitted first line of Tennyson's stanza which embodies Gaskell's theme: "O life as futile, then, as frail!" Philip speaks for law and authority in the early sections of the novel, when the issue comes up of the government's right to impress unwilling natives to serve in the war against France. The headstrong inhabitants of Monkshaven are opposed to the press-gangs, but Philip wonders what option the country has if it is to protect itself. Later in the book, when Sylvia's father, Daniel Robson, has been arrested for his part in the destruction of the press-gang's headquarters, Gaskell notes that the "authorities were quite justified in the decided steps they had taken [in making examples of such men as Robson], both in their own estimation then, and now, in ours, looking back on the affair in cold blood" (p. 300). Where she had supported Frederick Hale's part in a mutiny in *North and South,* here, in her antiromantic mood, she speaks for the side of authority and self-restraint. But she is not able to maintain a consistent attitude in this respect, and neither is Philip.

Philip is temperamentally more akin to the secondary heroine of the novel, Hester Rose, than to Sylvia: both he and Hester are hardworking and self-denying, at home in the shop or in a domestic setting. But while Hester shows her Gaskell spirit by suppressing the love she feels for him—"Never was such a quiet little bit of unconscious and unrecognized heroism" (p. 357)—he proves, in his tenacious and futile attempt to win the heart of the capricious˙and willful Sylvia, the truth of what Hester's sternly Methodist mother calls "the vanity of setting the heart on anything earthly" (p. 445). If Philip Hepburn's thwarted career confirms Gaskell's realistic bias, it is with the dashing Charley Kinraid, "the nearest approach to a hero [Sylvia] had ever seen" (p. 75), that the novelist identifies her romantic energies. Storytelling is the fabrication of lies and the endorsement of acts of subterfuge, yet Sylvia and her mother treat Kinraid's (and Daniel Robson's) "acted, as well as spoken, lies . . . as fine and spirited things" (p. 104). Kinraid's sailor's yarns are reminiscent of the tall tales of Will Wilson in *Mary Barton* and Peter Jenkyns in *Cranford;* and the novelist, who had several seafaring men in her family background, was as susceptible to and delighted by them as Sylvia herself. Charmed by his manner and ignorant of his reputation as a philanderer, Sylvia engages herself to Kinraid. It is at this point that the split focus of the novel becomes bothersome, for while Kinraid's lies are seen as the stuff of romance, Philip's lie—his failure, that is, to tell Sylvia that he has witnessed Kinraid's capture by the press-gang so that she, believing her fiancé to have been drowned, will be free to marry him—results in tragic suffering for himself and his unwilling bride. Gaskell's divided sympathies for hero and counterhero are demonstrated in her attempts to convey a sense of the two men's guilt, Kinraid as a lady-killer and Philip as a liar, and yet also absolve them both: Philip means well because he assumes that Kinraid will be as untrue to Sylvia as he has been to other women, while Kinraid turns out to have been faithful to her after all.

A mistakenly sentimental gesture is Gaskell's decision to have Kinraid marry someone else, when he returns from the war, for the sake of proving to Sylvia "the value of such enduring love as Philip's had been" (p. 517). But the novelist is too realistic-minded to expect that Sylvia will be able to love anyone purely on the basis of such tenacious devotion. The scene of reconciliation that takes place between Sylvia and Philip on his deathbed is unconvincing despite being well intended, as was the similar scene in *Mary Barton*. Gaskell is truer to her realistic instinct, and closest to real tragedy, in *Sylvia's Lovers*, when she treats of "the resisting forces which make all such harmony and delight impossible" (p. 417). (She is speaking of the irreconcilable marital differences between Philip and Sylvia, but she might as well be speaking of the deathbed scene.) Hester Rose, the prototypical Gaskell heroine, is thwarted in her chivalric attempt to reunite the pair, because for Philip Hepburn to achieve a romantic reunion with his wife, as the novelist keenly observes, "he had need be other than Philip Hepburn" (p. 508).

Romantic aspiration frustrated by realistic limitation is the theme of the novel; but in the depiction of Sylvia Robson, Gaskell pays homage to the unselfconscious, pre-Victorian world. To the heroine of *North and South*, Margaret Hale, Gaskell permitted a measure of the independence and self-reliance that the ladies of Cranford had mistakenly believed to be theirs; in the ignorant and impulsive Sylvia, the novelist allowed a character to roam free without a moral harness thrown over her. If Margaret Hale, Hester Rose, and Ellinor Wilkins (in *A Dark Night's Work*) point the way to Gaskell's definitively "good" heroine, Molly Gibson in *Wives and Daughters*, Sylvia is linked with Molly's half-sister Cynthia, delightful as a character in spite of and largely because of her willfulness. Sylvia's sense of harmony with nature connects her to the Lucy Gray type of Gaskell heroines, but instead of being subdued by nature, like Maggie Browne in "The Moorland Cottage," she is aroused. As a figure in a romantic landscape, Sylvia prefigures the heroine of Gaskell's greatest short story, "Cousin Phillis" (1864), written immediately after *Sylvia's Lovers*, and she foreshadows Hardy's heroines.

Sylvia's Lovers may be seen, then, as the attempt of a domesticated Romantic to look back on the not-too-distant past, before the Evangelically inspired Victorian stress on standards of conduct had tamed the wild passions of individualistic English men and women. But while Gaskell welcomes the moral advances made, the attempt by Christian Socialists and others to bring together in her own time "the laws of man and the laws of Christ" (p. 71) which are so conspicuously discordant in the world of *Sylvia's Lovers*, she also savors characters like Sylvia, Kinraid, and Daniel Robson, who occupy the realm she once described to Eliza Fox as her "idea of Heaven": "a place where we shan't have any consciences."[49] Nevertheless, despite the creation of admirably drawn characters and setting, Gaskell in *Sylvia's Lovers* was finally unable to contain romantic and realistic-minded figures in the same book. In "Cousin Phillis" and *Wives and Daughters* (1864–66) she did just that. They are her masterpieces of psychological realism because she was able to transpose the struggle within her own mind to the minds of her characters, and they are her artistic masterpieces because she allows the two sets of attitudes, Romantic and Victorian, to co-exist without intrusions of didactic moralizing. In both works the Romantic impulse, whether taking the form of Byronic pre-sumptuousness or Wordsworthian quiescence, is seen as a danger to the individual rather than to society. A moral purpose is not disavowed—Molly Gibson is a better person than Cynthia, and Cynthia recognizes that fact—but Gaskell sees no further need to transform her characters into effigies. Nothing human is henceforth repugnant to her.

With "Cousin Phillis" and *Wives and Daughters* Elizabeth Gaskell becomes the equal of Charlotte Brontë, Anthony Trollope, and George Eliot, like them joining disciplined Romantic aspirations to Victorian humanism. The tone of calm in these works is attributable to the artistic assurance she attained near the end of her life, her divided nature having peace at last in the refuge of art. In her final masterworks she no longer feared the artistic impulse. The story of "Cousin Phillis" is simplicity itself, harkening back to the world of the *Lyrical Ballads:* a young woman's peace of mind is disturbed, perhaps destroyed, when she is abandoned by the man she loves. But Gaskell is also, like Hardy in *The Woodlanders,* depicting the calm of a rural community violated by the invasion of well-intending scientists who symbolize in their very vocation an end to rural values and peace. The narrator of "Cousin Phillis," a brash young man of such naiveté and transparency of mind as to serve as perfect witness (and unwitting accomplice) to what transpires, relates how in his involvement with the building of a railroad line he came to introduce his engineer friend Holdsworth to his country relations, the Reverend and Mrs. Holman, and their un-spoiled daughter Phillis. "My cousin Phillis," he recalls, "was like a rose that had come to full bloom on the sunny side of a lonely house, sheltered from storms"; and he proceeds to link her with Wordsworth's Lucy Gray, "A maid whom there were none to praise, / And very few to love" (VII, 78). Holdsworth is an unconscious villain; like Kinraid, he fascinates the Holmans with the accounts of his worldly adventures, although the minister suspects "that his careless words were not always those of soberness and truth" (p. 58). But Phillis believes his promise, expressed to the narrator who unwisely repeats it to her, that he will "come back like a prince from Canada," where he is being sent on an engineering assignment, "and waken her to my love" (p. 64). The subsequent news of his marriage to a Canadian girl brings on brain fever in Phillis, and the story ends on an unresolved note with Phillis hoping to will a return "to the peace of the old days" (p. 109). The poignance of the ending is all the more effective to the reader who is familiar with Elizabeth Gaskell's lack of faith in one's ability to will anything of the kind.

The intrusion of romance into everyday life is also central to the theme of *Wives and Daughters*, but while the novelist demonstrates the perils and follies of romance in the figures of Hyacinth Gibson, her daughter Cynthia, the would-be Romantic poet Osborne Hamley, and the pseudo-Byronic land-agent Preston, she no longer condemns such models of willful behavior, nor treats them like naughty characters in one of Maria Edgeworth's moral tales. On the contrary, she finds an element of pathos in these individuals who cling to romantic poses and sentiments which have become obsolete in the new age of railroads and scientific facts. The change in modes is demonstrated in the contrasting figures of Lord Cumnor, the leading citizen of Hollingford, who quotes Byron, and his son and heir Lord Hollingford, who cultivates the new science. (Commenting on Molly's unpoetical nature, Mrs. Gibson boasts that Cynthia can recite "The Prisoner of Chillon" by heart.) It is Gaskell's realistic-minded characters, Roger Hamley, Dr. Gibson, and Molly, who embody the tendency in Victorian life and literature to invest everyday life with a new form of romanticism. The selfish and superficial Mrs. Gibson is to be pitied, in the end, because of her inability to grasp the facts of any other reality than the bright surfaces she clutches at. Her continual mouthing of romantic clichés and tags of sentimental nonsense, which she genuinely believes in, and her reiterated refusal to face up to the existence of death— a remarkable achievement for a doctor's wife—underlie the sadness beneath the more obviously comic situation of one who has lost all hold on reality. Her daughter Cynthia is not so self-deluded in this respect, but Cynthia's realization that facts be-yond her control—inheritance, upbringing, emotional and finan-cial insecurity in her youth—have shaped her into the antithesis of her half-sister Molly conveys a sense of melancholy. "I might be a heroine," she self-mockingly assures Molly," . . . but I shall never be a good woman . . . steady, every-day goodness is be-yond me" (VIII, 254).

The perils of romance are seen in the two subplots of the novel that involve romantic "secrets." Cynthia's secret is her engage-ment to Preston, made as a result of financial need and at the time of her mother's virtual abandonment of her during her ado-lescence. Despite the security that her mother's marriage to Dr. Gibson has afforded her, Cynthia feels herself still in the power of a man she hates, "cruel in his very soul—tigerish, with his beautiful striped skin and relentless heart" (p. 550). Molly's heroism saves Cynthia from the clutches of this combination Byron and Lovelace, but Molly is thereby subjected to the mali-cious gossip of the Hollingford ladies (Cranford ladies turned harpies) who think she has compromised herself by being seen talking to Preston. Gaskell saves Preston from the role of roman-tic villain he has consciously adopted for himself, for she shows the helplessness of his possessive love for Cynthia, a trait that links him to Philip in *Sylvia's Lovers*. The other secret in the novel involves the behavior of Squire Hamley's elder son, Os-borne; and while Gaskell skillfully keeps the Cynthia-Preston strand of *Wives and Daughters* from lapsing into sensationalism, she subtly and touchingly explores the tragic implications of Osborne's self-destructive romanticism.

Having inherited the native English yeomanly self-will of his father and the "unworldly and romantic" nature of his mother (p. 62), Osborne Hamley is encouraged to think himself a veri-table Romantic genius. Before she has the chance to meet him, Molly fancies Osborne to be something of a "troubadour" or "a knight, such as he wrote about in one of his own poems" (p. 167); but this inflated sense of self-importance, fostered by his parents, leads Osborne into a romantic misalliance with a French nurserymaid, which he is forced to keep secret from his parents who expect him, as heir to Hamley Hall, to marry well. Os-borne's relationship with his French bride is an attempt to live a

Rousseauesque "ideal state of love" (p. 352), and when Aimée becomes pregnant he nourishes "visions of poetical and romantic reconciliations brought about between [the now estranged] father and son, through the medium of a child" (p. 385). The discrepancy between Osborne's romantic view of himself and the grief he occasions to himself and everyone he loves as a result of this romantic role-playing is movingly described. As a visitor to Hamley Hall, Molly indulges in romantic reveries inspired by the pages of Scott's *The Bride of Lammermoor;* but when she becomes acquainted with Osborne's "concealed romance," the very sort of "love-story" with which "she had always wanted to come into direct contact," it makes her "very uncomfortable" (p. 244). Not daring to speak the truth to his father, Osborne sickens under the continual strain of living a double life—a theatrically romantic idyll with his wife and a tense everyday life with his father—and he eventually dies of the same sort of heart trouble that earlier claimed his mother.

The self-consciously romantic "hero" and "heroine" of *Wives and Daughters,* Osborne and Cynthia, are obliged, for the sake of financial and emotional security, to prey upon the real hero and heroine of the book, Roger and Molly. Roger, who (in his mother's apologetic words) lacks the "sentiment and imagination" of his genius brother (p. 89), and who prefers a work of "natural history" to "poetry, and books of romance, or sentiment" (p. 72), represents the Victorian allegiance to reality, which constitutes heroism of a new sort. This awareness of the everyday world, with regard to both the newly discovered scientific facts and the sadness of the human condition, constitutes a burden to whoever is clear-sighted and humane enough to grasp it. Hence, it is Roger who, early in the book, offers the advice to Molly that enables her to restrain the sorrow she feels at the news of her father's remarriage: "One has always to try to think more of others than of oneself" (p. 133). And it is Roger who provides the money and the sympathy that Osborne needs to sustain himself and his wife, even as it is Roger who offers his father the only consolation left to him after his wife's death and the estrangement of Osborne's affections. Gaskell admitted modeling Roger on her distant relation, Charles Darwin; in her novel Roger goes on a voyage similar to the young Dar-

win's aboard the *Beagle*, for the sake of easing his family's financial difficulties, but with the result of establishing himself as one
of the new scientific heroes whom W. R. Greg had hailed as the
modern successors to the poets and artists of old.

Roger's habit of relieving the burdens of others, all the while
ignoring his own wants, is similar in nature to the role of Molly's
father, Dr. Gibson. Elizabeth Gaskell had a special and typically
Victorian admiration for dedicated medical figures like Sir James
Kay-Shuttleworth and Florence Nightingale, whose families she
knew well; and this hero worship is imparted in her fiction in
such characters as Dr. Gibson, Mr. Harrison (in "Mr. Harrison's ⟩
Confessions," 1851), and Ruth Hilton in her phase as devoted
nurse. Doctors embody selflessness in their choice of profession,
in contrast to the lawyers in her work who invariably personify
willfulness and worldliness. Molly inherits from her father a
Wordsworthian sense of the beauty and comfort of nature, and
for a time she tries to copy his habit of trying to anesthetize his
feelings rather than allow them to be expressed, which she interprets in the light of Wordsworthian quiescence. There is
something both absurd and sympathetic in Gibson's belief "that
still his reason was lord of all" (his marriage to Hyacinth dis-
proves that boast readily enough) and his "contempt for dem-
onstrative people, arising from his medical insight into the consequences to health of uncontrolled feeling" (p. 33). He seeks,
early in the novel, to keep Molly from defining "her present
feelings [toward her new stepmother] by putting them into
words" (p. 152); but Molly learns that suppression of the self,
aggravated by the demands for sympathy that the other characters consciously and unconsciously make on her, can lead to a
dangerously self-destructive role.[50] Where the Romantics had
feared self-consciousness and had idealized preconscious states
of existence, the more perceptive and articulate among the Victorians, including Elizabeth Gaskell, were forced to bear up
without Romantic illusions about human nature and were obliged
to articulate their awareness of life's complexity and sadness.

That a life of "bearing up" for the sake of others can lead one
to a martyrdom from which nobody benefits is vividly demonstrated in the fate of Mrs. Hamley.[51] While she is alive she keeps
the family happy and united by providing a mothering sympathy

for her husband and sons; but at her death the family unit dissolves: "the keystone of the family arch was gone, and the stones of which it was composed began to fall apart" (p. 284). In bearing the burden of her family, she has fostered illusions of familial solidarity in Squire Hamley and Osborne that nothing but Osborne's death can clear up. At her death, Molly comes to fill something of the vacuum left in the Hamley household; the squire admits as much when he speaks of Molly as "ready to do anything one asks her, just as if doing it was the very sort of thing she liked best in the world" (p. 454). Molly's subordination of self is in line with the ethic of Gaskell's previous heroines; but Molly's refusal to numb her feelings, her clinging to a sense of identity through it all, and her development of a strength lacking in the others permit her a measure of independence too, of the sort Gaskell had permitted only once before in her work, in Margaret Hale's case. (And Margaret's independence was linked to her status as orphan and heiress.) In "deadness" lies comfort, Molly realizes, but there is a value in the self that her father and Roger have overlooked. "Thinking more of others' happiness than of her own was very fine," she surmises (p. 152); "but did it not mean giving up her very individuality, quenching all the warm love, the true desires, that made her herself?" Molly's willingness to question the feminine model of self-suppression keeps her from becoming the sort of abjectly dutiful onlooker that Tolstoy depicts in the figure of Sonya in *War and Peace*.[52] The Wordsworthian conquest of self is ultimately seen in a negative light in Molly's fearful reverie of "being carried on in earth's diurnal course, with rocks, and stones, and trees, with as little volition on her part as if she were dead" (p. 432). Molly's developing assertiveness parallels her author's increasing self-respect and pride in her artistic mastery, a development that is the inverse of Charlotte Brontë's flight from her Romantic impulse. For all her dutifulness there is nothing artificial or masochistic in Molly's character (as there is in Sonya); like Margaret Hale and like Elizabeth Gaskell, she is trying to resolve for herself "that most difficult problem for women, how much was to be utterly merged in obedience to authority, and how much might be set apart for freedom in working" (*North and South*, p. 416).

The delicate balance that Molly achieves between the posture of Wordsworthian quiescence and her native strength of character makes her the most forthright and clear-sighted character in the novel. Without illusions but rich in understanding and sympathy, Molly may well be the finest single achievement of Elizabeth Gaskell's formidable literary career. There is more sparkle in the characterizations of Cynthia and Mrs. Gibson, but in Molly the novelist was able to bring off that rarest of fictional triumphs, a realistic depiction of a good person, lacking the absurdity of a Don Quixote or the mental derangement of a Prince Myshkin or the stunted innocence of a Little Nell which their creators had thought necessary in order to make such goodness appear credible and interesting. Molly resembles her creator in the "steady, every-day goodness" and universal tolerance of her nature, her ability to feel the human tragedy in even Mrs. Gibson's situation—a sort of tolerance that the more intellectually gifted George Eliot was denied.[53] Author and character alike are weighed down by the burden of reality, a sense of the enduring sadness of the human condition; but in *Wives and Daughters*, Elizabeth Gaskell, writing in behalf of the Victorian humanism that replaced without wholly discarding the Romantic sense of life's infinite possibilities, demonstrated that the burden might be lightened by resources of humor and sympathy and hallowed by the power of artistic grace.

SIX

George Eliot:
The Romantic Legacy

Sometimes Maggie thought she could have been contented with absorbing
fancies; if she could have had all Scott's novels and all Byron's poems!—
then, perhaps, she might have found happiness enough to dull her sensi-
bility to her actual daily life. And yet . . . they were hardly what she
wanted. She could make dream-worlds of her own—but no dream-world
would satisfy her now. She wanted some explanation of this hard, real
life: . . . she wanted some key that would enable her to understand,
and, in understanding, endure, the heavy weight that had fallen on her
young heart.

The Mill on the Floss

But were not men of ardent zeal and far-reaching hope everywhere
exceptional?—the men who had the visions which, as Mordecai said,
were the creators and feeders of the world—moulding and feeding
the more passive life which without them would dwindle and shrivel
into the narrow tenacity of insects, unshaken by thoughts beyond
the reaches of their antennae.

Daniel Deronda

With George Eliot, the Romantic impulse in Victorian fiction
reaches its climax. The most highly cultivated of the great English novelists, she knew and was imbued with the works of not
only the native Romantic tradition but the Continental and
American varieties as well. Even with her vast intellectual resources, however, Eliot suffered from many of the disabilities
nineteenth-century women novelists were heir to—not the least
of which was the sense that giving way to her imagination by
writing novels was morally wrong. Like Charlotte Brontë and
Elizabeth Gaskell, she was often fearful of the imaginative energies that alternately sustained and gripped her. Instead of suppressing her creative instincts as Brontë eventually elected to do,
Eliot followed Gaskell's example in adopting the reverential and

duty-oriented Wordsworthian mode in order to justify her first literary efforts. But the Romantic impulse was stronger in Eliot than in most Victorian novelists; and despite the continual attempt to purge her characters of their romantic longings, to subject them to the burden of reality, her own yearning after a means of Romantic apotheosis and self-transcendence intensified with each novel she wrote. An examination of her literary career from the *Scenes of Clerical Life* to *Daniel Deronda* shows how insistent her Romantic demon became in spite of her efforts to tame it or disguise its existence.

The affinities between Eliot and Wordsworth have been observed from the time of her earliest reviews to the present. The large number of references to and quotations from him in her work and letters amply supports the claim that he was her favorite author. She constantly cites him in defense of her views of the sacredness of feelings, the moral properties of the imagination, the supreme importance of one's ties to the past, the therapeutic value of one's devotion to nature and childhood experiences. But while the themes in her books are often Wordsworthian, the impulse behind their writing was not. Quiescence, fortitude, recognition of human limitations, and sympathy for the downtrodden form noble themes, to be sure, but novels are not written in that spirit of self-suppression and renunciation which Eliot repeatedly offers as the message to her characters and readers alike. The novels and the life give off an impression rather different from the icon of George Eliot, almost repellent in its self-denying magnanimity, which Eliot herself encouraged in her later years and which many of her admirers have harkened back to, in one disguised form or another, during the hundred years following her death. The extent of her unWordsworthian Romantic will to power needs to be assessed lest we allow her to be turned into a figure too good to be true or to be read. George Eliot the novelist retained much of the ambitious, headstrong, vain, self-righteous nature of her youth (as we see it in her letters); and many of the finest, if also some of the weakest, of her characterizations show the force of her self-awareness and self-chastisement.[1]

Very early in her life, as J. W. Cross reveals, George Eliot "became possessed with the idea that she was going to be a personage in the world"; and he relates an appealing account of the four-year-old child "playing on the piano, of which she did not know one note, in order to impress the servants with a proper notion of her acquirements and generally distinguished position." Even her adolescent outbursts of Evangelical self-abasement, as Gordon Haight shrewdly observes, betray a tendency toward exhibitionism. The desire to be "chief actress" in a drama of imaginative wish-fulfillment or saintly self-suppression is as evident in the picture of Eliot reflected in her earliest letters as in the marvelous depictions of Maggie Tulliver and Dorothea Brooke. But Hetty Sorrel, Rosamond Vincy, and Gwendolen Harleth reveal the less sympathetic side of the same vanity and need for mastery; and the severity with which Eliot explodes these women's frail illusions is mandated by the extent to which their fantasies represent, in exaggerated form, aspects of her own romantic drives. Her "besetting sin," as she confessed to her Aunt Evans (the model in later years for Dinah Morris in *Adam Bede*), was "an ever struggling ambition," "a desire insatiable for the esteem of my fellow creatures." She was determined not only to receive affection but to make an effect. As Eliot declares of Maggie Tulliver's passionate efforts to achieve "self-renunciation," "her own life was still a drama for her, in which she demanded of herself that her part should be played with intensity."[2] Eliot's wish to be seen as a "personage" is reflected in many ways: in, for example, her pride in her social caste, which is illustrated in her tributes to her father as a reincarnated noble Roman (in the form of Adam Bede and Caleb Garth) and in her fury when he was mistakenly called a "mere farmer"; in her awareness of herself as a novelist vastly superior to the likes of Dinah Mulock, with whom she had been compared ("we belong to an entirely different order," she retorted, and called Miss Mulock "a writer who is only read by novel readers, pure and simple, never by people of high culture"); or in the frequent expressions of exultation that she had been able to "touch the hearts of my fellow men," especially the "young men" among her reading audience whose testimonials she craved.[3]

"Perhaps no man," as she says of Savonarola, with whom she identified to some extent, "has ever had a mighty influence over his fellows without having the innate need to dominate, and this need usually becomes the more imperious in proportion as the complications of life make Self inseparable from a purpose which is not selfish."[4] Eliot was a devotee of the charismatic Byron before she discovered Wordsworth; and when speaking of the authors who impressed her most in her youth and later years, she invariably stressed the emotional power of their work over her feelings. Careful scrutiny of her letters and essays indicates that while she praised the self-disciplining aims of realism, she was more often swept away by the ardor of the Romantics; and it was her ambition to exert that power over others which she envied in Byron and Schiller, Rousseau and George Sand, Carlyle and Ruskin. In addition, Eliot aspired to the vatic role of the poet-sage, the idea of which Carlyle had transmitted to English readers from its source in German Romanticism, and which admirers of Shelley claimed for him as well. In her attempt to raise the novel to the status that Thomas De Quincey and John Stuart Mill had thought only poetry capable of attaining, Eliot came uncomfortably close to self-glorification. All too conscious of the high seriousness of her aesthetic mission, she equated criticism of her work with criticism of the mission itself; and the least pleasant parts of her correspondence (and that of George Henry Lewes included among the Haight edition of her letters) are the insistences that her work receive the fullest measure of intelligent sympathy it deserves and that she be shielded from any adverse comments. Lewes eventually censored the mail addressed to her, directing friends not to discuss her work unless they piled on the requisite amount of incense. "It is a wretched weakness of my nature to be so strongly affected by these things," she wrote to her patient publisher, John Blackwood, of the insufficiently intelligent praise offered by reviewers of *Adam Bede*, "—and yet how is it possible to put one's best heart and soul into a book and be hardened to the result— be indifferent to the proof whether or not one has really a vocation to speak to one's fellow-men in that way? Of course one's vanity is at work; but the main anxiety is something entirely distinct from vanity."[5]

One reason she delayed for so long in satisfying the "vague dream of [hers] that some time or other [she] might write a novel"[6] was Eliot's suspicion that the form was unsuitable for her ambitions, powerful though the hold might be on her of the fictional imagination; but the delay also testifies to her fear of the imagination. Eliot's lurid description (at age nineteen) of the "pernicious" power of novels and romances over her childhood strikingly resembles the similar confession of Rousseau (who would soon become a favorite author):

> I shall carry to my grave the mental diseases with which they have contaminated me. When I was quite a little child I could not be satisfied with the things around me; I was constantly living in a world of my own creation, and was quite contented to have no companions that I might be left to my own musings and imagine scenes in which I was chief actress. Conceive what a character novels would give to these Utopias.

A year later Eliot reiterated the theme to her Evangelical mentor, Maria Lewis, in a manner resembling Charlotte Brontë's confessions to Ellen Nussey: "My imagination is an enemy that must be cast down ere I can enjoy peace or exhibit uniformity of character."[7] There is a certain irony in the fact that whereas the youthful Marian Evans scorned novels for exerting such strong power over her errant imagination, the mature George Eliot despised novels for not living up to her highest standards. By then, she had learned to transmute the power of the imagination into a moral force which she herself could exert, influencing others morally by stimulating their nobler feelings. So long, however, as she linked the creative imagination with the egoistic Byronic-Rousseauesque sensibility that set the artist apart from his fellow men, Eliot would not proceed beyond praising the power of that sensibility; she dared not adopt it for herself. Poets, as Byron allegedly told Lady Blessington, are cursed by having imaginations which are "warmer than our *hearts*, and much more given to wander, the latter [not having] the power to control the former"; the result is that "we are rendered incapable of sympathy," since by being transported by the "power of imagination . . . to other scenes, . . . we are always so much more occupied by the ideal than the present, that we forget all that is actual."[8] Eliot's discovery in the works of Wordsworth,

Shelley, and perhaps above all Schiller that the imagination could be made to serve the highest ideals of humanity was therefore a revelation to her.

In George Eliot's essays, most of them written before she wrote her novels, we see very clearly her indebtedness to Romantic theories concerning the aims and methods of artistic creativity, the nature of genius, and the importance of inspiration. Even the two pieces most often cited in support of Eliot's position as a literary realist, the praise of Ruskin for teaching the truth of realism ("the doctrine that all truth and beauty are to be attained by a humble and faithful study of nature, and not by substituting vague forms, bred by imagination or the mists of feeling, in place of definite, substantial reality") and "The Natural History of German Life," which argues that the writer is morally bound to be a realist if he means to (as he must) extend his readers' sympathies, betray a Romantic sensibility. The praise of Ruskin's doctrine is accompanied by praise for Ruskin's prophetic manner—his rhetorical-vatic ability to "compel men's attention and sympathy." "Very correct singing of very fine music," she remarks, "will avail little without a *voice* that can thrill the audience and take possession of their souls." In the same article, she praises the notably unrealistic Meredith novel *The Shaving of Shagpat* and points out the supernatural thrills to be found in Wilkie Collins's stories. "The Natural History of German Life" calls attention to W. H. von Riehl's studies of the German peasantry as a potential source of inspiration to English writers, who might henceforth portray the mass of people seen hitherto only in Wordsworth or Scott. Like Wordsworth and Rousseau, Eliot sees the peasantry as close to nature and hence to the moral norm of human behavior; and if in her pastoral novels Eliot was to reflect something of this German Romantic idealization of the *Volk*, in *Daniel Deronda* and *The Spanish Gypsy* she would also expand on the Romantic theories of race that she found in Riehl.[9]

Other noteworthy essays are concerned with Wagner's early operas (here Eliot shows sympathy for the self-denying Wagnerian heroines), Carlyle's power to arouse his reader (more important, as she views it, than the actual Carlylean ideas), the modern relevance of the *Antigone* (in daring "to be right," the reformer or martyr "must also dare to be wrong—to shake faith, to wound friendships, perhaps to hem in his own powers"), the moral significance of Goethe's *Wilhelm Meister's Apprenticeship,* and the beauties of Heinrich Heine's work. Eliot's three most famous essays—denunciations of "Silly Novels by Lady Novelists," who write out of vanity rather than to fulfill the seriousness of the artistic calling, and attacks on the poet Edward Young and the Evangelical preacher Dr. Cumming for preferring an ego-gratifying but insubstantial kingdom in heaven to the real world which requires men's deepest sympathies—can be seen as assaults on her own youthful predilections, although the lack of tolerance with which she wittily attacks these writers' egoism and lack of tolerance suggests a certain self-righteousness on her part. The laudatory reviews of Harriet Beecher Stowe's depiction of life among the blacks and of Riehl's depiction of German peasantry reveal Eliot's unconscious need to patronize, which later creeps into *Scenes of Clerical Life* and *Adam Bede* at those moments when the narrator manages simultaneously to look down on the forgettable souls she is immortalizing and on the reader for refusing to see the nobility of her subject. The review of Stowe's *Dred* is followed by a consideration of Charles Reade's *It Is Never Too Late to Mend,* which Eliot criticizes for its lack of inspiration and genius. Reade shows talent in making "effective use of materials, but nowhere of the genius which absorbs material, and reproduces it as a living whole, in which you do not admire the ingenuity of the workman, but the vital energy of the producer." Genius, she maintains, is the attribute of "the writer who thoroughly possesses you by his creation," the writer who has *himself* been "thoroughly possessed by his creation."[10]

The Romantic focus in the essays, as in the novels to come, is on feeling, feeling as the means and end of art and life. "After all has been said that can be said about the widening influence of ideas," as she was to write in *Romola,* "it remains true that they would hardly be such strong agents unless they were taken in a solvent of feeling." Eliot's susceptibility to the power of music, and especially to opera, was in part owing to that fusion in Romantic music of cause and effect: feelings aroused in support of the value of feelings.[11] Having abandoned all faith in a supernatural deity, Eliot placed her trust instead in what Leigh Hunt called "The Religion of the Heart." To a friend of her youth, Eliot loftily declared herself to be "influenced in my own conduct . . . by far higher considerations, and by a nobler idea of duty, than I ever was while I held the evangelical beliefs" now discarded. Where Evangelical beliefs reflected an egoistic desire to seek rewards in heaven, the religion of the heart decreed that it was one's responsibility to feel and act in behalf of others: the cultivation of feeling necessarily led to the expression of fellow-feeling. "Our duty to others," Hunt writes, "consists in imagining ourselves in their places, and doing them good accordingly." Eliot read *The Religion of the Heart* when it first appeared and liked it well enough to borrow Hunt's attack on "Other-Worldliness" ("the piety of the world to come" which is a disguised form of "self-seeking, without thought of others") in her own critique of Edward Young.[12]

Eliot's faith in the inherent goodness of feelings was encouraged by her readings in Wordsworth, Rousseau, and Schiller, and undoubtedly heightened by a work by the mentor of her youth, Charles Bray's *The Education of the Feelings*. Bray affirms the gospel of feelings: "Custom and tradition no longer rule men's minds, and it is to the dictates of our highest moral faculties—to the moral law written by God in our hearts, that we must look for a more definite ruler in their place."[13] For Eliot everything worthy of survival—from the memories of childhood celebrated in *The Mill on the Floss* to the Jewish people as depicted in *Daniel Deronda*—survives because of the durability and necessities of feeling. Along with Schiller, Rousseau, and Wordsworth, Eliot believed in the intrinsically reverential quality of the feelings: sentiments serving as deterrents to willfulness rather than as prods. Those who err in her novels do so, accordingly, because of a deficiency of feeling. Civilization itself depends, she wrote in one of her last essays, on the retention of feelings: "We have been severely enough taught," wrote Eliot in the wake of the 1870 Franco-Prussian war, ". . . that our civilization, considered as a splendid material fabric, is helplessly in peril without the spiritual police of sentiments or ideal feelings."[14] The possibility that feelings might be misapplied, in the service of nationalist ends, for example, seems not to have occurred to her. Eliot's belief in the majesty of feeling and in the supreme majesty of "ideal feeling," forms the basis of her Romantic outlook; but the natural transition she makes from feeling to ideal feeling reveals how readily she absorbed and combined aspects of French, German, and English Romantic views on the subject.

The argument that Romanticism originated in France rests on the commanding influence of Jean Jacques Rousseau. The Geneva-born philosopher created a revolution based (in Ernst Cassirer's view) on "the force of feeling" in reaction against the rationalist intellectual assumptions of the eighteenth century. Rousseau "opposed the essentially static mode of thought of the century with his own completely personal dynamics of thought, feeling, and passion."[15] A man who thinks, Rousseau wrote in the *Discourse on Inequality*, is a perverted animal, since reason only "engenders egotism and reflection strengthens it." "All the evil I ever did in my life," he admitted, "was the result of reflection; and the little good I have been able to do was the result of impulse." George Eliot's formulation of the "truth of feeling" is predicated on this Rousseauesque declaration: the intellect, as she wrote to Sara Hennell (Bray's sister-in-law), only causes division among men, while feeling unites them. "Speculative truth begins to appear but a shadow of individual minds, agreement between intellects seems unattainable, and we return to the *truth of feeling* as the only universal bond of union."[16]

Eliot's enthusiasm for Rousseau, shared by few of her Victorian contemporaries, transcended disagreement with many of his religious and political doctrines. Freed from the Evangelical strictures against pleasurable feelings, she found in Rousseau a source of emotional liberation: his "genius," she affirmed, "has sent that electric thrill through my intellectual and moral frame which has awakened me to new perceptions, which has made man and nature a fresh world of thought and feeling to me." To William Hale White she declared that it was "worth while to undertake all the labour of learning French if it resulted in nothing more than reading one book—Rousseau's 'Confessions' "; and to Emerson she attributed to the *Confessions* her first awakening "to deep reflection." Her fondness for the *Con-*

fessions ("Individuals are precious to me," as she admitted, "in proportion as they unfold to me their intimate selves") remained such that she visited Les Charmettes, the site of Rousseau's idyll with Madame de Warens, both with George Henry Lewes and with J. W. Cross, the latter occasion during her honeymoon.[17] With Rousseau she shared a preference for country to city life, an abiding love of music, a veneration for "the wisdom of the child" ("true wisdom," she declares in her first published essay, which directly acknowledges her debt to Rousseau and Wordsworth, ". . . consists in a return to that purity and simplicity which characterizes early youth, when its intuitions have not been perverted"), a belief in the therapeutic value of tears shared in unison ("Nothing," wrote Rousseau, "draws two hearts together so much as the pleasure of weeping together"), and a sense of belonging to an elite of individuals who suffer because of the delicacy of their sensibilities.[18]

Rousseau is, after Wordsworth, the most important presence in George Eliot's thought and work; and one can cite countless direct and indirect borrowings, from the scene in *The Mill on the Floss* when Maggie Tulliver allows herself to drift down the river (based on a famous passage in the *Confessions*) to the scene in *Middlemarch* when Dorothea Brooke and Rosamond Vincy break down the social barriers between them by weeping in each other's arms. Adam Bede's gospel of feeling is similar to that which Rousseau propounds in *Émile* ("The decrees of conscience are not judgments but feelings"), and Adam himself, in his guise of "idealized artisan," is a reflection, as Barbara Hardy points out, of the "Noble Savage" whose life is a rebuke "to those who are more sophisticated but less noble."[19] From Rousseau's novel *La Nouvelle Héloïse* came the situation of the tutor, lacking wealth but rich in sensibility, who is loved by an heiress. Charlotte Brontë had already borrowed this motif for *Shirley*, and Eliot was to follow suit in the pairings between Esther Lyon and Felix Holt and Dorothea Brooke and Will Ladislaw. Julie's "talent of loving" is duplicated, with even more pathos, in the case of Maggie Tulliver; and Stephen Guest's proposal to Maggie is based on the argument used by Saint-Preux to Julie that love like theirs can only be based on "the purest laws of nature."

"The heart's impulse is blinder" than the sway of reason, as one of the characters in *La Nouvelle Héloïse* observes, "but it is more irresistible; the way to ruin is to put oneself under the necessity of resisting it."[20]

That Eliot allowed herself to be swayed, in the end, more by Wordsworth than by Rousseau is reflected in her decision not to allow Maggie to be overcome by Stephen's argument that they yield to their "heart's impulse" toward each other in defiance of their presumed obligation to others. While Eliot trusts to the release of impulse in *Romola*—as demonstrated in the scene in which Romola allows herself to drift passively down the Arno— she fears in *The Mill on the Floss* that the gratification of one's feelings may lead to antisocial behavior, may even arouse one's inner demon. The Maggie who resists Stephen's plea is a reincarnation of the Marian Evans who feared what might happen to her after her father's death. "It will seem as if a part of my moral nature were gone," she wrote to the Charles Brays. "I had a horrid vision of myself last night becoming earthly sensual and devilish for want of that purifying restraining influence." Eliot had learned from Bray the need to distinguish between conflicting sets of feelings: one kind relating "only to individuals, the other . . . [to] the whole human race, or rather the whole sensitive creation." Bray believed in the necessity of educating the feelings so that when such a conflict arose one would choose to restrain one's selfish feelings in preference to more altruistic sentiments.[21]

Another potential danger in Rousseau's ethic of feelings is that it can—and did, in his case—direct one away from the capacity for empathy. Finding in his imagination a higher source of moral value than that which he discerned in his fellow men, Rousseau moved inevitably in the direction of misanthropy. "If I do not enjoy living among men," he admitted, "it is less my fault than theirs"—a sentiment shared by the protagonist of Eliot's Rousseauesque parable, "The Lifted Veil." Cassirer has convincingly argued that Rousseau's stress on feelings led ultimately to an "ethics of obligation," that Rousseau identified man's better impulses with obedience to the rule of law, religion, and society as set forth in *The Social Contract*; however, Eliot's interpretation of the positive social implications of Rousseau's theories did not prevent her also holding the Victorian prejudice (expressed by Lewes) that his was the libertarian "spirit which animated the [French] Revolution." Kant knew better, according to Cassirer, and Rousseau's influence in Germany "rested primarily on the ethical ideals and demands which he advocated." If Cassirer is correct, it is a confirmation of Rousseau's influence on Eliot that the Romantic German writer who so strongly shaped Eliot's idealist goals, Friedrich Schiller, derived much of his idealism from Kant's interpretation of Rousseau.[22]

George Eliot's indebtedness to Rousseau's disciples Madame de Staël and George Sand has been admirably discussed by Ellen Moers, Patricia Thomson, and Robert Colby.[23] Although their influence was of a lesser nature than Rousseau's, the two women novelists translated his views into themes and characters that the Victorian reading public could respond to. His large conception of feeling received a narrower, if more highly colored, reincarnation as Sand's cult of "romantic passion." Thomson sees Sand as "the missing link" between the generation of Scott and Jane Austen and that of Eliot and the Brontës. Herself a disciple of the great French and English Romantic writers, Sand helped transmit a popularized form of Romantic ideals and methods, a concern for justice and women's rights, a faith in the masses, all expressed through glasses so rose-colored as to make even her most subversive ideas seem sentimentally reassuring. When Richard Simpson observed of Eliot, in 1863, that she had dethroned religion and in its place had deified passion, he was linking her with the feminine tradition of Charlotte Brontë, Madame de Staël, and George Sand. Eliot read the Sand novels and thrilled to their power; the Berry novels in particular (*La Mare au Diable*, *La Petite Fadette*, and *François le Champi*), with their evocations of pastoral simplicity and innocence, undoubtedly contributed something of the glow that permeates the landscapes in *Adam Bede* and *The Mill on the Floss*.[24] (One almost suspects that Maggie Tulliver's idealization of her childhood is based on a reading of Sand's novels rather than on her actual experience in St. Ogg's.) George Henry Lewes was, in his reviews of her work, one of Sand's staunchest English supporters;

but Eliot's enthusiasm dimmed in later years, and she eventually reproached Sand's "teaching" for being "nonsensical if it did not deserve to be called wicked," a flattering of the ego "with the possibility that a complex and refined human society can continue wherein relations have no sacredness beyond the inclination of changing moods."[25]

Byron, himself an ardent admirer of Rousseau, allegedly told Madame de Staël that her novel *Corinne* "would be considered, if not cited, as an excuse for violent *passions*, by all young ladies with imaginations *exalté*, and that she had much to answer for." For Maggie Tulliver, such a book as *Corinne* does "no good," as she admits to Philip Waken, in that it confirms her sense of the injustice meted out to the "dark unhappy ones" of romantic fiction. For if Corinne is the incarnation of the woman of genius —"the myth," as Ellen Moers declares, "of the famous woman talking, writing, performing, to the applause of the world"—she is also Rousseau's martyr of sensibility par excellence.[26] As a great actress, singer, dancer, improvisatrice, Corinne embodies all that the Romantics revered in Italy, the country where nature and art reign supreme. But she also suggests the Romantic conception of the artist as a figure set apart from ordinary mortals, unable to find satisfaction in love or domestic happiness. Like Werther or Childe Harold, she makes a career out of suffering: Corinne's greatest performance takes place when she endures the grief caused her by Lord Nelvil, who has abandoned her to marry her dutiful, modest, blond half-sister Lucile. In Eliot's adaptations of Corinne, most notably the singer-protagonist of her play "Armgart," the artist is made to atone for having preferred a career to domestic duties. "Too much ambition has unwomaned her," Eliot notes, unsympathetically, of Armgart—a sentiment that reverberates throughout the Eliot novels.[27] In any case, the "violent passions" that Byron saw as the effect of *Corinne* on impressionable young ladies are not echoed in the Eliot heroines, who either suppress what passion they feel or disguise it by making it serve the ends of society. Poor Maggie Tulliver yearns for a world where the "dark woman" is allowed to triumph for a change; but if fiction allows little solace, St. Ogg's offers none at all, and Maggie is denied even those operatic outbursts of grief which Corinne pours forth by way of artistic compensation.

With the publication, six years after *Corinne*, of *De l'Al-lemagne* (1813), Madame de Staël made it clear to French and English readers that the torch of Rousseau had passed to Germany, where the cult of sensibility had become transformed into the cult of genius, and where Rousseau's mythical Noble Savage was revealed to have taken up residence among the German *Volk*. German Romantic critics, such as August Wilhelm Schlegel, encouraged support for the artist whose mission it was to express the truth of what he found within himself, not to reproduce the inferior reality of the objective world. According to Schlegel's younger brother Friedrich, the artist required complete freedom from the conventionalities if he was to serve as a "mediator," submitting "to the world his vision of the infinite."[28] One distinctly modern art form favored by the younger Schlegel was the novel (his newly honorific use of the word "romantic" was partially linked to his endorsement of the *"Roman"*); but while he lavished praise on Goethe's *Wilhelm Meister* and allowed some value to realistic fiction, Friedrich Schlegel's deepest sympathies were for those works of Cervantes, Sterne, and Jean Paul Richter in which the novelists' subjective qualities were allowed free rein. Schlegel's conception of a novelistic form encompassing irony and fantasy, rhapsody and myth was to be passed on to George Meredith rather than George Eliot; but his and his brother's sense of the artist's mission, which they took from Schiller, was to filter into Eliot's definition of her role as author. The Schlegels and other members of the "Romantic School" (in Heinrich Heine's derisive phrase) underwent an evolution from individualistic defiance of restraints to a religious reaction, a withdrawal into the world of the past and an endorsement of the conservative political regime of the day; and in this respect their development paralleled that of Coleridge, Wordsworth, and Southey.[29]

A steady stream of German ideas and German romances flowed into England as a result of the enthusiasm of Coleridge, Scott, Matthew Lewis, Byron, Bulwer Lytton, De Quincey, and Carlyle, among others. George Eliot's absorption of German

Romanticism was hardly unique; but the manner in which she drew upon so many of its disparate channels indicates the complexity of her intellectual and emotional needs. From Goethe and Schiller, the two fountainheads of German Romanticism, she received that fusion of realistic and idealistic standards which animates her finest fiction, and she inherited their mantle as artist-sage.[30] Although in *The Mill on the Floss* she denied Novalis's optimistic contention that "character is destiny"—seeing all too clearly the environmental and hereditary pressures that constrained her protagonists—Eliot nevertheless occasionally yearned after a mystical self-transcendence in defiance of scientific and realistic proscriptions. From Hegel and the young Hegelians, notably Ludwig Feuerbach, she received assurance for the secularized faith she was painfully constructing. And in Heine, whom she was among the first of English critics to call attention to, she found a liberating sense of romantic irony and a commitment to liberal values. Both Heine and Eliot were Romantic humanists, scornful of the perpetuators of illusions whether expressed in the form of metaphysical systems or in regressive or solipsistically oriented beliefs.

As Eliot was the wife of Goethe's English biographer, her high regard for Goethe is hardly surprising. At least one reviewer of *Adam Bede* noted the resemblance between Gretchen in *Faust* and Hetty Sorrel, not only in Hetty's fate but in the borrowing of the scene in which she decks herself with the jewels her lover has given her. On a more important level, the similar emphasis both writers placed on the ethic of renunciation was not ignored; and when Cross, in his biography of Eliot, called attention to her "many-sidedness," he used the term most often associated with Goethe's genius. For Lewes (as for Carlyle, to whom Lewes dedicated the biography) the "keystone" of Goethe's character was his "self-mastery," the subduing of his "rebellious impulses" for the sake of the harmony and Olympian detachment of his maturity; Eliot's adoring disciple Edith Simcox similarly spoke in awe of her idol's "beautiful" ordering of her "primitive passions of irresistible strength." However, where Lewes's Goethe was the apostle of objective realism, the artist as scientist, the poet as possessor of his passion but not one himself possessed, Eliot's Goethe was more Romantic in nature. She treasured the "strain of mysticism in his soul," that aspect of his poetic nature which involves "the delighted bathing of the soul in emotions which overpass the outlines of definite thought," while Lewes was put off by the haziness and mysticism in the second part of *Faust*—as indeed he was put off by all such abstract poetic effusions.[31]

The object of Eliot's greatest adulation among German writers was Goethe's friend and rival, Schiller; and to Schiller along with Wordsworth goes the credit for Eliot's transformation of Rousseau's ethic of feeling from a personal to a public frame of reference. But where Rousseau had sanctioned the flow of feeling in the young George Eliot, Schiller fired her with a devotion to lofty feeling. Tutoring Mary Sibree in German, Eliot chose Schiller's plays because of their "manifestations of nobility of character, and sympathy with human struggles and sufferings under varied conditions." At one point, Mary Sibree later recalled, Eliot said of Schiller's plays, "Oh, if *I* had given these to the world, how happy I should be!"[32] Where Goethe had seemed detached from the world, Schiller was the model for young idealists in need of a champion of humanity. To use the terms which Schiller himself popularized, Goethe was a "realist," resigned to the external world of men and nature as he found it, while Schiller was an "idealist," finding in himself higher standards than those practiced by most men and "always pining," in Lewes's phrase, "for something greater than Nature." The idealist, Schiller admitted, trusting to the power of will and hoping to improve the human condition, often falls into the error of thinking "so highly of mankind that he thereby falls into the danger of despising man." The realist, in contrast, "shows himself to be a philanthropist but simply without entertaining any very high idea of humanity."[33]

While Hegel specifically exempted Schiller's heroes from the status of "World-Historical Individuals," claiming that their ideals are too high to be "realized," Heine praised Schiller for the practical nature of his influence. "Goethe's works," charged Heine, "do not beget deeds as do Schiller's."[34] Schiller's heroes rarely achieve their lofty goals, but they achieve the status of heroes in his plays and in this way influence others. It is the *image* of the hero that matters in the long run, not the achievement or frustration of his goals. As George Eliot says in her highly Schilleresque play *The Spanish Gypsy:*

> The greatest gift the hero leaves his race
> Is to have been a hero.

It is precisely the responsibility of art, Schiller argued, to show the potentiality of idealism despite the evidence to the contrary. "Man has lost his dignity," he proclaimed, "but Art has saved it and expressed it for him." The artist's task is to avoid the extremes of a self-absorbed enthusiasm that flees contact with the world and a commonsensical approach that declares that whatever is is right; he must instead strive "from the union of the possible with the necessary to bring out the ideal."[35] Where Goethe and Schiller agreed, in the end, was in their devotion to the artistic calling as the highest of missions, comparable to the role played by religion in the past, and (as Lewes notes) "by whose aid the great world-scheme was to be wrought into reality . . . They believed that Culture would raise Humanity to its full powers; and they, as artists, knew no Culture equal to that of Art."[36]

It was in reading Schiller, I suspect, that Eliot first realized the idealistic potential of the imagination; and it was Schiller's lofty conception of the role of the artist that she ultimately adopted for herself. At about the time that she was tutoring Mary Sibree, Eliot defended "works of imagination," although she had attacked them in her Evangelical phase. Such writings, she now maintained, "perform an office for the mind which nothing else can."[37] Schiller's fusion of Plutarch and Shakespeare into a dramatic conception of heroism is at the heart of Eliot's design in *Adam Bede, The Spanish Gypsy,* and *Daniel Deronda;* and Schiller's idea of the "idyll" lies behind Eliot's intention in *Silas Marner.* Schiller's reputation among the early Victorians was immense: the young Thackeray, for example, regarded him as a poet second only to Shakespeare. In the defiantly anticonventional theatrical heroes created in his youth, notably Karl Moor in *The Robbers,* Schiller created the vogue of the outlaw-hero which was later to be adopted by such romantic English novelists as Bulwer Lytton in *Paul Clifford* and *Eugene Aram* and (satirically) Disraeli in *Contarini Fleming*. Even the youthful Carlyle was spellbound by this Byronic prototype: "We may exclaim against the blind madness of the hero [Moor]," Carlyle declared; "but there is a towering grandeur about him, a whirlwind force of passion and of will, which catches our hearts, and puts the scruples of criticism to silence."[38] Schiller himself repudiated the implications of *The Robbers*, without, however, substantially changing the flawed character of his heroic beings. Heroes and heroines who yearn after an ideal unrealizable on earth, who are tormented by internal weaknesses as well as external constraints, appear in Eliot as well as in Schiller; and, often, the greater the ardor the greater appears the flaw.

Schiller's finest heroic figure is probably Wallenstein, whose act of betrayal (like that of Karl Moor) is the result of external circumstances rather than any internal evil. Moor and Wallenstein look to the lofty impulses of their hearts, as opposed to the petty rules and intrigues of the society they inhabit, for justification for actions that serve a higher end than the world can fathom. The noble figure brought to bay by a world that has the conventional "wisdom" on its side is a likely pattern for such Eliot characters as Tertius Lydgate and Maggie Tulliver, more likely than the model offered (in Maggie's case) by Corinne. Eliot's defense of Maggie has a Schilleresque ring to it if we think of Moor, Wallenstein, Johanna (Schiller's Joan of Arc), or Posa (in *Don Carlos*): "If the ethics of art do not admit the truthful presentation of a character essentially noble but liable to great error—error that is anguish to its own nobleness—*then*, it seems to me, the ethics of art are too narrow, and must be widened to correspond with a widening psychology."[39] Max Piccolomini, Wallenstein's ardent young supporter who is in love with his daughter Thekla, defends his leader's perplexing actions on the ground that Wallenstein has always acted in accordance with the rule of Nature and that his disobedience to the Imperial Court has been occasioned by the court's treachery and ingratitude toward him; but Max is torn between his own obligations to the Austrian court and his love for Thekla and her father. Silva's dilemma in *The Spanish Gypsy* duplicates Max's, while Silva's fiancée Fedalma, the gypsy's daughter called to a heroic undertaking which requires that she forsake the man she loves, is a combination of Thekla and the heroine of *The Maid of Orleans*. (Johanna's heroic career stands in such stark contrast to Maggie Tulliver's as to seem a kind of mockery of it: a country girl called to the highest of missions, Johanna reconciles foes, errs only when she falls in love, allows herself to be falsely accused as a result, rejects her lover, and looks to vindication after her death.) Eliot's indebtedness to Schiller's plays may perhaps also be seen in her language and settings: his fondness for Shakespearean rhetoric and his historian's attention to realistic detail may have encouraged Eliot's not always successful attempts to juxtapose lofty rhetoric and minutely detailed backdrops in *Romola* and *Daniel Deronda*.

Eliot's debt to Ludwig Feuerbach has been considered often enough, although it seems a disservice to her genius to yoke her to his system of "sentimental clichés."[40] From Hegel, Feuerbach's mentor, Eliot drew support for her view of the will in history. Hegel's "World-Historical Individual" is a man who, at a time of need among his people or in a period of social decline when a new course of action must be taken, arises in order to accomplish "that for which the time [is] ripe." Such men are themselves subjects of the world spirit, which directs its future aim (the spread of freedom, in Hegel's view) through them: they thus demonstrate the power of will while remaining passive in the service of necessity. Daniel Deronda, the hero of Eliot's last novel, is characterized in terms of his "classical, romantic, world-historic position"; and Eliot's belief in determinism, encouraged alike by her Calvinist streak and the scientific theories of the day, and her counterbelief in the need for idealistically motivated, Schilleresque heroes found a common ground in Hegel's hero, who is both a determined and a determining force.[41]

Feuerbach broke with Hegel over the issue of the rationally motivated "World Spirit" which Hegel saw as ruling the course of history. Along with other of the young Hegelians, Feuerbach transferred his attention away from rational ideals and toward a celebration of sensuous, temporal, human-oriented reality. The only deity worthy of worship was man himself; love of God became redefined as love of one's fellow men; and "feeling" became the ultimate criterion for all human endeavor. Feeling was equivalent to God; feeling meant fellow-feeling; religion was to be reconstructed on the basis of the needs of the heart and the desires of the imagination. It is difficult nowadays to imagine how George Eliot and others of her generation could devour *The Essence of Christianity* and confuse its gaseous sentimentalism with genuine substance; but Eliot (who translated the work into English in 1854) claimed that she agreed "everywhere" with Feuerbach's ideas—an indication of how starved she must have been for a faith that placed mankind (a highly abstract Feuerbachian conception) at its center.[42] The Romanticism implicit in the activity of the young Hegelians resided in their determination to transfer the center of reality from external to subjective sources, culminating in Max Stirner's retreat into an "I" emptied of all value or meaning. Feuerbach's sentiments, for all their soothing vagueness, could provide little other than emotional reassurance to Eliot; it was the strength of her native English Romantic heritage that satisfied the deepest needs of her aesthetic-humanistic yearnings.

The similarity between George Eliot's and Wordsworth's themes, choice of subject matter, and artistic aims is so striking that it is misleading to speak of the relationship between these writers as strictly a matter of "influence." When, on her twentieth birthday, Eliot told Maria Lewis of her newly purchased volumes of Wordsworth's *Poetical Works*, she noted that she had "never met with so many of [her] own feelings, expressed just as" she might have done herself.[43] Eliot's readings in Rousseau and Schiller had demonstrable effects: Rousseau roused her by the "electric thrill" of genius to "new perceptions," and she was always henceforth to see literary genius in terms of its ability to produce an emotional effect; Schiller showed her that the artist's power and imagination could raise men's feelings to noble, heroic aims and ideals. Wordsworth's appeal may be said to have confirmed her in what she already felt and knew (as her response to his poems suggests) and to have persuaded her that she too had a fund of materials that could be put to literary use. When, for example, she said of *Silas Marner* that its substance would not interest anyone but herself "since William Wordsworth is dead," she was reiterating her sense of their shared affinity for lowborn characters whose lives carry symbolic resonance. Basil Willey, seeking an explanation for why Eliot's intellect did not "devour her creative instinct more completely than it did," notes that for Eliot as for Wordsworth "the heart in her was kept alive by the recollection of her early life, and of the scenes and people associated with the feelings of childhood."[44] The transition from the humbly realistic style of the *Lyrical Ballads* to the lofty manner of *The Excursion* was made as inevitably and swiftly in her case as in Wordsworth's; and for both writers the attraction to the invigorating effects of childhood and nature deepened—or hardened—into a conservative reverence for a world of the past which was in part a mythic construction rather than the reflection of actuality.

Michael Cooke's recent study of the "Romantic Will" suggestively argues that Wordsworth's stoicism ran counter to his own poetical gifts, undermining the forces of inspiration and energy that the creation of Romantic poetry required. Too much praise of quiescence numbs one's poetical imagination; and while Wordsworth's poetry provided splendid therapy for anxious Victorians who needed peace of mind, it could not be as much of an imaginative stimulus as the work of a lesser poet like Byron.[45] It is interesting to note in this context that while three favorite Eliot authors, Wordsworth, Rousseau, and Schiller, all named Plutarch as their favorite writer, Rousseau's and Schiller's enthusiasm was roused by the chronicler of great deeds, while Wordsworth was struck by Plutarch's stress on self-discipline and duty. Schiller's Wallenstein is a great figure despite his ambitious weakness; Wordsworth's Dion, on the other hand, is an object lesson in the futility of great enterprise carried out by an undisciplined hero. Where Eliot's "good" characters often fail to capture modern readers' interest is in that very aspiration to self-disciplined perfection, the refusal to touch pitch. (Henry James criticized Daniel Deronda, as he had in earlier reviews chastised Felix Holt and Adam Bede, for not having been created "more peccable.") There is something rather sad in the last image we have of Mary Garth in *Middlemarch*, married to Fred Vincy and self-effacingly raising her sons according to the gospel of Plutarch, which had been embodied in her father. It is the very fact that Mary was conceived along Wordsworthian lines that allows her to dissolve into so pallidly dutiful a character, a far cry from the promising figure of wit and energy she seemed in the early portions of the novel.[46] Nonetheless, the most serious case of Wordsworthian blight on Eliot's creative imagination occurs in *The Mill on the Floss*, her most Wordsworthian novel, in which the heroine is paralyzed by a myth of the past and a myth of her own childhood.

The abundance of Wordsworthian lines used as epigraphs or quoted in Eliot's novels and letters indicates how thoroughly she had assimilated his work. Eliot's Wordsworth was a weightier figure than Elizabeth Gaskell's favorite poet, although Gaskell was better aware than Eliot of the deadening effect of Wordsworthian quiescence. When Eliot speaks, for example, of "feeling 'the weight of all this unintelligible world,' " she is reflecting a profounder sense of Wordsworth's philosophical significance than Gaskell was aware of when she quoted the reassuring words "We have all of us one human heart" in her letters and novels. Asked by Frederic Harrison for poetic lines suitable for use as a Positivist credo, Eliot supplied ponderous lines from *The Prelude*, expressing the poet's reverence for the spirit of the past that lives in the present. Her youthful fondness for Wordsworth's "On the Power of Sound" shows to what degree she was willing to confuse sage-like pronouncements with poetry (a confusion which is reflected in her own painfully well-meaning poetry); and the passages she marked from *The Prelude* are almost invariably ones that speak of the ties that bind nature to men and men to men, of the therapeutic value of nature and memory on one's feelings, and of the resultant expansion of sympathy—the passages, in short, in which the Wordsworthian themes are stated rather than illustrated.[47] Eliot's famous pronouncement to Charles Bray that "if Art does not enlarge men's sympathies, it does nothing morally" is a Victorian restatement of Wordsworth's thesis in the Preface to *Lyrical Ballads* that the "purpose" of poetry is moral, the expansion of the reader's sympathy. The "only effect," she added, "I ardently long to produce in my writings, is that those who read them should be better able to *imagine* and to *feel* the pains and the joys of those who differ from themselves in everything but the broad fact of being struggling erring human beings."[48] The self-conscious nobility of statements like these, which swell the nine volumes of the *Letters,* indicates how seriously she meant to be taken; and one must look to her acquaintance with Romantic writers other than Wordsworth to understand the flourishing of many of her finest creative abilities.

Victorian reviewers noted that the presence of Sir Walter Scott was virtually as important in Eliot's work as that of Wordsworth. Both may be said to have kindled Eliot's "Tory imagination," but where a Wordsworthian reverence for nature led to that support for the status quo which Eliot describes in the *Impressions of Theophrastus Such,* Scott's influence was initially of a rebellious kind. It was to Scott that the young George Eliot "attributed the first unsettlement of her orthodox views" when she discovered that virtuous action, such as is exemplified in Scott's life and work, need not be instigated by religious dogma.[49] Scott remained a "sacred name" throughout her life, the novelist she delighted in reading to her father and then to Lewes (despite initial antipathy on his part). It may not be too much of an overstatement to say that from Scott she learned the lesson of tolerance, even if hers was never quite the good-humored tolerance he displayed toward the characters of opposing religious and political points of view in his books. Scott's love of the common man, completely lacking in condescension, is repeated up to a point in Eliot's artisans and workmen; and his appreciation of singular types of characters is reflected in such wonderful Eliot creations as Mrs. Poyser in *Adam Bede,* Rufus Lyon in *Felix Holt,* and the Ezra Cohen family in *Daniel Deronda.* Bob Jakin in *The Mill on the Floss* is probably modeled on the peddler in Scott's *The Pirate;* and the contrast between the "dark unhappy" Minna and the blond, dutiful Brenda Troil in the same Scott novel finds echoes in *The Mill on the Floss* and *Middlemarch.* With *Romola* Eliot took on the challenge of writing a Scott historical romance; and while contemporary reviewers praised the nobility of her conception, they missed Scott's gusto, "his dynamical force in making you plunge into [the past] with as headlong an interest as into the present."[50] Where Wordsworth had endeavored to awaken in his reader a sympathy for humble beings and objects, Scott also sought to widen the reader's sympathy for adherents of alien modes of culture and thought; and Eliot's treatment of Judaism in *Daniel Deronda* and of the gypsies in *The Spanish Gypsy* shows the degree to which he helped develop her romantic enthusiasm for people from seemingly alien or outcast ways of life.

Toward the poet of Romantic alienation, Byron, Eliot's feelings were ambivalent. By the age of twenty, she had read *Childe Harold* for the "second time" and had managed to find in it a therapeutic message of the need to subdue one's personal sorrows by reflecting on "the revolutions and woes beneath which the shores of the Mediterranean have groaned." (Dorothea Brooke, too, subdues her unhappiness in *Middlemarch* by thinking of the griefs of others.) At the height of her religious fervor, when she saw works of fiction as impediments to righteous behavior and thinking, Eliot exempted "Byron's Poetical romances" from the works presumably to be placed on the Evangelical index. And in her post-Evangelical phase, she interrupted her attack on Dr. Cumming's "Evangelical Teaching" with a sentimental defense of Byron (whom Cumming had anathematized): "Who that has a spark of generous feeling, that rejoices in the presence of good in a fellow-being, has not dwelt with pleasure on the thought that Lord Byron's unhappy career was ennobled and purified towards its close by a high and sympathetic purpose, by honest and energetic efforts for his fellow-men?"[51] The liberal climate of the *Westminster Review* during the period when Eliot edited and contributed to it would have guaranteed Byron's not being viewed there with the moral severity he encountered in religious journals of the period.

Ruby Redinger speculates that Eliot's later revulsion of feeling toward Byron was related to Harriet Beecher Stowe's revelation concerning his alleged relations with his half-sister, a hideous contrast to Eliot's celebration of her love for her brother Isaac as set down in the "Brother and Sister" sonnets or *The Mill on the Floss*.[52] In fact, Eliot's attack on Byron in *Felix Holt* preceded the Stowe article by three years. The animosity she expresses in that book reveals, as is usually the case when Eliot was attacking something, that she was chastising something that had been dear to her in her own youth. After Felix Holt's description of Byron as "a misanthropic debauchee" whose "corsairs and renegades, his Alps and Manfreds, are the most paltry puppets that were ever pulled by the strings of lust and pride,"

Eliot's subsequent personal dismissal of him as "the most *vulgar-minded* genius that ever produced a great effect in literature" seems anticlimactic. It is clear from her early letters, however, that Byron had had much the same effect on her as on Esther Lyon in *Felix Holt*; and while she adopted a condescending attitude toward Byron's chief male disciples among Victorian novelists, Bulwer Lytton and Disraeli, she greatly admired the most fervid worshipper of Byron among the great women writers, Charlotte Brontë. The young Marian Evans who deplored Jane Eyre's *not* going off with the married Rochester changed into the George Eliot who refused to allow Maggie Tulliver to yield to Stephen Guest's more honorable proposal. Yet even in her last novel Byronic traces remain: in her portrait of Mallinger Grandcourt in *Daniel Deronda*, Eliot drew a stunning portrait of a Byronic "misanthropic debauchee"; and her inspiration for Gwendolen Harleth derived from seeing Byron's grandniece gambling in Hamburg.[53]

Another reason for Eliot's change of attitude toward Byron might have been the influence of George Henry Lewes, who scorned the author of *Don Juan* for his egoism and cynicism and who idolized Shelley as the apostle of "Love and Hope." A full-length study of Shelley's hold on the Victorians would provide a useful gauge to the attitude of loathing and adoration felt by so many of the great Victorians toward the Romantics who had simultaneously nourished their creative sensibilities and disturbed their moral beliefs. I have indicated something of this mixed feeling toward Byron; but Shelley's influence was less substantial and more mythical in nature than Byron's. The diffuseness of his style and the loftiness of his subject matter, together with the shortened life that bore all the characteristics of a martyrdom in behalf of truth, helped to ensure that Shelley would never be seen "plain" in the nineteenth century. As the defender of liberty and justice at a time of political conservatism in England, Shelley might have been created by Schiller as an embodiment of the German "beautiful soul." Where Bulwer Lytton spoke of Wordsworth as "the apostle, the spiritualizer of those who cling to the most idealized part of things that are," he hailed Shelley as "a more youthful genius bodying forth the beauty of a time to be." "It is our best consolation," intoned

Mary Shelley in the 1839 Preface to his *Collected Poems*, "to know that such a pure-minded and exalted being was once among us." Robert Browning, a decade later, described Shelley as a divine "seer," the very model of the subjective poet who finds in his heart the Platonic Ideas, the man of unimpeachable moral purity (Browning was greatly shaken when he subsequently heard the story of Shelley's treatment of Harriet Westbrook), the youthful idealist whose sympathy for suffering mankind was such that "had [he] lived he would have finally ranged himself with the Christians."[54]

Eliot's fondness for Shelley was devoid of what she laughingly called "the imbecility of that pious dictum—that if Shelley had lived till now he would have been a Christian." Lewes, to be sure, had characterized Shelley as a preeminently "religious" poet—Cross would similarly later speak of Eliot's "religious mind"—but his was a religion not in the narrow, ego-gratifying guise that Eliot found so reprehensible in Protestantism, but a religion in the service of humanity.[55] The sight of "dear Shelley's tomb" in Rome consoled Eliot with the thought that "he is at rest, where no hatred can ever reach him again." Having just completed *The Mill on the Floss*, in which her martyr-heroine seems better off dead than being subjected to more of the environmental and genetic factors operating against her in St. Ogg's, Eliot could not fail to be moved by Shelley's attitude in the face of repeated adversity. For Shelley, indeed, it was the poet's responsibility to redeem "from decay the visitations of the divinity in man"; by reflecting a higher sphere of actuality than mere external reality in his work, the poet "defeats the curse which binds us to be subjected to the accident of surrounding impressions."[56] Shelley's existence was proof that idealism could arise on English soil, that an English writer could strive to combat the mood of despair in his time (as Shelley declares in the Preface to *The Revolt of Islam*) by "kindling within the bosoms of [his] readers a virtuous enthusiasm for those doctrines of liberty and justice, that faith and hope in something good, which neither violence nor misrepresentation nor prejudice can ever totally extinguish among mankind." Neither Shelley's belief in Necessity nor Eliot's acceptance of the law of consequences could destroy their idealism where the future was concerned. In her last novel, *Daniel Deronda,* Eliot allowed her hero's Shelleyan idealism to bear fruit. It is fitting that Deronda should be introduced to "The Philosophers" club at the Hand and Banner (where he will learn much of significance for his future) at precisely the moment that *Prometheus Unbound* is being recited. He enters just in time to hear Shelley's metaphor of the avalanche, which is applied in Deronda's case to the regeneration of Judaism under his leadership: "As thought by thought is piled, till some great truth / Is loosened, and the nations echo round."[57]

That Eliot's appreciation for Shelley intensified with her love for Lewes can be seen if one regards Dorothea Brooke and Will Ladislaw as the youthful embodiments of Eliot in her Schiller phase, yearning after "some lofty conception of the world which might frankly include the parish of Tipton and her own rule of conduct there," and Lewes in his "learned savage" phase, when he impressed and shocked Elizabeth Lynn Linton with his charm, audacity, and shamelessness. ("Frankly sensual, frankly self-indulgent and enjoying," she recalled, "he was the born Epicurean—the natural Hedonist.")[58] Young Lewes was a free-thinker and a self-styled martyr, who was drawn to Spinoza (as he admitted) out of "rebellious sympathy with all outcasts," and who found in Shelley an "angel-martyr" who, in contrast to the other major English Romantic poets, had offered the only viable "Gospel" for the nineteenth century: belief in "progression, humanity, perfectibility, civilization, democracy." As a friend of Leigh Hunt, who fanned his Shelleyan ardor, Lewes helped to perpetuate the Shelley myth in his 1841 essay for the *Westminster Review;* and a year later, in an article on "Hegel's Aesthetics," he demonstrated appreciation for the German Romantic conception of the poet as seer, whose work makes its effect on the reader by reproducing the poet's own sensibility, not by imitating reality as Aristotle had assumed. "Poetry," he claimed, "is *substitutive* and suggestive, not imitative," making an effect with *"words, not images."* This very Romantic sense of the power of the poet over the reader and over the age he lives in led Lewes to attack the regressive or passive roles played by Scott (for harkening back to "the dead spirit of chivalry"), Wordsworth (for abandoning his liberal ideals in favor of "an impossible state of country life or nature"), Coleridge (for "dreaming in the slumbers of the past, but unsettled, remote, altogether vague and intangible"), and Byron (for accurately reflecting the "unbelief" of the age but withdrawing into a life of gloomy self-abandon). Meanwhile, under the guidance of views on love and marriage right out of *Queen Mab*, Lewes and his young bride Agnes began to practice the contempt for marital fidelity which would, in the end, render impossible a legal marriage with George Eliot.[59]

When Lewes and Eliot were introduced, he had already separated from his wife, who continued to bear children to Leigh Hunt's son Thornton. Lewes's "learned savage" phase was behind him, and under Eliot's influence this charming Ladislaw-like figure of "heart and conscience [as she soon discovered] wearing a mask of flippancy" turned to the biography of Goethe and the scientific studies on which his modern reputation rests. Eliot herself had passed through a Shelleyan phase, acting as the apostle of free intellectual inquiry to John and Mary Sibree, deploring, in Shelleyan manner, the "diabolical [marriage] law" endorsed by Charlotte Brontë in *Jane Eyre* "which chains a man soul and body to a putrefying carcase," and yearning to "be doing some little toward the regeneration of this groaning travailing creation."[60] The happiness of their years together need not blind us to the many fundamental differences of outlook between Eliot and Lewes. She loved Wordsworth and preferred the country to the city, while he had assailed *The Prelude* for "the wretched absurdity" of its view that "man, to keep himself pure and pious, should shun cities and the haunts of men, to shut himself in mountain solitudes." Eliot clung to a romantic sense of the past, while Lewes sneered at the "Romanticist" as "one who, in literature, in the arts, in religion, or in politics, endeavours to revive the dead past."[61] Theirs was not so much a union of empiricist and idealist, realist and romantic, as a marriage of complementary forms of Romanticism: his idols were Goethe and Shelley, clear-eyed prophets and energetic amateur scientists; hers were Schiller, Rousseau, and Wordsworth, dreamy enthusiasts and ardent apostles of culture through the education of the feelings. When she drew herself and Lewes as Dorothea and Ladislaw, she had attained a knowledge of self and society unsurpassed among English novelists; and in that marvelous anatomy of Romanticism which exists in *Middlemarch*, the marriage of Shelleyan and Schilleresque characters symbolizes the triumph of the Romantic legacy.

ROMANTIC APPLICATIONS

Immersed in the Romantic tradition, George Eliot brought to the novel a sense of high seriousness that had hitherto been associated with Romantic poetry. For the first time in England, the writing of novels was seen as a "vocation" rather than a craft, while the novelist's role became that of a seer rather than a propagandist or an entertainer. Eliot's sense of the creative process, as well as of artistic responsibility, is thoroughly Romantic. Explaining her difficulty with the writing of *Romola*, Eliot contended that "great, great facts have struggled to find a voice through me, and have only been able to speak brokenly." This recalls Shelley's description of the creative mind as "a fading coal, which some invisible influence, like an inconstant wind, awakens to transitory brightness" and which begins to fade once the poet actually begins to write. To J. W. Cross, Eliot declared that "in all that she considered her best writing, there was a 'not herself' which took possession of her, and that she felt her own personality to be merely the instrument through which this spirit, as it were, was acting."[62] She had criticized Charles Reade for lacking this quality—the being "possessed" by a power that thereby enables the writer to possess his reader—which she defined as "genius."

In her correspondence with her publisher, John Blackwood, Eliot repeatedly refused to make changes in her work if that meant violating the sacred source of her creative energies. The novelist who preached the need for compromise to her characters and readers refused to budge whenever Blackwood indicated, for example, that she had disobeyed her realistic canons by resorting to melodramatic scenes and gestures. "I am unable to change anything," was the invariable response. Even as she recognized that fiction could not carry its proper moral weight unless it aroused readers' sympathies toward real individuals with real sorrows, Eliot nonetheless would not violate what her imagination *saw* and her emotions *felt* to be true.[63] The standards were subjective, but subjective in the Romantic sense whereby the artist reflected a higher and more extensive truth in himself than that which he found outside himself. Eliot was indignant when Dinah Morris's sermons and the characters in *Adam Bede* were thought to be reproductions of actual speeches and individuals: the reality expressed in that novel, she protested, was the "truth in art," not the truth of verisimilitude. While writing *Romola*, Eliot confided to Blackwood that "the real" could not be achieved in fiction without the "greater quality" of imagination. "Any real observation of life and character must be limited, and [so] the imagination must fill in and give life to the picture."[64]

For Eliot the novelist was thus a mirror *and* a lamp, committed to reality but compelled to satisfy the internal compulsion of the imagination. The realistic standards that Eliot demanded that the reader of her first published works of fiction, the *Scenes of Clerical Life* (1857) and *Adam Bede* (1859), accept need not be taken, therefore, as her only views on the subject.[65] As is invariably the case when she adopts a hectoring tone—for example, toward the reader who might not extend sympathy to Dinah Morris, accustomed instead "to weep over the loftier sorrows of heroines in satin boots and crinoline, and of heroes riding fiery horses, themselves ridden by still more fiery passions"—Eliot is criticizing in exaggerated form her own propensities or reflecting on the sins of her youth. In her novels the romantic element survives, even though it is sometimes disguised in modest trappings. On the eve of creating her first work of fiction, Eliot expressed an anxious desire "to know the names of things." (She was on vacation with Lewes, who was collecting information for his projected book *Sea-side Studies*.) "The desire," she added, "is part of the tendency that is now constantly growing in me to escape from all vagueness and inaccuracy into the daylight of distinct, vivid ideas." Realism, as expressed here and in her first fictions, was a form of self-therapy; but despite her applause for the "brave clearness and honesty" that she saw three years later demonstrated in the realistic data collected in Darwin's *Origin of Species*, she persisted in being more interested in "the mystery that lies under the processes" of evolution.[66] The "mystery" is not opposed to reality; rather, reality is part of the mystery.

The three *Scenes of Clerical Life* were undertaken in the spirit of "clearness and honesty," a conscious attempt (as has often been pointed out) to imitate the "programme" of Wordsworth's Preface to *Lyrical Ballads* and show the humble side of human creation speaking in its own, poetically unadorned voice.[67] The characters are meant to be so "palpably and unmistakably commonplace" as to serve as a cathartic dose of reality to the reader accustomed to dine on romance.[68] For all that, the painful self-consciousness with which Eliot lectures her readers on the need for sympathy suggests that she is not entirely convinced of her own words. "I wish to stir your sympathy with commonplace troubles," she intones, in so salubrious a manner that one secretly wishes that she will make our flesh creep instead. "Depend upon it," she declares, managing to patronize reader and characters in the same breath, "you would gain unspeakably if you would learn with me to see some of the poetry and the pathos, the tragedy and the comedy, lying in the experience of a human soul that looks out through dull grey eyes, and that speaks in a voice of quite ordinary tone" (I, 94, 67).

Despite her pronouncements to the contrary, the staples of romance abound in the *Scenes* in the form of angelic martyrs, noble and ignoble sinners, and melodramatic events—and romanticism itself emerges in the author's need to construct ideals and ideal figures who can transform, or transcend, the texture of reality. Each of the stories contains a type of idealized character who reappears in much of Eliot's later work. Amos Barton, "unmistakably commonplace" though he is, is allowed "a large, fair, gentle Madonna" (I, 24) for his wife, a figure of loving devotion, oblivious to his neglect of her. Eliot's predisposition toward such self-denying women was to color her attitude toward women's rights: although she expressed concern in later years that "we women are always in danger of living too exclusively in the affections"—to the point where they threaten to become models of "dog-like attachment"—she specifically exempted "married constancy" from the alternative proposed for women, that of the chance to have a "share of the more independent life." Like Mrs. Garth in *Middlemarch*, Eliot was "apt to be a little severe towards her own sex, which in her opinion was framed to be entirely subordinate."[69]

Milly Barton's alter ego is Caterina Sarti in "Mr. Gilfil's Love-Story," who embodies what Eliot saw as distinctly *feminine* "criminal impulses." A musician of Italian origin, she is the first of Eliot's romantically colored aliens, a victim of her Mediterranean-inspired passions and of Eliot's belief in racial determinism. The scene in which Caterina rushes with a dagger toward the man who has trifled with her affections reveals a melodramatic streak in Eliot which the novelist insisted to Blackwood was true to life.[70] Something in Eliot's nature made her underscore, in novel after novel, a willful streak in her female characters that leads them to commit or nearly to commit murder in one form or another: there are murderers in deed, like Hetty Sorrel in *Adam Bede* and Madame Laure in *Middlemarch*; thwarted would-be murderers, like Bertha Latimer in "The Lifted Veil" and Gwendolen Harleth in *Daniel Deronda* (who like Caterina carries a dagger); unintending accomplices in their husbands' deaths, like Dorothea Brooke (whose championing of Will Ladislaw's claim brings on Casaubon's first heart attack) and Romola (who gives Baldassarre alms which he uses to buy a knife); and quasi-murderers, like Rosamond Vincy (whose willfulness in going horseback riding brings on a miscarriage, and who later serves as Lydgate's "basil plant"). A terror of some demonic presence within her, abetted by the Evangelical mistrust of the will, drove her to the repeated use of melodrama in order to articulate that dread in her fiction: the "wilful sin" that Dinah Morris attempts to exorcise from Hetty Sorrel is another name for what Eliot feared as the sinful *will*.

The third, and most important, of the characters in the *Scenes*, in terms of Eliot's later romantic development, is the Evangelical minister Tryan in "Janet's Repentance." Tryan is the first of Eliot's magnetic figures who calm those in emotional distress—in this case curing Janet Dempster of her alcoholism—by the very force of personality. Tryan is provided with a lurid past history, ostensibly so that Eliot can enunciate the Feuerbachian theme of the companionship of suffering, but perhaps more likely because of the operatic appeal of the noble sinner.[71] De-

spite Eliot's intention in the first of the *Scenes*, "Amos Barton,"
to accommodate the reader to everyday reality, by the third
story she was only too willing to find some means for her heroine
to soar above what U. C. Knoepflmacher calls "the imperfect and
erratic universe to which [the novelist] had been forced to
consign her idealism." Eliot began the *Scenes of Clerical Life*
intending to argue to her readers, as she often argued to herself,
the need to face life honestly and without the opiate of illusion;
but her endorsement of Tryan's Evangelicalism, not to mention
her resorting to Tryan's mesmeric personality, is proof that to
Eliot illusions are necessary too so long as they allow one to
subordinate self and rise "to a higher order of experience" (II,
163). In the *Impressions of Theophrastus Such*, Eliot defended
the retention of illusions on the ground that "they feed the ideal
Better, and in loving them still, we strengthen the precious habit
of loving something not visibly, tangibly existent, but a spiritual
product of our visible, tangible selves." Even so, it would not be
entirely unfair to Eliot to say that the finest of the *Scenes of
Clerical Life* is about a woman whose craving for alcoholic
stimulants is subdued by a spiritual opiate.[72]

The vast increase in creative authority that separates *Adam
Bede* from the *Scenes of Clerical Life* does not quite conceal the
unresolved split in George Eliot's nature between the desire
for honesty and clarity and the need for ideals, or even illusions.
By resorting to the Loamshire countryside as background for her
novel, Eliot drew reassurance from the Wordsworthian conception of nature and the Schilleresque idea of the idyll: here, at
least, was a refuge from the ugliness and moral confusion of
urban life. The appeal of Methodism, as Dinah Morris admits, is
strongest in industrial centers like Leeds, where the soul is "hungry" and the body "ill at ease" among "those high-walled streets,
where you seem to walk as in a prison-yard" (p. 80). In *North
and South* Elizabeth Gaskell came out on the side of the energy
and potential for heroic will in the northern industrial towns
and warned against the stultifying influence of rural life. Eliot,
by contrast, idealizes country life for its stoic and quiescent
attitudes; the offenders in her pastoral idyll are those who dream
of a more headstrong alternative to the submissive ethic decreed
alike by the Wordsworthian position and the scientific facts of

life. Whether grounded in Dinah Morris's religion based on feelings, in Adam Bede's reliance on the work ethic, or in Martin Poyser's devotion to his native roots, the theme in *Adam Bede* is the necessity for the subordination of the will. Survival itself is connected with staying in one's proper place: as Martin Poyser remarks, fearful of the prospect of moving from his farm, "We should leave our roots behind us, I doubt, and niver thrive again" (p. 294).

Comparing the Evangelicalism preached by Tryan in "Janet's Repentance" with the Methodism expounded by Dinah Morris, one notes that while in "Janet's Repentance" religion provides a numbing of the heart's anguish, in *Adam Bede* it produces an excitation of the heart's feelings. Up to a point Methodism speaks for the Romantic faith in feelings. Indeed, in Dinah Morris, Methodism seems a surrogate for Romanticism itself. In the manner of a Romantic "genius" (as Eliot defines the word in her comments on Reade), Dinah possesses others by being herself possessed: when she delivers her outdoor sermon, Eliot writes, "she was not preaching as she heard others preach, but speaking directly from her own emotions, and under the inspiration of her own simple faith"; the effect she makes on others is not through the message she delivers but through the "electric thrill" (to borrow Eliot's phrase when describing the effect of Rousseau) of Dinah's "sincere unpremeditated eloquence" (pp. 25, 29).[73] It is this intense commitment to the power of fellow feeling that enables Dinah to break through to the unfeeling Hetty Sorrel after Hetty has been convicted of murdering her infant child. Dinah's and Hetty's mutual shedding of tears works a Rousseauesque magic which no rational logic can account for; Eliot has dehumanized Hetty too thoroughly in the course of her narrative to allow us to accept her tearful confession as anything other than a quasi-religious miracle. That one need not be a Methodist—or, indeed, religious in any denominational sense— is made clear in Adam Bede's similar equation of feelings with righteousness. "It isn't notions sets people doing the right thing," intones Adam—"it's feelings" (p. 154).

Adam is the prototypical Rousseau hero, a man opposed to reflection as at best a waste of time, one who acts according to the natural tendency toward goodness and obedience that his untutored feelings have guaranteed "Feeling's a sort o' knowledge," as Adam affirms (p. 425). When Arthur Donnithorne, the young country squire whom Adam reveres for his rank, compliments Adam on his aboriginal superiority—"I think your life has been a better school to you than college has been to me" (p. 143)—he is underscoring Eliot's comparison of her hero with the Noble Savage. But Adam is a domesticated version of Rousseau's mythic figure; and he is imbued with a native strength of character which allies him with the similar adaptation of Rousseau accomplished by Schiller in *Wilhelm Tell*. Eliot admitted that the confrontation scene in the Grove between Adam and Arthur, whom Adam has just witnessed kissing Hetty, "came to [her] as a *necessity*" while hearing Rossini's opera based on Schiller's play.[74] She was probably thinking of the climactic moment in *Wilhelm Tell* when Tell revenges himself upon the overbearing Gesler. In Schiller's play (and Rossini's opera), the Swiss tyrant who has disrupted Tell's domestic peace is murdered; in Eliot's novel, however, Adam immediately apologizes for having knocked down his once-beloved master. For where liberating action is the crux of a romantic play, stoical forbearance is the key to Eliot's novel, in which she allows her romantic sensibility to expand to a very small degree before it inevitably contracts. In this, she was following Wordsworth's lead: the Romantic will is absorbed by a principle of quiescence; and it is crucial for Eliot's Wordsworthian finale that her hero surrender his proud ways—what his mother, at the beginning of the book, calls his "peppery-like" self-righteousness (p. 16)—and that her heroine give up her preaching career in favor of married life with Adam. Along with Eliot's other stoic heroes, Caleb Garth and Felix Holt, Adam believes in the Carlylean gospel of work as a means of stifling sorrow or doubt: "there's nothing but what's bearable," he affirms, "as long as a man can work" (p. 99). But work, in the Eliot novels, is largely seen as a male prerogative.

The result of having one's feelings aroused, according to Eliot (as to Wordsworth before her), is that the individual will submit himself to the principles of rank, order, and control existent in nature. Eliot's epigraph to the novel, from *The Excursion*, emphasizes her agreement with Wordsworth's belief in lowly wisdom:

> So that ye may have
> Clear images before your gladdened eyes
> Of nature's unambitious underwood
> And flowers that prosper in the shade. And when
> I speak of such among the flock as swerved
> Or fell, those only shall be singled out
> Upon whose lapse, or error, something more
> Than brotherly forgiveness may attend.

She does not, however, carry out the intent, as promised in the quotation, of extending "brotherly forgiveness" to the offending Hetty Sorrel. Hetty's most unforgiveable offense is her refusal to submit to the idyllic way of life Eliot celebrates in the novel.[75] Unlike Gaskell's Ruth, who finds temporary refuge in the world of her imagination to console her for the misery of her daily life, Hetty seeks the "pleasant narcotic effect" of dreams and illusions out of ignorance that the real world is better than the vain luxuries of her imagination. Eliot's dissection of Hetty, which at times resembles the breaking of a butterfly on a wheel, betrays a sense of insecurity as to exactly how desirable or plausible the Loamshire way of life really is. For Hetty inhabits a world of nonhuman, or subhuman, volition into which all the supposedly consoling and restraining forces of nature and human idealism make no inroad.

Eliot's overzealous attempt to make Hetty appear the one alien figure in the novel—the single character denied the power to feel and hence the only person capable of committing a crime —has the reverse effect of making the reader wonder if Eliot is not disturbed by the possibility that Hetty's amoral willfulness is the rule and Adam's and Dinah's Wordsworthian submissiveness the exception.[76] There is no room for Hetty in a pastoral idyll built out of romantic wish-fulfillment, and so she must be made to seem unnaturally (or naturally?) hard-hearted; even her love for Arthur Donnithorne is without passion, since to Eliot's romantic mind passion was next to goodliness. (Because Arthur is capable of feeling and affection, he is capable of suffering and therefore reforming—and hence Eliot encourages us to sympathize with him.) Wordsworth, in "The Thorn," had depicted a child-murderer whose crime could be comprehended as an act of madness, a woman who had been jilted by her lover and whose intensity of grief could allow us to pity her. A soulless "water nixie" (p. 212) straight out of a German romance, Hetty must appear so repellently unhuman as to deny the reader the chance to feel sympathetic toward her, since sympathy for Hetty, paradoxically, would explode the moral basis of the book. Dinah Morris's exhortation to her audience to "tear off those follies!" (p. 28) is applied directly to Hetty's case; Hetty must be exorcised from the novel, for rather than being an individual possessed of folly, she is folly incarnate.

The need to tear away follies, to strip away illusions, to attain a sense of clarity and honesty and get back to the "truth of feeling" is undermined, however, by Eliot's equally strong sense of the need for illusions, for an assuring myth of the Loamshire countryside. According to the Romantic theory of perception, one's own personality is reflected in whatever one looks at, and one thus extracts a higher truth than the object in itself is capable of supplying. Like Wordsworth extracting from daisies and leech-gatherers comforting sermons, which are the reflection of his own feelings, Adam Bede is justified in idealizing Hetty even though she "really had nothing more than her beauty to recommend her" (p. 297). Such blindness to reality, Eliot affirms, is a proof of the nobility and beauty of Adam's illusions. "He called his love frankly a mystery . . . He only knew that the sight and memory of her moved him deeply, touching the spring of all love and tenderness, all faith and courage within him. How could he imagine narrowness, selfishness, hardness in her? He created the mind he believed in out of his own, which was large, unselfish, tender" (p. 298). Hetty's amoral existence apart from Adam's idealization of her is a proof that feeling is not necessarily knowledge, Adam's and Eliot's claims to the contrary. In *Adam Bede* Eliot wants her reader as well as her characters to see that life as it is is preferable to one's illusions, but she also endorses the need for illusions *lest* one see life as it really is. Yet the suspicion that Hetty's life may be closer to the order of nature than Adam's is the motivating force behind "The Lifted

Veil," the haunting parable of the need for illusions that Eliot wrote immediately after *Adam Bede*.

Where in *Adam Bede* Eliot sought, with qualified success, to express a Wordsworthian trust in nature and the efficacy of feeling, in "The Lifted Veil" (1859) she reverted to Rousseau's *Confessions* to show the fate of a more highly developed character than her Loamshire workman, a character living in a world where evil is the rule rather than the exception. Latimer, her protagonist and narrator, relates his past history in the form of confessions that are to be published after his death. Like Rousseau, he has been granted an "early sensibility to Nature," as well as a sensitivity too high-strung and self-centered to allow him "to trust much in the sympathy of [his] fellow-men."[77] Rousseau, speaking of his imaginative powers which compensated him for all that he had been denied, noted sadly that his youthful "love for imaginary objects and my facility in lending myself to them ended by disillusioning me with everything around me, and determined that love of solitude which I have retained ever since that time." Of Latimer and also of Maggie Tulliver, the heroine Eliot would create soon after writing "The Lifted Veil," it can be said that their hypersensitivity and romantic imaginations effectively deprive them of happiness in life; both are cut off from a world that is unloving, uncomprehending, and on occasion actively malign. Rousseau's pattern of development from trusting idealism to paranoia and misanthropy is duplicated by Latimer, who describes how as a student in Rousseau's native Geneva he copied Rousseau's example of seeking happiness by lying in a boat and letting it drift aimlessly on the water (pp. 284–285).[78] Eliot would reassert her Rousseauesque trust in nature in *Romola*, as evidenced in the great scene when the heroine of that novel entrusts her life to a boat drifting down the Arno. Before she could write *Romola*, however, she needed the experience of writing *Silas Marner*, in which her sense of trust was reconstructed, in order to counteract the negative implications of "The Lifted Veil" and *The Mill on the Floss*.

For the mood of her story, Eliot drew upon the gloomy fatalism of German romance, which was to exert considerable influence on the English "sensation" novels of the 1860s. "In the tragedy of fate," as René Wellek observes, "the German Romantics found a peculiar form for what is, it seems, the basic outlook on life, the attitude, the 'vision' of the German Romantics—their feeling for the uncanny, the menace, the sense of evil lurking behind the facade of the world."[79] English Romanticism, by contrast, is basically optimistic, expressing a faith in nature and the imagination, as in Wordsworth's case, in the values of love and hope, as with Shelley, or in the affirming powers of artistic instinct, as with Shelley's disciple Browning. The artist-heroes in Browning's poems have an intuitive grasp of life: "This world's no blot for us, / Nor blank," as Browning's Fra Lippo Lippi contends; "it means intensely, and means good." Although not a poet himself, Latimer is given the very poetic gift of insight and prophesy that seemed to Shelley and his admirers to point up the poet's divine nature, but which here proves to be a curse. Latimer likens his ability to have visions of the future and to read the minds of others to "a preternaturally heightened sense of hearing, making audible to one a roar of sound where others find perfect stillness" (p. 301). Eliot was to echo these words in the great passage in *Middlemarch* that she concludes by saying that luckily "the quickest of us walk about well wadded with stupidity." To hear the "roar which lies on the other side of silence" is the Romantic author's prerogative—and burden; and in one sense, the story reflects the Romantic theory of the creative process. But "The Lifted Veil" is also, as U. C. Knoepflmacher has admirably shown, an indication of Eliot's sense of the horror of reality, a proof that like Conrad's Marlow she had allowed herself to descend into the abyss of human nature and return to describe the "horror" of it.[80]

Eliot initially described "The Lifted Veil" as a "jeu de melancolie"; and her publisher, wondering what Bulwer Lytton (who was knowledgeable about German literature) would think of it, saw in the tale a reflection of the months of annoyance she had experienced while the authorship of *Adam Bede* was being assigned to other hands. Nearly a decade and a half later, the self-assured author of *Middlemarch* was to reinterpret her story as revealing Latimer's deficient powers of sympathy.[81] If one were to support Eliot's later reading, however, one would be obliged to conclude that the theme of "The Lifted Veil" is a defense of illusions that are palpably false. Latimer's ability to read the minds of his fellow men supports Eliot's basic theme that we are all egoists, but not Eliot's Romantic faith in the human capacity for being educated into an awareness of the needs of others. Under the "rational talk, the graceful attentions, the wittily-turned phrases, and the kindly deeds" of the people he meets, Latimer discerns with "microscopic vision" a view of human nature incapable of reformation: he sees "all the suppressed egoism, all the struggling chaos of puerilities, meanness, vague capricious memories, and indolent make-shift thoughts, from which human words and deeds emerge like leaflets covering a fermenting heap" (p. 295). If the Shelleyan consolation of hope is ruled out (Latimer describes himself as "without delusions and without hope"; p. 277), the saving value of love also proves ineffectual. Latimer's mistrustfulness toward human nature is temporarily put aside when he falls in love with Bertha, a "pale, fatal-eyed woman" who reminds him of the "Water-Nixie . . . of German lyrics" (p. 291). But after they are married, the one person whose mind Latimer has not been able to read—and hence, the one person who has been able to provide him with an illusion of love—is revealed to be a shallow, selfish individual who is plotting her husband's death. Latimer's vision of his own death, hastened by the indifference and neglect of his servants, which opens the story, reveals all too clearly how little reason there is for people to trust in others. Anna Karenina has a similarly nihilistic vision just before she kills herself, but Tolstoy allows us to believe that there are extenuating psychological reasons for Anna's views. In "The Lifted Veil" Eliot permits no such consoling thought, confirming instead the fatalism of German romance and the misanthropic position of Rousseau.

In *The Mill on the Floss* (1860) George Eliot's Wordsworthian and Rousseauesque affinities clash head on: faith in one's ties to the past contends with the hunger of the imagination; the values of childhood are opposed to the needs of passionate feeling. Eliot's heroine, Maggie Tulliver, has the "hunger of the heart"[82] and the hypersensitivity of a Rousseau protagonist (not to mention Rousseau and the young Eliot herself), but she finds herself in an unromantic and uncomforting world very different from that which she "fashioned . . . afresh in her own thoughts . . . The world outside the books was not a happy one, Maggie felt: it seemed to be a world where people behaved the best to those they did not pretend to love, and that did not belong to them. And if life had no love in it, what else was there for Maggie?" (pp. 207–208). Maggie possesses that mixture of narcissim and idealism which makes Rousseau so alternately perplexing and appealing a figure; and even as Eliot implies that Maggie's craving for fulfillment is doomed, she makes us sympathize with her heroine's yearning for a means to transcend the unattractive reality of St. Ogg's. Eliot superbly delineates both the needs of Maggie's ardent inner nature and the outer world of "oppressive narrowness" that constrains her. Like one of Schiller's frustrated heroes, large-souled but doomed to live among petty natures, Maggie is consigned to the world of the "emmet-like Dodsons and Tullivers," whose "sordid-life" is "irradiated by no sublime principles, no romantic visions, no active, self-renouncing faith—moved by none of those wild, uncontrollable passions which create the dark shadows of misery and crime— without that primitive rough simplicity of wants, that hard submissive ill-paid toil, that childish spelling-out of what nature has written, which gives its poetry to peasant life" (p. 238). The tone of this passage (even with Eliot's reference to the "uncontrollable" aspect of romanticism) is very different from Eliot's defense of realism in *Adam Bede* and the *Scenes of Clerical Life;* the romanticism lacking in St. Ogg's is not a meretricious concern with fancy dress and bogus passions but the Romanticism of Schiller, Rousseau, and Wordsworth. Whereas virtually all the major figures in *Adam Bede,* aside from Hetty Sorrel, exemplify Wordsworthian principles, Eliot's Wordsworthian sensibility, which directs, and finally mars, the development of *The Mill on the Floss,* makes an appeal that in this novel only Maggie Tulliver can respond to.

It is noteworthy that Maggie's beloved brother Tom is unaffected by her Wordsworthian attachment to the poetry of earth and the past. He lacks the affection for the daisied fields and "capricious hedgerows" that constitute "the mother tongue of our imagination," transforming the delighted perception of childhood into love (pp. 37–38); that spirtualized devotion to the scenes of one's youth which acts as a moral restraint against ambition when one enters the world of "getting and spending." "Heaven knows where that [ambitious] striving might lead us," Eliot declares, "if our affections had not a trick of twining round those old inferior things [dear to us in our childhood]—if the loves and sanctities of our life had no deep immovable roots in memory" (p. 135).[83] Tom has something of the stoical Wordsworthian commitment to duty; but his actions are directed by the Dodson family attachment to things rather than sentiments, by a sense of honor that concerns itself with financial rather than emotional debts. Tom Tulliver's inability to share or comprehend his sister's imaginative nature allows him to work steadily at his goals without qualms of indecision or delusions of grandeur. Eliot delineates Tom's character so painstakingly— and with genuine admiration for his practicality and rectitude of conduct—that we are allowed to see exactly how pathetically false is Maggie's image of him. For Maggie the protective brother of her emotional needs is turned into an icon that she confuses with the reality: when Maggie recalls the happy "days [when] Tom was good to me" (p. 294) and speaks of her devotion to her earliest memory, "standing with Tom by the side of the Floss, while he held my hand" (p. 268), she is respecting the Wordsworthian faith in memory in a manner that keeps her from either action or clear vision.

Despite the theatricality of the language (Maggie has been chief actress in her fantasies for so long that, as Eliot later says of the Princess in *Daniel Deronda*, she tends to "act her own emotions" at times), Maggie has one powerful moment of truth when she compares her innocent wrongdoing to the narrowness of mind that prevents Tom from seeing "that there is anything better than [his] own conduct and [his] own petty aims." In doing "wrong"—such as befriending Philip Wakem, son of the Tullivers' archenemy—Maggie admits to having exhibited "feelings that [Tom] would be the better for"; and she reproaches him for his lack of pity, recognizing at last that he has "always enjoyed punishing me—you have always been hard and cruel to me" (p. 304). But the intrusion of realism into Maggie's romantic view of Tom and herself cannot last for long; and Eliot resorts to the melodramatic stratagem of exhibiting, a few pages later, their father's deathbed scene so that Book Two of the novel can end with the image of brother and sister weeping and clinging together. Whereas she differentiates between Hetty Sorrel's hard nature and Adam Bede's mistaken, if noble, idealization of her, Eliot is determined to force Tom to live up to Maggie's idealization of him at the expense of the reader's credulity and Eliot's own painstakingly realistic portrait of Tom.

Although *The Mill on the Floss* is often taken to be two novels inexpertly joined together, the one dealing brilliantly with Maggie's and Tom's childhood experiences, the other too hastily with their adult positions, the book is in fact carefully divided into three parts: the early childhood scenes, which end with the Tulliver financial collapse;[84] the episodes of youth and growing estrangement between brother and sister, which end with the deathbed reconciliation; and the sequence dealing with young adulthood, in which brother and sister show to what ends their practical versus emotional trainings have been heading. Charles Bray's *The Education of the Feelings*, which Eliot much admired, might be cited here for having contributed something to the development patterns of brother and sister. Bray advocates the educating of the feelings in children so that they will learn in time to choose to act in behalf of others, rather than out of selfish motives. He warns, for example, against the acquisitive nature of boys who are "brought up to consider the acquirement of property as almost the chief end and aim of their existence"; but he also deplores the manner in which children's imaginations are corrupted by works of fiction that make them entertain "false expectations" of what life has to offer.[85] In *The Mill on the Floss* Maggie develops in the way advocated by Bray—proving that she has rejected the romantic fantasies of her youth when she rejects Stephen Guest's proposal in Book Three—but there is no corresponding development in Tom. Instead, he represents the acquisitive nature of the Dodsons, albeit in its finest form. Eliot's sense of psychological and social reality decreed that she show brother and sister developing away from each other, but her romantic sensibility decreed that they be reunited in the face of that reality. Each of the three books ends with brother and sister clasping each other in a Rousseauesque communion of grief; but preceding that sentimental scene in every case is an account of the unhappiness Maggie suffers at Tom's hands.

One way to explain the unresolvable division that runs through the novel is to say that while Eliot analyzes life from a realistic-scientific point of view, she puts her materials together with an artistic-romantic desire to transcend that reality.[86] The presiding myth of Eliot's novel concerns the patron saint of St. Ogg's, the boatman who rows a woman and child (who turn out to be the Madonna and Child) across the turbulent river Floss with the explanation, "it is enough that thy heart needs it" (pp. 104–105). That each of the three books of *The Mill on the Floss* ends with brother and sister reunited testifies to the victory of heart's need over reality. But it is not enough to say that romantic values triumph in the end; Eliot's Romanticism was also split between the Wordsworthian desire to freeze Maggie in a posture of reverent quiescence and the Rousseauesque wish to see her accomplish her heart's need in a more dynamic manner. Maggie's romantic dualism persists throughout the novel: on the one side is her willfulness, her habit of rushing "to her deeds with passionate impulse"; on the other are the force of her imagination, which makes her see the "consequences" of her acts in exaggerated detail (p. 58), and the force of her emotional hunger, which makes her fear her own nature lest she lose the love of those around her. As Maggie develops and her sense of the need to restrain herself intensifies, so too does the willfulness, expressing itself in occasional outbursts of "anger and hatred towards her father and mother, who were so unlike what she would have them to be—towards Tom, who checked her, and met her thought or feeling always by some thwarting difference." To her horror, Maggie finds herself growing akin to one of the Byronic rebels she once enjoyed reading about; the fits of anger "flow out over her affections and conscience like a lava stream, and frighten her with a sense that it was not difficult for her to become a demon" (p. 252). Unable to direct that ardor to any constructive use, Maggie determines to hide it under what Philip Wakem calls a "veil of dull quiescence"; but, as he wisely cautions her, there is no "safety in negations. No character becomes strong in that way. You will be thrown into the world some day, and then every rational satisfaction of your nature that you deny now, will assault you like a savage appetite" (p. 288).

The flaw in the moral climax of the novel, Maggie's rejection of Stephen Guest, is, as many critics have pointed out, the abstract quality of Maggie's argument in favor of the "sacred ties" (p. 417) that bind her to the past.[87] It is one thing to praise, as Eliot did in an 1855 essay, the "beauty and heroism of renunciation," but to situate such heroic renunciation in St. Ogg's is both dishonest and absurd.[88] Neither Stephen nor Maggie is formally engaged to anyone else, and Stephen, in beseeching her to marry him, argues both the Shelleyan position that it is wrong to others as well as to oneself to marry where there is no love and Rousseau's position that the dictates of love preclude all social obstacles because such love is a virtuous expression of the purity and truth of feeling. The passive abandonment to feeling typified by Rousseau's drifting on the lake is repeated in *The Mill on the Floss* when Maggie allows herself to drift down the river Floss with Stephen. Drift involves movement as well as emotional satisfaction, however, and Eliot wishes to freeze her heroine in place. Eliot's instinctive terror of the self forces Maggie to invoke duty and renunciation and the ties of the past as deterrents to the claims of impulse; but the sense of duty and renunciation works only on the private stage of Eliot's and Maggie's saintly histrionics, and the devotion to the ties of the past is a devotion to a myth of the past that Maggie has created in defiance of reality. Eliot's choice of Wordsworthian myth over both reality and Rousseauesque Romanticism is a prelude to the final reconciliation between brother and sister, united "in an embrace never to be parted," once again living the days (never glimpsed in the novel and perhaps never having existed outside of Maggie's imagination) "when they had clasped their little hands in love, and roamed the daisied fields together" (p. 456).

This freezing of action into a permanent reconciliation scene provides a sentimental satisfaction of sorts. However, Eliot's determination in *Romola,* the novel that was intended to follow

The Mill on the Floss, to provide an exalted role for a Maggie Tulliver-like heroine indicates that she could not accept Maggie's death as the only solution to her heroine's and her own divided loyalties. But before she could write *Romola*, Eliot needed to reaffirm her faith in both the internal world of feelings and the external world of fact. It was with the writing of *Silas Marner* (1861) that she recaptured her trust in the romantic sensibilities that sustain rather than inhibit life. Taking her epigraph from Wordsworth's "Michael" ("A child, more than all gifts / That earth can offer to declining man, / Brings hope with it, and forward-looking thoughts"), Eliot doubted that anyone but herself would be interested in its subject matter "since William Wordsworth is dead."[89] However, *Silas Marner* is a hopeful companion to Wordsworth's tragic tale. In the poem, an aged sheepfarmer loses his son to the corrupting forces of city life; in the novel, a weaver disillusioned by the hypocrisy and deceit that flourish in the city renews his faith in life when he moves to the country and adopts a young girl. Where Maggie Tulliver had sought refuge in a dubious myth of the past, Silas Marner learns to find trust in the timeless, idyllic world of Raveloe. Maggie and Silas are both romantic aliens, but where Maggie's romantic feelings make her an outcast in St. Ogg's, Silas is integrated into the Raveloe community at precisely the moment when his feelings are reawakened.

The optimistic format of the story derives less from Wordsworth than from Schiller's concept of the idyll. Schiller defined sentimental (as distinct from naive) poetry as the idealistic yearning after a seemingly lost or unobtainable world: but whereas in satire and elegy the poet reveals the distance between the ideal world desired by the individual and the debased society he inhabits, in the idyll he projects a vision of the integration of the individual with society, "a free uniting of inclination with the law, of a nature illuminated by the highest moral dignity, briefly, none other than the ideal of beauty applied to actual life." Only in the idyll is it possible to reconcile "*all opposition between actuality and the ideal*" and "therewith all conflict in the feelings likewise." The goal of the idyll is "calm," according to Schiller, but calm is derived not, as in Wordsworth, by the numbing of one's impulse but rather by the "balance" achieved between aspiring individual energies and the soothing influence of a humane community. The very writing of the idyll, thus, implies "hope . . . and forward-looking thoughts" on the part of the writer.[90]

As a young man whose best friend has caused him to appear a thief, and hence to be shunned by the Dissenting congregation he belongs to and forsaken by his fiancée, Silas Marner has as much reason as Latimer in "The Lifted Veil" to believe that "there is no religion possible, no worship but a worship of devils" (p. 330). The injured young man believes that "there is no just God that governs the earth righteously, but a God of lies, that bears witness against the innocent."[91] For George Eliot, however, there is no divinity distinct from the human community, and Silas's reawakening comes two decades later when a child wanders into the cottage where he lives his outcast existence and redirects his attention from material to spiritualized human values. If feeling is to be the key to Silas's conversion, the agent of that feeling is the child of Romantic lore. As Schiller proclaimed of this veneration for childhood values, "We are touched not because we look down upon the child from the height of our strength and perfection, but rather because we *look upward* from the *limitation* of our condition, which is inseparable from the *determination* which we have attained, to the unlimited *determinacy* of the child and to its pure innocence." Where wisdom and worldly experience teach mistrust and self-mistrust, childhood innocence is the perfection of trust and reverence. In her early essay "The Wisdom of the Child," Eliot echoes Schiller's (and Rousseau's) position in a manner that points toward *Silas Marner:*

> A truce to your philosophers whose elevation above their fellow-beings consists in their ability to laugh at the ties which bind women and children, who have looked just so far into the principles of ethics as to be able to disconcert a simple soul that talks of vice and virtue as realities. The child which abstains from eating plums, because grandmamma forbade, is their superior in wisdom; it exercises faith and obedience to law—two of the most ennobling attributes of humanity, which these philosophers have cast off . . . Self-renunciation, submission to law, trust, be-

nignity, ingenuousness, rectitude,—these are the qualities we delight most to witness in the child, and these are the qualities which most dignify the man.

Innocence, trust, and a sense of "unlimited determinacy" dependent on faith in forces that he obeys without needing to understand are attained by Silas through his adopted daughter's influence.[92]

In the early essay Eliot paid homage to Rousseau and Wordsworth; and in *Silas Marner*, after her unsuccessful attempts to disguise or suppress the Romantic impulse behind her first creative works, Eliot at last found the means to imbue her subject with Romantic hopefulness without being markedly unfaithful to realism. Beginning with *Romola* the message for the novelist and her romantic-minded heroes and heroines alike is Dolly Winthrop's words of comfort to Silas, "all as we've got to do is to trusten" (p. 217). The purest, if perhaps most ingenuous, examples of trust rewarded in her work are *Silas Marner* and the poem "How Lisa Loved the King" (1869). Eliot's intention is very clearly to integrate character and society (as in a Schiller idyll) so that instead of the latter contaminating the former, the former will enrich the latter. But while the Romantic mission intensified—and the role of Eliot's chosen protagonists clearly reflects the role she had adopted for herself—the awareness that the inhibiting factors of life are often fatal to idealism deepened. From *Romola* (1862–63) to *Daniel Deronda*, the novels are set in more complex environments than Loamshire or St. Ogg's or Raveloe and in times of transition and social stress, with the result that the members of her romantic elite have the opportunity to become modest (and not so modest, in the case of Savonarola and Deronda) versions of Hegel's "World-Historical Individuals," reshaping and redirecting their societies, even though their contributions may be unacknowledged. Those who have not been granted romantic wings, however, are forced to grovel in a reality that seems increasingly unendurable. From *Romola* on, Maggie Tulliver's dual nature splits into antipodal characters—with Romola, Fedalma (in *The Spanish Gypsy*), Dorothea Brooke, and Daniel Deronda embodying her ardent idealism and heroic aspirations and Tito Melema, Don Silva,

Tertius Lydgate, and Gwendolen Harleth demonstrating the suppressed diabolism, the divided loyalties, the "spots of commonness," and the temporal frustration that are also parts of Maggie's nature.

Romola, at first glance, seems like Maggie Tulliver transplanted to an age and a cultural milieu, early Renaissance Florence, that allow her to express her romantic aspirations. Like Maggie, Romola has inherited something of her father's pride, but old Bardo, for all his flaws, has a patrician's and scholar's gravity worthy of his daughter's respect;[93] and where Maggie longs to find a hero in St. Ogg's who will help her in her emotional hour of need, Romola has just such a hero in the figure of Savonarola. Even the allegiance to the ties of the past, which seems like a figment of Maggie's imagination, is demonstrated persuasively in Romola's loving duty to her father. There is nothing abstract in Romola's scorn for the hedonistic position her husband Tito takes after he has sold Bardo's library, which had been intended to remain as a memorial to the old scholar. Where Tito in self-defense expounds the epicurean doctrine of living for oneself and for the moment, Romola relies on the more concrete claims of the sentiments:

> You talk of substantial good, Tito! Are faithfulness, and love, and sweet grateful memories, no good? Is it no good that we should keep our silent promises on which others build because they believe in our love and truth? Is it no good that a just life should be justly honoured? Or, is it good that we should harden our hearts against all the wants and hopes of those who have depended on us? What good can belong to men who have such souls? To talk cleverly, perhaps, and find soft couches for themselves, and live and die with their base selves as their best companions.

Whatever reasonable "arguments" Tito may cite—Benthamite self-interest transmitted back to the Renaissance where it appears as epicureanism—Romola's sense of "duty" supersedes. "It was a yearning of *his* heart," she declares, "and therefore it is a yearning of mine."[94]

As the foil to Romola, in whose ardent nature self-denial and self-expression struggle to find a common ground, Tito Melema is one of Eliot's superbly drawn male characters. But where Romola expresses an unselfconscious version of Maggie Tulliver's saintly side, Tito speaks for the rebellious nature that seeks a more earthly satisfaction. Intelligent and personable, Tito represents the amoral side of the Renaissance man, trusting to Fortune and rejecting the claims of the past, or what he interprets as outworn moral standards, in order to satisfy his own individual desires; he is the sort of individualist whom the great historian Jacob Burckhardt saw exemplified both in the heroic figure of the Renaissance artist and in the less inspiring form of the Renaissance criminal. Tito is neither artist nor criminal, though he has the aesthetic sensitivity of the one and the lack of scruples of the other, but his lack of allegiance to any of the opposing political factions coupled with his Machiavellian adroitness and his scholarly abilities give him an entrée into the competing Florentine political circles. These wily Florentines hope to take advantage of his cunning even as he plots to use others for his own advancement. As an alien in Florence, brought up in the Hellenic outlook wherein beauty and material satisfaction constitute the only values in life, Tito "has a lithe sleekness about him," as Romola's godfather early on perceives, "that seems marvellously fitted for slipping easily into any nest he fixes his mind on" (I, 113). The neo-Platonism that flourished in fifteenth-century Florence allowed for the invalid assumption that one as handsome as Tito must be good. But lacking the feelings that root one to the past and that alone restrain egoism, he is denied what Eliot in *Theophrastus Such* characterized as the "spiritual police of sentiment." Freed of these restraints, Tito first betrays his foster-father—"Do I not owe something to myself?" he asks (I, 152), refusing to provide the ransom to free Baldassarre, and then denying the old man when he unexpectedly turns up in Florence—then betrays the wishes of his father-in-law with regard to the library, and ultimately helps to betray both Savonarola and Florence's political independence. His development from amiable youth, when his only flaw seems to be an excessive regard for his own "pleasure," to treacherous manhood is portrayed with marvelous truth and subtlety; he stands as sharply defined and attractively menacing on Eliot's canvas as one of Antonello da Messina's painted condottieri.

In her depiction of Savonarola, too, Eliot achieves a commanding likeness, but one that derives from her romantic sympathy for a Schilleresque figure whose noble idealism is marred by his surmounting ambition. He is the most notable—and perhaps the only really credible—embodiment in Eliot of what is described in *Romola* as "that subtle mysterious influence of a personality by which it has been given to some rare men to move their fellows" (I, 241). In his political trilogy, Disraeli celebrated the magnetism of romantic genius which, when transferred to the public arena, is able to exert benign mastery over others by the force of feelings; but what for Disraeli seemed largely a matter of charisma is seen by Eliot as a moral instrument for good with potential dangers. Initially, Savonarola's religious power over his audience is reminiscent of the effects of Evangelicalism as preached by Tryan in "Janet's Repentance," a force that subdues (as in Romola's case) the rebellious will and encourages "subjection of selfish interests to the general good" (I, 359). But there are also negative strains in Fra Girolamo's rhetoric that remind us of Eliot's denunciations of religion in the hands of Young and Dr. Cumming—the appeals to superstition, to fanaticism, to ambitious motives in his hearers, all of which reflect the flawed nature of his sense of mission. Savonarola hopes to purify the church of simony and other forms of internal corruption, and to redirect the Florentine state toward more humanitarian ends; but to attain the ecclesiastical and political power he needs to achieve these high aims, he resorts to questionable methods, and he begins to identify the interests of the state with his own interests. Like Robespierre, Savonarola is driven to self-delusion: "The cause of my party," as he tells a shocked Romola, "*is* the cause of God's kingdom" (II, 309). The bonfires that he has built so that earthly "vanities" can be extinguished once and for all inevitably anticipate the festivals decreed by Robespierre in behalf of the earthly kingdom of virtue. But for Savonarola as for Robespierre, costly sacrifices (including human sacrifices) must be made in the name of the public good. Eliot surmises that at some point he must have discerned in the primitive and sadistic aspect of the bonfires "the difficulty weighing on all minds with noble yearnings toward great ends, yet with that imperfect perception of means which forces a resort to some supernatural constraining influence as the only sure hope" (II, 198–199). However, since in the end Savonarola, like Schiller's Wallenstein, is destroyed not by his personal defects but by the intrigues of ambitious natures lacking any ideals, flawed or otherwise, Eliot ends the book with a Schilleresque tribute to his heroic endeavor: "a man who had sought his own glory indeed, but sought it by labouring for the very highest end—the moral welfare of men—not by vague exhortations, but by striving to turn beliefs into energies that would work in all the details of life" (II, 430–431).

Romola herself, who is compared to Savonarola in terms of their "kindred ardour" (II, 228), strives in the course of the novel to find a belief that will release such energies. She moves away from the austere paganism of her father, which finds less attractive expression in Tito Melema, practices for a time the self-renouncing religion preached by Savonarola, and finally emerges as a distinctly ideal figure in her own right. Romola is seen in a succession of noble roles—as Antigone to her father's Oedipus, as a Florentine Florence Nightingale during the time of plague and famine—without seeming more or less than human in her aspirations and rebelliousness. Her disillusionment with Savonarola and her unhappy marriage force her to a universal dilemma, the problem of "where the duty of obedience ends, and the duty of resistance begins" (II, 255). Ultimately, she must turn away from the less desirable ties to the past and from the influence of magnetic personalities to face the "moment when the soul must have no guide but the voice within it" (II, 306). It is at this point that Eliot resorts to one of the most flamboyantly romantic gestures in all her work: she resolves her heroine's dilemma by allowing Romola to drift passively down the Arno, placing her trust in "destiny." It is in this scene, as Laurence Lerner notes, that Eliot's Romantic faith in impulse and her Victorian sense of duty merge as a single conviction: "The yielding of self-indulgence has led directly to the yielding of service." This beautifully written episode, which culminates in Romola's arrival at a plague-infested village where in her care for the ill she is mistaken for the Madonna and, after her departure, made into a local legend, was the source, as Eliot admitted, of her inspiration to write this book, the "romantic and symbolical elements" from which the novel sprang. Where in "The Lifted Veil" Eliot had intimated the negative aspect of her artistic gift, in the figures of Romola and Savonarola she depicted the more idealistic and ambitious side of her artistic vocation.[95]

But it is at the moment when Romola is transformed into the effigy of the ardent young woman as protective Madonna that she becomes too "ideal" a figure (as Eliot herself apologetically admitted) to be taken seriously. The novelist who froze Maggie Tulliver into the posture of noble sacrifice with which *The Mill on the Floss* somewhat desperately concludes cannot in the end find a more dynamic role for Romola, despite the potential of the Renaissance setting, than that of protector of Tito's other wife, the happily bovine Tessa, and her two children, whom Romola is last seen coaching in the need to feel "for the rest of the world as well as ourselves" (II, 445). Despite the flatness of the ending, however, *Romola* is the most seriously under-rated of George Eliot's novels. If her historical romance does not have Scott's liveliness, it does have much of the intelligence and color of a Browning poem laid in the same period. The idea for *Romola*, coincidentally, came to Eliot in the same year, 1860, that Browning picked up *The Old Yellow Book* in a Florentine bookstall. One recalls Eliot's reference in *Middlemarch* to the recent past when "Romanticism" had not yet "helped to fill some dull blanks [of Roman history] with love and knowledge." *Romola* and Browning's poems alike achieve such Romantic aims —not attempting to escape the problems of the present by withdrawing into the past, as Lewes had accused the Romantic poets (aside from Shelley) of doing, but stressing the "vital connections" between present and past.[96] As if to demonstrate the universality of her theme, Eliot decided in her next novel, *Felix Holt* (1866), to transplant Savonarola to a period closer to her own time while dealing with some of the same problems and aspirations that move Romola, Tito, and the noble Fra Girolamo.

Unfortunately for the new novel, its hero does not turn into an effigy, as do Maggie and Romola; he begins as one. So upright that an act of homicide on his part is quickly overlooked, Felix Holt is the most imposing and the most insufferable of Eliot's

Rousseauesque heroes, the Noble Workman turned Carlylean critic of modern society. Holt clearly echoes Savonarola in his desire to reform society: Eliot's full title, *Felix Holt, the Radical*, is explained not in terms of his political views, which are somewhere to the right of Edmund Burke's, but by his intention to "go to some roots a good deal lower down than the franchise," to find the means for a moral revaluation of modern life.[97] His hope, as he explains to the admiring Esther Lyon, is to move to a large town and be "a demagogue of a new sort; an honest one, if possible, who will tell the people they are blind and foolish, and neither flatter them nor fatten on them" (II, 41). Holt sees himself, with frank self-admiration, as a proletarian St. Francis who will preach the truth to his generation and to his class. (He suggests to Esther that she follow St. Theresa's example.) The first we see of Eliot's hero is his acceptance of the life of poverty, refusing to live on the proceeds of his late father's quack medicine and choosing instead to become a watchmaker, in the manner of such uncommon common men as Spinoza, who worked as a lens-maker, and Charles Kingsley's Alton Locke, the tailor.[98] "This world is not a very fine place for a good many of the people in it," he gives as his credo. "But I've made up my mind it shan't be the worse for me if I can help it" (I, 91). However, if Holt seems to be repudiating the sort of ambition to which Savonarola succumbed, Eliot invests him with a romantic magnetic power every time he opens his mouth or even looks at others. In physiognomy he "might have come from the hands of a sculptor in the later Roman period" (II, 309); consequently, his working-class audiences are as much overwhelmed by "the grandeur of his full yet firm mouth, and the calm clearness of his grey eyes" (II, 87) as by his political message to them, which is the Wordsworth-Burke view that they should be reverential toward their betters and not demand reforms that will disrupt the organism of society.

The most interesting aspect of Eliot's treatment of Felix Holt is the linking of his mesmeric hold over others with his sexual magnetism. Holt's personality, rather than his Carlylean rhetoric, exerts an influence over Esther that turns her into an adoring slave-maiden straight out of Byron's poems, which Holt professes to despise. "He was like no one else to her," she muses after Holt expounds his social views: "he had seemed to bring at once a law, and the love that gave strength to obey the law" (II, 45). A contemporary reviewer of the novel, noting how Eliot inverts the conditions that make for heroism without denying the heroic role to Holt, connected him with the sort of overbearing, uncivil lovers found in women's novels, presumably those of Charlotte Brontë.[99] But if the relationship between Felix Holt and Esther Lyon, the poor but noble working man and the heiress who craves a superior-minded male, recalls the union of Louis Moore and Shirley Keeldar in *Shirley*, it also harkens back to the linkings of Saint-Preux and Julie in *La Nouvelle Héloïse* and the overbearing hero and his female acolyte in Byron's works. After meeting Esther, Felix expresses an initial disdain for her cultivated posture (he has caught her reading Byron) with a patently sexual arrogance: " 'A peacock!' thought Felix. 'I should like to come and scold her every day, and make her cry and cut her fine hair off' " (I, 106–107).

The manner in which Esther Lyon is transformed from an independent-minded woman of wit and sensitivity into a dependent figure who hopes to do only what Felix will deem right for her provides an indication of George Eliot's sense of women's place. Eliot holds up Mrs. Transome to Esther as an example of how the desire for independence and mastery robs a woman's spiritual nature. Admitting to Edith Simcox that "she had never all her life cared very much for women" (except as her disciples), Eliot in the same breath held up the "womanly ideal" for approval.[100] In *Felix Holt* Esther is redeemed by the power of her devotion to Felix; for his sake she repudiates the romantic fancies of her youth—rejecting the more polished figure of Harold Transome in his favor—with the Brontë-esque proviso that her "husband must be greater and nobler than" she is (II, 356). Eliot's advocacy of an idealism to which one can devote oneself is translated from religious (as in "Janet's Repentance") to sexual terms. "The best part of a woman's love is worship" (II, 177), she notes; and Felix is responsible for Esther's awareness of the beauty of self-suppression. He enunciates the Comtist position of woman as an ennobling influence—a Madonna in the house— who makes "a man's passion for her rush in one current with all the great aims of his life" (II, 39).

Esther's first, and presumably last, exertion of will in the novel occurs when she appears in court to speak in favor of Holt, who is being tried for having accidentally killed a constable during a mob riot which he had sought to disrupt by the force of his personality. Holt has already defended and absolved himself on the strength of his "sacred feelings" (II, 306); but Esther's appeal to the court, based on her feelings for him, is enough to secure a pardon. "When a woman feels purely and nobly," Eliot declaims, "that ardour of hers which breaks through formulas too rigorously urged on men by daily practical needs, makes one of her most precious influences." She has in fact attained that wisdom of the child which makes for obedience and righteousness: "Her inspired ignorance gives a sublimity to actions so incongruously simple, that otherwise they would make men smile. Some of that ardour which has flashed out and illuminated all poetry and history was burning to-day in the bosom of sweet Esther Lyon. In this, at least, her woman's lot was perfect: that the man she loved was her hero; that her woman's passion and her reverence for rarest goodness rushed together in an undivided current" (II, 313). For woman to be worthy of appreciation, as Eliot admitted to Edith Simcox, she must needs be patronized. But Eliot's own role in *Felix Holt* is synonymous with that of her righteous hero, exhorting others to submit but himself wielding the most romantic fantasy of power.

Despite George Eliot's apparent return to the novel of realistically detailed common life set in her favorite period, the years when the First Reform Bill was being discussed, there is much in *Felix Holt* to support Joan Bennett's contention that it is her "most romantic" book.[101] It is romantic in its choice of a dominating hero of impeccable moral standards and a dominated heroine whose love for him redeems her and saves his life. ("Hang it!" says one of the Tory magnates who has heard her appeal in court, "the fellow's a good fellow if she thinks so"; II, 321.) It draws upon the romantic convention of the missing heir to an estate (Esther), the coincidental turning-up of characters at the right moment, and the family secrets that come out at the most melodramatic opportunity. (Harold Transome, striking the lawyer Jermyn with his riding-whip, is told, "*I am your father*"; II, 327.) Eliot was not overly good at plot-making, and

she resorted time and again to the most hackneyed of melodramatic devices to tie her characters' fates together. But in
Felix Holt, for the first time, she sought intentionally to harness
melodrama and "sensationalism" into the service of her belief in
determinism and nemesis, and to use romantic characterizations
to express her social views. Moreover, the endorsement of romantic values in the Felix-Esther plot did not prevent her from
attacking what she deemed to be spurious romantic views in
the Harold Transome-Mrs. Transome counterplot of the novel,
a pattern that she would repeat in *Middlemarch* and *Daniel
Deronda*.

If Felix Holt is Eliot's example of the romantic lowly figure
raised high—Noble Workman turned unacknowledged legislator
of Treba Magna—Harold Transome and his mother represent
Byronic aristocrats brought low. Harold enters the novel in
deliberate imitation of Byron (even his name is Byronic): after
years spent in the East he has returned to his native town, bringing with him Oriental ideas of love and mastery. His later admission to Esther that the mother of his son was "a slave—was
bought, in fact," comes as a shock to her view of "Oriental love
[which she had] derived chiefly from Byronic poems" (II, 273).
Harold intends to apply his Byronic sensibility to radical politics
—the sort of career Disraeli had intimated in *Vivian Grey* that
Byron might well have adopted had he returned to England. "He
was at once active and luxurious," writes Eliot, "fond of mastery,
and good natured enough to wish that every one about him
should like his mastery" (I, 39). In the course of the novel,
Harold's faith in the power of his will is undermined by the
calamitous results of his attempt to secure a seat in Parliament,
by the discovery that Esther and not he is the true heir to the
Transome estate, and finally by the news of his identity as
Jermyn's son.

In the depiction of Mrs. Transome, Eliot goes beyond taming
the will (or the illusion of will) as in Harold's case; for having
spurned the "womanly ideal" of self-denial, Mrs. Transome is
transformed into a melodramatic version of the Wandering Jew,
an outcast in the house she seems to be ruling over.[102] Mrs.
Transome's observation that her willful son is attracted to Esther
because of the independence of spirit he sees in her, but plans to

subdue it after marrying her, foreshadows the relationship between Gwendolen Harleth and Mallinger Grandcourt in *Daniel
Deronda*, but it also betrays Mrs. Transome's sense of her own
degraded status: "This girl has a fine spirit—plenty of fire and
pride and wit. Men like such captives, as they like horses that
champ the bit and paw the ground: they feel more triumph in
their mastery. What is the use of a woman's will?—if she tries,
she doesn't get it, and she ceases to be loved. God was cruel
when he made women" (II, 202). Mrs. Transome's forlornly
independent role in *Felix Holt* underscores the "true" romanticism of Esther's wisdom in abandoning her claim to the Transome
estate, thereby repudiating the false romance of her youthful
dream to become a fine lady, and in preferring instead to subjugate herself to the man she loves. However, Mrs. Transome's
words remind us that Felix's hold on Esther is a sublimated version of the same kind of male mastery; and her presence in the
novel intrudes a jarring note in that, as in the case of Hetty
Sorrel or the Princess in *Daniel Deronda*, it raises doubts as to
whether this despairing, isolated figure represents merely the
exception to Eliot's hopeful Romanticism or its threatening
obverse.

The most conspicuous examples of George Eliot's Romanticism
can be found in her verse play The *Spanish Gypsy* (1868) and
in her motivation for writing it. It is necessary to include a discussion of the play in a study of her novels because of the manner in which *The Spanish Gypsy* draws together the often submerged romantic themes and aspirations of her earlier works
and uses them in a way which points to her two great final
achievements, *Middlemarch* and *Daniel Deronda*. The romantic
sensibility that led only to frustration in *The Mill on the Floss*
is here celebrated in operatic manner: indeed, Fedalma, the
gypsy queen of the play, fulfills one of Maggie Tulliver's youthful ambitions. In Eliot's first works of fiction there was usually
an outcast figure who represented a threat to the established
order, even though he or she was often superior in sensibility
to members of that order: Caterina Sarti in "Mr. Gilfil's Love
Story," Latimer in "The Lifted Veil," and Maggie Tulliver are

the most obvious cases. With *Silas Marner* Eliot allowed the outsider to be integrated into the community, and indeed went so far as to allow the former alien to achieve a moral triumph over the reigning squire, Godfrey Cass. The formula was repeated in *Felix Holt*, where a working class hero is allowed a major victory over the local gentry in terms of superior moral strength. *Romola* represented a partial exception to the pattern: Savonarola exerts a powerful moral force, but is defeated by his unworthy enemies; Tito has a material success, but is undone by his own lack of principles; and Romola achieves apotheosis as the protective Madonna, but is left without much compensation in human terms. In *The Spanish Gypsy* Eliot allowed each of her three principals a heroic role, although it might be added that she saved the most heroic role of all for herself.

The determination to glorify outcasts—whether they be the gypsy race of her play, the Jews and artists of *Daniel Deronda*, or the Shelleyan aesthete Will Ladislaw and his Schilleresque bride Dorothea Brooke in *Middlemarch*—has discernible roots in George Eliot's personal history. By the late 1860s Eliot's literary gifts had secured for her a footing in the world that her relationship with Lewes, and her being a woman, might once have seemed to preclude. But more significant than the fact of her literary notoriety was her sense of being established in the high Romantic line—principal soprano in that "choir invisible" which influences the lives of its auditors and helps in the making of the future. Eliot no longer identified with her hapless heroines, except, as in the case of Gwendolen Harleth, in reflection of her past history. Instead, she projected herself into the figures of Savonarola, Felix Holt, and Daniel Deronda, the Romantic heroes who are determined to see their ideals embodied in their and others' daily life. The all-too-conscious sense of her superiority as she announced that her new book was *"not* a novel," that it was not, heaven forbid, written in the spirit of "money-getting," did not prevent her from nagging her publisher for the largest circulation, the best financial arrangements, and the most thorough publicity campaign (not to mention his continuing reassurance of her genius) for her works. It was not, as she assured Blackwood, that she took herself seriously—but, after all, there were all those "strengthening testimonies" to the power of her work by "young men" that had to be taken into account.[103]

Whereas Wordsworthian quiescence had been the theme of Eliot's early works, the Schilleresque noble exertion of the will is hailed in her late works. In the case of her gypsy queen, Fedalma, obedience is indeed required, but in the form of a "grand submission" that requires her to abandon the prospect of domestic happiness as Don Silva's wife in order to preside over the destiny of her people. The idea of the play appealed to Eliot's dual romantic sensibility: one could have greatness thrust upon one in the manner of Hegel's "World-Historical Individuals." Fedalma's father, the gypsy chief Zarca, avers:

> you were born to reign.
> 'Tis a compulsion of a higher sort,
> Whose fetters are the net invisible
> That holds all life together.

Eliot's inspiration for the play, she admitted, was a Titian painting of the Annunciation: a young woman "chosen to fulfill a great destiny, entailing a terribly different experience from that of ordinary womanhood."[104] Her own heroine is "compelled to give way in the end," the individual being always at the mercy of external forces. But in the "collision between the individual and the general," which Eliot saw as the inevitable subject of tragedy, "it is the individual with whom we sympathise, and the general of which we recognise the irresistible power." Thus, the tragic hero, she notes, inevitably plays the role of Prometheus, splendid if ultimately frustrated. All three heroic figures in her play are "rendered vain" in the end: Silva's "tragedy of entire rebellion"; Fedalma's "grand submission," which Silva's rebelliousness renders ineffectual; and Zarca's "struggle for a great end rendered vain by the surrounding conditions of life." But it is not what happens to the tragic figures that matters; what is important is the *image* of the hero that is transmitted to future generations—the resultant glorification of heroic will, which, even when proven illusory, provides the illusion that men must live for if their life is to have meaning. As Zarca explains to his daughter (pp. 162–163):

No good is certain, but the steadfast mind,
The individual will to seek the good:
'Tis that compels the elements, and wrings
A human music from the indifferent air.
The greatest gift the hero leaves his race
Is to have been a hero. Say we fail!—
We feed the high tradition of the world,
And leave our spirit in our children's breasts.

As Eliot had learned from Schiller, art immortalizes what life consumes.

Although Eliot realized that *The Spanish Gypsy* was "eminently unsuited for an *acting* play," she thought it had operatic possibilities; "and I hope it will take that shape," she told Blackwood. To speak of *The Spanish Gypsy's* resemblance to a Schiller play is virtually the same as to speak of its operatic potential. The major themes of Schiller's plays—the conflict between love and honor (or duty to family), the contrast between rebellious will and the glories of self-sacrifice—made them perfectly suitable for the operatic stage, where even a passive hero can make an effect and the frustrating of will can be transcended in the form of a great aria.[105] In her play Eliot drew upon two Schiller works, *Wallenstein* and *The Maid of Orleans*, for the portrait of a young woman torn between her duty to her father (as is Thekla) or her nation (like Schiller's Johanna/Joan of Arc) and her love for a young nobleman of a different caste, and for her depiction of a young man caught between love for the daughter of an enemy chief (whom he also respects, as is the case with Max Piccolomini) and loyalty to his position as nobleman and soldier.[106] As opera, *The Spanish Gypsy* might have some redeeming quality: Fedalma's dilemma would be that of Verdi's Aida; Silva, in forsaking his military obligation for the sake of a beautiful gypsy, would follow Don José's example in Bizet's *Carmen;* and his repentant pilgrimage to Rome at the end would invoke Wagner's Tannhäuser. There would even be a great duet for hero and heroine at the end. (Eliot had originally planned to kill them off, but changed her mind.) But without arias or duets, we are left with an endless libretto, with characters who lack resemblance to human beings, and with ideals of dubious value.

The operatic analogy in Eliot's mind would play a significant role in her last two novels. Her interest in the power of music and the role of the musician reaches its ultimate expression in *Daniel Deronda*, but even in *Middlemarch* Ladislaw is first attracted to Dorothea by the power of her voice, while Lydgate is taken in by Rosamond Vincy's bogus "melodic charm." The structure of *Middlemarch* might be said to consist of a series of romantic duets, the more harmonious and genuinely romantic the better for each of the principals involved.

The greatness of *Middlemarch* (1871–72) depends to a certain extent on the convincing sense of perspective achieved by George Eliot, her ability to see her own obsessions and illusions with the same amount of clarity with which she perceives the various follies and frailties of members of her fictional community.[107] In this respect, the novelist attained the position of its chief opponent of illusions, Mary Garth. "Honesty, truth-telling fairness," Eliot declares, "was Mary's reigning virtue: she neither tried to create illusions, nor indulged in them for her own behoof, and when she was in a good mood she had humour enough in her to laugh at herself" (p. 84). For Mary life is a comedy in which she has resolved "not to act the mean or treacherous part." But Eliot notes that such a view of life might have led to a cynical attitude on Mary's part had it not been for the restraining force provided by parents capable of inspiring gratitude and teaching her by their example "to make no unreasonable claims" (p. 232). Such clear-sightedness is not enough, however; in Mary it leads to a Wordsworthian stoicism in which she forswears all active role in life for herself, choosing instead to be the good angel who reclaims Fred Vincy from a headstrong and hedonistic life. Her contempt for illusions is reminiscent of Harold Transome's when he hears Rufus Lyon's insistence that politics be made to serve the interests of morality: "If a cynical sprite were present," writes Eliot, ". . . he might have made himself merry at the illusions of the little minister who brought so much conscience to bear on the production of so slight an effect." But, she adds, "what we call illusions are often, in truth, a wider vision of past and present realities—a willing movement of a man's soul with the larger sweep of the world's forces—a movement towards a more assured end than the chances of a single life" (*Felix Holt*, I, 273–274). If Mary Garth were truly the central figure of *Middlemarch* and if the rejection of illusions were Eliot's only theme, it would be a rather bleak book—wonderfully therapeutic, perhaps, but as "melancholy" as some of Eliot's first readers, to her surprise, found it.

Instead, the book contains its wonderful mixture of clarity and ideal vision, comic exposure and tragic pathos combined with a sense of heroic potential, which is unique among the great English novels. It is important to keep in mind that *Middlemarch* does not so much weigh reality against Romanticism as balance kinds of Romanticism against each other: Mary Garth's Wordsworthian quiescence is one possibility, but Eliot's readers surely find more of the author's own feeling expressed in the union of Dorothea Brooke and Will Ladislaw, in which her Schilleresque ardor and earnestness complement his Shelleyan impudence and latent heroism. Gordon Haight has suggested that many modern readers' "discontent with their marriage springs largely . . . from our lack of sympathy with their romantic philosophy."[108] But it is precisely toward this triumph of their Romanticism that *Middlemarch* tends: Dorothea's and Will's victory is all the more notable in the context of a novel in which all forms of delusions of grandeur—whether Brooke's political or Bulstrode's religious ambitions, Casaubon's scholarly or Fred Vincy's gentlemanly pretensions—are scotched. The extent of their success, and Will Ladislaw's in particular, can be gauged if it is compared to the unhappy career of Tertius Lydgate, whose brief rise to eminence followed by virtual banishment from Middlemarch is the substance of romantic tragedy.

At one point Eliot considered giving Lydgate the surname of Tristram, to emphasize the appalling result of his love for Rosamond Vincy, although with a hint too of the futility of the power of his will such as is found in Sterne's protagonist.[109] Like Elizabeth Gaskell, who had selected a young scientist as the hero of *Wives and Daughters* to represent the new romantic values that she saw replacing the Byronic fashions of her youth, Eliot associates Lydgate's scientific ambitions with his romantic nature. Where Keats had compared the enrichment of his imagination to Herschel's astronomical discoveries, Lydgate actively views himself as a scientific explorer, finding in the medical profession "the most perfect interchange between science and art" (p. 108), and seeing in "the dark territories of Pathology . . . a fine America for a spirited young adventurer" (p. 109). For a would-be scientific genius no less than a romantic genius, however, independence is a necessity. Warning him of the need to remain "independent" if he is to achieve his ambitions, Mr. Farebrother reminds Lydgate that "very few men can do that. Either you slip out of service altogether, and become good for nothing, or you wear the harness and draw a good deal where your yokefellows pull you" (p. 129). Lydgate, like Gwendolen Harleth in *Daniel Deronda*, assumes that he will always have the reins in his hands; however, circumstances, joined to his internal weaknesses and external mishaps, conspire to tie him firmly in the end to the commands of Rosamond Vincy. His misapprehension as to the nature of women is the cause of his undoing: a reformer in scientific matters, Lydgate is sadly conventional in his belief that a man's wife should be a pattern of ornamental charm. What he seeks is a performance of femininity such as attracts him first to the seemingly helpless, but as it proves murderous, French actress Madame Laure and then to Middlemarch's star performer, Rosamond. Her romanticism is of the shallow nature that delights in Thomas Moore's poetry and that sees in her husband-to-be a dashing outsider with aristocratic connections straight out of a silver-fork novel. She responds to Lydgate more for the sake of his relations than for his scientific ideals, which she hopes to cure him of in time. What feelings she has for him, when she momentarily thinks herself neglected, are the sham romantic feelings of a Lizzy Eustace (in Trollope's *The Eustace Diamonds*), regarding herself "as forlorn as Ariadne —as a charming stage Ariadne left behind with all her boxes full of costumes and no hope of a coach" (p. 221).

The marriage scenes between Lydgate and Rosamond, his romantic idealism having no effect on her romance fantasies, which cloak a will infinitely stronger than his, are among the most harrowing in all of literature. "Their impressiveness," as Henry James notes, "and (as regards Lydgate) their pathos, is deepened by the constantly low key in which they are pitched. It is a tragedy based on unpaid butchers' bills, and the urgent need for small economies." James's description of Isabel Archer as an ardent nature who dreams "of freedom and nobleness" and who is "ground in the very mill of the conventional" applies even more strongly to Lydgate.[110] Eliot compares his fate with that of the Byronic malcontent: "Some gentlemen have made an amazing figure in literature by general discontent with the universe as a trap of dullness into which their great souls have fallen by mistake; but the sense of a stupendous self and an insignificant world may have its consolations. Lydgate's discontent was much harder to bear: it was the sense that there was a grand existence in thought and effective action lying around him, while his self was being narrowed into the miserable isolation of egoistic fears, and vulgar anxieties for events that might allay such fears" (p. 473). In the end, one is reminded of Edward Trelawny's and Thomas Moore's reflections, with regard to Byron, that genius and marriage don't mix. Lydgate's marriage proves as damaging to his career as Byron's was ruinous to his reputation; and in both cases, men of imaginative energy and reformist zeal become exiles from a world that is all the poorer for the loss.

Where Lydgate suffers romantic alienation, Will Ladislaw is transformed from the very image of a romantic interloper (a gypsy with white mice—"a sort of Byronic hero—an amorous conspirator," in the view of the Middlemarchers; p. 278) to an effective political reformer. "I come of rebellious blood on both sides," Ladislaw admits (p. 269), referring to his father, a Polish patriot, and his mother, a stage actress; but the double heritage proves useful, allowing him to follow in Disraeli's footsteps and convert the postures of romance into the politics of Romanticism. At one point Eliot apparently considered giving Ladislaw a Jewish background[111]—to point up the parallel with Disraeli perhaps, but also to emphasize his alien status and to utilize what Disraeli and, increasingly, Eliot saw as the romantic nature of Judaism. In her last novel, *Daniel Deronda*, Eliot expanded on the theme of the romantic outsider metamorphosed into the new ruling elite, selecting Jews and artists for her heroes and heroines. In *Middlemarch* her aim is less ambitious and more successful, as her treatment of Ladislaw's development indicates. He enters the novel as a self-proclaimed Shelleyan "genius," opposed to all "fetters," and demanding only that he be placed "in an attitude of receptivity towards all sublime chances."[112] His "generous reliance on the intentions of the universe with regard to himself" (p. 61) is a slightly higher, more aesthetic, version of Fred Vincy's similar trust in Providence. However, Providence, or George Eliot, is kind to both figures, allowing each to be redeemed from a life of aimless self-indulgence through the force of a woman's love. Ladislaw is changed, in short, from a character with Shelley's looks and mannerisms— with his "Ariel" smile and his "hair [which] seemed to shake out light" (pp. 152, 155) and his contempt for all forms of constraint—to a man with Shelley's ideas and radical idealism, and with Shelley's romantic view of women.

"He seems to me a kind of Shelley, you know," Brooke, with rare perception, says of Ladislaw, whom he has invited to Middlemarch to help with own political plans. Not, Brooke adds, that Ladislaw is guilty of "laxities or atheism . . . But he has the same sort of enthusiasm for liberty, freedom, emancipation" (p. 263). As his protégé develops a flair for political rhetoric, Brooke sees him as "a sort of Burke with a leaven of Shelley" (p. 366); and he regrets that there isn't a "pocket-borough to give" him (as there was for Burke), since "You'd never get elected, you know" (p. 337). With the Reform Bill on the horizon, Ladislaw grows increasingly interested in a political career —initially, like the young Disraeli, putting his rhetorical gifts to use for others' benefit, then thinking along more ambitious lines. Like Disraeli's Vivian Grey, he begins to have romantic fantasies of political self-importance, first seeing himself as the power behind Brooke, then imagining himself wielding the power openly. "There will be a great deal of political work to be done by-and-by," he explains to Dorothea (who has begun to idealize Ladislaw, as she had idealized his cousin Casaubon earlier), "and I mean to try and do some of it. Other men have managed to win an honourable position for themselves without family or money" (p. 395). Just as Disraeli's political heroes are enabled to succeed thanks to the help of women, Ladislaw's political career is fueled by Dorothea's high regard for him. But where the desire to see her own ambition embodied in another drove her to an unhappy first marriage with Casaubon, her ability to see her own idealism reflected in another (reminiscent of Adam Bede's view of Hetty Sorrel) has the effect of making Ladislaw strive to live up to her ideal of him. It is her belief that he has always "acted in every way rightly" (p. 464) that determines Ladislaw to do so in fact. As a result of her faith in him, he becomes, as we learn, "an ardent public man, working well in those times when reforms were begun . . . and getting at last returned to Parliament"—despite Brooke's prediction to the contrary—"by a constituency who paid his expenses" (pp. 610–611).

But just as Ladislaw's regeneration is owing to Dorothea's ardent idealism, she too is transformed from what he early described as one possessed by a "fanaticism of sympathy" (p. 163) to a woman responsive to beauty and physical charm. Neither character is perfect nor meant to be so: we see many examples of Ladislaw's youthful petulance and impetuosity throughout the novel—from his "arrogantly merciless" disdain toward Bulstrode (p. 457) to the "poisoned weapons" of reproach he hurls at Rosamond Vincy in his desire to "shatter [her] with his anger" (pp. 570–571)—but then we are also reminded from beginning to end that Dorothea will always manage not only to get her way but to satisfy her desires in a way meant to intimidate those who disagree with her. Their illusions are not so much dispelled as put to socially productive use; and while Ladislaw is allowed his political triumph, Dorothea too is granted the more modest-sounding but no less heroic role of one whose "unhistoric acts" are responsible "for the growing good of the world" (p. 613). Eliot's finale to *Middlemarch* is a confirmation of Dorothea's goal to widen "the skirts of light and [make] the struggle with darkness narrower" (p. 287). Earlier, Ladislaw defined the sensibility of the poet, which he shared, in Shelleyan terms: "to have a soul so quick to discern that no shade of quality escapes it, and so quick to feel, that discernment is but a hand playing with finely-ordered variety on the chords of emotion—a soul in which knowledge passes instantaneously into feeling, and feeling flashes back as a new organ of knowledge" (p. 166). But, as Dorothea reminds him, a poet is obliged to write poems—after all, Latimer in "The Lifted Veil" had just such a sensibility for all the good it did him or allowed him to do. And as Shelley in his Prefaces reminds us, the aim of poetry is to arouse the reader's imagination to the point where he becomes aware of the needs of others. The Shelleyan stress on sympathetic feeling and the Schilleresque call for idealistic action merge in the active public career of Eliot's hero and heroine; and the novel ends on a note of hope in the power of romantic ideals to work miracles in spite of clear-sighted objectors to the contrary. It is noteworthy that in our last impression of Dorothea she has not been frozen into a saintly posture, as was the case with Romola and Maggie Tulliver.

Despite the frustration of some of its characters' wishes, *Middlemarch* offers the gospel of "love and hope" that Lewes had cherished in Shelley's poetry. In *Daniel Deronda* (1876), Eliot's Romanticism is even more apparent; but while in one respect this novel represents the culmination of her Romantic sensibility, in another it expresses a Romanticism born out of desperation and wish-fulfillment, a Romanticism no longer at home on English soil. In the same passage of *Middlemarch* where Eliot describes Ladislaw's career as a political reformer, she interjects the reminder that such "hopefulness . . . has been much checked in our days," and she ominously adds that Dorothea's and Ladislaw's son, "who might have represented Middlemarch," declines a political career "thinking that his opinions had less chance of being stifled if he remained out of doors" (pp. 610, 612). The sense that modern England allows little room for hope or love or romantic fulfillment is all too evident in *Daniel Deronda*, the only Eliot novel set in the modern period. The confines of provincial St. Ogg's that served to defeat Maggie Tulliver's aspirations are here seen as the barriers surrounding modern England, which must be bodily escaped, or transcended through the artistic imagination, if one is not to be reduced to a life of pettiness and emotional and cultural deprivation. The Romantic idealism and adventurousness that Eliot sets in opposition to the barrenness of mid-Victorian England foreshadow the Romantic Revival of the 1880s and 1890s, although Deronda's trip to Palestine, which concludes the novel, is related more to the romantic voyages of discovery in Byron, Disraeli, or Charles Kingsley than to the pure escapism that was to be the aim of H. Rider Haggard and Robert Louis Stevenson.[113]

Eliot's celebration of the powers of the artistic imagination places her firmly in the Romantic tradition. However, her linking of Judaism with the heritage and future of Romantic values, while inspired by both Disraeli and the Jewish literature she read in preparation for the novel, was something new.[114] The sense of artistic vocation that is reflected in the great composer and musician Julius Klesmer, "a felicitous combination [as we are told] of the German, the Sclave and the Semite,"[115] is of a grander dimension than any of the worldly concerns of the novel's English-born characters, aside from Deronda. Where Ladislaw had represented the Shelleyan conception of genius as a process of being finely receptive, Klesmer speaks for what Shelley also saw as the *power* of the artistic genius: "We help to rule the nations and make the age as much as any other public men. We count ourselves on level benches with legislators" (I, 363). "My rank as an artist," he contends, "is of my own winning, and I would not exchange it for any other" (I, 374). Mrs. Arrowpoint, whose heiress-daughter's subsequent marriage to Klesmer demonstrates the superiority of the artist caste to that of mere aristocracy (and represents the ultimate expression of the Saint-Preux and Julie, tutor and heiress, plot), mouths the conventional definition when she says of Klesmer that genius does not follow the rules; "it comes into the world to make new rules" (I, 152). But the artistic life requires severe discipline: one does not become a genuine artist, as Klesmer tells Gwendolen Harleth, on the basis of beauty or by sheer will, as she had supposed; one must be animated by a sense of "inward vocation" (I, 282) and be prepared to work hard. "Genius at first is little more than a great capacity for receiving discipline," he notes (I, 385), gently persuading her to give up the idea of a stage career. However, Eliot does not include all artists in her lofty view: Deronda's childhood friend, the painter Hans Meyrick, seems too lightweight a figure in his habits and tastes to reassure the reader that the future of English art is in good hands; and the sort of musical vocation that Klesmer and Deronda's future bride Mirah Cohen embody is of a markedly Teutonic nature. Gwendolen's singing of a Bellini song is castigated by Klesmer: mere bel canto, he charges, "expresses a puerile state of culture—a dandling, canting see-saw kind of stuff—the passion and thought of people without any breadth of horizon." Art, to be truly great, must express "deep, mysterious passion," "conflict," a "sense of the universal"; it must make men large "as they listen to it" (I, 67–68).

George Eliot turns the artist into so lofty a personage that it soon becomes apparent that actual artists, as in Meyrick's case, cannot live up to her ideal. Klesmer and his conception of artistic genius virtually disappear after the first third of the novel, and Mirah gives up her vocation to become Deronda's wife. Most important, Deronda's long-sought mother, the legendary opera singer known as that Alcharisi (the Princess Halm-Eberstein in her married state) turns up late in the novel to demonstrate the fact that the sacrifices made in the name of art are of no avail in the end. "My nature gave me a charter," she tells Deronda (III, 183) in explanation for her abandonment of both him and her Jewish heritage; but it is clear in Eliot's late works, as the figures of Mrs. Transome and Armgart show, that the independent life is not for a woman. In Gwendolen, the desire for independence releases that murderous instinct which Eliot saw as a distinctly feminine trait.[116] The Princess complains of the penalty of having had "a man's force of genius" while suffering "the slavery of being a girl" (III, 131)—and a Jewish girl, at that, for whom independence is an act of sacrilege—but in so doing she admits that genius is a male prerogative. Eliot's bleak sense of the constraints that are women's due and glory takes us back to her first domestic heroine, the "gentle, uncomplaining" Milly Barton, who unquestioningly clings to the "loving woman's world [that] lies within the four walls of her own home" (I, 96–97).

Having thus denied the practice of the artistic vocation to women, Eliot would seem to have repudiated her own right to continue as a Romantic seer. It was perhaps partly out of the need to stifle any self-doubt that Eliot embraced the idea of Judaism as a means of defending her Romanticism; for Judaism, as she had come to view it, represented the apotheosis of the Romantic sense of vocation and mission, but without requiring an expenditure of will on the part of Jews. In the figure of Deronda, the English-born gentleman who is set apart from his fellows (like Latimer and Maggie Tulliver and Eliot herself) on account of his hypersensitivity, but who has a noble vocation willed to him as a result of genetic and racial forces beyond his control, Eliot was able to conceal her ever-increasing ambition under the cloak of necessity.[117] Like Fedalma in *The Spanish Gypsy*, Deronda is fated to dominate others by the force of his magnetic personality, a force that he tries to seem unaware of, and to lead his outcast nation to the promised land. It is indispensable not just to the plot of *Daniel Deronda* but to Eliot's sense of her own mission that her hero discover that he is a Jew, for in Judaism Eliot observed the triumph of the Romantic principle: in the survival of a nation through the power of shared memories and feelings, Eliot saw a Darwinian justification for the survival of the idealism of the authors dear to her, Wordsworth, Rousseau, and Schiller. Her celebration of a faith in which individual sacrifices were made for thousands of years in behalf of the "living force of sentiment in common" is a rebuke directed to the English of Eliot's time whom she saw degraded by the pursuit of materialist self-indulgence. The George Eliot who sought in a Wordsworthian manner to raise the artistic status of humble life in her first novels developed into the Schilleresque sage identifying with an entire nation who seemed of little importance in the eyes of mid-Victorian England but who, to Eliot, represented the perpetuation of those ideals which alone make life endurable. "The pride [as seen in Judaism] which identifies us with a great historic body," as she wrote in *Impressions of Theophrastus Such*, "is a humanizing, elevating habit of mind, inspiring sacrifices of individual comfort, gain, or other selfish ambition, for the sake of that ideal whole" (pp. 207, 221).[118] It is for rejecting this tradition that the Alcharisi, for all the comfort and fame she has received, is ultimately found wanting and left in bitter isolation: she has denied the fellow-feeling and love (which for her is synonymous with "subjection"; III, 185) that alone might have brought her satisfaction.

Isolation, in fact, seems the fate of all characters in the novel who are not connected in some way with a large, self-denying mission that has been thrust upon them. Eliot attributes Gwendolen Harleth's egoism and lack of fellow-feeling to the lack of a childhood home "endeared to her by family memories." But while this gives Eliot the opportunity to echo the Wordsworthian faith in "human life . . . well rooted in some spot of native land" (I, 26), it seems rather harsh for her to condemn her character for actions that are the result of her rootless upbringing. It is precisely this expanded devotion to roots that makes Deronda's pilgrimage to Palestine so necessary and that makes Zionism a movement of Romantic rather than religious significance. Like the national unification movements in Greece and Italy, Zionism (for Eliot) is seen as the reification of national sentiment. It is time, as Mordecai Cohen (Mirah's brother and Deronda's spiritual mentor) proclaims, to "Revive the organic centre: let the unity of Israel which has made the growth and form of its religion be an outward reality" (II, 387). In contrast to Gwendolen, Mordecai and Mirah exemplify throughout the novel the passionate belief in imagination and sentiment as the forces that change and dignify the world. Neither brother nor sister, interestingly, is an orthodox believer: her religion, like his, "was of one fibre with her affections, and had never presented itself to her as a set of propositions" (II, 128). Instead, theirs is the Romantic religion, like that described by Wordsworth in *The Excursion*, of the heart's need that inspires reverence and obedience, and also the Romantic faith in "visions," as espoused by Shelley and Schiller. Such visions are, in Mordecai's words, "the creators and feeders of the world" (II, 335). Mirah's defense of the truth of the imagination is strikingly Keatsian: "If people have thought what is the most beautiful and the best thing, it must be true" (II, 288). And Mordecai himself is movingly identified with Keats in the lines chosen by Eliot as epigraph to the chapter in which Deronda begins "to feel his imagination moving without repugnance in the direction of Mordecai's desires" (II, 407): Mordecai, strong in visionary life but mortally ill, is compared to Keats's "sick eagle looking at the sky" (II, 398).[119]

In Deronda, Eliot sought to resolve that polarity in Romanticism which had disrupted her previous work and which plagued many of the Romantic poets: the need to believe in the power of will to translate vision into fact, and the counteracting sense of fatalism or stoicism which threatened to turn into either nihilism or a quiescence that ran counter to the driving energies of Romanticism. Where Disraeli had jauntily sung the romance of the will, yet created essentially passive heroes, Eliot united passivity and will in the figure of her Hegelian "world-historic" hero (III, 308). It is Deronda's duty not only to be the receiver of his grandfather's religious yearning but, on a more secular level, to play the role of Schiller's Don Carlos to Mordecai's Posa: to be one of the men Mordecai calls upon to ensure a "place for resistance in this generation," resistance to the common-sensical claims advanced by Mordecai's assimilation-minded fellow Jews who meet at the Hand and Banner, resistance in favor of "the life of his people [which one feels] stirring within his own" (II, 378). Everything from Deronda's childhood on points to a Romantic career. Even his sense of parental depriva-tion (the mistaken feeling that he is Sir Hugo Mallinger's illegiti-mate son rather than his ward) can be "compared in some ways with Byron's susceptibility about his deformed foot" (I, 259). But where the Byronic hero would allow the sense of "entailed disadvantage" to turn him into a misanthropic "Ishmaelite," Deronda at thirteen is of "the rarer [and Shelleyan] sort, who presently see their own frustrated claim as one among a myriad, [and for whom] the inexorable sorrow takes the form of fellow-ship and makes the imagination tender" (I, 262). Eliot compares the rarity of Deronda's "subdued fervour of sympathy, [his] activity of imagination on behalf of others," as evidenced in his college life, with "another sort of genius" such as was seen "in the poet who wrote Queen Mab at nineteen" (I, 267). In Shelley and Deronda, we glimpse precocious youths in training for the role of "resistance" to the world they live in.

Deronda's Rousseauesque passivity of character, which Eliot links with his "receptivity," is responsible for the fateful moment when, as a result of his habit of indulging "himself in that solemn passivity" (I, 282) whereby he lets his boat drift on the Thames according to the tide, he is carried toward Mirah Cohen as she attempts suicide. It is by rescuing Mirah and going in search of her long-lost brother that Deronda comes in contact with his own lost religious background and his own destiny. The coincidence of events strikes him even before he discovers his Jewish identity: of a "romantic" nature, he is aroused by "that young energy and spirit of adventure which have helped to create the world-wide legends of youthful heroes going to seek the hidden tokens of their birth and its inheritance of tasks" (II, 361). Eliot early defines her hero's romanticism in terms of "a fervour which made him easily find poetry and romance among the events of everyday life"; but despite her efforts to ground his romantic yearnings in the world of "the microscope and . . . railway carriages" (I, 305), she betrays a disgust for the world on his part and her own so strong that in the end even Sir Hugo's fear of "eccentricity" of action on Deronda's part is of no avail. "At this stage of the world," Sir Hugo warns, "if a man wants to be taken seriously he must keep clear of melo-drama" (III, 265). Sir Hugo's is a reaction the reader of George Eliot often feels when melodrama and sensationalism are made to serve the ends of reality, and his warning seems especially significant in her last novel, for, even as Sir Hugo is speaking, his ward is ascending into the romantic stratosphere.

The need for romance to satisfy her "soul-hunger" (the phrase she applied to Dorothea Brooke) is most evident in Eliot's cele-bration of Mordecai's visions and enthusiasm. At times, in *Daniel Deronda*, she comes perilously close to committing the sin, which she deplored in the poet Young, of displaying a "defi-cient human sympathy, that impiety towards the present and visible, which flies for its motives, its sanctities, and its religion, to the remote, the vague, and the unknown."[120] The rare (for her time) tolerance and sympathy displayed toward the Jews does not prevent Eliot from showing a lack of such sympathy for independent-minded women, for Gwendolen Harleth, and for the stolidly contented Englishmen presented in the novel. It is such visionaries as Mordecai, she protests, who nourish the "world—moulding and feeding the more passive life which without them would dwindle and shrivel into the narrow tenacity of insects, unshaken by thoughts beyond the reaches of their antennae" (III, 213). But since Eliot makes it clear that one must *inherit* the sensibility that allows one to rise above the insects (one remembers her description of the "emmet-like Dodsons and Tullivers" in *The Mill on the Floss*), she allows her Romantic vision to warm only the elite of readers toward whom she directed her books. One does not have to be Jewish to respond to the Deronda portions of the novel, but it certainly helps to be Romantic.[121]

Gwendolen Harleth, alas, is neither. Her dilemma is that she must surrender all sense of self-esteem without being compensated with the powers of imagination or vision. From her first dazzling appearance in the novel, Gwendolen seems like a figure in a romance—as the "problematic sylph," the "Lamia beauty" (I, 7, 11) whom Deronda sees gambling at a German spa—but it is Eliot's purpose to sink Gwendolen in the mire of reality. Gwendolen is not without a sense of dread, which is evident in her childlike bursts of terror and in her Pascalian awe at the discoveries of astronomy, which conjure up a "vastness in which she seemed an exile." And despite her efforts to feel that she lives in a world "in which her will [is] of some avail" (I, 90), it is this sense of vulnerability that makes her susceptible to Deronda's claims on her conscience. The freedom of "will" that Gwendolen clings to is brutally exposed in the course of the novel, even though Eliot, forgetfully, thrusts Gwendolen into a charade where she seems to be "choosing" to marry Grandcourt freely—and is hence guilty of the "willing wrong" (II, 123) for which she is reproached by Grandcourt's ex-mistress and by Gwendolen herself—when she is in fact doing what her relatives and her poverty have forced on her. Ruby Redinger has persuasively indicated the extent to which Eliot drew upon her youthful self for the portrait of Gwendolen: her exhibitionism, her terrors, the sense that without self-abasement something demonic within her would emerge. "On one level," Redinger notes, "Gwendolen embodies the inner forces of egoism, hostility, and aggressiveness that George Eliot had long feared would master her; and Daniel is the incarnation of counteracting ideals."[122]

Eliot's epigraph to the novel—"Let thy chief terror be of thine own soul . . ."—speaks both for the Gwendolen side of the novel and for Eliot's latent Evangelicalism, in which the human will was ever a potential criminal. Deronda's most embarrassing moment in the novel occurs when he must play the Saviour to her repentant Magdalene: he feels that her "self-abhorrence," after the accidental death of her husband, must be sustained, and that "her remorse was the precious sign of a recoverable nature; it was the culmination of that self-disapproval which had been the awakening of a new life within her; it marked her off from the criminals whose only regret is failure in securing their evil wish. Deronda could not utter one word to diminish that sacred aversion to her worst self—that thorn-pressure which must come with the crowning of the sorrowful Better, suffering because of the Worse" (III, 232–233). Neither Feuerbach's religious sentimentalism nor Rousseau's faith in human goodness and feelings could absolutely override, in the end, Eliot's stern view that self-contempt is the beginning of wisdom. Yet, if Gwendolen represents Eliot's fearful sense of her own potential for ill, Deronda is the ultimate expression of her childhood fantasy of becoming an exalted personage. The Gwendolen side of Eliot must be abased so that the Deronda side can grant absolution. As the Spanish Gypsy was the embodiment of Maggie Tulliver's ambition, Daniel Deronda is the apotheosis of Eliot's identification of herself with the Romantic seer and messiah. She admitted a similarity of viewpoint extending back from *Daniel Deronda* to the *Scenes of Clerical Life*, and noted that "the principles which are at the root of my effort to paint Dinah Morris are equally at the root of my effort to paint Mordecai."[123] However, where in *Adam Bede* the spirit of Wordsworthian Romanticism was seen to inspire and subdue the Loamshire inhabitants, in *Daniel Deronda* such salvation is open only to a handful of the chosen. Gwendolen gets over her fantasy of being a "princess in exile" (I, 30, 55) quickly enough; but while she ceases to be a princess, she and the other English characters in the novel remain in a state of spiritual exile, locked within the iron gates of reality. Meanwhile, Daniel Deronda, a real princess's son, as it happens, and Eliot's other surrogate romantics are allowed to emigrate to the land of heart's desire.

SEVEN

Death and Circuses: Charles Dickens
and the
Byroads of Romanticism

I am the modern embodiment of the old Enchanters, whose Familiars tore
them to pieces. I weary of rest, and have no satisfaction but in fatigue.
Realities and idealities are always comparing themselves before me, and I
don't like the Realities except when they are unattainable—then, I like
them of all things. I wish I had been born in the days of Ogres and
Dragon-guarded Castles . . . There's a frame of mind for you, in 1857.
Charles Dickens

It has become the fashion in recent years to label Dickens a "Romantic" novelist, but Dickens is both more and less than what the epithet implies:[1] more, because he is indebted to so many other literary traditions; and less, because his Romantic sympathies are frequently at odds with his anti-Romantic views. A listing of some of the sources of Dickens's literary inspiration is in order here: his trust, for example, in the benign workings of Providence, assisted by the actions of benevolent individuals, derives from such eighteenth-century writers as Fielding and Goldsmith; his sense that life is charged with wonder and fantasy owes a good deal to his youthful absorption in fairy tales and the *Arabian Nights;* the insatiable desire to produce an "effect" in his work—a *coup de théâtre* that occasionally undermines the moral intention behind his fiction—is partly the result of his retention of the Regency culture that flourished in his youth, that mixture of Byronic posturing, popular melodrama, and Gothic horror stories which were later to recombine in the form of the sensation novel; and with all these echoes of the past, Dickens also emerges in his novels as a prototypical Victorian, devoted to the work ethic and to a new earnestness of spirit and conduct.[2]

For all that, the Romantic strain in his work is genuine. Unlike Charlotte Brontë and George Eliot, who had drunk deeply of their Romantic heritage, Dickens was an instinctive Romantic. His celebration of the imagination as a means of personal and social salvation and his identification with the child's point of view, for example, are characteristics that derive from his life rather than from his readings. His knowledge of the Romantic poets was spotty; and aside from a rare quotation or two from Byron and Wordsworth, or the fact of his visit to Keats's and Shelley's graves in Rome, there is no reason to dispute Philip Collins's statement that Dickens's Romantic ideas owe little to the poets and "more to the Romantic middlemen—essayists such as Lamb, De Quincey and Leigh Hunt." The Romantic author Dickens is closest to is Carlyle; but the bulk of the Carlylean views he echoes in his work are, with a few exceptions, ones that he would have expressed had he never known or read Carlyle.[3] Dickens's Romanticism seems, in many ways, a simplified and sentimentalized version of the Wordsworthian-Coleridgean trust in the spontaneous, untutored imagination placed in opposition to the scientific-rationalist strain of the eighteenth and nineteenth centuries. To say, however, that he confutes "Utilitarianism" with "life" (as F. R. Leavis does of the Dickens of *Hard Times*) is to indicate only that he yearns for an uncomplicated form of existence in which man's innately benign disposition will be allowed to flourish without hindrance from higher authorities.[4]

Nevertheless, Dickens does not reject the material fruits of progress and mechanization that, unobtrusively, guarantee one's comfort, and he demands a strong police force to deal with the class of criminals and ruffians whose existence (the result of innate, not environmental, evil) forces him to qualify his Romantic sense of man's inherent goodness.[5] Despite the idealized depictions of rural life in his novels, Dickens prefers the energy and activity of the city to the serenity of the country: he and Elizabeth Gaskell are alike in seeing the country as a source of tranquillity for the city-dweller, but for the country-dweller as an enervating way of life that suggests the calm of death. (Sometimes Dickens was attracted to the country for that very reason.) Like Wordsworth, he prefers the status quo: despite the nostalgic descriptions of the age of the stagecoach in his novels, he has little of the Romantic sense of the past, and his idea of social change, as Orwell notes, amounts to "a moralised version of the existing thing." But where the conservative poet idealized a rural way of life that had already largely disappeared, Dickens's place is with the newly emergent middle class, and his allegiance is not to the past or to religious authority but to the sanctities of the domestic circle: the Victorians' version of the Roman worship of the household gods. One sees in Dickens the Wordsworthian gospel of quiescence and forbearance translated into what one reviewer praised as the novelist's "beautiful dogma of meekness,"[6] and adapted for domestic consumption; but a Byronic current of willfulness and rebelliousness is also increasingly evident in his work and character.

"Like Byron," declared a *Quarterly* reviewer in 1839, Dickens "awoke one morning and found himself famous, and for a similar reason: for, however dissimilar the men and their works, both were originals, and introduced a new style of writing . . . both touched a string which vibrated with another pitched to the same key in their readers' hearts." But where Byron had touched a chord of melancholy and discontent, Dickens sounded the strains of a more domestic and restraining harmony. It was his aim not to look to the exotic East for literary inspiration but to find the materials that provoke wonder close at hand: in the modern city and in the middle- and lower-class household.[7] Beginning with the *Sketches by Boz* (published in book form in 1836–37), Dickens was to show what a contemporary described as "the romance, as it were, of real life." Twenty years would pass before another budding writer, the author of *Scenes of Clerical Life*, would be praised for her "just appreciation of the romance of reality," but the phrase chosen to characterize her early efforts indicates that she was seen as a descendant of Boz, who had first "opened the inexhaustible mine of the domestic life of the masses" to fictional excavation.[8] The reviewers who compared Dickens's achievement to those of Crabbe and Wordsworth in this respect would not have displeased Dickens: he

admitted a youthful liking for Crabbe, although he felt with
Wordsworth that Crabbe showed "a dreary want of fancy";[9]
and in his sense of the moral superiority of the poor—the Betty
Higdens and Trotty Vecks of this earth—to those in higher
spheres of life, Dickens offered a watered-down version of
Wordsworth's belief in the Preface to *Lyrical Ballads* that "the
essential passions of the heart find a better soil" in such plain
folk. (Unlike the Romantic poet, however, Dickens did not
restrict his attention to the rural poor.) The contemporary
phrase, repeated by many of his admirers, that Dickens's "fellow-feeling with his race in his genius"—in marked contrast
to the Byronic aloofness appreciated by an earlier generation—
is confirmation of the fact that Dickens was, whether he or his
contemporaries realized it or not, an obvious heir to the poet
who had declared the following as his aim:

> What nobler marvels than the mind
> May in life's daily prospect find,
> May find or there create?
>> (Prologue to *Peter Bell*, ll. 143–145)

The novelist's most obvious tribute to Wordsworth occurs in the
Preface to *Bleak House*, where he claims to have "purposely
dwelt upon the romantic side of familiar things." One inevitably
remembers Wordsworth's design in *Lyrical Ballads*, as later
recounted by Coleridge, "to give the charm of novelty to things
of every day, and to excite a feeling analogous to the supernatural, by awakening the mind's attention from the lethargy
of custom, and directing it to the loveliness and the wonders of
the world before us."[10]

Dickens's enthusiasm for the author of *Scenes of Clerical
Life* reflects the kinship he felt with her aims; the creator of
Daniel Deronda was also committed to the romance of everyday
life. But although she shared many of his weaknesses—the addiction to "sensational" elements in her plots, the overuse of coincidence, the idealization of woman's domestic role—George Eliot
sharply criticized Dickens for his lack of verisimilitude in por-
traying the masses, his tendency to exaggerate their external
traits and to ignore their psychological dimension altogether.
Eliot's dissatisfaction may have been the cause of George Henry

Lewes's drastic shift in attitude toward Dickens. As a young Hegelian who believed that the primary aim of art was not mimetic but emotive, Lewes in 1837 praised Dickens's truthfulness, finding *Oliver Twist* "pregnant with philosophy and feeling." In 1872, however, Lewes was distressed with Dickens's violation of the rules of fictional realism. Although he called attention to the novelist's "glorious energy of imagination," he deplored the fact that the Dickensian imagination was powerful enough to make unreality (or what Lewes decried elsewhere as "falsism") seem like reality. Eliot's and Lewes's attitude toward Dickens reflects something of their reaction against their own youthful Romantic sensibilities: the young Eliot had preferred the "truth of feeling" to the intellectual and scientific views of the 1830s and 1840s, which were increasingly dividing men and alienating man from a sense of his intrinsic purposiveness; but the mature Lewes criticized the absence of "thought" in Dickens, noting that "the logic of feeling seems the only logic he can manage." What seemed like powers of "hallucination" to Lewes in 1872 had once resembled the powers of "genius" and a truth to "poetry": the ability of the artist to "see" what others have missed, showing us "how blind [we were] to what we also might have seen, had we used our eyes."[11] Although Dickens insisted that he was basically a realist, he had, like Lewes, defined genius in terms of this very ability to see what others, viewing his work, regard only as exaggeration: the viewer, being "partially blind," as Dickens complained, therefore "accuses [the genius] of wilful invention."[12]

Ultimately, as Dickens himself came to realize, his art was a combination of realism and romanticism, of observation filtered through the spectacles of romance. What Trollope deplored as Dickens's peculiarity of style another critic praised as his singularity of vision, the author half-creating and half-perceiving in a Romantic manner: "To read one of his romances is to see everything through the author's eyes; the most familiar objects take an air of strangeness when surveyed through such a medium." Dickens admitted as much, but claimed the same was true for George Eliot and Elizabeth Gaskell, who, making "the most opposite use of the same material," testify to the truth that "we are all partly creators of the object we perceive."[13] The belief that the imagination attains a higher truth than mere visual accuracy was shared by Bulwer Lytton, who invoked the Hegelian claims for the autonomy of the creative mind that Lewes had once held. Although Eliot may have altered Lewes's Romantic view in this respect, she herself in *Daniel Deronda* paid a Dickensian tribute to the truth of the seemingly fantastic; but where Dickens drew fire for his obstinate assertion that such things as spontaneous combustion could and did occur, she was intellectually astute enough to cite Aristotle as her source for the proposition that "It is a part of probability that many improbable things will happen."[14]

In at least one respect, the author of *Daniel Deronda* was more Romantic-minded than Dickens or even Charlotte Brontë, for where the Brontë and Dickens protagonists are made to awaken from their romantic illusions, Eliot's hero awakens *to* a sense of his romantic birthright. Deronda shares the sensibility of Arthur Clennam in *Little Dorrit* and Esther Summerson in *Bleak House:* deprived of a secure social and familial footing at the outset of his life, he refuses, like them, to become a Byronic misanthrope, to regard his sense of shame (at his presumed illegitimacy) as a reason to despise and revenge "himself upon mankind in general, by mistrusting them one and all" in the manner endorsed by "divers profound poets and honourable men." The preceding remark is made apropos of Tom Pinch in *Martin Chuzzlewit*, who feels that while others may choose to follow in Byron's footsteps and "consider it a very fine thing to be discontended and gloomy, and misanthropical, and perhaps a little blasphemous, because they cannot have everything ordered for their individual accommodation" (*MC*, pp. 767–768), he is determined to assert a trust in humankind and to act in an altruistic manner. The same goal is shared by Esther and by Clennam, who refuse to allow a taint of birth to darken their outlook or hold them aloof from others. This refusal to turn "misanthropical, Byronic, and devilish"[15] is a sign of Dickens's rejection of Romantic egoism in favor of Victorian selflessness; yet if Dickens thereby distorts the nature of Byron's achievement, he also exhibits a fascination with the popular version of the Byronic figure of imperious will and mesmeric power. On the other hand, the role of forbearance and self-suppression that

Dickens allots to his true heroes and heroines is in its way a popularized version of the Wordsworthian strain in Romantic poetry. Indeed, if Byron and Wordsworth can be said to represent the polar attractions of Romanticism, Dickens shows a divided loyalty to both figures, along with a pronounced antipathy.

According to his friend and biographer John Forster, Dickens had "little love for Wordsworth"; and notwithstanding his professed admiration for "We Are Seven," there is little evidence that Dickens knew Wordsworth's work to any great extent. An important indication of Dickens's attitude toward Wordsworth is reflected in his advice to Angela Burdett-Coutts as to what kind of reading material the women of Urania House (the home she had established for the reformation of prostitutes) might be permitted to look at. One of the teachers had suggested Wordsworth and Crabbe as suitable authors, and Dickens agreed: "I think the library might be extended in this direction, with great advantage. All people who have led hazardous and forbidden lives are, in a certain sense, imaginative; and if their imaginations are not filled with good things, they will choke them, for themselves, with bad ones."[16] This use of Wordsworth as a kind of medicine for the rebellious imagination also appears in Charlotte Brontë's and Elizabeth Gaskell's work; and it is noteworthy that Dickens's closest link with Wordsworth can be seen in the figures of sickly children (Oliver Twist, Little Nell, Paul Dombey) or in individuals like Betty Higden in *Our Mutual Friend* whose "resolution and independence" are tantamount to a death wish. Wordsworth is celebrated in the form of passivity and quiescence, while Byron is invoked in such a figure of malign energy as Daniel Quilp in *The Old Curiosity Shop* or in the criminality and hypnotic quality of a John Jasper in *The Mystery of Edwin Drood*. If the Wordsworthian side of Dickens's nature inclines him toward the pathetic and sentimental mode, the Byronic appeal is seen in his comic and horrific characters. The Byronic figure, above all, is one who makes an "effect," who seeks to exert power by the way he acts, dresses, or gazes at others.

An early Dickens sketch of "The Poetical Young Gentleman" dwells on the appeal of Byron to the young man of the 1830s (such as Trollope was later to describe in Johnny Eames and Charley Tudor), who "turned down [his] shirt collar" and exhibited a countenance "of a plaintive and melancholy cast, his manner . . . abstracted and [bespeaking] affliction of soul."[17] Such a figure has boundless admiration for murderers (men of "great spirit, . . . full of daring and nerve") and for scenes of gloom, the former showing force of will and eloquence and the latter reflecting the poet's requisite state of mind. He is full of poetical quotations, and his own speech contains nothing but "superlatives" as adjectives. Thus far Dickens might be drawing a preparatory sketch for Dick Swiveller in *The Old Curiosity Shop*, but in the would-be poet's "plaintive lament that he is no longer a child, but has gradually grown up," there is a hint of Harold Skimpole as well. In the early novels, the Byronic sensibility is reserved mainly for comic characters like Chevy Slime in *Martin Chuzzlewit* ("I have a soul that rises superior to base considerations"; p. 108) or Miss Knag's brother in *Nicholas Nickleby* (so "conscious of his own superiority . . . that he took to scorning everything, and became a genius"; p. 223). Two of Dickens's greatest characters, Dick Swiveller and Mr. Toots in *Dombey and Son*, are followers of the Byronic mode in speech and dress, but their innate good nature enables them to cast off the Byronic trappings and live selfless lives. (Mr. Toots's relations with his boxing companion, the Game Chicken, might well have seemed to Victorian readers to be a parody of Byron's exploits with "Gentleman" Jackson.) However, in the protagonists of his last two novels, Eugene Wrayburn in *Our Mutual Friend* and John Jasper in *Edwin Drood*, Dickens hinted that the Byronic element he alternately satirized and reviled was a disturbing aspect of his own personality.

The split between Dickens's sense of himself as a vulnerable, almost passive, individual and the different sense of Dickens that we get in his letters, and in the recollections of his friends and relations, as a willful, commanding presence, a benign ogre with friends but refusing to be dictated to or reasoned with by wife or publisher, is reflected in the opposing series of portraits in his fiction of suffering children and domineering ogre-figures, in his good, forbearing heroes and heroines and his evil (or comic-wicked) or willfully idle characters. Where the Wordsworthian side of Dickens calls fond attention to those who are innocent and patient—those who like Emily Norton in Wordsworth's *The White Doe of Rylstone* epitomize "female patience winning firm repose"—his own nature seems closer to Childe Harold, who "would not yield dominion of his mind," or to the Corsair, who exerts a "commanding art" over his followers. It is this Byronic sensibility that became linked with the artist's will to create and to exert power over fictive characters and real audiences alike. Whether engaged in pseudoscientific experiments involving mesmerism[18] or in the Public Readings near the end of his life, Dickens sought to exert his will over others much as had Byron's flawed heroes:

> that commanding art
> That dazzles, leads, yet chills the vulgar heart.
> What is that spell, that thus his lawless train
> Confess and envy, yet oppose in vain?
> What should it be, that thus their faith can bind?
> The power of Thought—the magic of the Mind!
> (*The Corsair*, 1. 177–182)

The young Dickens who hoped to create a "considerable sensation" with "The Stroller's Tale" in *The Pickwick Papers* and the Dickens of the Readings who gloated over the great "effect" planned with the recital of the death of Nancy in *Oliver Twist* ("I have no doubt that I could perfectly petrify an audience") are alike men tempted to embody the Byronic powers of magnetism, however irresponsible or self-destructive the effort might prove. Francis Jeffrey's praise of *Dombey and Son* includes the observation that Dickens had captured "the searching disclosure of inward agonies of Byron, without a trait of his wickedness."[19] But where Byron's great effect had been displayed in the erotic-criminal nature of his heroes (the side that appealed so strongly to Charlotte Brontë's imagination), Dickens's greatest effect lay in his death scenes—whether achieved by means of the comical-sadistic relish with which he dispatches his criminals or through the calculated, albeit often quite genuine, pathos accompanying the deaths of children.

Dickens's awareness of the self-indulgent aspect of the Byronic author led him to criticize a would-be poet for his excessive subjectivity: "It is not the province of a poet to harp upon his own discontents," he warned, "or to teach other people that they ought to be discontented. Leave Byron to his gloomy greatness, and do you

> Find tongues in trees, books in the running brooks,
> Sermons in stones, and good in everything."

To the same correspondent, Dickens decried the assumption that "genius" need not be bound to rules of industry or earnestness: "Whatever Genius does, it does well," he observed; "and the man who is constantly beginning things and never finishing them is no true Genius, take my word for it." The development of Dickens's mature genius coincided with his emergent Victorianism, his desire to make an effect for its own sake giving way (as he claimed with the writing of *A Christmas Carol*) to the discovery of the "immense effect [he] could produce" for the good of society.[20] It was at this point, in the 1840s and 1850s, that his arrested sense of self-pity, directed back to his own childhood suffering, expanded into a sense of pity and outrage on behalf of other sufferers in the modern world. Children in his books would henceforth be abused not by fairy-tale ogres but instead by neglectful social conditions. Dickens's heightened sense of the responsibilities of the artist no doubt abetted his taking on editorial duties in the 1850s and 1860s, rather than the other way around. And the turning against the Byronic characters in the novels of this period reflects this sense of heightened social responsibility: James Steerforth and Harold Skimpole are not sources of mirth, as had been the case with Chevy Slime and Miss Knag's brother, but are menaces to society. Even so, the need to make an effect, a flamboyant exertion of will, persisted and intensified, as did the passive side of Dickens's nature.

Dickens's passive strain reflects his lifelong sense of vulnerability, the memory of his childhood experiences in the blacking factory having become an unexorcisable, if stylized, part of his identity.[21] Forster astutely attributes the development of Dickens's indomitable will to this sense of childhood deprivation: "a passionate resolve [discernible in the young Dickens], even while he was yielding to circumstances, *not to be* what circumstances were conspiring to make him." The consolation of art, as Forster notes elsewhere, was that "Against whatever might befall he had a set-off in his imaginative creations, a compensation derived from his art that never failed him, because there he was supreme. It was the world he could bend to his will, and make subserve to all his desires." The hardening of Dickens's will and the channeling of vast resources of his energy into creative and personal power were not effected without some resultant flaws in his personality:

> What it was that in society made him often uneasy, shrinking, and over-sensitive, he knew; but all the danger he ran in bearing down and overmastering the feeling, he did not know. A too great confidence in himself, a sense that everything was possible to the will that would make it so, laid occasionally upon him self-imposed burdens greater than might be borne by anyone with safety.[22]

As he got older, and especially when his domestic world began to collapse in the mid-1850s, Dickens began to find less and less consolation in the act of creation, the therapy of creation that had sustained him through such crises as the death of his sister-in-law, Mary Hogarth. It is at this point that his letters reveal a manic desire for action of all kinds, theatricals, walking tours, readings, so that he might burn up some of that energy which had made him "incapable of rest." The "habit of suppression," which he recognized as part of his nature, was giving way; and what Dickens had foreseen happening to many of the inhabitants of Urania House began to apply to himself: "There is no doubt that many of them would go on well for some time, and would then be seized with a violent fit of the most extraordinary passion, apparently quite motiveless . . . There seems to be something inherent in their course of life, which engenders and awakens a sudden restlessness which may be long suppressed, but breaks out like madness." To Forster he wrote in 1856:

> However strange it is to be never at rest, and never satisfied, and ever trying after something that is never reached,

and to be always laden with plot and plan and care and worry, how clear it is that it must be, and that one is driven by an irresistible might until the journey is worked out. It is much better to go on and fret, than to stop and fret. As to repose—for some men there's no such thing in this life.

"I am the modern embodiment of the old Enchanters, whose Familiars tore them to pieces," he once declared. "I weary of rest, and have no satisfaction but in fatigue. Realities and idealities are always comparing themselves before me, and I don't like the Realities except when they are unattainable."[23] The "ideality" of his last novels, *Our Mutual Friend* and *Edwin Drood*, seems suspiciously like a romance of withdrawal from life—either in the form of fairy-tale denials of reality or in the final relief of death. In the end, the Byronic willfulness and Wordsworthian quiescence seem like alternative forms of the same Dickensian death wish.

The connection between Romanticism and death is pronounced in the Dickens novels in which Byronic and Wordsworthian characters and forces meet each other head-on, *The Old Curiosity Shop* and *Our Mutual Friend*. I will discuss these most markedly Romantic of his novels in the last section of this chapter, along with the novel in which Dickens displays his Romantic sympathies to less negative, though also less powerful, effect, *Hard Times*. Dickens's finest achievement, however, lies precisely in those novels in which he rejects the excesses of Romanticism, in which he seeks a position midway between the extremes of Romantic willfulness and Romantic quiescence: *David Copperfield*, *Bleak House*, *Little Dorrit*, and *Great Expectations*. In the first two books especially, Dickens presented a Victorian vision of restraint, moderation, and self-denial; but he also created two memorable figures whose existence poses a threat to that Victorian balance, Steerforth and Skimpole. Dickens had already attempted a critique of Romanticism in *Barnaby Rudge* (1841), a historical novel in the manner of Scott which deals with some of the same themes George Eliot was to consider in her historical novel, *Romola*: "The question where the duty of obedience ends, and the duty of resistance begins," and the dilemma of a well-intending leader corrupted by the exercise of power.[24] (To Forster's surprise, Dickens sympathized with Lord Gordon.) Angus Wilson has suggestively argued that Dickens carefully chose as three of the leaders of the Gordon Riots a Byronic malcontent, Sim Tappertit, who wishes that he had "been born a corsair or a pirate" and who hears within him "a voice . . . whispering Greatness" (*BR*, pp. 66–67); a Rousseau-esque noble savage, Hugh, who embodies the anarchic-destructive forces of the state of nature; and a Wordsworthian "idiot boy" in Barnaby himself. Of the title character Wilson observes, "Barnaby represents the extreme freedom of fancy that in some aspects of Romanticism broke down the old eighteenth-century order; and . . . Dickens here expresses his fear of such total dismissal of the real world for the world of shadows, a fear, strong, perhaps, because the dismissal of reality in so many of his moods was both dear and easy to him."[25] The Romantic "dismissal of reality" in favor of a world of the imagination provides the impetus for *The Old Curiosity Shop, Hard Times,* and *Our Mutual Friend;* but elsewhere Dickens devotes his artistic attention to the education of such "romantic" young men as David Copperfield and Pip away from the illusions and fancies that darken their lives.

The contemporary reviewer of *David Copperfield* (1850) who called attention to Dickens's "deep reverence for the household sanctities, his enthusiastic worship of the household gods," underscored Dickens's Victorian point of view.[26] As Charlotte Brontë had done three years earlier in *Jane Eyre*, Dickens planned his fictionalized autobiography in the form of a pilgrim's progress from Romantic self-preoccupation to Victorian expression of sympathy. Many of the fancies and stylized traumas of childhood constitute the materials for David's (and Dickens's) later artistic career: "When I tread the old ground," David recalls, "I do not wonder that I seem to see and pity, going on before me, an innocent romantic boy, making his imaginative world out of such strange experiences and sordid things" (*DC*, p. 169). But while the young David feels keenly his sufferings at the hands of the Murdstones and in the warehouse of Murdstone and Grinby, magnifying his experience in his childish mind so that he seems to be at the mercy of wicked ogres and regarding his life as a "labouring hind" as a terrible violation of his princely birthright, the mature David resolves both to apply his will so that he may never "be houseless any more" and also "never [to] forget the houseless." David is learning to see beyond his own suffering and thereby achieve an authorial empathy with others (pp. 199, 815). David is not, to be sure, a rebellious child like Jane Eyre, and he never entirely exorcises his childhood vision of a world of threatening monsters. (What is that "ugly and rebellious genii" Uriah Heep, p. 747, if not the incarnation of David's youthful reading of fairy tales?) Nonetheless, in his transformation from devotee of the selfishly Byronic James Steerforth to acolyte of the selfless Agnes Wickfield, we see, in an allegorical form reminiscent of *Jane Eyre* (where Brontë transforms her selfish Byronic hero into a self-denying husband fit for her heroine), the making of a Victorian sensibility.[27] It is worth noting, however, that for Brontë and Dickens a self-deprecating heroine is essential to the final outcome: however, where Brontë had turned the devoted slave-maidens of Byron's poetry into dutiful Victorian mates, modifying the eroticism of the originals until they became models of marital respectability, Dickens in his anti-Byronic temper arrived at this image of feminine self-suppression, minus all eroticism, in the form of the Victorian housewife, guardian of the domestic temple.

If Agnes is the reward for David's arrival at his Victorian journey's end, David's first wife Dora plays a role in the novel analogous to Steerforth's in showing the hero the excesses of a Romantic way of life. Dickens's psychological acuity is demonstrated in the manner in which his hero falls in love with a "child-wife" who is the reincarnation of his child-mother. The novelist's celebration of the child's imaginative point of view in his earlier fiction is a sign of his Romantic sympathies: Paul Dombey's wish that he remain a child rather than be coerced by Dr. Blimber into the unnatural state of intelligent adulthood, or Scrooge's realization that his happiest time of life was his childhood and his wish that he might regress to the state of his innocence ("I'd rather be a baby. Hallo! Whoop!"; *Christmas Books*, p. 72) are examples of Dickens's Romantic sense that to be very young is very heaven. However, the thought that innocence immunizes one from the corruption of worldliness and getting and spending gives way in *David Copperfield*, where to be young is to be helpless and to be helpless is to spur on the triumphs of the victimizers of the world. That David marries Dora is proof of his vestigial Romantic nature: her childish impracticality seems proof of her desirable innocence. David's Aunt Betsy sees Dora as "a favourite child of nature . . . [a] thing of light, and airiness, and joy" (p. 543). Like Harold Skimpole, Dora is aware of her childishness, though unlike Skimpole she does not use it to disguise a parasitic disposition. By retaining her light and airy ways in marriage, however, Dora guarantees that she will never make an independent gesture of her own, and she transforms the servants and tradesmen she deals with into victimizers: "there is contagion in us," David ruefully notes. "We infect every one about us" (p. 693). The Romantic impulse that attracts David to Dora is finally evaluated as the "mistaken impulse of an undisciplined heart" (p. 664).

David's earthly pilgrimage brings him into contact with the innocent and the powerful, the born victims and the victimizers. It is his decision not to be one or the other, neither Mrs. Copperfield nor Murdstone, neither Wickfield nor Heep, that enables David to maneuver successfully between the dangers and temptations of life. Dickens plays with the comic possibilities of his innocent characters—Mr. Dick and his kite, Tommy Traddles's misfortunes in school and at the hands of Micawber, Doctor Strong's role as "a very sheep for the shearers" (p. 238)—but as the novel grows increasingly serious such comical characters prove themselves capable of earnest, diligent behavior. David's determination never to be helpless again enables him to attain something of the Dickensian will and the concomitant powers of self-reliance, dedication, and orderly work habits that enable him to become a novelist in the manner of his creator. But David is denied any of the Dickensian energy that would enable us to conceive of him masterfully bending the created world to his will. Dickens's strategy in denying the reader a glimpse of the power-hunger inherent in the creative process is probably prudent, although such a glimpse would thereby enable the reader to see more clearly the ambivalent hold that Steerforth has on Dickens's and David's imagination. For if the magnetic power of the artist were to be seen as akin to the Byronic hold on the individual, we might see that it takes more than "thorough-going, ardent, and sincere earnestness" (p. 606) to account for the masterpieces of Victorian fiction.

David speaks of the Byronic "spell" that Steerforth casts upon him—his "inborn power of attraction" to which "it was a natural weakness to yield" (p. 104)—but just as Dickens assures us of David's literary gifts without showing anything of the needed artistic energy, he is more inclined to tell us about Steerforth's power than to show it in action. The manner in which Steerforth imposes upon David's good nature tells us more about David's vulnerability than about his friend's magnetism. One of the few illustrations of Steerforth's charm (in both senses of the word) is supplied in a passage that Dickens unfortunately cut from the novel, part of the scene in chapter xxi where the two friends visit the Peggottys together for the first time. Hearing the perpetually despondent Mrs. Gummidge avow that she is "a lone lorn creetur'," with whom "everything goes contrairy," Steerforth jovially responds, "Why, we must be designed by Heaven for one another! I'm a lone lorn creature myself, and everything has gone contrary with me from my cradle . . . Come! Let us be lone and lorn together. Everything shall go contrairy with us both, and we'll go contrairy with all the world." Mrs. Gummidge is unable "to resist this league"; and at such a moment Steerforth is indeed irresistible.[28] We are reminded of those delightful moments when Byron himself would comically deflate the image of the gloomy Byronic hero.

Elsewhere, we see the negative impact of Steerforth's mastery over Mr. Mell, Rosa Dartle (in whom the devotion of the Byronic slave-maiden has turned to bile), or Little Emily; but even here we see the result rather than the process of his willfulness. David too readily acquiesces when Steerforth's mother claims that he has a right to exert his superior power wherever he chooses: David inclines to the view that to bow before his friend is a matter of "grace" (p. 296). In his aloofness and restlessness, his determination to dominate others and his inability to control himself, Steerforth inevitably calls to mind Childe Harold:

> untaught to submit
> His thoughts to others, though his soul was quell'd
> In youth by his own thoughts; still uncompell'd,
> He would not yield dominion of his mind
> To spirits against whom his own rebell'd;
> Proud though in desolation . . .
>
> (*Childe Harold*, 3.12. 3–8)

The portrait of Steerforth is considerably less persuasive than Disraeli's tribute to Byron, Lord Cadurcis in *Venetia*. (Both authors, curiously, provide a Shelleyan death for their Byronic figure.) But in choosing to treat the Byronic persona in a serious, albeit largely negative, manner, rather than in the comical fashion of his previous caricatures of Byronic misanthropy, Dickens indicated something of the darkly ambivalent hold such a figure was beginning to exert on him. Steerforth's lack of a "judicious father" who might have provided some sense of guidance for him ("I wish with all my soul I could guide myself better!"), his restlessness and inability to find an object in life to satisfy him, his fear of his own headstrong nature ("I have been afraid of myself"; p. 322), all serve to remind us of Dickens's own situation.

The battle between David's good, self-denying Victorian angel, Agnes, and his bad, willful, Romantic angel, Steerforth, could not be resolved as easily for David's creator as for David himself. Where energy and willfulness seem to partake of evil, the Dickensian protagonists must gravitate toward figures and resolutions that resemble relaxation or atrophy of will. After Dora's death, David finds consolation in the Wordsworthian sedative of Nature's serenity (p. 815); and even before David consciously realizes that Agnes is the wife he deserves, he thinks of her as the source of "peace and happiness. I come home now, like a tired traveller, and find such a blessed sense of rest!" (p. 567). The novel concludes, to be sure, with Aunt Betsy's tribute to David's attainment of Victorian investiture: "I wanted to see how you would come out of the trial, Trot; and you came out nobly—persevering, self-reliant, self-denying!" (p. 776). But we also have David's reminder early in the book that but for having had an Aunt Betsy—and but for his childhood Byronic sense that he was superior to the other laboring hinds in the ware-

house—he might have become "a little robber or a little vaga-
bond" (p. 161). In the end, the victory of good over bad angel,
with the household hearth replacing the restless voyaging of
a Byronic self-exile, is as much an assertion of triumph as it
is a matter of proof. In the year following the publication of
David Copperfield, Tennyson, echoing Goethe's belief in the
need to sublimate self, wistfully asserted it to be true "That
men may rise on stepping-stones / Of their dead selves to
higher things" (*In Memoriam*, ll. 47–48). In the most Victorian
of his novels, Dickens also turned to Goethe and to the gospel
of eternal womanhood to point him upward, hoping with as
much mingled doubt and faith as Tennyson "that real love and
truth are stronger in the end than any evil or misfortune in the
world" (p. 511).

Aunt Betsy's injunction to David that he be self-reliant, that
he trust only to his own "strength of character" (p. 275), is
echoed in *Bleak House* (1853) in John Jarndyce's advice to his
ward Richard Carstone that he "trust in nothing but in Providence and your own efforts" (*BH*, p. 180). But Richard, who
should fulfill the role of Victorian hero by awakening from
Romantic illusions and working diligently in his own behalf,
refuses to shake off the soothing thought that he will be taken
care of once his Chancery suit is settled. There to support his
folly is the example of Harold Skimpole, who seems to vindicate
the Disraelian romantic notion that all things come to those who
wait. Professing an ignorance of worldly affairs, Skimpole is
"constantly being bailed out—like a boat . . . Somebody always
does it for me. *I* can't, you know, for I never have any money"
(p. 523). Skimpole is Richard's Romantic bad angel, while hardworking and self-denying Esther Summerson is his good angel;
yet it is typical of Dickens's darkening mood in the 1850s that
the bad angel should not only prove the source of the hero's
undoing but also cast into doubt the role of the artist in Victorian
society.

The Romantic idealization of the artist as a law unto himself
reaches its ultimate exaggerated expression in Skimpole, in whom
the Shelleyan doctrine of the poet's innate superiority to others
by reason of his intense powers of imagination has been divorced
from the Shelleyan view that the poet's imagination will make

him feel deeply with humanity and hence enable him to become its benefactor. In a world overrun by parasitism in which the acknowledged legislators of England—the representatives of government, law, religion, and aristocracy whom we see in the novel—only perpetuate, when they do not cause, continuing abuses, it is the unacknowledged legislators who must fight injustice. In Skimpole, however, the artist has become another parasite, regarding the American slaves, for example, as figures in a landscape, giving "it a poetry for me, and perhaps that is one of the pleasanter objects of their existence" (p. 253). Although he can sing "quite exquisitely" about the peasant boy ("Thrown on the wide world, doom'd to wander and roam, / Bereft of his parents, bereft of a home"; p. 436), Skimpole has no sympathy for the real thing, Jo, when he turns up at Bleak House, stricken with fever. His advice to Jarndyce is that Jo be turned out of the house and left to fend for himself—preferably exhibiting some trace of "misdirected energy that [might get] him into prison. There would be more of an adventurous spirit in it, and consequently more of a certain sort of poetry" (p. 434). Skimpole's cruelest act, however, occurs when he sells Richard to the lawyer Vholes (who undertakes to look after his interests in the Chancery suit) and then prates about his friend's "youthful poetry" of hope. As the hopeful dreams fade, and as Richard's health gives way, Skimpole abandons him, lamenting the decline of poetry in that quarter to amuse him further. In Skimpole, one sees the transformation of Romanticism into aestheticism: all life exists as a spectacle for one to feed on; and the idea of the moral responsibility of art has come to seem an impertinence.

The lethal implications of Skimpole's airy philosophy, which make an already bleak world bleaker, were very much in Dickens's mind during the 1850s and 1860s. Although he believed that imagination was necessary for the welfare of society (in *Hard Times*, he holds up fancy as a narcotic for victims of society), Dickens worried that the imagination might seek only its self to please. If a child's sensibility is truly the happiest of states, as Blake or Wordsworth or Dickens himself often seemed to suggest, what if everyone refused to grow up? Jarndyce excuses Skimpole's misdeeds and irresponsibility on the ground of his redeeming childishness; but when pressed to answer the question of why Skimpole remains a child, he responds, "Why . . . he is all sentiment, and—and susceptibility, and—and sensibility—and—imagination. And these qualities are not regulated in him, somehow. I suppose the people who admired him for them in his youth, attached too much importance to them, and too little to any training that would have balanced and adjusted them; and so he became what he is" (pp. 592–593). Jarndyce's Romantic need to justify Skimpole (like David's praise of Steerforth) is meant to show us his own innocence; but by encouraging Skimpole in his parasitic role, Jarndyce is partly accountable for the devastation he causes. Dickens leaves it to Inspector Bucket to analyze Skimpole's behavior correctly: "Whenever a person proclaims to you 'In worldly matters I'm a child,' you consider that that person is only a-crying off from being held accountable, and that you have got that person's number, and it's Number One" (p. 775).

The odious role in which Dickens casts Skimpole may seem surprising, since Dickens is not only satirizing his own disposition to treat things in a fanciful and exaggerated manner but calling attention as well to two persons close to him: his father and his old friend Leigh Hunt. Dickens had already shown something of his father's irresponsibility in Micawber, although the presence of Steerforth and Heep in *David Copperfield* had served to deflect attention away from Micawber's parasitic nature. "Skimpole," as G. K. Chesterton observes, "is the dark underside of Micawber"; and the elder Dickens's combination of high spirits and financial improvidence encouraged his son to regard him, at times, as "a drag-chain on my life." "How long he is, growing up," Dickens complained at one point.[29] The various children in his fiction who become fathers to their childlike parents must have been suggested, in part, by Dickens's own experience. In the portrait of William Dorrit, Dickens was to remove all traces of comedy from such a figure; and while Dorrit is arguably Dickens's closest approximation to a tragic character, concealing with rhetorical bravado the sense of his complete helplessness, he is also a parasite where his daughter Amy is concerned. The connection between Skimpole and Hunt was perceived by Forster before *Bleak House* was published, and

Forster (who had introduced Dickens to Hunt a decade and a half earlier) persuaded Dickens to tone down the resemblance. For one thing, the original name of Leonard was changed to Harold Skimpole—enabling the reader to think of Childe Harold. Even with the changes, however, and despite a public "Remonstrance" to the effect that he had only drawn upon the "airy quality" of Hunt's "gay and ostentatious wilfulness" in looking at certain aspects of life, Dickens privately maintained that Skimpole was "the most exact portrait that was ever painted in words! I have very seldom, if ever, done such a thing, but the likeness is astonishing. I don't think it could possibly be more like himself [that is, Hunt]."[30]

Why Dickens should have chosen to associate Hunt's likeness with Skimpole's villainy will always remain a subject for speculation. It has been suggested that Dickens, in his determination to raise the professional status of the writing profession, objected to Hunt's Bohemian manner, his preference for being supported by friendly patrons rather than turning to the public or to the literary guild that Dickens was instrumental in founding. The Hunt who had written in his *Autobiography* of the pleasures of having rich patrons "amiable enough to render obligation delightful" is akin to the Skimpole who tells his patron Jarndyce, "I almost feel as if *you* ought to be grateful to *me*, for giving you the opportunity of enjoying the luxury of generosity" (p. 71). The young Dickens was honored to meet Hunt—to feel himself close to one who had known Byron and Shelley—and he was not unflattered when the *Sketches by Boz* was attributed in some quarters to Hunt. He sent Hunt copies of his early work and received the older writer's flattering assurance that he was comparable to Shakespeare.[31] In 1847 Dickens arranged a theatrical benefit in Hunt's behalf, and he may have felt some gratification in serving as the benefactor to a senior literary figure. Dickens was also proud of his link with Scott as a result of having the Waverley novelist's friend George Hogarth for a father-in-law; but this did not prevent his irritation at what he felt to be his in-laws' sponging on him. The sense that he served as Jarndyce to a flock of Skimpole-like relatives perhaps exacerbated Dickens's irritation when he came to draw the portrait; but he may also have been influenced by the accounts of "Hunt's half-fawning, half-arrogant manner" in the days of his dependence on Byron in Italy. In *Lord Byron and Some of His Contemporaries* (1828), Hunt, in seeking to deny the unflattering accounts of his relationship with Byron, only made matters worse, harping on Byron's miserliness and exposing his own ingratitude and paranoia. Dickens may have echoed Hunt's disagreeable self-revelation in the passages of Skimpole's autobiographical writings where he claims to have "been the victim of a combination on the part of mankind against an amiable child"; and Hunt's ingratitude toward Byron may have suggested Skimpole's charge that his former benefactor Jarndyce was in fact "the Incarnation of Selfishness" (p. 831). Despite his detestation of the Byronic mode of behavior, Dickens had enough respect for Byron the man to disapprove of Harriet Beecher Stowe's famous attack on the poet. "Wish Mrs. Stowe was in the pillory," he protested.[32]

The notion that a Romantic writer was above "principle and purpose" (p. 522), incapable of work or concern for others, was to Dickens's Victorian sensibility a matter of repugnance. Skimpole's "Drone philosophy"—whereby he expects the bees to do all the work while he enjoys the sweets of their labor (p. 93)— echoes the Dandiacal point of view in Carlyle's *Sartor Resartus;* and Carlyle's contempt for the modern dandies and his celebration of earnest and self-denying labor are very much felt in the Dickens novels of the 1850s. It is left to a very few Dickens characters, however, to illustrate the work ethic: Caddy Jellyby in the dancing academy, Allan Woodcourt in his medical profession, and Esther Summerson in her capacity as mistress of Bleak House. It was perhaps a mistake on Dickens's part to make Esther such a good character from the start, giving her no romantic illusions to overcome in the manner of a David Copperfield or no rebellious streak to subdue in the manner of a Jane Eyre. But since the novelist needed a foil to Skimpole, he exaggerated her goodness even as he exaggerated Hunt's potential for villainy. It is curious (as J. Hillis Miller has noted) that from Esther's perspective, life seems to have a purpose and direction that seem less obvious from the point of view of the novel's omniscient narrator.[33] Dickens relies on Esther's benign disposition so that her narrative will balance the omniscient narrator's grim picture. Where in *Middlemarch* George Eliot had sought to deflate the egoism deriving from each character's limited angle of vision, Eliot herself showing the larger point of view which indicates some sense of Providence and interconnection in the world, in *Bleak House* Dickens adopted the opposite method: like Tennyson in *In Memoriam*, he relied on the limited vision of a loving heart to project a sense of Providence that he implied may not, in fact, exist.

Where the emphasis in Dickens's most Victorian novels is on the need for the redirection of will by men and women of benevolent dispositions, in his most Romantic novels the stress is on the need for withdrawal—into the realm of fancy or into a romance of death. Early and late in his career, Dickens idealized and feared the display of energy. It was artistic energy that had allowed him a significant measure of power over his audience, and it was energy that he celebrated in the London scenes of his novels and sketches.[34] Wordsworth had seen London at its fairest when "the very houses seem asleep; / And all that mighty heart is lying still!" Dickens, on the other hand, delighted in the "moving mass" and the "ceaseless roar" of people, the movement and color and variety found only in the city (see *Nicholas Nickleby*, pp. 408–409). But Dickens could also visualize London from a Romantic point of view—in terms of "crowded, pent-up streets" (*OT*, p. 237), as in the prison-city of *Oliver Twist* and *Little Dorrit*—and in such moods the country offers more than a sense of momentary relief: it provides a peace and tranquillity that look suspiciously like death. In *Oliver Twist* Dickens intones (p. 237),

> The memories which peaceful country scenes call up, are not of this world, nor of its thoughts and hopes. Their gentle influence may teach us how to weave fresh garlands for the graves of those we loved: may purify our thoughts, and bear down before it old enmity and hatred; but beneath all this, there lingers, in the least reflective mind, a vague and half-formed consciousness of having held such feelings long before, in some remote and distant time, which calls up solemn thoughts of distant times to come, and bends down pride and worldliness beneath it.

It should be noted that the Wordsworthian "intimations of immortality" that Oliver feels in the country do not make him a spontaneous, unthinking child of nature—like the children in Wordsworth's poetry—but instead make him look forward to the time of his own death when the peace of pre-existence will be transferred to the calm of eternity. Where the child in "We Are Seven" is oblivious to the fact of death, Dickens's children seem oblivious to the fact of life.

Dickens's treatment of death and nature inspired his most maudlin sentiments on occasion; but just as he described in Skimpole a Romantic virtue carried to such extremes as to become loathsome, in his depictions of dying children and nature-graveyards he drew on Wordsworthian premises and carried them to grotesque, though not unwarranted, lengths. A Romantic like Wordsworth might replace his youthful energies with stoical precepts, might make his retreat into the realm of the imagination seem a religious act, but Dickens lacked the "philosophic mind" that found compensation for the loss of such energies.[35] Instead of having an intellectual stoicism that might allow him to see through death, Dickens saw death as the source of release from the compulsions and frustrations of the will. The problem with his treatment of death in the novels arises from the fact that he does not fully believe in—or understand—what he is sentimentalizing. The aspect of *The Old Curiosity Shop* (1841) that has so disgusted modern readers is already present in *Oliver Twist* in the opposition between the malign but vital force of Fagin and his associates and the innocence and moribund passivity of Oliver and Rose Maylie. When Oliver prays to Heaven "to spare him from such deeds; and rather to will that he should die at once, than be reserved for crimes, so fearful and appalling" (p. 146), Dickens is expressing a repulsion toward more than criminal acts of will. Oliver's deepest happiness, significantly, is occasioned by "that deep tranquil sleep which ease from recent suffering alone imparts; that calm and peaceful rest which it is pain to wake from. Who, if this were death, would be roused again to all the struggles and turmoils of life; to all its cares for the present; its anxieties for the future; more than all, its weary recollections of the past!" (p. 78). The sentiment recurs in Dickens's last completed novel, *Our Mutual Friend*.

Dickens uses the death of children, as Philip Collins remarks, to "make a final indictment of the adult world's misdeeds, but the atmosphere of peace and blessedness in which they die is not merely intended to comfort the distressed reader. 'Now more than ever seems it rich to die': these children repudiate the adult world, and Dickens is not sorry to see them thus escape from the 'contagion of the world's slow stain.' "[36] There are, to be sure, more than Romantic echoes in this infantine expression of the death wish. Dickens also draws on Shakespeare when he eulogizes death (the passage from *Oliver Twist* just quoted suggests Hamlet's defense of suicide), and when he depicts the preternaturally wise child, like Nell or Paul Dombey, who seems too good to live: in the words of Richard III, "So wise so young, they say do ne'er live long." What Dickens most obviously borrows from Wordsworth is the sense that by dying young Lucy Gray has been saved from the anxieties of age or the taint of worldliness and that by dying innocent she will never be disturbed by sensual instincts. (This Romantic view of the purity of childhood was severely challenged by Freud.) But where Lucy dead is seen as an eternal part of nature—a spirit "upon the lonesome wild," untouched by "earthly years"—Nell is an effigy of immobility in death as in life.

To the illustrator chosen to depict Nell in death, Dickens insisted that the scene exhibit "the most beautiful repose and tranquillity, and . . . have something of a happy look, if death can." The "effect" is meant to be that of a *tableau mourant*, with Nell as a ghostly actress hypnotizing the audience out of the sorrow they might otherwise feel. Attempting to console a grief-stricken couple who had lost their son, Dickens assured them that they might now have his image "*As a child*, In Heaven" forever.[37] Dickens's clinging to the image of Mary Hogarth (whose death inspired Nell's) for so many years enabled him to remember her always as frozen in the innocence of youth—and encouraged him, unfortunately, to regard woman's role as the personification of unchanging repose. "Think what earth is," the schoolmaster says over Nell's dead body, "compared with the World to which her young spirit has winged its early flight; and say, if one deliberate wish expressed in solemn terms above this bed could call her back to life, which of us would utter it!" (*OCS*, p. 539). The child's death is better than the adult's continuing existence: could it be that the thousands, including Dickens himself, who wept over Nell's death were really weeping for their own protracted suffering? The less Dickens himself could subscribe to this morbid celebration of death ("I can't preach to myself the schoolmaster's consolation," he told Forster, "though I try"),[38] the more he contrived, nevertheless, to invest the fact of death with a fairy-tale glamor in his writings.

In *The Old Curiosity Shop* death becomes the consummate romance: for Nell, a fairy-tale innocent in a world of fairy-tale, as well as realistic, horrors, the land of heart's desire is beyond the grave, where her mother has already "flown to a beautiful country beyond the sky, where nothing died or ever grew old" (p. 49). The Romantic quest for permanence leads, perhaps inevitably, to a worship of death. Nell and her grandfather flee the city not because they are pursued by the evil dwarf Quilp, but because she is determined that her grandfather will not be corrupted further by the temptations of city life. As they wander through the countryside, Nell, like Oliver, is especially drawn to the country graveyards, where children like herself have been transplanted to "a bright and happy existence" and hence spared "the pain of seeing others die around them, bearing to the tomb some strong affection of their hearts" (p. 194). Nell places her faith in the Wordsworthian Nature, who never betrays the heart that loves her ("Let us walk through country places, and sleep in fields and under trees, and never think of money again," she says trustingly; p. 71), yet she is sadly aware that the people closest to her are not so reliable. Dickens comes closest to Wordsworth in *The Old Curiosity Shop* in the contrast he makes between the demonic energy exhibited in the industrial town Nell and her grandfather pass through and the "freedom of pure air and open country" where such evils don't exist (p. 334). When people are immured in confined spaces, energies smolder and burst forth in ugly form, as is seen in the band of Chartists rushing forth by night "on errands of terror and destruction" (p. 336). In this novel, as in *Hard Times*, Dickens could show understanding of why and how such energies are unleashed, but his mistrust of energy and his distaste for rebellion forced him to look away from social solutions that did other than numb the rebellious instinct, forced him to look instead to the panacea of death and circuses.

Dickens's conscious design in *The Old Curiosity Shop* was to chronicle a pilgrimage from urban energy to pastoral peace, from the death-in-life of the city to the life-in-death of the country. There is no more reason to mourn Nell's death, from this point of view, than there would be to mourn Christian's in the Bunyan allegory to which Dickens makes constant reference. But the artistic delight with which he examines the urban culture he is affecting to despise, the exuberant creative energy with which he invests the figure of Daniel Quilp, who is meant to convince us of the destructive nature of that element, fatally undermines the Romantic-religious allegory. In Quilp, Dickens created (as Albert Guerard has perceived) a surrogate artist-figure, a monstrous embodiment of comic-sadistic power. In his terrorizing of Nell and her grandfather, in his tyranny over his all-too-compliant wife, Quilp parodies the Byronic hero in all his fatal attraction, even as he also resembles the wicked dwarf of fairy tales. It is tempting to associate Quilp with the Id or with the destructive nature of the will;[39] but there are too much stylization and comedy in his behavior, and in Dickens's manner of describing him, to warrant too close a scrutiny along those lines. Nor, for that matter, should one idealize Quilp as a representative of the life force. The grotesque antics that he performs before others cannot be taken too seriously: his is less the embodiment of evil than a pantomime performance of it. It is notable that in the grisly death Dickens provides for him— meant, obviously, to contrast with Nell's peaceful end—the novelist has unconsciously *become* Quip in the sadistic relish with which he disposes of the dwarf.

In *The Old Curiosity Shop* an exaggerated version of Wordsworthian quiescence is set off by a deformed version of Byronic magnetism; and while Dickens's sentimental nature inclines him in one direction, his creative drives direct him elsewhere. Unfortunately, both paths, the Wordsworthian and the Byronic, lead to the grave; and it is by another route that Dickens envisages a more invigorating form of consolation. The subplot of the novel, featuring Dick Swiveller and the Marchioness, parodies features of the main plot; a diminutive creature, like Nell, she is at the mercy of an ogre-mistress (Sally Brass), while he is a cockney version of the Byronic gentleman. Their meeting ground is their faith in the power of imagination to ward off the corrupt and corrupting influences around them.[40] The Marchioness's rescue of Dick from the illness that has very nearly killed him (which prefigures Lizzie Hexam's rescue of Eugene Wrayburn in Dickens's last completed novel) forms a contrast to Dickens's celebration of Nell's death, and it undermines the allegorical significance of that death. For appalling as life may seem to the narrator of Nell's death, it has compensations for the good-hearted who can use the power of their imagination to redeem life by coloring it to their point of view. "If you make believe very much," as the Marchioness says of the power of fancy to make "orange-peel and water" taste like wine, "it's quite nice" (p. 481).

The Romantic gospel Dickens offers in *Hard Times* (1854) might well be called the doctrine of "orange-peel and water" writ large. The world of Sleary's Circus does wondrous battle against a universe of muddle and destruction. At the founding of his popular journal *Household Words* in 1850, Dickens insisted on the need to include something of fancy and romance in every issue. In answer to those who, disturbed by the lack of constructive thought in Dickens's social criticism, see the novelist offering escapist fancies in place of solutions, it might be said that for Dickens escapism *was* a solution. *Hard Times* is a sequel to the series of Christmas Books Dickens wrote in the 1840s. There, the problems of modern life were resolved in a glow of affectionate feeling;[41] in *Hard Times*, Dickens suggests that without stimulants to the affections, without the nursing of a sense of wonder, a social revolution might well ensue. His injunction that the "common people" be provided with "the utmost graces of the fancies and affections" lest, deprived of romance, they turn "wolfish . . . , and make an end of you" (*HT*, p. 163), is simplistic at best. Convinced that power was corrupting, whether employed by the millowners or the workers' unions, Dickens nevertheless recognized the horrors of the average worker's life. He has no disagreement with Stephen Black-pool's declaration, "Look how we live, an' wheer we live, an' in what numbers, an' by what chances, and wi' what sameness; and look how the mills is awlus a goin, and how they never works us no higher to onny dis'ant object—ceptin awlus, Death" (pp. 149–150). But Dickens's Romantic stress on the primacy of feelings ensured that he, like Charlotte Brontë in her industrial novel *Shirley,* would hold grateful deference more worthy of respect in the workers than assertions of independence. (In *Bleak House,* Dickens is far more sympathetic to Captain George, the devoted army man who becomes Sir Leicester Dedlock's manservant, than he is to his brother, Rouncewell the ironmaster.) The imaginative sense of wonder, as Wordsworth affirmed in *The Excursion,* inevitably leads to a sense of reverence and forbearance. Coleridge asserted that reading the *Arabian Nights* in his childhood had habituated his mind to a sense of the "*Vast,*" culminating in his religious convictions. To Dickens, for whom the Coketown churches cannot offer the sort of solace to the fancy that he deems necessary, only a perpetual immersion in the *Arabian Nights* or children's tales, along with repeated visits to Sleary's Circus, will allay the anxieties of the masses.

Hard Times offers the basic Dickensian Romantic solution: the genii of "fancy" winning over the ogres of "fact." Wordsworth, Keats, and Disraeli had shown a similar determination to disregard facts in favor of the imagination; Dickens reduces this notion to its barest bones. In the process, his principal characters are reduced to walking demonstrations of the virtues of a life of fancy or the deadness of a life without it. Sissy Jupe, whom Dickens holds up as a paragon for her innocence in the ways of the world, is little more than a cardboard figure, labeled "wisdom of the Heart" (p. 223). The scene in which she subdues Louisa Gradgrind's would-be seducer, James Harthouse, by the sheer force of innocence is a marvel of fairy-tale logic. In Louisa, the daughter of a Utilitarian philosopher whose sternly realistic views Dickens sees causing a blight in England, Dickens had a character with genuine tragic potential. Having been deprived of the "dreams of childhood—its airy fables; its graceful, beautiful, humane, impossible adornments of the world beyond," she suffers a spiritual anguish of terrible force. The

Wordsworthian "root of piety" has been torn out of her life: "Her remembrances of home and childhood were remembrances of the drying up of every spring and fountain in her young heart as it gushed out. The golden waters were not there" (p. 197). One wishes that a more intelligent and passionate author than Dickens—George Eliot or Charlotte Brontë—had written the scenes in which Louisa very nearly succumbs to Harthouse's appeals. But having sketched in the background leading up to her great temptation, Dickens backs away suddenly; and she is finally, and unforgivably, reduced to another cardboard object lesson, which Dickens labels "the pride of [Gradgrind's] heart and the triumph of his system, lying, an insensible heap, at his feet" (p. 219).

Without the opiate of fancy, everything in life seems bleak and unendurable, an unfathomable "muddle." Louisa Gradgrind's realization that her father's philosophy leads to the same nihilistic conclusions as Harthouse's Byronic cynicism serves to remind us that for Dickens all intellectual systems were worthless:[42] "Where was the great difference between the two schools, when each chained her down to material realities, and inspired her with no faith in anything else? . . . Upon a nature long accustomed to self-suppression, thus torn and divided, the Harthouse philosophy came as a relief and justification. Everything being hollow and worthless, she had missed nothing and sacrificed nothing" (pp. 166–167). Only by instinct can one arrive at what George Eliot called the "truth of feeling," or at what the circus-owner Sleary sees as proof "that there ith a love in the world, not all Thelf-intereth after all" (pp. 292–293). But this belief in love is illustrated by the actions of a devoted dog, not by the domestic circle that Dickens apotheosized in *David Copperfield* and *Bleak House*. In the novels that followed *Hard Times*, Dickens stressed the value of the affectionate domestic household that is missing in that book; but by the time of *Our Mutual Friend*, in which the Harthouse-Gradgrind philosophy is again subdued by the force of devoted affection, a happy lovefilled household had come to seem as rare and wonderful and unreal as something out of a fairy tale.

Our Mutual Friend (1865) can perhaps be best appreciated as Dickens's valedictory statement as a creative artist: in it the mingled strands of his literary heritage—fairy tales, melodramas, eighteenth-century fiction, and Romantic fancies—come together to form his most comprehensive, though by no means his best, book. With almost his last gasp of Romantic optimism, he affirms his faith in the powers of imagination, benevolence, and womanly devotion to carry one through. The power of imagination is embodied in the crippled doll's dressmaker Jenny Wren, Dickens's reincarnation of Little Nell, who now, rather than seeking a fairy-tale resolution in death, makes a fairy-tale affirmation of life by pretending that it is death. The scene in which Jenny invites the victimized Jew Riah to join her on the London rooftop where they can pretend they are dead is a marvelous expression of poignant fancy: when the material pressures of the world keep men and women in a state of living death, the solution is to immerse oneself in a fantasy of non-being. To be "called back to life" (*OMF*, p. 281), as Jenny sees it, is to be reminded of all the heartache and the thousand natural shocks that flesh is heir to. Jenny's Elia-like reveries of being watched over by angel-children, and her ability to breathe the perfume of imaginary roses, are "pleasant fancies . . . given the child in compensation for her losses" (p. 239), and to miss the pathos of her situation, as well as to overlook the flashes of childish-sadistic glee in Jenny as modern admirers of her "escape artistry" have done, is to overrate the power of imagination as something sufficient in itself in Dickens's larger scheme.[43]

For it is to the younger Dickens's figure of the benevolent old gentleman, and to the literary cliché of the power of a good woman's love to work miracles, that the older Dickens turns in his search for forces that will bring about happiness and harmony. In Nicodemus Boffin, the loyal servant turned wealthy benefactor, Dickens combines the eighteenth-century good-hearted patron with the fairy godfather of children's tales. It is by his wizardly devices that Bella Wilfer is transformed from a petulant, avaricious young woman to the devoted wife of John Harmon with a newly developed "perfect genius for home" (p. 681). In choosing to disguise his true nature in order to test her good (and Silas Wegg's bad) qualities, Boffin echoes old Martin Chuzzlewit's stratagem to test the worth of his grandson and the duplicity of Pecksniff. It is a sign of the bleak and tired tone of the novel that Boffin and his wife seem the only vital presences; and the glee with which Dickens describes their acting talents reminds us of his own love of theatrical role-playing.[44] The Boffins don't inhabit the novel; they perform in it. In the parallel plot of *Our Mutual Friend*, which involves the physical and moral reclamation of a latter-day Byronic dandy, Eugene Wrayburn, at the hands of Lizzie Hexam, Dickens also drew upon a situation from a previous novel, in this case the Marchioness's rescue and nursing of Dick Swiveller; yet despite the rhetorical flourishes with which Wrayburn acts out his repentance, it is the earlier version of the scene that carries genuine conviction. One problem with the Eugene-Lizzie plot is the unnatural burden placed on Lizzie: she must be resourceful enough to rescue him from death but passive enough to be eternally grateful for the dubious honor he grants her. Eugene's moral transformation has been cited as one of the rare examples in Dickens where a character shows himself capable of change, but Dickens is, in part, updating the eighteenth-century convention of the reformed rake, which Richardson drew upon in *Pamela*. Moreover, the situation of a gentleman marrying a woman beneath him in social status is less daring than it might seem—certainly less daring than the Veneering circle regard it —if we think of the fairy tale of King Cophetua and the beggar maiden.

Although Dickens's portraits of women are more realistic in his later novels than in his early work, they remain less than fully convincing: the passion in the male figures' attitudes toward the women they love has deepened more than the reality of the women. (In his expression of Pip's feeling for Estella, for example, Dickens has strengthened his earlier heroes' psychological identity without making Estella a figure of much complexity in herself.) Bella's devotion to her husband in the face of her "trial" is no doubt very charming, but it leaves her permanently immured in Dickens's fairy-tale dollhouse. Moreover, in Lizzie's devotion to Wrayburn Dickens apotheosizes the virtue of womanly self-suppression, even as he shows the danger of that sacrifice in the figure of Bradley Headstone. Where Wrayburn and Headstone devote their energies to pursuing Lizzie, she in turn is armed only with "a woman's heart" that never, as she protests, seeks "to gain anything" (p. 527). Where a male, like John Harmon, may "repress [himself], and force [himself] to act a passive part," he does so with "a settled purpose" (p. 521), in Harmon's case, to test Bella; but with his purpose accomplished, his will is reasserted in moderate form. In the Dickensian woman's case, the exertion of will is always bad—witness Miss Wade and Mrs. Clennam in *Little Dorrit*—and the passive role is held up as the most fulfilling.

In Betty Higden, Dickens makes a rare allowance for a woman's independent character, but hers is a negative version of the "resolution and independence" of Wordsworth's leechgatherer: her native streak of self-sufficiency is devoted to the principle that she be allowed to die in the manner she chooses, not to end up at the mercy of the poorhouse. The Wordsworthian idealization of peasant fortitude finds its ultimate expression in Betty Higden's flight toward self-obliteration, just as (at the opposite Romantic pole) the Byronic heroism of energetic self-will finds dual expression in the contrasting figures of Wrayburn and Bradley Headstone. In Lizzie's two suitors the Byronic magnetism has been split off from the Byronic willfulness: Wrayburn is the better of the two because he has a faded gentlemanly charm that Dickens was beginning to find attractive in his old age and because he lacks will.[45] In the schoolmaster Headstone the will explodes in the frenzy of animal energy that Dickens saw as the inevitable result of sustained self-suppression: "Tied up all day with his disciplined show upon him, subdued to the performance of his routine of educational tricks, encircled by a gabbling crowd, he broke loose at night like an ill-tamed wild animal" (p. 547). The Byronic idleness and irresponsibility of a Steerforth or a Harthouse is forgiven in Wrayburn because, in the end, he is a victim rather than a victimizer. "Better to be Abel than Cain," one of Dickens's chapter titles, might serve as a motto for the entire novel. In his original plan, Dickens had intended to have Eugene die of Headstone's assault on him: thus he, along with the schoolmaster and Betty Higden, would have demonstrated that, as in the cases of Quilp and Nell, the contending Romantic attractions of Byronic willfulness and Wordsworthian quiescence inevitably shade into death wishes.

For Dickens at this stage in his life, driven by energies that brought him no possibility of relief, death was beginning to take on an ominous attractiveness, culminating in the *Oliver Twist* readings in which, as he acted out the deaths of Sikes and Nancy, he committed a kind of suicide nightly. The death wish that had first appeared in Oliver's desire to lie at rest forever resurfaces in *Our Mutual Friend* in the extraordinary passage in which Dickens describes the villainous Rogue Riderhood's struggle to return from the dead: "And yet—like us all, when we swoon—like us all, every day of our lives when we wake—he is instinctively unwilling to be restored to the consciousness of this existence, and would be left dormant, if he could" (pp. 444–445). This Romantic fixation with death reaches its literary climax in *The Mystery of Edwin Drood*, whose schizophrenic hero-villain, John Jasper, unites the Wordsworthian and Byronic polarities. With his mesmeric hold over others and his murderous will, Jasper reflects the Byronic Corsair as adapted for the sensation novel of the 1860s.[46] Mr. Grewgious's characterization of him as "a brigand and a wild beast in combination" (*ED*, p. 245) points up the likeness. But the presumed murderer of Edwin Drood is also the victim of opium dreams, the genuinely innocent seeker of his nephew's murderer. Jasper's vow to destroy the murderer is a preparation for a scene that Dickens did not live to write: the willful and the quiescent, victimizer and victim, confronting one another in the same being.

In *Our Mutual Friend*, however, Dickens ultimately resisted the morbid tendency of his Romantic instincts and returned to the Victorian romance of harmonious domestic life to ward off ill thoughts. Wrayburn is morally transformed by Lizzie's love into a protective, if somewhat patronizing, husband; and even Jenny Wren is allowed to exchange her fancies for a retarded but devoted follower in Sloppy. Above all, in the union of Bella and John Harmon, blessed by their godparents, the Boffins, Dickens made his last Tennysonian appeal to the strength of love as the great buttress against moral and material contamination. This presentation of domestic concord as the ultimate escapist fantasy is a victory of sorts for Dickens's creative power over the sense of drift and desolation evident in his private life. While writing *The Old Curiosity Shop*, twenty-four years earlier, Dickens had described to Forster the wonderfully mesmeric power his creative gifts had had upon him at a time of deep personal unhappiness: "But may I not be forgiven," he asked, "for thinking it a wonderful testimony to my being made for my art, that when, in the midst of this trouble and pain, I sit down to my book, some beneficent power shows it all to me, and tempts me to be interested, and I don't invent it—*but see it*, and write it down . . . It is only when it all fades away and is gone, that I begin to suspect that its momentary relief has cost me something."[47]

EIGHT

George Meredith:
A Romantic in Spite of Himself

---

*The hero is chargeable with the official disqualification of
constantly-offending prejudices, never seeking to please; and
all the while it is upon him the narrative hangs. To be a
public favourite is his last thought. Beauchampism, as one
confronting him calls it, may be said to stand for nearly
everything which is the obverse of Byronism, and rarely woos
your sympathy, shuns the statuesque pathetic, or any kind of
posturing. For Beauchamp will not even look at happiness
to mourn its absence; melodious lamentations, demoniacal
scorn, are quite alien to him. His faith is in working and
fighting. With every inducement to offer himself for a
romantic figure, he despises the pomades and curling-irons
of modern romance, its shears and its labels: in fine,
every one of those positive things by whose aid, and by some
adroit flourishing of them, the nimbus known as a mysterious
halo is produced about a gentleman's head.*

Beauchamp's Career

As the possessor of intellectual powers second only to George
Eliot's and of imaginative energies exceeded only by those of
Dickens among the great Victorian novelists, George Meredith
is the proper figure with whom to conclude a study of the Romantic impulse in nineteenth-century fiction. It may be, as Oscar
Wilde and others have suggested, that Meredith was too highly
endowed for his own good. The Meredith novels strike many
readers as undigested and undigestible mixtures of painful psychological realism and extravagant comic romance. There is much
truth to Wilde's admiring claim that Meredith "is not a realist"
at heart, "that he is a child of realism who is not on speaking
terms with his father" and who "by deliberate choice . . . has
made himself a romanticist." But Meredith was also a child of
romance and Romanticism who determined to convey a vision

of reality in his novels that would accommodate the fantastic as well as the earthly. His novels are perhaps the finest examples in English before Joyce of the sort of grandiose Romantic fiction conjured up by Friedrich Schlegel: a genre ambitious enough to contain irony and romance and myth.[1] However, for all the strength of his Romantic sensibility, Meredith was also the single major Victorian novelist to defy the Romantic devaluation of women—to treat women as individuals worthier of a higher role in life than serving to inspire, or merely serving, the male Romantic genius.

Meredith's first novel was published a year after the death of another poet-novelist in whose work the spirit of the *Arabian Nights* mingled with Byronic Romanticism, Charlotte Brontë; and it appeared a year before the first work of fiction, *Scenes of Clerical Life*, of a philosopher-novelist similarly motivated by realistic and Romantic premises, George Eliot. Acknowledging the receipt of *The Shaving of Shagpat: An Arabian Nights Entertainment* (1856), Dickens assured its author that the book could not have been sent to a more favorably disposed reader: "I take it home to-night to read, and shall not be unworthy to enter on its perusal, as one of the most constant and delighted readers of those Arabian Nights Entertainments of older date than they have ever had, perhaps."[2] The *Arabian Nights* had a lifelong appeal to all the novelists considered in this book: even the archrealist Anthony Trollope, in a waggish mood, once promised to inscribe a copy of the *Arabian Nights* to "Kate Field, from the Author." In her review of Meredith's novel, George Eliot called *The Shaving of Shagpat* "a work of genius," regarding its "Oriental forms" with the sort of critical enthusiasm she is sometimes thought to have reserved for the soberly realistic doctrine of Ruskin. Reading the *Arabian Nights* in childhood was a momentous event to Coleridge and Newman: Coleridge claimed to have become so "habituated *to the Vast*" as a result that he was later enabled to discount the evidence of sensory experience when he formulated his metaphysical beliefs; while Newman clung to the view that the Tales had provided his youthful imagination with a sense of authority higher than that of the "material world."[3] From a metaphysical point of view, the *Arabian Nights* demonstrated the superiority of the spiritual to the phenomenal world; but the Tales also did much to illustrate a cardinal element of Romantic theory: the primacy of the imagination over the world of facts. In many ways, the Romantic impulse in Victorian fiction was stimulated by the spirit of romance—both the Eastern variety as expressed in the Tales and the European chivalric tradition as manifested in Ariosto or the *Amadis de Gaule*.

In "A Gossip on Romance," Robert Louis Stevenson cites the *Arabian Nights* as the supreme example of the natural human craving for escapist "Adventure" pure and simple, literary daydreams detached from the threats and confusions of modern life. In the Sleary's Circus portion of *Hard Times*, Dickens presents a slightly moralized version of Stevenson's romantic credo —that the creative artist is obliged "to satisfy the nameless longings of the reader, and to obey the ideal laws of the day-dream." For Dickens, the problems of industrialism and mechanistic codes of behavior could not be solved, could only be evaded through visits to the circus (where a more selfless ethic than that of the Coketown manufacturers is displayed) and through readings in romances and fairy tales. Meredith's novelty in *The Shaving of Shagpat*, therefore, was in using a fundamentally escapist literary form for highly serious ends.[4] The first of his novels contains the themes of much of his later work—the ordeal that a hero must undergo, the need to conquer egoism and ego-bred illusions, the superior wisdom of women, and the value of comedy to social well-being—but it also reveals his love for a form that is synonymous with magic and adventure and boyish wish-fulfillment. Asked in old age which books had had the most "formative" effect on him, Meredith listed the *Arabian Nights* first—to indicate that it had been the earliest book to arouse his imagination, but also to demonstrate its continuing hold on him in the company of the more corrective influences of "Gibbon, Niebuhr, Walter Scott; then Molière, then the noble Goethe, the most enduring."[5]

More perhaps than any other romance, the *Arabian Nights* supported the youthful fantasies of Dickens, Charlotte Brontë, and Meredith that they were destined for a special fate and a noble role in life. Unlike the chivalric romances in which only high-born heroes can aspire to perform acts of valor or marry beautiful princesses, the *Arabian Nights* allows for the triumph of outsiders—cobblers, porters, and even tailors' sons, the most famous of whom is Aladdin. In addition, the heroes of the *Arabian Nights* receive their rewards with a minimum of exertion on their part: such things are ordained by fate (or Allah) to happen. (Hence, Darsie Latimer, in Scott's *Redgauntlet*, allows himself to imagine becoming the "hero of some romantic story" without expending "any effort or exertion"; while Rosamond Vincy, in Eliot's *Middlemarch*, dreams of "ideal happiness" such as is "known in the Arabian Nights, in which you are invited to step from the labour and discord of the street into a paradise where everything is given to you and nothing claimed.")[6] No doubt the childish feeling of having been born to higher things than their immediate background seemed to allow for encouraged many future Victorian writers to view their creative powers as a kind of magic: the novelist creating a world out of nothing was the successor to the genii of their childhood readings. In Meredith's case, such creative ambitions combined with the family romance believed in by his father and grandfather, tailors both, that they were descended from Welsh royalty. As a child, Meredith kept away from others his age and indulged in fantasies of being a "gentleman" with purer blood and finer prospects than the tradesmen's children he met.[7] Harry Richmond's youthful sense that he can read the minds of others, in proof of his superiority to them, is a fictional reflection of Meredith's self-conceit at this age; but it is also a demonstration of his "magical" powers. In *Evan Harrington* (1860) and *Harry Richmond* (1871), Meredith laughed at his romantic pretensions; but he also saw to it that romance conquered in the end or else, when thwarted, exacted a fearsome revenge on reality. Evan, whose fictional career was meant to be that of a tailor masquerading as a gentleman, comes off as a gentleman temporarily masquerading as a tailor; and the conquest of romance in *Harry Richmond* or in *Beauchamp's Career* (1875) is achieved at very high cost. If Meredith could never quite remove romance from his novels, this was because he realized that such an exorcism would be tantamount to artistic suicide. As in the case of Charlotte Brontë, the Meredithian battle against romance and Romantic values was a battle against the creative impulse itself, which he fortunately (unlike Brontë) managed to lose enough of the time so that he could continue to write.

Just as the Victorian novelists' reaction against the Romantic values that were dominant in their childhood may be seen as a reaction against the very forces that had nourished their creative ambitions, so too can their occasionally ambivalent attitude toward romance be seen as a form of self-scourging. To Meredith, romance was the breeding ground of egoism: "romance," as Gillian Beer says apropos of *Harry Richmond*, "is the desire for omnipotence, the will to make the world and its people approximate to one's vision of them." Where the Victorian novel stresses the supremacy of the objective world in opposition to its inhabitants' subjective desires, the romance follows a pattern in which (in Robert Kiely's words) "The ego absorbs all and temporarily becomes the world."[8] Meredith's greatest novel, *The Egoist* (1879), deals with the comic victory of the "world" over the egoistic Sir Willoughby Patterne; but it might be wondered if, having achieved this masterpiece of romantic self-exposure, Meredith could ever put his creative energies to satisfying use again. As it happened, the novels that followed *The Egoist* are his most unabashedly "romantic," both in the cultivation of a style so singular as to seem (to many readers) virtually unreadable, and in the development of plots in which an individual consistently defies the laws of household or country in behalf of a higher, more personal standard of moral authority. Mrs. Berry's statement in *The Ordeal of Richard Feverel* (1859) that even with a father's injunctions one "musn't go again' the law of his nature" points the way to the Shelleyan temper of the late Meredith novels. Similarly, Meredith's assertion that poets like Tennyson and Browning cannot be appraised in any other light than their singularity of style and vision—"They are to themselves 'both law and impulse' "—is a reminder that creativity is individualism in action, albeit individualism in potentially the noblest of roles.[9]

Although Meredith's birthdate (1828) puts him in a later generation than Dickens or Trollope, by temperament he belongs to the generation before them, that of Byron, Stendhal, and Scott. A testimony to his affiliation with this second generation of Romantics can be seen in his love of the chivalric romances whose themes turn up in so many of his novels. Chivalry, according to Scott in his essay on the subject, provided a code of behavior for medieval knights whereby individualistic energies could be channeled into selfless functions. Although the love of glory might tempt a knight toward "Enterprises the most extravagant in conception, the most difficult in execution, the most useless when achieved" (one thinks of Beauchamp's career as a frustrated version of this goal), the love of God and reverence toward one's lady provided a tempering and civilizing influence. Chivalry declined, Scott explains, when it was discovered that disciplined troops achieved better results in battle than single, frequently reckless, knights, and also when the display of romantic selfless devotion, such as that of a Sir Lancelot, proved less persuasive a model than the self-indulgence of a Sir Tristram. However, the chivalric ideal survived, in large measure, because of Scott's Tory convictions regarding the duties of the ruling class, his belief in the need for "individual freedom to defend the social order," which his novels did much to popularize for nineteenth-century readers.[10]

For Scott, the ideal hero of romance was Amadis de Gaule, the very model of "chivalrous constancy" in his devotion to the equally faithful Oriana, and the prototype for Meredith's gallant Evan Harrington.[11] The favorite romance of Scott's generation, however, was Ariosto's *Orlando Furioso*—to whom Meredith paid oblique tribute in *Evan Harrington* by selecting for his hero's name that of the Ferrarese poet's Renaissance translator. (Evan's high scruples with regard to honor, even when they threaten to deny him the hand of the heroine, call to mind Ruggiero's lofty sense of honor, which very nearly costs him the hand of his beloved Bradamante.) The very "term 'romantic poetry,' " René Wellek observes, "was used first of Ariosto and Tasso and the medieval romances from which their themes and 'machinery' were derived." Where Plutarch's celebration of patriotic valor and duty had provided the favorite reading and inspiration for Rousseau, Schiller, and Wordsworth, Ariosto's mixture of exuberance and irony appealed to the second generation of Romantics, in love with heroism provided that it sometimes mocked its own pretensions. As a student, Scott insisted, to his teacher's disgust, upon Ariosto's superiority to Homer; and in later years he admitted to rereading Ariosto (and Boiardo) once a year. "Ariosto formed my character," admits Stendhal's autobiographical Henri Brulard; and the hero of *The Charterhouse of Parma* wanders with sublime innocence into battle, thinking that he is reliving the exploits of Ariosto and Tasso. "It was Byron," as Barbara Reynolds has recently noted, "who, above all, possessed an exceptional capacity for assimilating and recommunicating the spirit of Ariosto, for capturing his ability to pass from one thing to another with the greatest ease, to throw out reflections apparently casual but full of profundity. The light raillery, the good-natured fun, the tolerant cynicism, the philosophy of humour are qualities which the mature Byron shares with Ariosto." Meredith lacked Byron's lightness of touch; but his treatment of heroism in *The Ordeal of Richard Feverel* and *Beauchamp's Career* owes much to the Ariosto-Byronic combination of serious regard for and gentle satire of its ambitions and frustrations. And Meredith too was possessor of a "philosophy of humour."[12]

A number of Meredith's characteristic creative virtues and flaws may well owe something to Ariosto's example. The apparent lack of structure in a Meredith novel—the abrupt shifts from scene to scene or from comedy to tragedy, for example—is reminiscent of Ariosto's practice. Asked to describe the format of *Childe Harold*, Byron maintained that he was working "on Ariosto's plan that is to say on no plan at all"; similarly, he claimed the sort of license in describing Don Juan's career that Ariosto had taken.[13] *The Ordeal of Richard Feverel* was assailed for inconsistencies in tone and for daring in treatment that would have gone unnoticed in Ariosto. The most obvious of Meredith's borrowings from the *Orlando Furioso* is the mythic airborn creature, the hippogriff, whom Wilfrid Pole in *Sandra Belloni* (1864) metaphorically mounts during his sentimental flights. The novelist's most significant link with the poet, however, involves their attitude toward women. Ariosto's heroines are models of valor (Bradamante, Marfisa), devotion (Isabella, Fiordiligi), and instinctive intelligence. Jealous male historians, Ariosto claims, have conspired to minimize the role of women in history (*Orlando Furioso*, 37.23); but it will be his aim—and here he was followed by Scott and Meredith—to redress the balance, to hymn the heroic potential and the actual achievements of women. His romance, accordingly, is filled with tributes to quasi-mythical female warriors (Bradamante is established as the mythic ancestor of the ruling Este family of Ferrara) and to real figures like the poet Vittoria Colonna. Ariosto's hope that the Italian states might one day abandon their petty intrigues among themselves and unite against the common enemy was echoed three and a half centuries later in Meredith's novel about the rivalries and egoisms that stand in the way of a unified Italy, *Vittoria* (1867). That novel's heroine, whose name perhaps derives from Vittoria Colonna although her artistic nature reminds one also of a Corinne turned political activist, is the first of Meredith's "New Women" in whom the courage, dedication, and spontaneous wisdom of the Ariosto heroines are resurrected to memorable effect.

Among nineteenth-century English novelists, only Scott, who also looked to Ariosto, created women of such heroic potential. Scott's heroes may be passive by nature, but such vigorous heroines as Diana Vernon (*Rob Roy*) and Flora MacIvor (*Waverley*) goad the men to rebellious action. In this respect, Meredith, by turning back to the romance tradition, bypassed the Romantic poets' celebration of woman's quiescent and submissive, albeit "inspirational," nature (Shelley is a partial exception here), which Victorian novelists like Dickens and George Eliot picked up on. Meredith's dissimilarity to the novelists who were his contemporaries can be seen in his obstinate reliance upon plots and characters that derive from the old romances. He was probably, after George Eliot, the best-read of the major Victorian novelists, but he drew upon a different frame of literary and social reference. Where George Eliot's sense of "duty" originated in her childhood Evangelical beliefs, Meredith's belief in human "obligation" seems linked in large part to his love of chivalric romance. From his choice of high (or at least nobly) born protagonists, his reliance upon plots in which characters must prove their worthiness, one might reasonably deduce that for Meredith a romance impulse was more significant than the Romantic impulse that animated Dickens, Eliot, Gaskell, or even, on occasion, Trollope. Meredith's combined spirit of seriousness and self-mockery might seem out of place in the

Victorian intellectual milieu, which placed such high value on "high seriousness" and on the responsibilities of the artist. It would be a good many years before Meredith found a Victorian audience to respond to what seemed an eccentric style and perverse choice of subject matter. However, Meredith readily admitted his links with Continental European Romanticism; and much of the anti-Romantic satire that Meredith turns upon his heroes, and some of the solemnity with which he regarded his artistic calling, reflect his reluctant indebtedness to the native Romantic tradition as well.

From Goethe, for example, whom he called "the pattern for all who would have a directing hold of themselves," Meredith received philosophical and literary aid: lessons in the need for seeing the world and oneself objectively, and a fictional form, the *Bildungsroman*, in which to apply that lesson to his protagonists. (Three Meredith novels, which I will consider later, are descendants of *Wilhelm Meister's Apprenticeship*: *The Ordeal of Richard Feverel*, *Harry Richmond*, and *Beauchamp's Career*.) Professor Julius von Karsteg in *Harry Richmond* is in many ways a mouthpiece for Goethe's views: from him Harry hears of the necessity for the sublimation of self and for striving in behalf of noble aims. Meredith's belief that idealism in art is desirable only if it is based on a realistic foundation (such realists as Shakespeare and Goethe, he claims, "have the broad arms of Idealism at command" only because they themselves are firmly rooted to earth) has its nonaesthetic application in von Karsteg's warning to Harry that he may aim at a star so long as he does so with his head. Meredith was more appreciative of Goethe's oriental-inspired poetry than the sentimental posturings of *Werther*—which, as far as he was concerned, had had a detestable influence similar to that of Byron's early work.[14]

A connoisseur of German poetry, Meredith was especially fond of Heine's lyricism: he once considered giving a lecture on Heine that would complement his lecture on comedy. From Heine (and from Jean Paul Richter) Meredith learned to become a master of romantic irony, which allowed him to preach a lofty philsophy of nature and art and human potentiality while simultaneously interjecting himself facetiously into his fiction—thereby breaking the illusion of fictive reality for the sake of demonstrating the artistic process at work. Oskar Walzel's description of Nikolaus Lenau's "nature mythology"— Lenau's attempt to "combine nature and humanity into something 'organically alive' which would represent symbolically the sublimer spiritual unity of natural and human life"—sounds suspiciously like a description of Meredith's nature poetry. (The young Meredith wrote on this "remarkable" Austrian poet for *Fraser's Magazine* in 1852.) Another link between Meredith and the German Romantics involves their advocacy of women's rights; however, *The Egoist* and *Diana of the Crossways* are considerably more advanced, in this respect, than Friedrich Schlegel's once-notorious *Lucinde* (1799), in which woman's passivity is raised to a transcendental-erotic level.[15] And if Meredith's first novel, *The Shaving of Shagpat*, reflects his fondness for the *Arabian Nights,* his second novel, *Farina: A Legend of Cologne* (1857), reveals the extent of his absorption in German folktales. Meredith's theory of the intellectual basis of comedy owes much to another favorite German author of his and Carlyle's, Jean Paul Richter; and traces of Richter's Sterne-derived whimsicality and his "eccentric individuality" of style can be found in *The Ordeal of Richard Feverel* no less than in *Sartor Resartus.* Richter's habit of "following 'steam baths of emotion' with 'cold showers of satire' " was to become one of Meredith's accustomed mannerisms.[16]

The young Meredith's education in Germany was responsible for his subsequent habit of regarding that country as the pre-eminent realm of romance, although Italy and France also had strong holds on his romantic imagination. The sensible, realistic-minded maidens in his novels are inevitably English-born (Janet Ilchester in *Harry Richmond* and Cecilia Halkett in *Beauchamp's Career,* for example), but his romantic heroines contain either Continental or Celtic blood: Princess Ottilia in *Harry Richmond,* Countess Renée in *Beauchamp's Career,* the heroine of *Vittoria,* Diana Warwick in *Diana of the Crossways,* and all the rest. As a poet of "Earth," however, Meredith belongs among the English Romantic poets. Where Goethe hymns "eternal womanhood" for drawing man heavenward, Meredith praises terrestrial womanhood for bringing man back to earth, where he belongs. For late nineteenth- and early twentieth-century admirers of Meredith's poetry of earth, only Wordsworth seemed worthy of comparison, even if, for some, Wordsworth's depiction of a comforting, maternal Nature seemed naïve in the wake of Darwin's discoveries. Meredith himself regarded Wordsworth as "the least dangerous of all preceptors to a youthful poet, and one whose sound and sonorous English, reverence for his art, and eternal dealing with the well-heads of Nature, can do nothing but good to a young and imaginative mind."[17] But where Wordsworth is ultimately more of a metaphysical than a descriptive poet, interested in the "mystery" that lies behind Nature and that obliges man to submit to a transcendent authority, Meredith's Nature is essentially palpable, a force that compels man toward self-discipline rather than points him upward. In his first published volume, *Poems* (1851), the young Meredith included tributes in verse to five Romantic poets. Southey and Coleridge are invoked, though not Byron; and Wordsworth's poetry is characterized in terms that provoke awe rather than joy ("The voice of great Nature; sublime with her lofty conceptions"). Meredith's favorite native Romantic poets, one would gather from this volume, were Keats and Shelley, the first for his gorgeous descriptions and language, the latter for his selfless idealism and sense of mission. (One of Meredith's finest lyrics of later years, "The Lark Ascending," was perhaps intended as a Victorian version of Shelley's "To a Skylark.") In the 1851 tributary poem, Shelley is characterized as a skylark fluttering "Deep in the heart-yearning distance of heaven." But the best-known of the 1851 poems is the Keatsian "Love in the Valley," a celebration of sensuous and sensual delights.

In some respects, the English Romantics left a dangerous legacy to aspiring Victorian poets. From Keats, it might be charged, Meredith learned the habit of writing too consciously for effect, of over-"loading every rift of the subject with ore."[18] And from Shelley, Meredith, like George Eliot, drew encouragement to regard himself too self-consciously as a divinely inspired being, set uniquely apart from his fellow mortals. The Romantic sense of having been born to communicate eternal wisdom in the form of subjective utterance degenerated in the late 1840s and early 1850s during the vogue of the Spasmodic poets. Meredith was briefly linked with the Spasmodics thanks to his friendship with R. H. Horne (who introduced him to Dickens); a typically Spasmodic effort was Meredith's 1851 sonnet to Alexander Smith, reproaching the author of *A Life Drama* for having dared to doubt the sanctity of poetic fame. ("Fame is the birthright of the living lyre!" Meredith replies to Smith, and to Milton before him.) One need only look at the letters he wrote in his twenties to see how seriously Meredith took his newly discovered poetic vocation.[19] The *Arabian Nights* fantasy of having been born for great ends combined with the Shelleyan-Spasmodic notion of the divinity of the poet, misunderstood or persecuted by others. Meredith was prepared, well in advance of the negative reception of his works, to don the martyr's crown of thorns along with the poet's laurels. An unhappy souvenir of Meredith's dalliance among the Spasmodics was his truculent attitude toward his critics, which sometimes extended toward his readers as well.

Meredith's artistic development might be said to have begun the moment he was able to turn the light of the comic spirit onto his own delusions of grandeur. Beginning with *The Shaving of Shagpat*, he made self-anatomy the great theme of his work; it was because he had swallowed so much of the Romantic sense of self, along with the romance-inspired fantasies of self-importance, that he was able to make Romanticism and romance prime targets in his novels. In later years, Meredith wrote poems satirizing the Romantic postures of Byron's Manfred, Victor Hugo's Hernani, and Matthew Arnold's Empedocles, egoists (in Meredith's view) who utter sentimental platitudes but ignore the obligations they owe to nature and reason. Meredith's contempt for "Byronics" did not, however, prevent a considerable admiration for and even a certain degree of identification with Byron: "He's abused, so I take to him," he once remarked. Visiting Venice in 1861, Meredith felt himself following in "Byron's and Shelley's footsteps." "I love both those poets," he confessed; "and with my heart given to them I felt as if I stood in a dead and useless time."[20] As Byron's reputation ebbed in the 1860s, Meredith considered the author of *Don Juan* a healthy alternative to Tennyson; and he was heartened when two of his friends, Swinburne and John Morley, wrote stirring defenses of Byron. He rejected the sickly posturing of a Manfred, but in Byron's "ruggedness" and "manliness" he found a needful tonic. "I adore his humour," he told Swinburne, "which is about the highest we possess." In his lecture on comedy, Meredith reaffirmed his high opinion of Byron's satiric powers; however, Byron in his histrionic "anti-social position" he viewed as a fit target for the comic spirit.[21] This description of Byron as both satirist and object of satire applies to Meredith too. Moreover, Meredith's greatest predecessor as Romantic anti-Romantic was Byron himself.

Byron's debunking of the myth of heroism has been cited as evidence of his legacy to the hero-less Victorian novel;[22] but like Ariosto before and Stendhal and Meredith after him, Byron knew the art of simultaneously winking at and keeping alive the wise absurdities of romance. A more serious attempt to keep the spirit of chivalric romance alive in the modern world was made by Scott. It is interesting to note that both Scott and Meredith have been credited with the "conquest of Romanticism" and the achievement of objective realism in the novel. Robert Kiely has corrected Georg Lukács's interpretation of Scott by showing that, while the novelist "ultimately repudiated" the lure of romance in favor of a more sensible and law-abiding code of behavior, nevertheless "what seems most stimulating to his creative imagination is almost invariably that which is unacceptable to his reason."[23] Scott's virtually irresolvable dilemma was Meredith's too: the conquest of romance and Romanticism implied not only the rule of reason and the triumph of civic order but the defeat of the creative impulse. Meredith cited Scott as the fourth of his "formative" influences; and the Meredith novel which most closely adheres to the pattern used by the author of *Waverley*—an impressionable hero's pilgrimage through the dual realms of romance and reason—was the book that guaranteed Meredith a role in the Romantic revival of the 1880s, *Harry Richmond*.

Meredith did not list Carlyle among the authors who most influenced his development as a writer; but *Beauchamp's Career* and Meredith's letters attest to the fact that he regarded Carlyle as a potent source of inspiration with dangerous tendencies. Like Scott and Byron, Carlyle was a Romantic anti-Romantic, anti-

Romantic in his crusade against the subjective impulse and Romantic in his subjective style and hero-obsessed vision. Meredith singled out for praise two aspects of Carlyle that he had also hailed in Byron: his robust sense of humor and his "manliness." But to his friend Frederick Maxse (the model for Beauchamp), Meredith cautioned that while Carlyle, as "the nearest to being an inspired writer of any man in our time[,] . . . does proclaim inviolable law: he speaks from the deep springs of life," Carlyle's practical solutions were suspect: "when he descends to our common pavement, when he would apply his eminent spiritual wisdom to the course of legislation, he is no more sagacious nor useful nor temperate than a flash of lightning in a grocer's shop."[24] Carlyle's analysis of the ills of Victorian society, his detestation of humbug, his critique of materialist values, and his championing of the laboring class are reason enough for Meredith's, and his Carlyle-inspired hero Nevil Beauchamp's, high praise. But Carlyle was unable to offer more than "heroes and rhetoric and romanticism in the pejorative sense" (in Arnold Kettle's words)—an unsatisfactory alternative to Dickens's prescription of circuses and romances—in response to the social-industrial muddle. Kettle links Carlyle and Meredith too closely together, seeing the author of *Beauchamp's Career* trapped behind the "paraphernalia of Byronism" that he had intended to cast away. But Kettle concludes his study of that novel with a brilliant afterthought:

> Romanticism in its various forms and aspects and implications is the great critical problem of English nineteenth-century literature, and it is a problem precisely because the Romantic impulse contains at the same time all that is best and worst in the literature of the time. If Meredith—or Carlyle—had drunk less deep of the Romantic draught they would certainly not be the writers they are; but it is also doubtful whether they would have become writers at all.[25]

It is ironic that the Romantic revolution originally instigated in behalf of the liberation of human political, social, imaginative, and creative energies should have come, by the mid-nineteenth century, to seem synonymous with self-indulgent and antisocial behavior. The altruism of a Shelley had metamorphosed into the irresponsibility of a Harold Skimpole. Similarly, Scott's revitalization of chivalric romance as a power intended to combat the egoistic and competitive spirit of the early nineteenth century had come to seem a defense of feudal authoritarianism. The defense of individual rights, in both cases, had been reinterpreted as a justification for singular behavior. Meredith's task in novels like *Harry Richmond* and *Beauchamp's Career* was to differentiate between the negative results of romance and Romanticism and their positive intentions. Whereas in *The Ordeal of Richard Feverel* Romantic values are transformed into destructive egoistic acts, in *Beauchamp's Career* the extinction of Romantic ambitions is seen to be disastrous to society. The triumph of civilization is Meredith's dream; but society purged of Romantic energies is no more satisfactory than Romantic energies allowed to flourish in opposition to society. Ideally, the individual and society should find a common ground; but in practice the two seem hopelessly antithetical. In *The Ordeal of Richard Feverel, Harry Richmond*, and *Beauchamp's Career*, the perils of romance and Romanticism are weighed against their positive values; but Meredith is finally unable to arrive at the synthesis he has attempted.

Both Sir Austin Feverel and his son Richard, the twin protagonists of *The Ordeal of Richard Feverel*, are worshippers of Romantic idols. Meredith demonstrates in their parallel careers how a perversion of Romantic values causes misfortune for virtually everyone the two have dealings with. The victim of an unhappy marriage, Sir Austin resolves to raise his son according to a "system" whereby he will be spared the misfortunes of his father. The Rousseauesque origins of this educational system have long been recognized: for both Sir Austin and the author of *Émile* an idealistic plan for the promotion of purity and natural wisdom in a young man is invalidated by egoistic flaws in the promoter's own nature.[26] The spirit of "system" crushes the native "instinct" which rises in natural rebellion against the system. Richard is as much a tragic victim, in this sense, as Louisa Gradgrind under her father's similarly well-intended educational system. (The relationship between *The Ordeal of Richard Feverel* and *Hard Times* is strengthened if we think of Mrs. Berry as Meredith's version of Sissy Jupe, embodying the "wisdom of the heart.") But the real Romantic villain of the novel is not Rousseau but Byron: it is through love of the Byronic mode that Sir Austin and Richard are responsible for the failures of their marriages; and it is by following the Byronic route—exacerbated, in Richard's case, by his overfondness for the postures of chivalric romance—that father and son are both transformed into Byronic misanthropes.

As the author of *The Pilgrim's Scrip*, a collection of mordant epigrams many of which contain ironic reference to his own flawed character, Sir Austin Feverel resembles both Byron and Meredith: satirists who are unwillingly the object of their own satire. The baronet is attached, while at college, to a young poet, Denzil Somers, whose "absence of principle" is overlooked on account of his presumed "genius." Somers acts like the popularized version of Byron: "being inclined to vice, and occasionally, and in a quiet way, practising it, he was of course a sentimentalist and a satirist, entitled to lash the Age and complain of human nature" (II, 4). To the dismay of the worshipper of genius, his friend and wife become lovers; and Sir Austin is transformed overnight from a Romantic sentimentalist to a latter-day Timon. Rather than reject the spurious aspect of his Byronic loyalties, he chooses to play the Byronic role himself, pouring forth his "bruised heart to the world" (p. 3) in the form of *The Pilgrim's Scrip*. (One recalls Arnold's description of Byron bearing "the pageant of his bleeding heart.") Self-exiled at Raynham Abbey, the baronet determines that his son's fate will not resemble his own.

Unfortunately, the Byronic virus is passed from father to son. "Had he not been nursed to believe he was born for great things?" (p. 501), Richard feels, as he prepares to show off his "heroic" nature. The father who had encouraged the self-indulgent behavior of his "genius" friend makes the further mistake of treating his son as another privileged being. As a result, Richard grows up convinced that all things are permitted him and that a special "fate" watches over him. His love of chivalric romance intensifies his egoism. Like a romantic hero, he regards all things beautiful as his by right: cousins "belong to" him; and no one may dare to trifle with "the boy with a Destiny" (pp. 115, 94). Those who interfere with his knightly prerogatives deserve to have their ricks burned (Farmer Blaize) or are "dragons" (the butler Benson) to be disposed of. "If we lived in [chivalric times], I should have been a knight," he tells the maiden he takes possession of, "and have won honour and glory for you. Oh! one can do nothing now" (p. 163). However, to the end of his "ordeal" Richard regards his own satisfaction as paramount: he carries off his bride Lucy, in defiance of both their families' wishes, in the spirit not only of love but of self-will. (One recalls that George Osborne, in *Vanity Fair*, chooses to marry Amelia Sedley as much out of obstinacy as for love.) When he bullies her into agreeing to marry him, Richard harps only on his rights in the matter: "Would you see me indifferent to everything in the world? Would you have me lost? Do you think I will live another day in England without you? I have staked all I have on you, Lucy. You have nearly killed me once. A second time, and earth will not be troubled by me" (p. 254). As a successful suitor, he plans to take the Byronic route: " 'The Alps! Italy! Rome! and then I shall go to the East,' the hero continued. 'She's ready to go anywhere with me, the dear brave heart! Oh, the glorious golden East! I dream of the desert. I dream I'm chief of an Arab tribe, and we fly all white in the moonlight on our mares, and hurry to the rescue of my darling! And we push the spears, and we scatter them, and I come to the tent where she crouches, and catch her to my saddle, and away! . . . what a life!' " (pp. 265–266). Thwarted in his schemes, Richard refuses to blame his own willfulness, choosing to see himself the victim of his father's plotting (the father, ironically, also sees Richard's actions as plots directed against him) or of fate itself.

Another author might have seen Richard's youthful attitude as mere boyish high spirits—a harmless phase, at worst. (One thinks of the Romantic posturing of Disraeli's Vivian Grey or Contarini Fleming.) Meredith's determination to show how Byronic-chivalric gestures can lead to a tragic conclusion was based on his own identification with the Feverel father and son. Because he was assaulting his own youthful pretensions, Meredith allowed no mercy to his semi-autobiographical projections. (Meredith himself, while a young man, had written in earnest the sentimental lyrics that he later, with savage self-irony, asscribed to Denzil Somers and Richard Feverel.) The knightly code of "honor" is shown to encourage self-indulgence rather than curb it, as Scott had believed to be the case. Richard's plan to champion fallen women, which leads to his seduction by Lady Bella Mount, was perhaps based on Meredith's bitter reflection on his own youthful folly in marrying his first wife.[27] In similar fashion, the triangle made up of Sir Austin, Lady Austin, and Denzil Somers recreates the situation that broke up Meredith's marriage: Mrs. Meredith's affair with Meredith's friend, the Pre-Raphaelite painter Henry Wallis. Richard's fantasy that he might "recast the civilized globe," beginning with "the release of Italy from the subjugation of the Teuton" (pp. 501, 487), is an overblown representation of Meredith's own conceit as a Spasmodic poet. (The liberation of Italy was, in fact, an ideal he believed very strongly in, as his novel *Vittoria* demonstrates.) Richard's increasingly egoistic behavior is an ironic confirmation of a Wordsworthian truism: the selfish child is father to the egomaniacal man. However, it is Sir Austin's egoism that has nourished the infant Frankenstein's monster. The author's inability to achieve a proper distance from his characters perhaps accounts for some of the inconsistencies in the book's reasoning: Meredith blames Sir Austin Feverel for maiming his son, but he blames the son too for blaming "fate" rather than admitting that he is himself responsible for what befalls him.

Another indication of Meredith's lack of complete authority in the writing of *The Ordeal of Richard Feverel* can be seen in the contrasting portraits of women. Assailing the chivalric romances for their part in pumping up Richard's ego, Meredith was not quite able, as yet, to treat women as other than romantic stereotypes: Lady Mount is the Alcina-Circe enchantress, whose existence would seem to vindicate Sir Austin's misogyny; while Lucy is the unblemished maiden of romance, Haidée to Richard's Don Juan. In the depiction of Richard's devoted cousin Clare, who dies of unrequited love for him, Meredith may have intended a grim rebuke to the fanciers of romance who overlook how many innocents are slaughtered for no other reason than finding themselves in the path of knightly "heroes." Mrs. Berry is cast as Nature's spokeswoman, a delightful fugitive from Dickens (with a touch of Juliet's nurse); while the bluestocking

Lady Judith Felle seems to have strayed from a silver-fork novel. That people may choose to wear such stereotypes as masks is a shrewd perception; but in his first major novel, Meredith imposed the masks upon his characters as often as he allowed them to select them themselves. Our sympathy for Lucy is heightened by our knowledge of the difference between her true nature and the mask she mistakenly dons. A Wordsworthian "daughter of earth" (p. 116), full of vitality and natural reverence, she is obliged by her love for Richard to impersonate "a dutiful slave" (p. 253) fit for a Byronic Corsair. Richard's love for Lucy is initially seen as the triumph of natural instinct over rational system;[28] but it is the rigid control over her emotions that Lucy is forced to exercise in the service of her lover that precipitates her tragic death. In an ironic reversal of roles, it is the innocent damsel who must bear the burden for the errant knight.

Lucy's Wordsworthian virtues are reminders that Meredith is not attacking all forms of Romanticism. In a passage seemingly unrelated to the novel, Sir Austin's admiring friend Lady Blandish reads a number of Meredith's favorite authors, including Gibbon and Boiardo, so that the Byron-Wordsworth opposition in the book can be made clear. As yet uncritical of Sir Austin, she is put off by Wordsworth's egotistical sublimity, yet is moved by the "greater egoist." Byron, she claims, "reminds me of a beast of the desert, savage and beautiful; and [Wordsworth] is what one would imagine a superior donkey reclaimed from the heathen to be—a *very* superior donkey, I mean." Asking Sir Austin why she loves "Wordsworth best, and yet Byron has the greater power" over her, she occasions a cynical reflection from him: "Because . . . women are cowards, and succumb to Irony and Passion, rather than yield their hearts to Excellence and Nature's Inspiration" (p. 187). Sir Austin's fate is to have made the same error—to have chosen irony as his mask and to have spurned the voice of nature. However, the image of the poets as desert animal and beast of burden (the rampant imagination versus the burden of reality?) superbly indicates why Byron should have had the greater appeal to Meredith, for all the meretricious implications of Byronism. Despite the Wordsworthian promptings of Nature speaking (chap. 42) which persuade Richard to abandon his Byronic pilgrimage and return to Lucy, ultimately it is the distorted Byronic self-image that determines Richard's final course of action, the duel to avenge his tarnished "honor." As self-alienated at the end of the novel as his father appeared at the beginning, Richard, through his Byronic posturing, has duplicated Manfred's great crime: "I loved her, and destroy'd her!"

In the contrasting figures of Sir Austin's nephews, Austin Wentworth and Adrian Harley, Meredith indicates the penalties and compensations of romantic behavior and the emotional deadness of a life without any Romantic values. Austin's youthful blunder in having married a housemaid is never accounted for in the novel; but the implication is that the act reflected some chivalric aspect of his nature (one recalls Osborne Hamley's similar misalliance in *Wives and Daughters*) which Austin was able to make better use of when he matured. When the novel begins Austin has passed his "ordeal" and become a Carlylean advocate of the need to be earnest and take responsibility for one's actions. Austin's every appearance in the novel ensures that the truth will be told and the right action performed; but, unfortunately, he is kept offstage too often to prevent the final catastrophe. (One of his romantic ventures is to follow up on Carlyle's suggestion in *Chartism*: to establish a foreign colony "for poor English working-men to emigrate to"; p. 162.) His cousin Adrian, however, is devoid of all Romantic sentiment. The "wise youth," he has the wisdom that comes from regarding all the world as a comic spectacle and the perpetual youth of one who will never cease being a spectator. While Sir Austin and Richard Feverel (and briefly, Austin Wentworth) misapply their Romantic impulse, Adrian has made the opposite error— has avoided the realm of romance (as Meredith says in *Diana of the Crossways*) and thereby escaped "*the title of Fool at the cost of a celestial crown.*"[29]

Romantic idealism is commendable, as Professor von Karsteg tells the hero of *The Adventures of Harry Richmond*, provided that it is supported by a framework grounded in reality. Whether Harry is to be viewed as "a most fortunate or a most unfortunate young man" depends on whether he has a "solid and adventurous mind" or is "a mere sensational whipster" (IX, 305, 316): whether he is a Romantic realist, who has *combined* the best qualities of his down-to-earth grandfather, Squire Beltham, and his highly imaginative father, Richmond Roy, or is merely a Byronic poseur like his father. Like *The Ordeal of Richard Feverel*, *Harry Richmond* is basically a novel about a father's negative influence on his son; but where Richard is encouraged to see himself as a knight-errant, Harry is brought up under the spell of the *Arabian Nights*. In both novels, romance is shown as a corrupting influence, delaying the hero from the inevitable moment when he must (in von Karsteg's words) "Look within, and avoid lying" (IX, 317). The charm of the novel, however, depends on Harry's determination *not* to look within, his addiction to the fantastic lies his father utters. Meredith's long-standing partiality for the *Arabian Nights* and his mastery of the romantic mode guarantee that despite the negative implications, which become increasingly obvious as the novel develops, the reader of *Harry Richmond* is as captivated as the young hero by the romantic point of view. A marvelous storyteller who claims to be descended from royalty, Richmond Roy is the most enchanting of Meredith's characters—but enchantment is not without a moral cost. When Harry admits that "There never was so fascinating a father as mine for a boy anything under eight or ten years old" (IX, 18), the effect is to make the son's maturity of vision seem less desirable than his childhood sense of wonder.

A second factor that obscures the novel's philosophical implications, but illumines its romantic appeal, is the author's use of the first-person narrative. Meredith disliked the "autobiographical" tendency in fiction, which had caught on following the success of *Jane Eyre*; but, like Charlotte Brontë, he felt it necessary to convey the seductiveness of romance as seen from his protagonist's dazzled, if limited, perspective.[30] Meredith refused to allow a similar method to illustrate Richard Feverel's and Nevil Beauchamp's romantic fixations lest the reader feel too much sympathy for their erring vision and lose sight of the author's anti-Romantic drift. His plan here was to show as vividly as possible Harry growing away from his father's influence: "Note as you read," he advised a friend, "the gradual changes of the growing Harry, in his manner of regarding his father and the world." Harry was intended for a *Bildungs-roman* protagonist, the kind of "mediocre hero" who either (in Lukács's interpretation of Scott) overcomes the spurious attractions of Romanticism and settles for the small but concrete domain of objective, domestic reality, or else learns (in the manner of Goethe's heroes) to combine Romantic with realistic values.[31] The problem is that by using the first-person narrative Meredith causes us to focus on and care for what Harry sees rather than what Harry is. Despite the length of the novel, the protagonist emerges as fairly colorless in contrast to the figures he has viewed and listened to: German royalty, fashionable Bath society, deranged sea captains, English gypsies, and the like. Moreover, Harry lacks the domestic responsibilities and vocational interests that Dickens, for example, makes use of to characterize David Copperfield. The more Harry develops, the more anonymous he becomes. His realization at the end "that there is more in men and women than the stuff they utter" (X, 340) shows an awareness of values that lie too deep for sight, but it is also a repudiation of the verbalizing ability that has allowed him any measure of distinctive identity as narrator.

Harry's insistence that "The individual's freedom was my tenet of faith" (X, 119) is never substantiated: on the contrary, he is forever at the mercy of what captivates his eye or imagination. Meredith's protagonist more fittingly describes himself as an "automaton" (X, 91) who lets others act for him; he is typically being "carried on" by the tide (chap. 39 title) or carried off "on a runaway horse" (X, 126). Robert Louis Stevenson described the lure of romance in terms of willing abandonment to "the poetry of circumstances";[32] and Disraeli's heroes inhabit such a perfect romance world, not needing to exert their will when others obligingly do the work for them. The parasitism that a life of "romance" entails can be seen in the way the women surrounding Roy devote themselves to his cause (and later to Harry's), much as do the women in a Disraeli novel. Meredith's objective in *Harry Richmond* is to confound the Disraeli celebration of romantic passivity, to jolt the hero and the reader into becoming responsible adults and applying their wills constructively. But Meredith's predilection for the *Arabian Nights* sabotages his good intentions: the imaginative license that Richmond Roy exerts in the novel is morally reprehensible but is no less commanding than the power of the Eastern genii, no less potent than that of a romantic novelist.

"My father was indeed a magician!" (X, 213), Harry says when the beautiful German Princess Ottilia, whom he has yearned for, seems to have been brought within his reach: Richmond Roy has seemingly duplicated the feat of the genie who united the Chinese Princess Badur with the Persian Prince Kamar al-Zaman. Despite the laws of the German Diet, which forbid a pure-blooded Princess to marry a commoner (X, 24), Roy has determined that his son will achieve the fate of Aladdin, and that he will establish royal credentials of his own. "His destiny is brilliant," he tells a dumbfounded Squire Beltham, Harry's grandfather who has raised Harry in his father's absence, at the opening of the novel, as Roy prepares to transfer his son from the solid world of Riversley Grange to his own *Arabian Nights*–colored domain. "He shall be hailed for what he is, the rightful claimant of a place above the proudest in the land" (IX, 13). Roy's conviction of being the son of royalty is so intermingled with his fantasy of being an "African magician" (IX, 38) that the reader cannot always distinguish between what may be true and what remains fantasy, cannot separate the solid from the vaporous. While young Harry luxuriates in "this Arabian life" (IX, 40), the *Arabian Nights* fantasies that his father reads to and acts out for him, Roy's devoted housekeeper, Mrs. Waddy, worries that all the rented splendors will "vanish" (IX, 37) like Aladdin's palace after he lost his lamp. Having been schooled by a magician, Harry takes it for granted that romance is his due: "adventures are what I call life," he maintains as a teenager, seeing himself as a combination of Sindbad and Telemachus. When he goes in search of his father, he is convinced that he is "subject to a special governing direction" (IX, 139, 178)—and so indeed he seems to be, since while the novelist warns against romantic presumptions, the narrative is constantly demonstrating their bases in fact. Harry's voyaging leads him to a German principality where he discovers his father (in one of Meredith's great scenes) impersonating a bronze horseman, and where he first meets Princess Ottilia. Roy's position at court is, fittingly, that of court jester: "He is our fun-maker," the Princess admits (IX, 185). Years later, back in England, the father provides "Princely entertainments" reminiscent of the "Arabian Nights" (X, 131) in order to advertise his son's standing as heir to Beltham's wealth. The money he stands to inherit from his grandfather and the royal tie he owes to his father do not, surprisingly, occupy Harry's mind. From his youthful point of view, nothing solid or unchanging (like his grandfather) is worthy of notice; only what is magical seems real and worthy of pursuit. It is because the Princess is beyond his reach that he wants her—"Of the real Ottilia I had lost conception," he admits (IX, 324)—and it is because he has been brought up as a latter-day Aladdin that he persists in his dream.

However, princesses are not to be stalked with imaginary nets. It becomes increasingly clear, as the novel proceeds, that for all Roy's romantic verbiage and trappings, he is capable of schemes and calculations of a sordid nature to achieve his aims. His repeated attempts to compromise Ottilia's reputation so that she will be obliged to marry his son, his lies to the newspapers, and his attempt to buy his way into the aristocracy all reveal a temperament that is far from noble. (At such times, as proud of himself as if he were a successful merchandiser or speculator, Roy calls attention to his "prudence and common sense"; X, 157.) It is never established, moreover, whether Roy is pushing his royal claims so that his son will benefit or is plotting a royal wedding for Harry so that his own claims will be advanced. Newspaper descriptions of Roy allow him a double focus: to be seen in terms of "romantic history" and "mythological heroes" or judged as an "adventurer," "the Perkin Warbeck of Society" (IX, 235–236). But Roy's actions seen up close reveal the predatory nature of romance. Because we see the father from the son's infatuated point of view, the parasitical aspect of his romantic and regal claims is never made obvious; the reader is allowed to wink at the truth, made to see the down-to-earth Squire Beltham's caustic descriptions of his son-in-law as examples of bad taste. It is because Meredith is almost as eager as Harry and the romantic-minded reader *not* to see Roy for what he is that Beltham's succinct characterization of him as "Tom Fool the Bastard" (X, 66) carries so little impact. The pursuit of romance involves deceit and self-deceit, as Harry realizes in his lucid moments (IX, 321); but when Janet Ilchester (Harry's neighbor and friend at Riversley Grange whom he lacks the common sense to recognize as his proper mate) urges him to make Roy "behave like a gentleman" (X,237), Harry is as reluctant to comply as the reader is to awaken to a real sense of Roy's nature or to a realistic awareness of the impossibility of Harry and Ottilia being married. However, when Roy ranks himself higher than Napoleon ("I have fought as many battles, and gained as startling victories . . . *he* was an upstart"; X, 203) or sees himself as "a God, . . . inaccessible to mortal ailments" (X, 251), the reader happily goes along with the romantic charade.

In Richmond Roy's pretensions to royal birth, Meredith was poking fun at more than the Meredith family romance: he was satirizing the Romantic claims for the truth of the imagination as well. But as the novel developed, Roy became real to Meredith—the novelist found himself listening to his character's claim to be "the son of a duke of blood royal."[33] It may well be that the moral blemishes attributed to Roy piled up in direct proportion to his increasing hold on Meredith's imagination. (There is the parallel case of Thackeray's attitude to Becky Sharp, which grows ever more morally offended as she becomes ever more irresistible.) By the time Squire Beltham amasses all the truth concerning Roy's predatory life and the mysterious payments made to him and then tells him off ("What's your boast?—your mother's disgrace! . . . You shame your mother, damned adventurer!"; X, 283), Roy should by rights explode. Instead, the Squire collapses and dies; and at the close of the novel, when Harry has finally turned his back on his romantic dreams, which he realizes to have been bred by egoism, and has returned to the solid, sensible values represented by Riversley Grange, he sees the house going up in flames. Roy, in a final gesture of romantic extravagance, has accidentally set fire to the house and exploded Harry's hard-earned sense of what is real and genuine.[34] Another indication of the extent to which romance overwhelms reality can be glimpsed in the City Company banquet scene, near the end of the novel, in which a half-crazed Roy bids "his audience to beware of princes," describing royalty as having "the attraction of the lamp, the appetite of the hawk, the occupation of the pumpkin: nothing . . . given them to do but to shine, destroy, and fatten" (X, 327). Meredith admitted to having toned down the speech for publication —it "would have satisfied a Communist Red, originally"[35]— but even so, Roy's remarks have two contrary effects. The satire directed against a royal Pretender has turned into a critique of *all* royalty as pretense ("feathered nonentities"), while Roy's claim that if he had been allowed his due England would be blessed with "Princes with brains, princes leaders, princes flowers of the land" has a curious ring of credibility. Meredith has given his romantic Pretender the best lines because Roy embodies the Romantic impulse that seeks power in one capacity or another.

The republicanism of Roy's remarks is one of a number of signposts in *Harry Richmond* pointing toward Meredith's next novel, *Beauchamp's Career*. The novelist's sense that he had allowed the Romantic imagination to exert too great a sway over himself and Harry may explain the comparative austerity of *Beauchamp's Career*, in which romantic expectations are thwarted at every turn. In both novels, a Romantic point of view is meant to be seen as disguised egoism. The end result of Roy's educating his son with romantic expectations is that Harry comes to expect all good things as his birthright. He blames "the Fates for harassing me, circumstances for not surrounding me with friends worthy of me. The central *I* resembled the sun of this universe, with the difference that it shrieked for nourishment, instead of dispensing it" (X, 184). The tone of the passage calls to mind the magnificent rebuke of Carlyle's hero in *Sartor Resartus*: "Art thou nothing other than a Vulture, then, that fliest through the Universe seeking after somewhat to *eat*; and shrieking dolefully because carrion enough is not given thee?" Arnold Kettle is correct in his surmise that *Beauchamp's Career* was written to promote the Carlylean doctrine of closing one's Byron and opening one's Goethe;[36] but that theme is already implicit in *Harry Richmond*. Where the later novel includes the semi-Carlylean (and part-Shelleyan) figure of Dr. Shrapnel, *Harry Richmond* contains Professor von Karsteg, who speaks directly for Goethe. Where Richmonds Roy has glorified his son's "destiny," the professor wants to know what is Harry's "aim." Encouraged by his father to adopt a passive role in life, Harry is directed by von Karsteg to take an active stand, to subdue egoism and to "strive" on behalf of others. The professor's criticism of England, of which Harry appears as a typically flawed exemplar, is directed at the quiescent nature of the English: unwilling to develop "a scheme of life consonant with the spirit of modern philosophy" but preferring to go along with what is "traditional"—preferring romance to reality, in other words. The "exact stamp of the English mind," he charges, is "to accept whatsoever is bequeathed it, without inquiry whether there is any change in the matter. Nobles in very fact you would not let [your nobles] be if they could. Nobles in name, with a remote recommendation to posterity—that suits you!" (IX, 314, 313).

Von Karsteg has only a small part in the published version of *Harry Richmond*, but his spirit is very much present in *Beauchamp's Career*. Young Nevil Beauchamp, born to a race of chivalric-minded noblemen who seem on the verge of extinction, initially believes that it is time for the nobles to "resume their natural alliance with the people, and lead them, as they did of old, to the battle-field"; but gradually he comes to see that the aristocracy should prove itself worthy of the name, that "that is no aristocracy, if it does not head the people in virtue—military, political, national: I mean the qualities required by the times for leadership." Beauchamp's youthful radicalism has much in common with that of the "Young England" Tories, as popularized in Disraeli's novels. But Disraeli's predecessor was Scott, who transformed the ideal of chivalric self-subordination into a "social philosophy" of "paternalism at home."[37] Beauchamp's feudal-based radicalism is roused, instead, by Carlyle's celebration of the heroic ideal (XI, 22). However, while Disraeli's optimistic Romantic nature allows him to provide victory for Coningsby and Egrement (in *Sybil*), showing how aristocrats working in behalf of the people make popular movements like Chartism irrelevant, Meredith's more "realistic" appraisal of the times and his less sympathetic attitude toward the leaders in power ensure only frustration for Beauchamp. Where Coningsby learns to combine traditional Conservative principles with a respect for the new romantic possibilities of Manchester, Beauchamp, in his determination not to compromise his ideals, remains steadfastly opposed to "unchivalrous" Manchester (XI, 29).

Meredith's hero's failure owes as much to his Romantic sense of self as to the country's resistance to his new crusade: just as the young Nevil takes it upon himself at one point to defend England's honor by challenging the French nation to a duel, so too does his inability to work with others, to accommodate his vision to the views of others, mar the practicability of his radicalism. "I see what others don't see," he maintains, "or else I feel it more; I don't know; but it appears to me our country needs rousing if it's to live. There's a division between poor and rich that you have no conception of, and it can't safely be left unnoticed" (XII, 45). The subjective basis of Beauchamp's idealism is the source of comedy in the early sections of the book, and of near-tragedy in the later sections. In most respects, he is a nobler version of Richard Feverel, inspired by the same knightly ideals but determined to help the "people" as Richard had deemed it his mission to save damsels in distress. It is noteworthy that while the first of Carlyle's panaceas (as prescribed in *Chartism*) for the "condition of England" crisis, emigration of unemployed workers to foreign colonies, was the aim of Austin Wentworth, it is Beauchamp's aim to promote Carlyle's second proposal, universal education. Unfortunately, his flaw, as Blackburn Tuckham, the Manchester-born, commonsensical foil to Beauchamp, realizes, is that "Beauchamp has no *bend* in him. He can't meet a man without trying a wrestle, and as long as he keeps his stiffness, he believes he has won" (XII, 208). Meredith uses the image of the unsuccessful wrestler earlier when he shows how Beauchamp's inability to comprehend his ultrachivalric Uncle Everard Romfrey (the name and character recall Scott's Sir Everard Waverley, who also plays the role of avuncular transmitter of the heritage of chivalry to an impressionable nephew) frustrates the well-meaning attempt to extract an apology from him. Romfrey, misled into thinking that Shrapnel has insulted a woman under his knightly protection, has horsewhipped the doctor; and no amount of reasoning on Beauchamp's part will make Romfrey see that he is at fault. Like uncle, like nephew. Beauchamp gloomily reflects, "he who alone saw the just and right thing to do, was incapable of compelling it to be done. Lay on his uncle as he would, that wrestler shook him off. And here was one man whom he could not move! How move a nation?" (XII, 110–111).

Beauchamp's perplexing mixture of hubris and self-effacement reflects something of his real-life model, Meredith's close friend Frederick Maxse, whose futile campaign for a Radical seat in Parliament provided material for the novel. Meredith's efforts to demonstrate the value of "Moderation" were of no avail: "You must have the world moving in your own fashion," he reproached Maxse. Meredith claimed afterward to have been more aware than the candidate of "the far striking deep root of Toryism in the soil of the country," although he observed cynically that "we could have bought the pure elector freely had we willed." In *Harry Richmond* Richmond Roy, making use of the right connections, has little difficulty in acquiring a seat in Parliament for his son Harry; but Maxse was penalized, as Meredith claimed, for acting "simply in a spirit of duty, that he might enter Parliament to plead the cause of the poor." Into Beauchamp's frustrated ability to "make himself understood" (XI, 22), however, Meredith also put a good deal of his own predicament as a novelist offering a morally therapeutic message to readers who resisted or refused to comprehend him. His reputation among critics as a writer of problematic "genius," "clever" but "obscure," and perhaps morally "impure," intensified his sense of paranoia toward reviews. In addition, his temporary estrangement from John Morley in 1871 made Meredith conscious of how unpleasantly his occasionally self-righteous manner could affect even those close to him.[38] As in *Richard Feverel* and *Harry Richmond*, the scourging of Nevil Beauchamp is an attempt at self-scourging; and the degree to which the hero is and is not George Meredith accounts, in part, for the mixture of irony and sympathy the author directs toward the hero's ambitions.

G. M. Young's observation that Meredith's hero "is at once in front of his time and behind it" captures the reason for his practical failure. Beauchamp condemns capitalism, for example, on the grounds that possessions detract from one's love of country (XII, 156); while his desire that the working people's burden be lightened is based more on a sense of chivalry than on a belief in economic or democratic rights. Even his great dream of founding a radical newspaper, *The Dawn*, rests on the egoistic assumption that he can single-handedly transform the condition of the working classes by educating them to a sense of their duties. "The enemy of the Ego," as V. S. Pritchett notes, "is passionately self-willed and self-absorbed."[39] However, the sense that Beauchamp is born at the wrong time links him with the heroes created by Romantic and post-Romantic authors who have felt themselves living both too late and too soon. Like Arnold's frustrated Empedocles, for example (whom Meredith mocked for his flight from responsibility and reason), Beauchamp has

> come too late . . .
> And the world hath the day, and must break thee,
> Not thou the world.
> (*Empedocles on Etna*, 2.16–18)

Meredith protests at the outset that "Beauchampism . . . may be said to stand for nearly everything which is the obverse of Byronism, and rarely woos your sympathy, shuns the statuesque pathetic, or any kind of posturing . . . With every inducement to offer himself for a romantic figure, he despises the pomades and curling-irons of modern romance, its sheers and its labels" (XI, 38–39). Nonetheless, it has been argued that there is too much "Byronism" in the novel, as the tone of special pleading in this passage indicates: where Beauchamp was intended for a "romantic Radical" (Kettle's phrase), he seems, in the end, more of a radical Romantic.[40] Meredith's predecessors, in this respect, are the creators of Don Juan and Fabrice del Dongo, who cast ironic reflections on their heroes' outdated Romantic values but who condemn even more the world in which such values are deemed superfluous. Beauchamp's personal development is toward the conquest of his romantic sense of self-importance; but the novel's implicit movement is in the opposite direction: "The fellow had bothered the world," as Romfrey observes, "but the world without him would be heavy matter" (XII, 260).

The sense, in the end, that Beauchamp has accomplished something heroic runs counter to the book's philosophical drift. Meredith's anti-Romantic intention was to deny hero and reader anything savoring of a heroic or Romantic victory. Lest one should regard Romfrey's eventual apology to Dr. Shrapnel as proof that Nevil does not fail in everything, Meredith is careful to show how circumstances rather than principles direct Romfrey's action; and he brutally kills off his hero to demonstrate self-conquest in its ultimate form. But Beauchamp's career is not devoid of achievement: there is the conquest of self, most vividly illustrated in his decision not to run off with the married Countess Renée, who was his first love; there is his work on behalf of the people, demonstrated when he is mourned by them during his illness and when he sacrifices his life to save "an insignificant bit of mudbank life" (XII, 315); and finally, there is his role in the intellectual development of Cecilia Halkett, the Tory heiress he comes to love but to whom he proposes too late. The tenuousness of women's place in the world is a prominent motif in *Beauchamp's Career*, and it is a sign of Meredith's increasing interest in the subject that he should allow Beauchamp (who does not, at the outset, think overmuch of women's abilities) to be the occasion for Cecilia's advancement and for the secure social position of both Renée and his uncle's wife Rosamond.[41] Even the manner of Beauchamp's death has Romantic connotations—a Shelleyan death by drowning. The Shelleyan side of Beauchamp's adviser Dr. Shrapnel is established at various times in the novel: in his declaration, for example, that principles transcend familial loyalties ("Sound the conscience, and sink the family!"; XI, 116), in his advocacy of female emancipation to the point where women can choose to leave their husbands if they no longer love them (XI, 305), and even in his vegetarianism. Not all of this rubs off on Nevil, to be sure—he is fiercely respectful of Renée's marital status—but there is more than a hint at the end of the novel that he is moving in a Shelleyan direction. "A translation of Plato," we find, "had become Beauchamp's intellectual world. This philosopher singularly anticipated his ideas" (XII, 310).

For the most part, however, Meredith succeeds all too well in *Beauchamp's Career* in assaulting the Romantic instinct, which had proved so troublesome and so irresistible in *Richard Feverel* and *Harry Richmond*. With Nevil's political and amorous failures and his death, objectivity and anti-Romanticism are accomplished with a vengeance. If history and romance alike reveal "the stench of the trail of Ego," then Meredith and Dr. Shrapnel proclaim, "death to ego" (XII, 11–12). The result, for the reader, is a book with perhaps more in it to admire than to like; but following its completion, Meredith was able to let up on his anti-Romantic crusade. With his next novel, *The Egoist*, Meredith demonstrated the need for responsible individuals to resist the thrall of a socially sanctioned egoism: "Clara and Vernon have to learn to 'be brave enough to be dishonourable,'" as John Goode has suggestively observed. The late Meredith novel heroes and heroines—Diana Warwick, Nesta Radnor, Matey Weyburn and Aminta, Carinthia Jane— learn to rise above the barriers of social forms and customs in order to speak in behalf of a higher law, that which "Nature" has implanted in them.[42] Meredith's increasing use of women characters to express his Romantic views should not go unnoticed in this context. The novelist's sense of women's emergent strengths developed as he himself developed: the stereotyped feminine characters of *The Ordeal of Richard Feverel* give way to the combination of stereotyped (the pastoral-sentimental maidens Mabel Sweetwinter and Julia Rippinger, the gypsy Kiomi) and nearly-three-dimensional figures in *The Adventures of Harry Richmond* (Princess Ottilia, Janet Ilchester) and *Beauchamp's Career* (Cecilia Halkett, Jenny Denham), and are finally succeeded in *The Egoist* by the triumphantly liberated Clara Middleton. Both as a Romantic outsider and as a disciple of Nature, Meredith identified with women's position; and by combining the romance sense of women's potential for leadership (which he had found in Ariosto) with the Romantic defense of the rights of the individual, he was able to create in his novels what had eluded Charlotte Brontë and George Eliot: the "New Woman."

Notes

Index

Notes

ONE Introduction

1. Arnold, "The Function of Criticism at the Present Time" (1864), *Essays in Criticism*, 1st ser., in *Complete Prose Works*, ed. R. H. Super, III (Ann Arbor: University of Michigan Press, 1962), 262. Neither here nor in the essays devoted to individual poets does Arnold use the term "Romantic"; he tends to unite the Romantics less in terms of common features than in terms of common liabilities, above all their lack of "ideas." Authors who consider the transition from Romantic poetics to Victorian fiction include Peter Conrad, in *The Victorian Treasure-House* (London: Collins, 1973), and John Speirs, in *Poetry Towards Novel* (New York: New York University Press, 1971), both of whom see a Shakespearean influence that finds its way into the novel by way of the Romantic poets; Karl Kroeber, in *Romantic Narrative Art* (Madison: University of Wisconsin Press, 1960), who notes a movement from Byron, Scott, and Crabbe to the novel; and Ioan Williams, in *The Realist Novel in England* (University of Pittsburgh Press, 1974), who does not allow sufficiently for the realist impulse within Romanticism itself. The links between Romanticism and native English traditions such as Puritanism are dis-

cussed by Walter E. Houghton in *The Victorian Frame of Mind* (New Haven: Yale University Press, 1957), e.g., in the sections on Enthusiasm and Hero-Worship.

2. Lewes, *The Story of Goethe's Life* (revised and abridged version of *Life and Works of Goethe;* Boston 1873), p. 119; Bulwer Lytton, *Zanoni,* bk. 2, chap. 7; Charlotte Brontë, Preface to Emily Brontë, *Wuthering Heights,* ed. William M. Sale, Jr. (New York: Norton, 1963), p. 12.

3. Jane Austen's last completed novel, *Persuasion,* shows indications that its author was not immune to the new Romantic sensibility: e.g., as Marilyn Butler observes in *Jane Austen and the War of Ideas* (Oxford: Clarendon Press, 1975), p. 278, in "the inference" that the heroine's "inner life has an unassailable quality and truth." Anthony Trollope, *An Autobiography,* ed. Frederick Page (London: Oxford University Press, 1950), pp. 173–174, 233–234.

4. Kingsley, "Thoughts on Shelley and Byron," reprinted in *Byron: The Critical Heritage,* ed. Andrew Rutherford (New York: Barnes & Noble, 1970), p. 350; Macaulay, "Moore's Life of Lord Byron," in *Critical and Historical Essays,* 2 vols. (London: Dent, Everyman's Library, 1967 reprint), II, 632, 635; Arnold, "Wordsworth" (1879), *Essays in Criticism,* 2nd ser., in *Complete Prose Works,* IX (1973), 51; "Heinrich Heine" (1863), *Essays in Criticism,* 1st ser., III, 132. As Leon Gottfried notes in *Matthew Arnold and the Romantics* (Lincoln: University of Nebraska Press, 1963), p. 98, "If the 'power of joy' is the keynote of [Arnold's] 'Wordsworth,' that of the 'Byron' essay of two years later may be said to be power, pure and simple."

5. Kingsley, "Thoughts on Shelley and Byron," p. 360; Lewes, "Percy Bysshe Shelley," *Westminster Review* 35 (1841): 303–344; Lewes, "Shelley and the Letters of Poets," *Westminster Review* 57 (1852): 502–511; Browning, introductory essay to *Letters of Percy Bysshe Shelley* (London, 1852), p. 7. In his 1841 essay, Lewes criticized the other Romantic poets for their regressive or negative social tendencies: Byron for his "licentiousness and misanthropy," Scott for his reactionary celebration of "the dead spirit of chivalry," Wordsworth (along with Southey and Coleridge) for the betrayal of his youthful liberalism and for his withdrawal "to an impossible state of country life or nature." "Shelley alone was the poet standing completely on his truth; giving up his life to it, and eternally preaching it" (pp. 311, 319–320).

6. Although many modern literary critics would rank Keats, Coleridge, and Blake higher than Wordsworth, Byron, and Shelley with respect to intellectual awareness and imaginative intensity, the Victorian writers I am considering would not have done so. Lewes, for example, characterized Coleridge as "dreaming in the slumbers of the past, but unsettled, remote, altogether vague and intangible" and saw Keats too as "remote and unsettled" ("Percy Bysshe Shelley,"

p. 320). As for Blake, Lewes declared in his 1872 study of Dickens's defective mental abilities, "in no other perfectly sane mind (Blake, I believe, was not perfectly sane) have I observed vividness of imagination approaching so closely to hallucination." Reprinted in *The Dickens Critics*, ed. George Ford and Lauriat Lane, Jr. (Ithaca: Cornell University Press, 1961), p. 59. Elizabeth Gaskell, after glancing at the Angrian fantasies created by Charlotte Brontë in her youth ("the wildest & most incoherent things"), remarked, "They give one the idea of creative power carried to the verge of insanity. Just lately Mr. M. Milnes [Lord Houghton] gave me some MS. of Blake's, the painter's to read,—& the two MSS (his & C.B.'s) are curiously alike." *Letters*, ed. J. A. Chapple and Arthur Pollard (Cambridge, Mass.: Harvard University Press, 1967), p. 398. In *Coleridge: The Moralist* (Ithaca: Cornell University Press, 1977), Laurence Lockridge brilliantly shows Coleridge's position midway between Romanticism and existentialism. And see George Ford, *Keats and the Victorians* (Hamden: Archon Books, 1962 reprint), for an indication of how some major Victorians scorned or misinterpreted Keats. Carlyle, for example, dismissed him as "a miserable creature, hungering after sweets which he can't get" (p. 4).

7. In different but equally stimulating ways, Georg Lukács, in *The Historical Novel*, trans. Hannah and Stanley Mitchell (Harmondsworth: Penguin Books, 1969), and Alexander Welsh, in *The Hero of the Waverley Novels* (New Haven: Yale University Press, 1963), point up Scott's achievement in creating a hero who is the antitype of the Romantic rebel. Cf. Stevenson in *Scott: The Critical Heritage*, ed. John O. Hayden (New York: Barnes & Noble, 1970), p. 476. George Whalley, in his discussion of how the term "romantic" came to be applied to the English Romantic Poets, slights Scott's significance in this respect. See "England: Romantic-Romanticism" in *"Romantic" and Its Cognates: The European History of a Word*, ed. Hans Eichner (University of Toronto Press, 1972), p. 162n.

8. For a skeptical view, see Ian Jack, in *English Literature: 1815–1832* (New York: Oxford University Press, 1963), who says, e.g., "Wordsworth, Byron, Shelley, and Keats did not regard themselves as writing 'romantic' poems and would not—in fact—have been particularly flattered if they had been told that that was what they were doing. They did not regard themselves as constituting a Romantic movement" (p. 410); for endorsement of the historical fact of a European Romantic movement, see René Wellek, "The Concept of Romanticism in Literary History," *Concepts of Criticism* (New Haven: Yale University Press, 1963), pp. 128–198. In a splendid new study, *Romanticism* (New York: Harper & Row, 1979), Hugh Honour observes that the common feature uniting the Romantics was their intense individualism. Writers who have suggestively linked the Romantic poets with other revolutionary tendencies of the day in-

clude Crane Brinton, in *The Political Ideas of the English Romantics* (Ann Arbor: University of Michigan Press, 1966 reprint); Northrop Frye, in *"The Drunken Boat:* The Revolutionary Element in Romanticism," in *Romanticism Reconsidered,* English Institute Papers (New York: Columbia University Press, 1963); and Carl Woodring, in *Politics in English Romantic Poetry* (Cambridge, Mass.: Harvard University Press, 1970).

9. Carlyle, "Corn-Law Rhymes," in *Works.* Centenary ed., 30 vols. (London: Chapman and Hall, 1898–1901), XXVIII, 136. For Byron's hold on Browning and Tennyson (and what replaced it), see, for example, William Irvine and Park Honan, *The Book, the Ring, and the Poet* (New York: McGraw-Hill, 1974), e.g., chaps. 2–3; Sir Charles Tennyson, *Alfred Tennyson* (New York: Macmillan, 1949), pp. 33–34, 451; Christopher Ricks, *Tennyson* (New York: Macmillan, 1977), pp. 13–14; and Ford, *Keats and the Victorians,* pt. 1. The standard work of Byron's nineteenth-century reputation is Samuel Chew's *Byron in England* (New York: Russell and Russell, 1965 reprint); and see Roland A. Duerksen, *Shelleyan Ideas in Victorian Literature* (The Hague: Mouton, 1966), and Frederick A. Pottle, *Shelley and Browning: A Myth and Some Facts* (Chicago: University of Chicago Press, 1923).

10. D. G. James contends, in *Matthew Arnold and the Decline of English Romanticism* (Oxford: Clarendon Press, 1961), that Arnold's rejection of Romanticism necessarily led to his own creative suicide. (A similar claim can be made for Charlotte Brontë). More positive considerations of Arnold's attitude toward the Romantics (including the fact that he helped to popularize their achievements) are made by Gottfried in *Matthew Arnold and the Romantics* and by William A. Jamieson in *Arnold and the Romantics* (Copenhagen: Rosenkilde and Bagger, 1958).

11. The quoted phrase is Jacques Barzun's in *Classic, Romantic, and Modern* (Garden City: Doubleday Anchor Books, 1961 rev. ed.), p. 94, and is echoed by Robert Langbaum, who in *The Poetry of Experience* (New York: Norton, 1963 reprint) defines true Romanticism as a "corrected empiricism," that is, a "formulation . . . evolved out of experience and . . . continually tested against experience" (p. 22). Where Langbaum emphasizes the continuity between the Romantic and Victorian writers, Michael Timko stresses the divergencies in "The Victorianism of Victorian Literature," *New Literary History* 6 (Spring 1973): 607–627. Whereas the Victorians, for example, defined man (Timko claims) in terms of his social and cultural context, the Romantics thought of man in terms of his relationship to nature and self.

12. I have cited Browning's 1888 revision of these lines. The original 1833 lines give the same meaning but are less emphatically

worded: "I'll look within no more— / I have too trusted to my own wild wants– / Too trusted to myself—to intuition. / Draining the wine alone in the still night . . ."

13. Karl Kroeber prefaces his study of *Romantic Narrative Art* with the admission that such terms as "Romantic," "Romanticism," and "Romantic style" are "artificial and inexact," as well as "vague and controversial," yet "are part of a convenient critical shorthand" (p. viin). In *The Romantic Novel in England* (Cambridge, Mass.: Harvard University Press, 1972), Robert Kiely allows the word "romantic" to refer to the genre of romance as well as to the Romantic movement, which occasions some confusion in definition. That aspect of Romanticism which trusts to the primacy of the imagination draws upon the romance tradition, a cardinal tenet of Romantic faith being the belief in the world recast by the individual imagination. However, one should not overlook the realistic strain in Romantic authors like Byron, Wordsworth, Crabbe, and Scott.

14. Crane Brinton noted the link between Byronism and Benthamism, liberalism and industrialism, in *The Political Ideas of the English Romantics*, e.g., pp. 185, 221–222. In this context, it is interesting to remember that Carlyle connected Byronism and Benthamism in a negative manner in *Past and Present*, while Edward Bulwer Lytton, as a Romantic individualist, was supportive of both figures in *England and the English* (1833). Morley's 1870 defense of Byron as the "poet of the Revolution" has been reprinted in *Byron: The Critical Heritage*, pp. 384–409, and Mill's essays *On Bentham and Coleridge* have been united by F. R. Leavis (London: Chatto & Windus, 1950). What Mill (like Coleridge before him) saw as the contrasting principles of "progression" and "permanence," Hoxie Neale Fairchild, in *The Romantic Quest* (New York: Columbia University Press, 1931), has redefined as the Romantic poles of "naturalism" and "medievalism": the former, which is based on a belief in man's innate goodness, "points toward liberalism," while the latter "encourages a glorification of tradition," which tends "toward conservatism" (pp. 240–241).

15. Louis Cazamian's thesis in *The Social Novel in England, 1830–1850*, trans. Martin Fido (London: Routledge & Kegan Paul, 1973) is that Romanticism provided the idealistic impulse that countered the competitive, materialist, individualist attitudes of the period: from Wordsworth, Coleridge, and Carlyle came the impetus that fed the humane vision of Dickens, Gaskell, Kingsley, and Disraeli. The influence of Wordsworth on the Oxford Movement is treated in Humphry House's "Wordsworth's Fame," in *All in Due Time* (London: Rupert Hart-Davis, 1955) and in Katherine Mary Peek's "Wordsworth in England: Studies in the History of His Fame" (Ph.D. diss., Bryn Mawr, 1943), which also points up Wordsworth's hold on Unitarianism and the Broad Church Movement.

16. The chief Wordsworthian text among modern studies is M. H.

Abrams's *Natural Supernaturalism* (New York: Norton, 1973), while Peter Thorslev's *The Byronic Hero* (Minneapolis: University of Minnesota Press, 1962) is the basic Byronic primer. The term "negative romanticism," as applied to Byron's posture of defiance but also to his refusal to accept a basis for affirmation, is used by both Langbaum in *The Poetry of Experience* (p. 16) and Morse Peckham in *The Triumph of Romanticism* (Columbia: University of South Carolina Press, 1970), pp. 21–23. An astute recent commentator on the "Romantic will," Michael Cooke, in *The Romantic Will* (New Haven: Yale University Press, 1976), e.g., p. 216, has observed in Romanticism "a movement for Prometheanism to stoicism," as reflected in the withdrawal from creative vision in Wordsworth (and, one might add, in Coleridge); and he suggests that Byron and Shelley might well have converted to stoicism had they lived long enough.

17. Peter Thorslev, in "The Romantic Mind Is Its Own Place," *Comparative Literature* 15 (Summer 1963): 250–268, views Satanic Prometheanism, which he finds in Byron above all, as synonymous with the creative impulse.

18. The transformation of romanticism into domestic realism is the subject of Vineta Colby's excellent *Yesterday's Woman: Domestic Realism in the English Novel* (Princeton: Princeton University Press, 1974).

19. See U. C. Knoepflmacher, "The Counterworld of Victorian Fiction and *The Woman in White*," in *The Worlds of Victorian Fiction*, ed. Jerome H. Buckley (Cambridge, Mass.: Harvard University Press, 1975), pp. 351–369.

20. Quoted in Edgar Johnson, *Sir Walter Scott: The Great Unknown*, 2 vols. (London: Hamish Hamilton, 1970), I, 328.

21. Kiely, *The Romantic Novel in England*, p. 151. One should remember, however, that Scott's reviewers differentiated between the chivalric romances and the more realistic Scottish novels.

22. Coleridge, reprinted in *Scott: The Critical Heritage*, p. 180. In *On the Constitution of the Church and State* Coleridge distinguishes between "the two antagonistic powers or opposite interests of the state": those of "permanence," represented by the landed classes, and those of "progression," represented by business and professional interests. *Collected Works*, ed. Kathleen Coburn, 16 vols. (Princeton: Princeton University Press, 1971–), X, 24–25.

23. Hazlitt, *The Spirit of the Age*, reprinted with *Lectures on the English Poets* (London: Dent, Everyman's Library, 1960 reprint), p. 228.

24. *Quarterly Review* (1817), reprinted in *Sir Walter Scott on Novelists and Fiction*, ed. Ioan Williams (New York: Barnes & Noble, 1968), pp. 238, 240, 256.

25. Quoted in Johnson, *Sir Walter Scott*, II, 904, 870. Scott's regard for Byron was mutual: Byron dedicated *Cain* to him, and the pirate-

heroes of his Eastern Tales owe something to the hero of Scott's *Marmion*. In 1810 Scott underestimated Wordsworth's and Coleridge's achievement—see "Of the Living Poets of Great Britain," reprinted in Kenneth Curry's *Sir Walter Scott's Edinburgh Annual Register* (Knoxville: University of Tennessee Press, 1977), pp. 75–79—but by 1816, with *The Antiquary*, he conceded that Wordsworth's celebration of figures of humble life was worthy of emulation. (In that novel Edie Ochiltree is compared to Wordsworth's Cumberland Beggar.)

26. Johnson, *Sir Walter Scott*, II, 1251.

27. *Redgauntlet*, chap. 9 of narrative section.

28. *Waverley*, chaps. 60, 24, 23.

29. See Welsh's comparison of Scott's dark and blond heroines in *The Hero of the Waverley Novels*, pp. 70–82. Harriet Martineau noted that the resourceful Scott heroines (Flora MacIvor, Diana Vernon, Jeanie Deans, Rebecca) show what women might become, while his insipid, domesticated heroines reveal what is wrong with ordinary "womankind"; see James T. Hillhouse, *The Waverley Novels and Their Critics* (New York: Octagon Books, 1970 reprint), p. 106. Even though Scott's dark heroines point to Meredith's New Women, Scott himself is capable of deploring the unfeminine willfulness of an Amy Robsart, her lack of past training in "submission and self-command" (*Kenilworth*, chap. 25). The submissive heroine may be the natural mate for the passive hero, but Scott nevertheless warms to the romantic adventurousness of his Amazon heroines.

30. *Ivanhoe*, chap. 29. Johnson sees in *Ivanhoe* a critique of feudalism, and in *Kenilworth* an exposé of the human cruelty lying behind the trappings of regal splendor (Johnson, *Sir Walter Scott*, I, 736, 758–759). Yet Scott persisted to the end in seeking to demonstrate that chivalric honor could be found somewhere on the stage of history: his last novel, "The Siege of Malta," represents chivalry's last stand in the face of changing times. See Donald E. Sultana, *"The Siege of Malta" Rediscovered* (Edinburgh: Scottish Academic Press, 1977).

31. *The Pirate*, chap. 42.

32. See Hillhouse, *The Waverley Novels*, p. 268; Jack, *English Literature: 1815–1832*, p. 408.

33. Among the influences noted by John Henry Raleigh in "What Scott Meant to the Victorians," *Victorian Studies* (Sept. 1963), pp. 7–34, are those he exerted together with Wordsworth: a new concern for the country over the city, an imaginative way of looking at landscape, and a regard for humble life (pp. 18–19). More specific instances of his power can be seen in George Eliot's admission that Scott was responsible for eroding her orthodox beliefs, in Charlotte Brontë's sense of confirmation, while reading Scott, of the dark side of human nature—see Elizabeth Gaskell, *The Life of Charlotte Brontë* (London: Dent, Everyman's Library, 1970 reprint), p. 80—and in

Meredith's utilization of Scott-inspired romance, as well as his sense that romance should play a key role in the *Bildungsroman* hero's development.

34. While both Welsh and Kroeber note Scott's importance in subordinating the individual to the context of law and to the structure of fictional narrative, the former sees this as a proof of Scott's eighteenth-century training, while the latter concludes from it that Scott was the father of the Victorian novel. Bagehot, reprinted in *Scott: The Critical Heritage*, pp. 407, 411.

35. Hutton, *Sir Walter Scott* (English Men of Letters series, 1878), excerpt reprinted in *Scott: The Critical Heritage*, pp. 489, 492. James's review of *Middlemarch*, which reveals something of his Romantic bias, can be found in *The Future of the Novel*, ed. Leon Edel (New York: Vintage Books, 1956): Dorothea Brooke, he insists, "is of more consequence than the action of which she is the nominal center" (p. 83).

36. Maurice, reprinted in *Scott: The Critical Heritage*, pp. 310, 313; Carlyle, "Sir Walter Scott," *Works*, XXXIX, 35, 54.

37. Carlyle, "On History" (1830), *Works*, XXVII, 86. Ten years later he amplified this to read (for the lectures *On Heroes, Hero-Worship, and the Heroic in History*) that history "is at bottom the History of the Great Men who have worked here" (*Works*, V, 1).

38. Carlyle, "Signs of the Times," *Works*, XXVII, 63, 75, 74; cf. Carlyle's famous comment on Scott as "the Genius of rather a singular age—an age at once destitute of faith and terrified at scepticism" (*Works*, XXIX, 49); *Sartor Resartus*, *Works*, I, 154.

39. See Williams, *The Realist Novel in England*, pp. 100–101; and, for the finest account of how Carlyle's early attempts at fiction found their way into *Sartor Resartus*, G. B. Tennyson, *"Sartor" Called "Resartus"* (Princeton: Princeton University Press, 1965), pp. 45–65.

40. Sanders, "The Byron Closed in *Sartor Resartus*," *Studies in Romanticism* 3 (Winter 1964): 81. Born the same year as Keats, Carlyle died the same year as Dostoevsky.

41. In "Characteristics" (1831) Carlyle explicitly includes Byron among those who have nobly "dared to say No, and cannot yet say Yea" (Works, XXVIII, 31).

42. Sanders, "The Byron Closed," p. 94.

43. Abrams, *Natural Supernaturalism,* pp. 311, 12, 134. Carlyle's Romanticism is considered by Frederick William Roe in *Thomas Carlyle as a Critic of Literature* (New York: Columbia University Press, 1910), e.g., pp. 34, 69, 75–76, and by René Wellek, with reservations, in "Carlyle and German Romanticism," in *Confrontations* (Princeton: Princeton University Press, 1965), pp. 34–81.

44. Morley, "Carlyle," *Critical Miscellanies,* I (London, 1871), 204–205, 217–218, 210; Hazlitt, *Characters of Shakespear's Plays*, re-

printed with *The Round Table* (London: Dent, Everyman's Library, 1960 reprint), pp. 214–215.

45. Carlyle, Introduction to his trans. of Goethe, *Wilhelm Meister's Apprenticeship and Travels, Works,* XXIII, 23–24; *The Life of Friedrich Schiller, Works,* XXV, 19.

46. Carlyle, "Corn-Law Rhymes," *Works,* XXVIII, 145, 162; *On Heroes, Hero-Worship, and the Heroic in History, Works,* V, 80.

47. Thackeray, *Letters and Private Papers,* ed. Gordon N. Ray, 4 vols. (Cambridge, Mass.: Harvard University Press, 1945–1946), II, 309; Carlyle, *The French Revolution, Works,* II, 149, 211; *Chartism, Works* XXIX, 157; *On Heroes, Hero-Worship, and the Heroic in History, Works,* V, 197.

48. In the essay "Biography," Carlyle granted the novelist, "Foolishest of existing mortals," some credit if he stuck to Reality for his subject (*Works,* XXVIII, 49–53). (Elizabeth Gaskell took her epigraph for *Mary Barton* from this passage.) Ioan Williams, in *The Realist Novel in England,* justifiably credits Carlyle with being the "Prophet of the Real" (chap. 8) as far as the Victorian novel was concerned; while Louis Cazamian, in *The Social Novel in England,* cites Carlyle as the "central" figure in the "interventionist reaction" against the forces of egoism and materialism (pp. 27, 83). Carlyle, *The Diamond Necklace, Works,* XXVIII, 329; Meredith, *Beauchamp's Career, Works,* Memorial ed., 27 vols. (New York: Scribner's, 1909–1911), XI, 22; Kingsley, *Alton Locke* (London, 1878 reprint), pp. 34, 100.

49. Quoted in Edwin M. Eigner, "Raphael in Oxford Street: Bulwer's Accommodation to the Realists," in *The Nineteenth-Century Writer and His Audience,* ed. Harold Orel and George W. Worth (Lawrence: University of Kansas Publications, 1969), p. 69.

50. Elizabeth Gaskell, *The Life of Charlotte Brontë,* p. 277.

51. See Thackeray, *Letters and Private Papers,* I, 51, 74, 98–99; Ray, *Thackeray: The Uses of Adversity (1811–1846)* (New York: Octagon Books, 1972 reprint), pp. 118, 128–129.

52. Mario Praz, *The Hero in Eclipse in Victorian Fiction,* trans. Angus Davidson (London: Oxford University Press, 1969 reprint), pp. 189–260; Ray, *The Uses of Adversity,* pp. 248–249. A reviewer for the London *Times* (1855) called attention to Thackeray's "chief and important defect, which is, that he fails on the side of imagination. He is always restricted to the domain of pure facts. He has no dreams, no superstitions, no tentative aspirations to the unseen. What he can see, hear, smell, touch, and taste he can describe, and even idealize, but he can go no further than the range of his five senses." Reprinted in *Thackeray: The Critical Heritage,* ed. Geoffrey Tillotson and Donald Hawes (London: Routledge & Kegan Paul, 1968), p. 229. This strikingly resembles Maurice's criticism of Scott twenty-five years earlier (see note 36).

53. Theodore Martin, "Thackeray's Works," *Westminster Review* (April 1853) (reprinted in *Thackeray: The Critical Heritage*, p. 179).

54. *Notes of a Journey from Cornhill to Grand Cairo*, chaps. 5, 6, 8. Thackeray's antiromantic method of description reaches a climax when he arrives at the Pyramids (chap. 15): "Several of us tried to be impressed; but breakfast supervening, a rush was made at the coffee and cold pies, and the sentiment of awe was lost in the scramble for victuals." Trollope's antiromantic series of "Tales of All Countries" owes much to Thackeray's example.

55. Chaps. 7, 1. There is some question as to whether the title of this work is in fact *Rebecca and Rowena: Romance Upon Romance*.

56. *The Luck of Barry Lyndon, a Romance of the Last Century* (retitled, for book publication, *The Memoirs of Barry Lyndon, Esq.*), chap. 4; Ray, *Thackeray: The Age of Wisdom (1847–1863)* (New York: Octagon Books, 1972 reprint), p. 144.

57. Masson's review comparing *Pendennis* and *David Copperfield* is excerpted in *Thackeray: The Critical Heritage*, p. 118; cf. Thackeray's reply, p. 128.

58. See Thackeray's 1845 review of Disraeli's *Sybil*, reprinted in *Contributions to the Morning Chronicle*, ed. Gordon N. Ray (Urbana: University of Illinois Press, 1955), pp. 77–78; Dickens, "In Memoriam," *Cornhill Magazine* (Feb. 1864), reprinted in *Thackeray: The Critical Heritage*, p. 321.

59. The Earl of Lytton, *The Life of Edward Bulwer, First Lord of Lytton*, 2 vols. (London: Macmillan, 1913), II, 89; Thackeray, *Letters and Private Papers*, I, 198.

60. Thackeray, *Catherine: A Story*, chaps. 3, 7. Cf. Geoffrey Tillotson, *Thackeray the Novelist* (London: Methuen, 1963 reprint): "Knowing so much about himself he was much aware of the weakness of ordinary men" (p. 251). See Robert A. Colby, "*Catherine:* Thackeray's Credo," *Review of English Studies* 15 (Nov. 1964): 381–396; and Colby, *Thackeray's Canvass of Humanity* (Columbus: Ohio State University Press, 1979), pp. 147–172. Thackeray, *The History of Henry Esmond*, ed. John Sutherland and Michael Greenfield (Harmondsworth: Penguin Books, 1970), p. 48.

61. Thackeray, *Letters and Private Papers*, I, 432–433.

62. *Vanity Fair: A Novel without a Hero*, ed. Geoffrey and Kathleen Tillotson (Boston: Houghton Mifflin, 1963), p. 19.

63. Macaulay, "Moore's Life of Lord Byron," p. 636; *Vanity Fair*, pp. 187, 552. Mrs. Oliphant, noting that the "rogues [in *Vanity Fair*] are clever and amusing, and all its good characters fools," added that "Amelia is a greater libel upon womankind than Becky herself" (*Thackeray: The Critical Heritage*, p. 204).

64. *The Life of Edward Bulwer*, II, 43. Michael Sadleir succinctly describes Bulwer's life as that of *"an intellect betrayed by character"* in *Bulwer: A Panorama (Edward and Rosina)* (Boston: Little, Brown,

1931), p. 34. Bulwer was fond of citing Shakespeare in support of his antimimetic views: Shakespeare, he claimed in the Introduction to *Zanoni*, "has never once drawn a character to be met with in actual life . . . or a personage who is real!"

65. *The Life of Edward Bulwer*, I, 27, 303; II, 498–499. Cf. Allan C. Christensen, *Edward Bulwer-Lytton: The Fiction of New Regions* (Athens: University of Georgia Press, 1976), p. 221. And see Edwin M. Eigner, *The Metaphysical Novel in England and America* (Berkeley: University of California Press, 1978): "Bulwer and Carlyle tried to save their own contemporaries by substituting the visionary and intuitive for the material and experiential" (p. 9).

66. Bulwer discusses Rousseau in *Pelham*, chap. 24, and in *Alice: or The Mysteries*, bk. 6, chap. 2.

67. Bulwer, *Zanoni* (1842), Introduction and bk. 2, chap. 9. (In the Introduction, he cites Wordsworth as a member of the "Dutch School," which prefers copying "simplicity and Betty Foy" to aspiring to Grecian truth and grandeur. Bulwer's position as the leading "idealist" among Victorian novelists is considered by Eigner; by Richard Stang in *The Theory of the Novel in England: 1850–1870* (New York: Columbia University Press, 1959), pp. 12–14, 153–155; and by Anthea Trodd (who considers the polarity between Thackeray and Bulwer) in "Michael Angelo Titmarsh and the Knebworth Apollo," *Costerus* 2 (1974): 59–81.

68. Quoted in *The Life of Edward Bulwer*, II, 86. And see the 1840 Preface to *Eugene Aram*: "Whenever crime appears the aberration and monstrous product of a great intellect, or of a nature ordinarily virtuous, it becomes not only the subject for genius, which deals with passions, to describe; but a problem for philosophy, which deals with actions, to investigate and solve: —hence, the Macbeths and Richards, the Iagos and Othellos."

69. Quoted in Ernest A. Baker, *The History of the English Novel*, 10 vols. (New York: Barnes & Noble, 1963 reprint), VII, 189.

70. Bulwer, *Pelham*, chap. 86. (In *England and the English*, Bulwer claimed that the silver-fork novel, of which *Pelham* is a notable specimen, by exaggerating the fashions of the day helped put an end to such dandiacal and frivolous attitudes.)

71. Bulwer, *Falkland*, bk. 4; *The Life of Edward Bulwer*, I 189; 1840 Preface to *Pelham*.

72. Bulwer, *Paul Clifford*, chaps. 18, 19; *Eugene Aram*, bk. 5, chap. 7. See Trodd, "Michael Angelo Titmarsh," pp. 71–73. (Trodd also sees Thackeray's portrait of the artist as an unexceptional young man in *Pendennis* as a rebuke to Bulwer's portrait of the artist-as-genius, above the rules of common morality, in *Ernest Maltrevers*.)

73. Bulwer's 1837 Preface to *Ernest Maltrevers*, also bk. 9, chap. 8; *Alice*, bk. 6, chap. 1.

74. Bulwer, *Ernest Maltrevers*, bk. 4, chap. 2; *Alice*, bk. II, chap. 8;

The Caxtons: A Family Picture, pt. 14, chap. 3; Thackeray, *Vanity Fair,* p. 553; *Ernest Maltrevers,* bk. 9, chap. 7. See Houghton, *The Victorian Frame of Mind,* chap. 13, "Love"; and Eigner, The *Metaphysical Novel,* pp. 120–138.

75. Bulwer, *Alice,* bk. 11, chap. 8. In "Stepfathers of Victorianism," *Virginia Quarterly Review* 6 (April 1930): 251–267, Lionel Stevenson notes the transition in Bulwer, as well as in Disraeli, from Byronic individualist to Victorian novelist with a purpose.

76. *The Caxtons,* bk. 1, chap. 5; bk. 16, chap. 4. Bulwer allows for a touch of chivalric romance in the portrait of Pisistratus's Don Quixote-like Uncle Roland. Where the father is commonsensical, the uncle is imaginative: "Proof, sir, is a handcuff," Roland tells his nephew, "–belief is a wing!" (bk. 3, chap. 4). Yet Roland fathers the destructively Byronic Vivian Caxton.

77. Charlotte Brontë, Preface to *Wuthering Heights,* pp. 9–12. See J. Hillis Miller, *The Disappearance of God: Five Nineteenth-Century Writers* (Cambridge, Mass.: Harvard University Press, 1963), pp. 157–211; Walter L. Reed, *Meditations on the Hero: A Study of the Romantic Hero in Nineteenth-Century Fiction* (New Haven: Yale University Press, 1974), pp. 85–119; Winifred Gérin, *Emily Brontë* (Oxford: Clarendon Press, 1971), pp. 44–46; Arnold Kettle, *An Introduction to the English Novel,* 2 vols. (New York: Harper Torchbooks, 1960), I, 139–155; Thomas Moser, "What Is the Matter with Emily Jane? Conflicting Impulses in *Wuthering Heights,*" *Nineteenth-Century Fiction* 17 (1962): 1–19; Patricia Meyer Spacks, *The Female Imagination* (New York: Knopf, 1975), pp. 134–142.

78. *Wuthering Heights,* p. 84. The review (quoted) from the *Britannia* is excerpted in the Norton edition of the novel, pp. 282–283.

79. *Wuthering Heights,* pp. 139, 13.

80. Charlotte Brontë, Preface to *Wuthering Heights,* p. 11; Arnold, "Haworth Churchyard."

T W O   Trollope, Byron, and the Conventionalities

1. *The Eustace Diamonds,* chap. 21. (Subsequent references to Trollope's novels will be given in the text. The dates of the novels, which are noted only when important, refer to the year the book was completed, not the year it was published.) Julius Mackenzie is the protagonist of Trollope's finest short story, "The Spotted Dog." Trollope's anti-Romantic bias, as evidenced in his short and longer fictions, is examined by David R. Eastwood in "Realistic Responses to Romantic Literary Conventions in Trollope's Short Fiction" (Ph.D. diss., University of Kansas, 1971) and by Robert Tracy in *Trollope's Later Novels* (Berkeley: University of California Press, 1978).

2. *The George Eliot Letters,* 9 vols., ed. Gordon Haight (New

Haven: Yale University Press, 1954–1978), IV, 9; Meredith, review of *Barchester Towers, Westminster Review* 68 (Oct. 1857): 594–596, reprinted in *Trollope: The Critical Heritage,* ed. Donald Smalley (London: Routledge & Kegan Paul, 1969), p. 54; Carlyle, quoted in N. John Hall, "Trollope and Carlyle," *Nineteenth-Century Fiction* 27 (Sept. 1972): 202; Trollope, *An Autobiography,* ed. Frederick Page (London: Oxford University Press, 1950), pp. 120–121.

3. On Carlyle: from the introduction of Trollope's uncompleted "History of Fiction," reprinted in Michael Sadleir, *Trollope: A Commentary,* 3rd ed. (London: Oxford University Press, 1961), p. 423. On Scott: Trollope's 1869 lecture "On English Prose Fiction as a Rational Amusement," *Four Lectures,* ed. Morris Parrish (London: Constable, 1938), p. 97. See J. A. Sutherland, *Victorian Novelists and Publishers* (Chicago: University of Chicago Press, 1976): "Byron and Scott . . . inaugurated the new era of huge readership and correspondingly huge payments" (p. 10), Bradford Booth cites Trollope's jottings on Scott in "Trollope on Scott: Some Unpublished Notes," *Nineteenth-Century Fiction* 5 (Dec. 1950): 223–230.

4. J. G. Lockhart, *The Life of Sir Walter Scott,* shorter version (London: Dent, 1906), pp. 500–501, 262, 486. See Trollope, *Letters,* ed. Bradford Booth (London: Oxford University Press, 1951), p. 178.

5. Lockhart, *The Life of Sir Walter Scott,* p. 628; Trollope, *Autobiography,* p. 146.

6. Trollope, "Novel-Reading," *Nineteenth Century* (Jan. 1879): 31–32; "On English Prose Fiction," p. 117.

7. Chivalric gentlemen include Sir Peregrine Orme in *Orley Farm,* Roger Carbury in *The Way We Live Now,* and William Whittlestaff in *An Old Man's Love;* the ugliest of Trollope's ugly duckling heroes is Felix Graham in *Orley Farm.* (Trollope also followed Charlotte Brontë's lead in creating physically unprepossessing protagonists.) Trollope's fondness for Jeanie Deans accompanies his criticism of Scott's paragon heroes and heroines (see "English Prose Fiction," pp. 117–118).

8. Scott, Preface to *Memoirs of the Marchioness de la Rochejaquelein* (Edinburgh, 1827), pp. 13–14. The 1874 Catalogue of Trollope's library (Forster Collection, Victoria and Albert Museum) lists only the original French edition. See Robert Polhemus, *The Changing World of Anthony Trollope* (Berkeley: University of California Press, 1968), pp. 20–23.

9. Carlyle, *Past and Present, Works,* Century ed., 30 vols. (London: Chapman and Hall, 1898–1901), X, 196; Trollope, "An Essay on Carlylism," *Saint Pauls* 1 (Dec. 1867): 292. See Ruth apRoberts, "Carlyle and Trollope," in *Carlyle and His Contemporaries: Essays in Honor of Charles Richard Sanders,* ed. John Clubbe (Durham, N.C.: Duke University Press, 1976), pp. 205–226; and Hall, "Trollope and Carlyle."

10. See, for example, Trollope, *Letters,* pp. 15, 150; and *Autobiography,* pp. 370–371 (cancelled passage). If Trollope sometimes overstates his case for the novelist as "preacher," one reason for this is his determination to repel Carlyle's assault on novelists as lying "windbags."

11. Carlyle, *Works,* X, 75.

12. apRoberts, "Carlyle and Trollope," p. 221; Trollope, "An Essay on Carlylism," p. 293. Carlyle was very much on the novelist's mind during the mid-1850s: between *The Warden* (1853) and *Barchester Towers* (1856), Trollope wrote *The New Zealander,* which expresses a Carlylean concern with changing times—although it also reflects some guarded hope for the future.

13. *Saint Pauls* 1 (Dec. 1867): 5. Where Matthew Arnold, a decade later, saw poetry taking upon itself much of the former role of religion, Trollope deemed the novel, because of its greater popularity, to be religion's true modern successor. Keats, *Letters,* ed. Hyder E. Rollins, 2 vols. (Cambridge, Mass.: Harvard University Press, 1958), I, 224; Trollope, *Letters,* p. 218.

14. Trollope, *Letters,* p. 217; *Autobiography,* pp. 229, 227. See James R. Kincaid, *The Novels of Anthony Trollope* (Oxford: Clarendon Press, 1977), p. 34, on the Trollopean narrator who by "Controlling the imagination . . . can thus educate it, make it grow. The strategy is typically Romantic, as are the pedagogical principles."

15. apRoberts, "Carlyle and Trollope," p. 224; Carlyle, *Sartor Resartus, Works,* I, 157; Trollope, *Autobiography* p. 362.

16. Quoted in Samuel Chew, *Byron in England* (New York: Russell & Russell, 1965 reprint), pp. 250–251.

17. Trollope, *Autobiography,* p. 42; *The Brontës: Their Lives, Friendships and Correspondence,* ed. T. J. Wise and J. A. Symington, 4 vols. (Oxford: Shakespeare Head Press, 1932), II, 210. (Charlotte Brontë's fear of the Romantic imagination is the theme of my chapter 4.)

18. *Autobiography,* pp. 42–43; *Letters,* p. 138. Two recent commentators have shown the strength of the "sensational" current in Trollope's work: P. D. Edwards in *Anthony Trollope: His Art and Scope* (Brisbane: University of Queensland Press, 1977), and R. C. Terry in *Anthony Trollope: The Artist in Hiding* (London: Macmillan, 1977). Terry makes a good case for Trollope's "emotional—even romantic—attitude to life, which he found it necessary to curb and control" (p. 15). Trollope himself thought little of his purely "true to life" novels like *The Belton Estate, Rachel Ray* and *Miss Mackenzie:* see *Autobiography,* p. 196. Terry suggests that when reading Trollope's claim that novels should be sensational, one may substitute the word "romantic" for "sensational" (p. 90).

19. James Pope Hennessy, *Anthony Trollope* (Boston: Little, Brown, 1971), p. 167. Other proofs of Trollope's intensely active

imagination are his ability to work on two novels–as he did with
Castle Richmond and *Framley Parsonage*—simultaneously, to live
intimately with his characters, and, as he admitted, to be able to pick
up the thread of a work left dangling for years and return to it with
his memory still fresh.

20. "Novel-Reading," p. 25; *Autobiography*, pp. 217–218; *The
New Zealander*, ed. N. John Hall (London: Oxford University Press,
1972), p. 186. The echo of Shelley seems curious coming from Trollope.

21. "On English Prose Fiction," pp. 104, 112, 117; *Autobiography*,
pp. 107, 145. See Peter Thorslev for the connection between Promethean ambitions and Byronic Romanticism in "The Romantic Mind
Is Its Own Place," *Comparative Literature* 15 (Summer 1963): 250–
268.

22. Sadleir, *Trollope: A Commentary*, pp. 339–340; Escott,
Anthony Trollope: His Work, Associates, and Literary Originals
(London: John Lane, 1913), p. 170.

23. *Letters*, p. 266; *Autobiography*, pp. 33, 22. See Frances Trollope's indignant poem on the refusal of Harrow church authorities
to allow a plaque to be put on Allegra Byron's grave, reprinted by
N. John Hall in *Salmagundi: Byron, Allegra, and the Trollope Family*
(Pittsburgh: Beta Phi Mu Chapbook no. 11, 1975).

24. Taylor, quoted in Chew, *Byron in England*, p. 253; White
("Mark Rutherford"), *The Revolution in Tanner's Lane* (London:
T. Fisher Unwin, 1929; first published 1887), p. 145.

25. *Autobiography*, p. 156.

26. Quoted in N. John Hall, "Trollope's Commonplace Book, 1835–
40," *Nineteenth-Century Fiction* 31 (June 1976): 19. Trollope's mar-
ginal commentary on his mother's poem to Byron, written at age
nineteen (*Salmagundi*, p. 57), betrays a sensibility at once steeped in
Byron and critical of him; his criticism savors of self-criticism.

27. *Letters*, pp. 118, 117.

28. R. H. Hutton, Trollope's favorite reviewer of his works, contrasted, to Trollope's disadvantage, Trollope's reliance on observation
with Charlotte Brontë's capacity to draw from her imagination. See
David Skilton, *Anthony Trollope and His Contemporaries* (London:
Longman Group, 1972). The Byron text used is the one-volume *Poetical Works* (London: Oxford University Press, 1945).

29. Meredith, *Letters*, ed. C. L. Cline, 3 vols. (London: Oxford
University Press, 1970), I, 297. Arnold's essay on Byron appears in
the second series of *Essays in Criticism*. For Ruskin's views of Byron
see Chew, *Byron in England*, pp. 235–236, 267–268.

30. Sadleir, *Trollope: A Commentary*, pp. 153–154.

31. Bradford Booth, *Anthony Trollope: Aspects of His Life and
Art* (Bloomington: Indiana University Press, 1958), pp. 141–142. In
Booth's opinion, Trollope's love stories were mostly written in "defer-

ence to the taste of the lending libraries" and are thus a sign of "superficiality" on his part. On this matter cf. Ernest Baker, *The History of the Novel*, 10 vols. (New York: Barnes & Noble, 1963 reprint), VIII, 144; and Trollope, *Autobiography*, pp. 224–226.

32. James, "Anthony Trollope," reprinted in *The Future of the Novel*, ed. Leon Edel (New York: Vintage Books, 1956), p. 256. Trollope's heroines also owe something to the faithful maidens of English ballad tradition.

33. *Autobiography*, p. 183. (Lucy Robarts appears in *Framley Parsonage*, Mary Thorne in *Doctor Thorne*, Emily Hotspur in *Sir Harry Hotspur of Humblethwaite*, Lily Dale in *The Small House at Allington*, Gertrude Woodward in *The Three Clerks*, and Hetta Carbury in *The Way We Live Now*.)

34. Escott, *Anthony Trollope*, p. 207; *Sardanapalus*, 1.2.645.

35. Among the several homilies in *The Small House at Allington* that strain toward a Byronic cynicism of tone is the following: "But men are cowards before women until they become tyrants; and are easy dupes, till of a sudden they recognize the fact that it is pleasanter to be the victimiser than the victim,—and as easy" (chap. 14). In *The Vicar of Bulhampton*, however, Trollope attacks the sexual double standard, refusing either to condemn the "fallen woman" Carry Brattle or to idealize her into a Magdalen figure (see *Autobiography*, pp. 332–334).

36. See Mario Praz's colorful account of the Byronic "Fatal Man" in *The Romantic Agony*, trans. Angus Davidson (London: Oxford University Press, 1970 reprint). Tracy sees in Thwaite "the Wordsworthian and Jefferson ideal of the educated worker" (*Trollope's Later Novels*, p. 148). Other Byronic prototypes are examined in Peter Thorslev, *The Byronic Hero* (Minneapolis: University of Minnesota Press, 1962).

37. Preface, *Philip Van Artevelde* (London, 1834), p. xviii. Trollope thought highly of this "long, sustained and precious song" (*New Zealander*, p. 175).

38. Suggesting a link between Trollope's speculator, Melmotte, and Charles Maturin's Gothic hero-villain, Melmoth, Tracy notes that in an intermediary work, *Melmoth Reconciled* (1845), Balzac alludes to "that race of corsairs whom we dignify with the name of bankers." Balzac, *Works*, New National ed., 18 vols. (New York: Hearst's International Library, n.d.), I, 2. See *Trollope's Later Novels*, p. 169.

39. See the interesting description of the Stanhopes in Polhemus, *Changing World*, pp. 39–45. Trollope's accounts of the marriages between Lord and Lady Lovel (*Lady Anna*) and the Sir Hugh Claverings (*The Claverings*), incidentally, bear a resemblance to the popular versions of Byron's marriage.

40. "The Spotted Dog," *An Editor's Tales* (London, 1870), pp. 236–237, 319; *Letters*, p. 118.

41. See Polhemus, *Changing World*, p. 163; J. Hillis Miller, *The Form of Victorian Fiction* (South Bend, Ind.: University of Notre Dame Press, 1968), pp. 123–139.

42. See A. O. Cockshut, *Anthony Trollope: A Critical Study* (New York: New York University Press, 1968 reprint), p. 172, for a suggestive account of the "destructive" effects of freedom on Trevelyan and others.

43. *Autobiography*, pp. 259–260. Trollope's detestation of Disraeli, as author and political leader, is taken up in the next chapter.

44. See Henry Milley, "*The Eustace Diamonds* and *The Moonstone*," *Studies in Philology* 26 (1939): 651–663.

45. *Letters*, p. 247.

46. See Ruth apRoberts, *Trollope: Artist and Moralist* (London: Chatto & Windus, 1971), pp. 191–197.

THREE   Benjamin Disraeli and the Romance of the Will

1. The most eloquent defenders of Disraeli's Romantic Toryism have been W. F. Monypenny and G. E. Buckle in the monumental *Life of Benjamin Disraeli* (New York: Macmillan, 1929, 2-vol. rev. ed.), Robert Blake in *Disraeli* (New York: St. Martin's Press, 1967), and Stephen Graubard in *Burke, Disraeli, and Churchill: The Politics of Perseverance* (Cambridge, Mass.: Harvard University Press, 1961). The case for the opposition was recently made by J. H. Plumb in "Nixon as Disraeli?" *New York Times Magazine* (Feb. 11, 1973), pp. 12–13, 61–65: "a fine orator, but deeply cynical, yet full of fantasy; he was careless of facts, misty in principles, a lover of monarchy, aristocracy, and empire; above all, he was a gambler in politics" (p. 63).

2. Bagehot, *The English Constitution* (London: Collins, 1963), p. 82: "It is often said that men are ruled by their imaginations; but it would be truer to say they are governed by the weakness of their imaginations" (and see pp. 250–251). Of Disraeli himself Bagehot declared in 1859, "No politician has ever shown, in the bad sense of the word, so *romantic* a political imagination,—in other words, a fancy so little imbued with the laws of real life, so ready to revolt against those laws, and put feeble idealities in their place. His ideal measures, like his ideal heroes, have always seemed the inventions of a mind on the rack to produce something grand or startling instead of something true and lifelike" "Mr Disraeli," *The Economist* 17 (July 2, 1859): 725–726; reprinted in *Bagehot's Historical Essays*, ed. Norman St. John-Stevas (Garden City, N.Y.: Doubleday Anchor Books, 1965), pp. 278–280.

3. *Can You Forgive Her?* (London: Oxford University Press, 1953, double vol.), I, 302–303. Direct and indirect attacks on Disraeli recur in Trollope's writings. In *The Way We Live Now*, for example, he speaks of that "hazy mixture of Radicalism and old-fogyism, of which we have lately heard from a political master, whose eloquence has been employed in teaching us that progress can only be expected from those whose declared purpose is to stand still" (London: Oxford University Press, 1951, double vol., II, 171). Trollope's dislike of Disraeli is discussed by Robert Tracy in *Trollope's Later Novels* (Berkeley: University of California Press, 1978) and by John Halperin in *Trollope and Politics* (New York: Barnes & Noble, 1977). Halperin identifies Disraeli as "the real political villain" of the Palliser novels (p. 175).

4. Wordsworth, quoted in Mary Moorman, *Wordsworth: The Early Years* (London: Oxford University Press, 1957), p. 116; Alexander Gilchrist quoting Blake, cited in Morton Paley, *Energy and the Imagination: A Study of the Development of Blake's Thought* (Oxford: Clarendon Press, 1970), p. 212 (from chap. 8, "The Sublime of Imagination"). And see M. H. Abrams, *Natural Supernaturalism* (New York: Norton, 1973), pp. 117–122 ("The Redemptive Imagination"). Keats, Letter of Nov. 22, 1817, in *Letters*, ed. Hyder Rollins, 2 vols. (Cambridge, Mass.: Harvard University Press 1958), I, 184–185.

5. *Novels and Tales*, Bradenham ed., ed. Philip Guedalla, 12 vols. (New York: Knopf, 1927), VIII, 253. (Subsequent quotations from Disraeli's novels refer to this edition, and the appropriate page numbers appear in the text.) "The Utilitarians in politics are like the Unitarians in religion," Disraeli noted in his diary in 1833; "both omit imagination in their systems, and imagination governs mankind" (Monypenny and Buckle, I, 241).

6. From General Preface to the 1870 collected edition. Reprinted in *Novels and Tales*, I, xv.

7. Blake, *Disraeli*, p. 506. Trollope, *An Autobiography*, ed. Frederick Page (London: Oxford University Press, 1950), p. 259. Trollope was not fond of "men of genius": "I can understand," he continues, "that Mr. Disraeli should by his novels have instigated many a young man and many a young woman on their way in life, but I cannot understand that he should have instigated any one to good."

8. *Henrietta Temple, Novels and Tales*, VI, 442.

9. Blake, *Disraeli*, p. 168.

10. Woodring, *Politics in English Romantic Poetry* (Cambridge, Mass.: Harvard University Press, 1970), p. 43. Coleridge's growing fear of the will and his flight from the imagination are examined by Laurence Lockridge in *Coleridge: The Moralist* (Ithaca: Cornell University Press, 1977), chap. 1. Creativity itself came to seem a "demonic" act of will to Coleridge (p. 69).

11. Thackeray, review of *Coningsby* (May 13, 1844), reprinted in *Contributions to the "Morning Chronicle,"* ed. Gordon N. Ray (Urbana: University of Illinois Press, 1955), p. 40.

12. The expression is applied to Walter Scott's Darsie Latimer (*Redgauntlet*, Letter 2).

13. Eliot and Disraeli shared, nonetheless, an interest in the metaphorical possibilities of Judaism. And she considered the potential conflict between romantic aspirations and realistic expectations in *Romola:* her version of a statesman who would misread facts in the interests of a higher truth is Savonarola, of whom Macchiavelli (in the novel) says to the poet Cei, "you yourself, my Francesco, tell poetical lies only; partly compelled by the poet's fervour, partly to please your audience; but you object to lies in prose. Well, the Frate differs from you as to the boundary of poetry, that's all. When he gets into the pulpit of the Duomo, he has the fervour within him, and without him he has the audience to please. Ecco!" *Romola*, 2 vols., in *The Works of George Eliot*, 24 vols. (Edinburgh: Blackwood Cabinet ed., 1878–1885), II, 160.

14. *Coningsby*, VIII, 126. Disraeli was pleased when *Vivian Grey* was puffed as a prose *Don Juan* and when *Contarini Fleming* was hailed as a prose *Childe Harold*. By contrast, Bulwer Lytton, whose youthful attachment to Byron was more extravagant than Disraeli's, shed his devotion in later years and in his novels characterized Byronism as a form of adolescent antisocial behavior.

15. *Byron's Letters and Journals*, ed. Leslie Marchand (Cambridge, Mass.: Harvard University Press, 1973–), II, 167; Thomas Medwin, *Conversations of Lord Byron*, ed. Ernest Lovell, Jr. (Princeton: Princeton University Press, 1966), p. 228.

16. Preface to *The Revolutionary Epick*, 1834, reprinted by W. D. Adams (London: Hurst and Blackett, 1904), p. xii. Cecil Roth, in *Benjamin Disraeli* (New York: Philosophical Library, 1952), p. 66, surmises that Disraeli's references to his background were efforts "to vindicate his position [in a party "in which the aristocratic faction was dominant"], as the greatest aristocrat of them all by virtue of his Jewish desecent." Byron (who was an admirer of Isaac D'Israeli's writings) himself provided rewritten Biblical texts, to accompany a musical setting, in his *Hebrew Melodies* (1815), which may have suggested something of the Biblical-Byronic cadences, as well as the theme of sympathy for the dispossessed, suffering Jewish nation, of Disraeli's *Alroy*. "It is odd that this should fall to my lot—who have been abused as 'an infidel,'" Byron wrote to his bride-to-be, "—Augusta says 'they will call me a *Jew* next' " (*Letters and Journals*, IV, 220).

17. In a defense of his Radical Tory principles ("What Is He?," 1833), Disraeli praised "an influence too much underrated in this age of bustling mediocrity—the influence of national character. Great

spirits may yet arise to guide the groaning helm through the world of troubled waters." Isaac D'Israeli archly wondered whose "proud spirit" his son had in mind (Monypenny and Buckle, I, 231).

18. See J. M. Thompson, *Louis Napoleon and the Second Empire* (New York: Norton, 1967), pp. 52, 11, 159. One of Louis Napoleon's closest friends thought him "master of the *charlatanerie* which carries away the French people," and noted that "His intellect is sterile. He can copy, and has done so successfully, but he cannot originate" (p. 93). Bagehot made the same observations with reference to Disraeli.

19. See Richard Garnett, "Shelley and Lord Beaconsfield," in *Essays of an Ex-Librarian* (London: Heineman, 1901).

20. Peter Thorslev, *The Byronic Hero* (Minneapolis: University of Minnesota Press, 1962), p. 143.

21. Monypenny and Buckle, I, 240.

22. See Roth, p. 63.

23. Monypenny and Buckle, I, 240.

24. Lionel Stevenson considers Disraeli's (and Bulwer Lytton's) transition from Byronic dandies to respectable Victorians in "Stepfathers of Victorianism," *Virginia Quarterly Review* 6 (April 1930): 251–267.

25. Disraeli's anti-Utilitarian views were shared by Carlyle, Coleridge, Dickens, and Newman. One of the wittiest of the Romantic attacks on Utilitarianism is Disraeli's delightful *Popanilla* (1828).

26. A good recent appraisal of the element of wish-fulfillment in Disraeli's early novels is Robert O'Kell's "The Autobiographical Nature of Disraeli's Early Fiction," *Nineteenth-Century Fiction* 31 (Dec. 1976): 253 284.

27. Browning conjectured that if Shelley had survived into middle age he would have become a good Victorian—like Browning himself. The conversion of a nonbeliever to a belief in Christian and domestic values through the agency of a young woman is a staple of the silver-fork novel, used, for example, in *Tremaine* (1825), Robert Plumer Ward's attempt at a Regency *Hamlet*. Disraeli copied the formula in *The Young Duke*, as did Charlotte Brontë in *Jane Eyre*.

28. An amusing counterpart to Cadurcis is Disraeli's portrait in "Ixion in Heaven" (1833) of Byron as Apollo, "whose love of fame was only equalled by his horror of getting fat." "Say what they like," the melancholy god reflects, "Immortality is a bore" (*Novels and Tales*, III, 119).

29. Moore's biography popularized the image of the antisocial genius. Trelawny reinforced the legend in his *Records of Shelley, Byron, and the Author* (1858, 1878), ed. David Wright (Harmondsworth: Penguin, 1973), p. 92: "Poets, like priests, have hosts of communicants, and should be sworn to celibacy. A catalogue of the domestic grievances of the poets and their wives, from the omniscient Shakespeare and solemn Milton, to scoffing Byron and the martyr

Shelley, would show that men of imagination all compact are devoid of what women call domestic virtues—that is, propriety of conduct and submission to the conventional customs of the time." Venetia's aunt flightily observes (p. 259), "everything is allowed, you know, to a genius!"

30. Blake, *Disraeli*, p. 146. Compare Monypenny and Buckle, I, 365, and B. R. Jerman, *The Young Disraeli* (Princeton: Princeton University Press, 1960), pp. 289–290.

31. Thackeray, *Contributions to the "Morning Chronicle,"* p. 42.

32. "A Defence of Poetry," in *Works*, ed. Roger Ingpen and Walter Peck, 10 vols. (London: Ernest Behn, 1930), VII, 118.

33. *Chartism* (1839), in *Works*, Centenary ed., 30 vols. (London: Chapman and Hall, 1898–1901), XXIX, 157. Disraeli's debt to Carlyle is best described in J. A. Froude's *Lord Beaconsfield* (New York: Harper, 1890).

34. "The Spirit of Whiggism" (1836), reprinted in *Whigs and Whiggism: Political Writings by Benjamin Disraeli*, ed. William Hutcheon (London: John Murray, 1913), p. 340. In her chapter on Disraeli in *A Dream of Order: The Medieval Ideal in Nineteenth-Century English Literature* (Lincoln: University of Nebraska Press, 1970), Alice Chandler contends that the ideals of Young England did find concrete expression in the prime minister's many acts of humanitarian legislation.

35. The best claim for taking *Tancred* seriously is made by Richard Levine in *Benjamin Disraeli* (New York: Twayne, 1968). John Holloway suggestively studies the relationship between Disraeli's extravagant effects and his serious purpose in *The Victorian Sage* (New York: Norton, 1965), e.g., p. 110.

36. See Monypenny and Buckle, I, 850: "*Tancred* strikes the reader less as the accomplishment of a political purpose, than as the sudden revolt of the author against the routine and hollowness of politics, against its prejudice and narrowness; and as an assertion of his detachment and superiority to it all by the glorification of his race and by the proclamation of the mystic ideas, inherited from the Jews, which marked him out from the commonplace mediocrities around him."

37. "Disraeli's Novels," in *Hours in a Library*, 2nd ser. (London: Murray, reprinted 1928), p. 117. Stephen makes much of Disraeli's spirit of self-mockery: the more serious he becomes, the more self-mocking.

38. Quoted in Monypenny and Buckle, II, 105. "There must be design," the hero of Disraeli's next novel, *Lothair*, affirms. "The reasoning and the research of all philosophy could not be valid against that conviction. If there were no design, why, it would all be nonsense; and he could not believe in nonsense" (*L*, p. 190).

39. Problematic though the cardinal's role in *Lothair* may be, his

defense of religion as the national bulwark against barbarism is undoubtedly Disraeli's own, influenced perhaps by Coleridge's *On the Constitution of the Church and State* (1830). "In fine," Coleridge contends, "Religion, true or false, is and ever has been the centre of gravity in a realm, to which all other things must and will accommodate themselves." *Collected Works*, ed. Kathleen Coburn, 16 vols. (Princeton: Princeton University Press, 1971–), X, 70. In "Falconet" Disraeli perhaps intended an account of the barbarians" invasion.

40. Carlyle, "Characteristics," *Works*, XXVIII, 26. And see Byron: "'Actions—actions,' I say, and not writing,—least of all, rhyme" (*Letters and Journals*, III, 220).

41. The title of "Falconet" was not chosen by Disraeli but by Philip Guedalla, who reprints it with *Endymion* (pp. 497, 495).

42. Blake, *Disraeli* p. 419.

43. The cardinals in both books were drawn from the same source, Cardinal Manning.

44. *Bagehot's Historical Essays*, p. 281.

45. Cazamian, *The Social Novel in England: 1830–1850*, trans. Martin Fido (London: Routledge & Kegan Paul, 1973), pp. 179–180; Philip Magnus, *Gladstone* (New York: Dutton, 1964), p. 270.

46. *On the Constitution of the Church and State*, p. 58. (Coleridge is paraphrasing Proverbs 29:18.)

F O U R   Charlotte Brontë and the Perils of Romance

1. Anthony Trollope, *An Autobiography*, ed. Frederick Page (London: Oxford University Press, 1950), pp. 252–253. Trollope links *Jane Eyre* with *Henry Esmond* and *Adam Bede* in opposition to the unrealistic novels of Bulwer Lytton and Dickens.

Citations from *The Professor*, *Shirley*, and *Villette* refer to the Shakespeare Head Brontë Edition (Oxford, 1931). In the case of *Jane Eyre* I have used the Clarendon Edition, ed. Jane Jack and Margaret Smith (Oxford University Press, 1969). Page numbers appear in the text. Criticized for melodramatic and coarse elements in her novels, Brontë invariably defended herself on the grounds of having been true to life. Even the miracle of Jane Eyre's hearing Rochester's voice across many miles was "a true thing; it really happened," as quoted by Elizabeth Gaskell in *The Life of Charlotte Brontë* (London: Dent, Everyman's Library, 1971), p. 296. What Keats called the "truth of the imagination" and George Eliot the "truth of feeling" was not sufficient for Brontë. Her Romanticism is usefully and variously defined by Ernest Baker in *History of the English Novel*, vol. 8 (New York: Barnes & Noble, 1950 reprint); Karl Kroeber in *Styles in Fictional Structure: The Art of Jane Austen, Charlotte Brontë, George Eliot* (Princeton: Princeton University Press, 1971); Algernon Charles Swinburne in "A Note on Charlotte Brontë," in *Complete Works*,

XIV, ed. Edmund Gosse and T. J. Wise (London: Heinemann, 1926); Kathleen Tillotson in *Novels of the Eighteen-Forties* (London: Oxford University Press, 1954); and Raymond Williams in *The English Novel: From Dickens to Lawrence* (London: Oxford University Press, 1970.

2. See Terry Eagleton, *Myths of Power: A Marxist Study of the Brontës* (New York: Barnes & Noble, 1975), e.g., p. 16: "Where Charlotte Brontë differs most from Emily is precisely in this impulse to negotiate passionate self-fulfilment on terms which preserve the social and moral conventions intact."

3. Margaret Blom, *Charlotte Brontë* (Boston: Twayne, 1977), p. 58. And see Valentine Cunningham on the "Methodist matrix" in the Brontë novels in *Everywhere Spoken Against: Dissent in the Victorian Novel* (Oxford: Clarendon, 1975), e.g., pp. 125–126.

4. Douglas Bush, *Mythology and the Romantic Tradition in English Poetry* (New York: Norton, 1963), p. 79.

5. *The Brontës: Their Lives, Friendships, and Correspondence*, 4 vols., ed. T. J. Wise and J. A. Symington (Oxford: Shakespeare Head Brontë Edition, 1932), II, 210; I, 122 (hereafter cited as *SHB*). Lawrence J. Dessner discusses Brontë's "literary culture" in *The Homely Web of Truth: A Study of Charlotte Brontë's Novels* (The Hague: Mouton & Co., 1975), chap. 2. Jane Stedman, in "The Genesis of the Genii," *Brontë Society Transactions* (1965): 16–20, argues that Brontë also drew upon the Reverend James Ridley's moralized pastiches of the *Arabian Nights,Tales of the Genii.*

6. *SHB*, III, 98; I, 122, 109; Gaskell, p. 80.

7. Eagleton, p. 76.

8. Stephen, *Hours in a Library*, 3rd ser. (London: John Murray, 1919 reprint), pp. 26–27; *SHB*, IV, 4. "Undoubtedly," Stephen adds, "such a position speaks of a mind diseased." However, Philip Momberger, in "Self and World in the Works of Charlotte Brontë," *ELH* 32 (Sept. 1965): 349–364, sees the Brontë protagonists in a more positive light as "outcasts" seeking a middle position between desires for assertive selfhood and social acceptance. The element of antagonism and self-division in Brontë's novels has been ably discussed, from a stylistic point of view, by Kroeber, and by Margot Peters in *Charlotte Brontë: Style in the Novel* (Madison: University of Wisconsin Press, 1973). Peters sees Brontë's basic theme as the "problem of asserting and maintaining one's identity in a world that functions upon different and chiefly hostile sets of values" (p. 121). "Perhaps only in Byron," she observes, "do we find so many conflicting personalities warring at once" (p. 161).

9. "Strange Events," in *Miscellaneous and Unpublished Writings of Charlotte and Patrick Branwell Brontë*, 2 vols., added to the Shakespeare Head Brontë Edition (Oxford, 1936–1938), I, 19 (Brontë was fourteen); *SHB*, I, 211, 139.

10. *SHB*, I, 157–158, 155, 241; Gaskell, p. 123. "Oh, my child-hood!" Lucy Snowe reflects in *Villette* (I, 134). "I had feelings: passive as I lived, little as I spoke, cold as I looked, when I thought of past days, I *could* feel. About the present, it was better to be stoical; about the future—such a future as mine—to be dead. And in catalepsy and a dead trance, I studiously held the quick of my nature."

11. Roe Head Manuscript, in *Misc. Writings*, II, 255–256; *SHB*, I, 297. "The fact," says Blom, "that both Branwell and Charlotte referred to their Angrian creation as the 'infernal world' and the 'world below' gives some indication of the moral judgment they passed upon the substance of their fantasies" (Blom, *Charlotte Brontë*, p. 22).

12. See Winifred Gérin, *Charlotte Brontë: The Evolution of Genius* (London: Oxford University Press, 1967), pp. 226, 251; and Fannie E. Ratchford, *The Brontës' Web of Childhood* (New York: Columbia University Press, 1941), pp. 157–165, 229.

13. *SHB*, I, 260.

14. A variation on the Pamela story, "The Cottage in the Wood" contains an orphan-heroine who refuses to become the mistress of a wealthy rake. She serves as the agent of his moral regeneration, and, after becoming an heiress (while he loses his fortune and barely escapes death), she marries him. "Her conscience now told her that she might indulge the pure passion," which rests "upon the immoveable basis of friendship and esteem" (Rev. Patrick Brontë, *Collected Works*, ed. J. Horsfall Turner [1898], pp. 117–118). For the Reverend Brontë see Annette Hopkins, *The Father of the Brontës* (Baltimore: Johns Hopkins Press, 1958), and John Lock and Canon W. T. Dixon, *A Man of Sorrows: The Life, Letters, and Times of the Rev. Patrick Brontë* (London: Nelson, 1965).

15. "Caroline Vernon," in *Legends of Angria*, ed. Fannie E. Ratchford and William DeVane (New Haven: Yale University Press, 1933), p. 303; Winifred Gérin, "Byron's Influence on the Brontës," *Keats-Shelley Memorial Bulletin* 17 (1966): 1–19.

16. "A Peep into a Picture Book," *Misc. Writings*, I, 361; "History of Angria III" ("Passing Events"), ibid., II, 167.

17. Jeffrey, *Edinburgh Review* (July 1814), reprinted in *Byron: The Critical Heritage*, ed. Andrew Rutherford (New York: Barnes & Noble, 1970), p. 60; Macaulay, "Moore's Life of Lord Byron," in *Critical and Historical Essays*, 2 vols. (London: Dent, Everyman's Library, 1967 reprint), II, 636.

18. Ratchford, *The Brontës' Web of Childhood*, pp. 73–75. The Brontë sisters in their role of genii had the power to revive those male figures Branwell chose to kill off. Even in fantasy, however, the female characters, such as Zamorna's wife Marian, once dead were irrecoverable.

19. "Passing Events," *Misc. Writings*, II, 134; "Mina Laury" and

"Caroline Vernon," *Legends of Angria*, pp. 206, 260; *SHB*, I, 174. Shirley was a masculine name when Brontë selected it for her heroine.

20. The apt phrase is Gérin's, *The Evolution of Genius*, p. 133.

21. See Gaskell, p. 57, and Gérin, *The Evolution of Genius*, p. 30, for vivid descriptions of Brontë's ability as a child to live in a fantasy world and simultaneously maintain a mature awareness of public events. According to Earl A. Knies in *The Art of Charlotte Brontë* (Athens: Ohio University Press, 1969), p. 83, Brontë's use of the irreverent Charles Wellesley to narrate the tales may have been a conscious attempt to keep her distance from Angria.

22. "The Duke of Zamorna," *Misc. Writings*, II, 373, 358.

23. "The Foundling," *Misc. Writings*, I, 239; "Captain Henry Hastings," in *Five Novelettes*, ed. Winifred Gérin (London: The Folio Press, 1971), pp. 202, 243. Tom Winnifrith, in *The Brontës and Their Background: Romance and Reality* (London: Macmillan 1973), has recently expressed the possibility that "The Foundling" and other Angrian stories attributed to Charlotte Brontë may be by Branwell (pp. 16, 225). But even if Branwell had a hand in the writing, the story is one that Charlotte draws upon in all her novels; moreover, her recently rediscovered tale "The Secret," published in *Two Tales by Charlotte Brontë: "The Secret" and "Lily Hart,"* ed. William Holtz (Columbia: University of Missouri Press, 1978), begins where "The Foundling" leaves off. See Otto Rank on the psychological implications of the "family romance"—the imagining of a noble lineage for oneself—in *The Myth of the Birth of the Hero* (New York: Vintage Books, 1960), p. 68ff.

24. *Anatomy of Criticism* (New York: Atheneum, 1967 reprint), p. 193.

25. Gaskell, p. 212; *SHB*, II, 152.

26. "The Foundling," *Misc. Writings*, I, 226.

27. Crimsworth's "dosing" his bride with Wordsworth echoes Byron's remark: "Shelley, when I was in Switzerland, used to dose me with Wordsworth physic even to nausea." Thomas Medwin, *Conversations of Lord Byron*, ed. Ernest Lovell, Jr. (Princeton: Princeton University Press, 1966), p. 194.

28. Currer Bell's 1850 Preface to *Wuthering Heights*; *SHB*, II, 153, 179, 201. Lewes himself (notwithstanding his advice to Brontë that she rely upon observation rather than inspiration) had commended Goethe for working "according to the impulse from within, not according to the demand from without." *The Story of Goethe*, revised and abridged version of *Life and Works of Goethe* (Boston, 1873), p. 119.

29. Much astute criticism has been devoted to the various ways *Jane Eyre* holds together by means of its imagery and symbol patterns. See, for example, Robert B. Heilman, "Charlotte Brontë, Rea-

son, and the Moon," *Nineteenth-Century Fiction* 14 (March 1960): 283–302; David Lodge, "Fire and Eyre: Charlotte Brontë's War of Earthly Elements" in *Language of Fiction* (New York: Columbia University Press, 1966); and Mark Schorer, *The World We Imagine* (New York: Farrar, Straus, and Giroux, 1968), pp. 80–96.

30. *SHB*, II, 197. According to Kathleen Tillotson, *Jane Eyre* "started a vogue for plain heroines and ugly masterful heroes" (p. 260).

31. Blanche Ingram and Bertha Rochester may derive from the same source in the Brontë juvenilia: Lady Zenobia Ellrington, a commanding beauty with a propensity toward acts of violence. Of Bertha, Robert B. Martin notes in *The Accents of Persuasion: Charlotte Brontë's Novels* (New York: Norton, 1968), p. 77: "The danger of the unreality of vision that man suffers when he gives himself over to unrestrained passion is one of the themes in the book, and Bertha becomes the objectification of the results of uninhibited license." Bertha's setting fire to Thornfield may have been suggested by Branwell Brontë's similar act, while under the influence of alcohol, at the parsonage. Branwell's real-life self-destructive behavior came to resemble a ghastly parody of the Angrian fantasies of untrammeled willfulness that he and his sister had created.

32. *SHB*, II, 244–245.

33. Although not all literary critics have approved of the domestication of the mythic elements in *Jane Eyre*, Brontë was using the motif of the reformed rake that extends back to *Pamela* (see note 14). The importance of Providence in *Jane Eyre* is treated by Barbara Hardy in *The Appropriate Form: An Essay on the Novel* (London: Athlone Press, 1964), chap. 3.

34. Jane's dual nature, as expressed here at its extreme, corresponds to the Romantic polarities as Michael Cooke has defined them in *The Romantic Will* (New Haven: Yale University Press, 1976), p. 220: "Within the poles of Prometheanism and stoicism, the romantic mind engages itself with the problematics of an assertion of being, centered in the self but radiating, with a tentative imperialism and at the same time a bold obedience, out into the world."

35. Rivers's antecedent in the Angrian stories is John of Fidena. See "A Peek into a Picture-Book," *Misc. Writings*, I, 358–359; and Holtz, Introduction to "Lily Hart," in *Two Tales*, pp. 74–75.

36. The decisive role played by nineteenth-century women novelists in transmuting Romantic into Victorian values is examined by Vineta Colby in *Yesterday's Woman: Domestic Realism in the English Novel* (Princeton: Princeton University Press, 1974). Brontë told Lewes that *Jane Eyre* had been "objected to at first" on the grounds that, like *The Professor*, it was realistic rather than romantic in coloring (*SHB*, II, 153). She described it to her publisher's reader (Williams) as "a mere domestic novel" (*SHB*, II, 151). There is truth,

however, in the contention of Lady Eastlake (Elizabeth Rigby) that "the popularity of *Jane Eyre* is a proof how deeply the love of the illegitimate romance is implanted in our nature." *Quarterly Review* (Dec. 1848), reprinted in *The Brontës: The Critical Heritage*, ed. Miriam Allott (London: Routledge & Kegan Paul, 1974), p. 107. Brontë may be credited with having transformed, with *Jane Eyre*, the focus of romance for Victorian fiction so that the love interest would be more important than the adventure—the reverse of Scott's method. For Brontë love was the greatest adventure in life (as Harriet Martineau complained in her review of *Villette*), and subsequent novelists, Trollope and Meredith among them, followed her example in this respect.

37. See Franklin Gary, "Charlotte Brontë and George Henry Lewes," *PMLA* 51 (1936): 518–542, for an account of Lewes's influence on her. Despite Lewes, however, she preferred Scott to Austen (see *SHB*, II 179). For a study of *Shirley* as a "social novel," see Asa Briggs, "Private and Social Themes in *Shirley*," *Brontë Society Transactions* (1958), pp. 205–219.

38. *SHB*, II, 215–216; III, 150.

39. Zamorna's typical posture is unyielding: "It is no part of my plan [he tells his wife] to allow the existence of a counteracting influence to my own in that heart and family where I ought to reign paramount" ("The Secret," *Two Tales*, p. 48). Gaskell, p. 175. At sixteen Brontë had compared the striking Angrian millworkers to rebels—led by the archrebel of the Angrian cycle, Alexander Rogue (later renamed Percy)—who make "exorbitant demands" ("The Bridal," *Misc. Writings*, I, 210–211). Her sympathy was invariably with the masters and commanders, Zamorna, Wellington, and the like.

40. Caroline's resemblance to Anne Brontë is stressed in J. M. S. Tompkins, "Caroline Helstone's Eyes," *Brontë Society Transactions* (1961), pp. 18–28.

41. *SHB*, III, 278.

42. In "The Problem of Unity in *Shirley*," *Nineteenth-Century Fiction* 12 (Sept. 1957): 125–136, Jacob Korg argues that Brontë's aim was to offer Romantic solutions to the problems of the day. Patricia Beer dismisses Brontë's solution as "sad, reactionary, mixed-up stuff" in *Reader, I Married Him* (New York: Barnes & Noble, 1974), p. 100.

43. *The Brontës: The Critical Heritage*, pp. 109–110.

44. The phrase is Martin's (*The Accents of Persuasion*, p. 145). *Villette's* claims to be the best of the Brontë novels, advanced by a number of recent critics, rests on the assumption that the book expresses Brontë's mature and realistic awareness of tragic life. "Her last novel is the culmination of her campaign to free herself from Angria," writes Robert A. Colby in *Fiction with a Purpose* (Bloomington: Indiana University Press, 1967), p. 209. Lucy "has made her

commitment to life," Knies contends, "and that is her triumph" (*The Art of Charlotte Brontë*, p. 197). It is curious that the paranoid perspective of *Villette* can be interpreted as a triumph of objectivity by a religious-minded author like Martin and by a psychoanalytical critic like Charles Burkhart in *Charlotte Bronte: A Psychosexual Study of Her Novels* (London: Victor Gollancz, 1973). Perhaps confusing masochism with stoicism, Burkhart declares, "The superiority of *Villette* is that it 'faces out the truth' " (p. 118). Lucy's embracement of her doom is seen as a "great acceptance" with an "authentic tragic ring" (p. 121). Calvin and Freud join hands. The classic study of the novel remains Colby's "*Villette* and the Life of the Mind," *PMLA* 75 (Sept. 1960): 410–419.

45. *SHB*, IV, 16, 22. In "The Secret," Paulina's antecedent Marian Hume thanks the "Great Genii who watched over" her at a time of peril (*Two Tales*, p. 64).

46. Ratchford, *The Brontës' Web of Childhood*, p. 240. No Brontë novel is so saturated with references to the *Arabian Nights*, one of the original influences on the Angrian tales. "The nearer she came to realism," Dessner notes of *Villette*, "the more potently did she reproduce the charms of Angria. She was irretrievably enmeshed in that 'web of childhood,' and her crusade against romance was foredoomed to subversion from within" (*The Homely Web of Truth*, p. 116).

47. *SHB*, III, 243 (see "A Romantic Tale," *Misc. Writings*, I, 9), 290.

48. Gaskell, p. 366; *SHB* III, 167, 189; IV, 18.

49. *SHB*, III, 15.

50. Both stories were written and left unfinished before her marriage. "The Story of Willie Ellin" and "Emma" deal with abandoned orphans and reflect Brontë's continuing preoccupation with foundlings—who may or may not find a secure haven in life. According to Elizabeth Gaskell, Mr. Nicholls "always *groaned literally*—when [Charlotte] talked of continuing" "Emma." Gaskell, *Letters*, ed. J. A. Chapple and Arthur Pollard (Cambridge, Mass.: Harvard University Press, 1967), p. 496.

51. *SHB*, III, 328. If we accept the view of a recent Brontë biographer, Margot Peters, in *Unquiet Soul: A Biography of Charlotte Brontë* (Garden City, N.Y.: Doubleday, 1975), that the novelist's decision to marry Nicholls constituted an acceptance of "life and reality" (p. 386), we must also be prepared to say that for Brontë a writing career and "reality" were mutually exclusive. As a recent author pontificates, "The long years of neurotic illness and depression [that is, Brontë's creative years] gave way to healthier activity and perhaps—one hopes but does not know—to a satisfactory sexuality." Helene Moglen, *Charlotte Brontë: The Self Conceived* (New York: Norton, 1976), p. 238. Having exorcised the Angrian ghosts in *Villette*,

Brontë was thus ready for a "mature" role in life. One problem with such psychoanalytical interpretations is that works of literature are turned into reflections of a disease, which their authors are better off without—even if the cure involves the loss of the creative impulse. Perhaps it is truer to say that in *Villette* Brontë exorcised something of her humanity.

F I V E   Elizabeth Gaskell, Wordsworth, and
the Burden of Reality

1. *Alton Locke* (London, 1878; first published 1850), p. 30. The hero of Kingsley's earlier novel, *Yeast* (1848), also goes through a Byronic-Shelleyan-Wertherean phase in his youth. Kingsley claimed that Wordsworth's nature-based philosophy saved him from "shallow, cynical, and materialistic views of the universe." Quoted in Humphry House, "Wordsworth's Fame," *All in Good Time* (London: Rupert Hart-Davis, 1955), p. 40. Charlotte Brontë, *The Professor* (Oxford: Shakespeare Head Brontë Edition, 1931), p. 224.

2. Edward Bulwer Lytton, *England and the English*, ed. Standish Meacham (Chicago: University of Chicago Press 1970), p. 283; Thackeray, *The Newcomes*, chap. 21.

3. Quoted in Mary Moorman, *Wordsworth: The Later Years* (London: Oxford University Press, 1965), p. 107. *The Excursion* is the classic Wordsworthian text praising the faculties of "Admiration, Hope and Love" (4.763) and exhorting quiescence ("Wisdom is ofttimes nearer when we stoop / Than when we soar," 3.231–232), but the *Lyrical Ballads* too encourage a "wise passiveness" on the part of man to the powers of nature. On Wordsworth's acceptableness despite the Evangelical ban on romantic literature see, for example, Francis Mineka, *The Dissidence of Dissent* (Chapel Hill: University of North Carolina Press, 1944), pp. 57, 123–125; and Richard Altick, *The English Common Reader* (Chicago: University of Chicago Press, 1957), pp. 108–115 (on the mistrust of literature), 122.

4. See Louis Cazamian, *The Social Novel in England: 1830–1850*, trans. Martin Fido (London: Routledge & Kegan Paul, 1973; first published 1903), pp. 76–82, for a somewhat simplified account of Romantic "idealistic" opposition to the selfishness and materialism of the industrial apologists of the early nineteenth century. In chaps. 7 and 8 Cazamian considers Gaskell's "Christian interventionism" and Kingsley's "Christian socialism." Wordsworth's beneficial hold on the Victorians has been succinctly treated in House's "Wordsworth's Fame"; M. H. Abrams, *The Mirror and the Lamp* (New York: Norton, 1958), pp. 326–335; and Abrams, *Natural Supernaturalism* (New York: Norton, 1973), pp. 134–140. For the link between Wordsworth and Maurice, see, for example, Olive Brose, *Frederick Denison Maurice: Rebellious Conformist* (Athens: Ohio University Press,

1971), pp. 16–17; and Katherine M. Peek, "Wordsworth in England" (Ph.D. diss., Bryn Mawr, 1943) pp. 147–152. Gaskell's letters are filled with admiration for Kingsley (her "hero") and Maurice ("Mr. Maurice has more influence over the more thoughtful portion of the English people than any one else I know of") and the Christian Socialist movement. Gaskell, *Letters,* ed. J. A. Chapple and A. Pollard (Cambridge, Mass.: Harvard University Press, 1967), e.g., pp. 90, 256–257, 79, 105. Moorman, *Wordsworth: The Later Years,* p. 182. Jonathan Wordsworth's study of the "deeply humane" aspect of Wordsworth in *The Music of Humanity* (London: Nelson, 1969) offers a useful corrective to the modern sense of the poet as aesthetic visionary.

5. Showalter, *A Literature of Their Own* (Princeton: Princeton University Press, 1977), p. 22. (Despite the prohibitions and guilt, the nineteenth century was a great age of women's literature.) Wright, *Mrs. Gaskell: The Basis for Reassessment* (London: Oxford University Press, 1965), p. 31.

6. Annette Hopkins, *Elizabeth Gaskell: Her Life and Work* (London: John Lehmann, 1952), p. 26. Gaskell's first known prose publication was a sketch of Clopton Hall (1938), which contains a grisly account of how the house is haunted by a woman buried alive in the family vaults. Reprinted in the Knutsford Edition of *The Works of Mrs. Gaskell,* ed. A. W. Ward, 8 vols. (London: Smith, Elder, 1906), I, 502–508. For a view from within the Gaskell circle of friends, see Margaret Shaen, ed., *Memorials of Two Sisters: Susanna and Catherine Winkworth* (London, 1908), p. 31.

7. See Ernest Baker, *History of the English Novel,* 10 vols. (New York: Barnes & Noble, 1950 reprint), VIII, 95–96; Winifred Gérin, *Elizabeth Gaskell: A Biography* (London: Oxford University Press, 1976), pp. 60–61; Hopkins, p. 273; and especially Wright, p. 34. The submissive ethic is also taught, to be sure, in the didactic tales of such authors as Maria Edgeworth and Hannah More.

8. House, "Wordsworth's fame," p. 42. Elie Halévy's *England in 1815* (London: E. Benn, 1949) is the classic account of the effect of Protestant, particularly Methodist, restraint on early nineteenth-century England. Both George Brandes, in *Main Currents in Nineteenth Century Literature,* vol. IV (New York: Boni & Liveright, 1923), and Cazamian consider the native individualistic tradition in English Romanticism; while H. G. Schenk relates Byron's ego-centered Romanticism to Continental rather than English Romanticism in *The Mind of the European Romantics* (Garden City: Doubleday, 1969), p. 141.

9. *The Political Ideas of the English Romanticists* (Ann Arbor: University of Michigan, 1966 reprint). The insistence on freedom to follow one's nature, Brinton suggests, could lead "into cotton manufacturing or into pantheism. Ruskin would not have cared to admit

it, but the industrial revolution he detested, and the 'iridescence, colour-depth, and morbid mystery' of things he loved, had the same historical origin" (pp. 221–222).

10. Keats, *Letters*, ed. Hyder Rollins, 2 vols. (Cambridge, Mass.: Harvard University Press, 1958), I, 293.

11. See Ellen Moers, *Literary Women* (New York: Doubleday, 1976), pp. 81–84; and Vineta Colby, *Yesterday's Woman: Domestic Realism in the English Novel* (Princeton: Princeton University Press, 1974). Victorian women were seen, and saw themselves, as "Custodians of the Standard"; as G. M. Young observes, in *Victorian England: Portrait of an Age* (London: Oxford University Press, 1960 reprint), pp. 3–4, "the evangelical faith in duty and renunciation" was "a woman's ethic."

12. Stephen's obituary tribute (*Cornhill*, 1881), reprinted in *George Eliot: The Critical Heritage*, ed. David Carroll (New York: Barnes & Noble, 1971), p. 474. Maurice, quoted in Charles Raven, *Christian Socialism, 1848–1854* (London: Macmillan, 1920), p. 90. Such figures as Benson and Harding are also descendants of the kind-hearted ministers and men of feeling in eighteenth-century fiction. Coleridge's *Lay Sermons* and Southey's *Colloquies of Society* contain some of the ideas later to be developed by the Christian Socialists (Raven, pp. 49–50).

13. See Brose, *Maurice*, pp. 217, 224–225. For Coleridge (a former Unitarian preacher) too, "To exult in our selfhood is an act both of freedom and of evil, because we have sought to raise our finitude to a state independent of God, and a self independent or 'free' of God is definitionally evil." Laurence Lockridge, *Coleridge the Moralist* (Ithaca: Cornell University Press, 1977), p. 64. Arthur O. Lovejoy, in "Coleridge and Kant's Two Worlds," *Essays in the History of Ideas* (Baltimore: Johns Hopkins, 1948), pp. 275–276, considers Coleridge's mistrust of will—his growing sense of man's innate "depravity"—as an aspect of rather than a revolt against Romanticism.

14. Raymond Holt, *The Unitarian Contribution to Social Progress in England* (London: Allen & Unwin, 1938), p. 26; Earl Morse Wilbur, *A History of Unitarianism in Transylvania, England, and America* (Cambridge, Mass.: Harvard University Press, 1952), pp. 377–378.

15. Martineau's biographer, R. K. Webb, has shown how her life of service exemplifies a current in Victorian life "which, far from stressing the insignificance of the individual [as in the case of Evangelicalism], raised him to the towering pinnacle of mastery of his own fate through mastery of the laws of the universe"; yet Martineau adopted Joseph Priestley's necessarianism, which declared free will to be illusory, and she glorified in the certainty that God had chosen her for suffering and self-abasement. *Harriet Martineau: A Radical Victorian* (New York: Columbia University Press, 1960), pp. 86, 80,

201–202. Gaskell's Unitarianism is considered by Wright in *Mrs. Gaskell*, pp. 23–50, and by Coral Lansbury in *Elizabeth Gaskell: The Novel of Social Crisis* (New York: Barnes & Noble, 1975), pp. 11–21. The individualist bias of Gaskell's religion can be seen in the letters to her daughter Marianne (*Letters*, pp. 520, 860).

16. *Letters*, pp. 430, 398. In his review of *Wives and Daughters*, Henry James remarks of the biography that "it tells the reader considerably more about Mrs. Gaskell than about Miss Brontë. *Notes and Reviews*, ed. Pierre de Chaignon la Rose (Cambridge, Mass., 1921), p. 155. Felicia Bonaparte develops this idea in her excellent 1977 English Institute paper, "Elizabeth Gaskell: The Gypsy Bachelor of Manchester."

17. *Letters*, p. 695. Elizabeth Gaskell was thirty-eight when her first novel, *Mary Barton*, was published. *My Diary* (London: privately printed by Clement Shorter, 1923), pp. 5, 10, 13, 16. Gaskell feared the loss of her child and also the possibility that Marianne might learn about death at too early an age. Gaskell's creativity was spurred by her sense of loss: her first poem, written a year after the diary was begun, was an elegy to the daughter who had died before Marianne's birth; her first novel was begun in an effort to subdue the grief she felt after her son's death. Gaskell shared with Tennyson, her favorite Victorian poet, an elegiac cast of mind. *Letters*, p. 541.

18. *Letters*, pp. 115, 109–110, 106, 107. Eliza Fox was the daughter of W. J. Fox, the reform-minded editor of the *Monthly Repository*. See Margaret Ganz, *Elizabeth Gaskell: The Artist in Conflict* (New York: Twayne, 1969), for a discussion of Gaskell's divided nature. *The Life of Charlotte Brontë* (London: Dent, Everyman's Library, 1971), p. 238. To underline this theme, Gaskell maintained that the very writing of the biography was a "grave duty laid upon me" (*Letters*, p. 349).

19. *Letters*, p. 107.

20. Frances Trollope's idea of a factory resembles something out of a Gothic novel, yet she had collected notes. According to her son Thomas Adolphus Trollope, "should any reader ever refer to those pages for a picture of the state of things among the factory hands at that time, he may take with him my testimony to the fact that there was no exaggeration in the outlines of the picture given." *What I Remember*, ed. H. van Thal (London: William Kimber, 1973), p. 138. It may be coincidental, but the kindly master whom Michael Armstrong works for after his escape from Deep Valley Factory is named Thornton. Michael is compared to a Wordsworthian child on a number of occasions.

21. Preface to *Lyrical Ballads*, in *Prose Works*, ed. W. J. Owen and J. W. Smyser, 3 vols. (Oxford: Clarendon Press, 1974), I, e.g., pp. 124, 126 (1800 text), 138–142 (1850 text). *Mary Barton, Works*, I, 284 (all further quotations are from the Knutsford Edition, except

in the case of the Oxford English Novels editions of *Cranford* and *North and South,* and are cited in the text); *The Excursion,* 1.924. The young Wordsworth had written, "Action is transitory . . . / Suffering is permanent, obscure and dark, / And shares the nature of infinity." *The Borderers,* 3.1539–1544.

22. *Letters,* p. 7. In the same letter Gaskell indicates that she is writing imitations of the Romantic poets, including Wordsworth, Coleridge, and Byron. Two years later, her husband William (Manchester's Unitarian minister) gave a series of lectures on "The Poets and Poetry of Humble Life," which she probably helped him prepare.

23. *Alton Locke,* p. 105; Gaskell, *Letters,* p. 33. Some of Gaskell's characters and situations may be derived from Crabbe (for example, the plot of *Sylvia's Lovers* perhaps owes something to "Ruth," in *Tales of the Hall,* in which the heroine loses her sailor-fiancé to a press-gang and is then courted by a dour, possessive teacher), but she shared Wordsworth's desire to spread "a veil of nostalgic sentiment over his [Crabbe-inspired] tales, so that even the most sordid have a pleasant meditative warmth." Judson Lyon, *The Excursion: A Study* (New Haven: Yale University Press, 1950), p. 39.

24. *Letters,* p. 82. The poem has been reprinted in Gaskell, *Works,* I, xxiii.

25. In a companion poem to "The Old Cumberland Beggar," "Animal Tranquillity and Decay," Wordsworth celebrates this attainment of perfect "peace" in the insensibility of old age. Gaskell expands on the role of the Cumberland Beggar: in addition to being the occasion for sympathy on the part of others, Alice Wilson also becomes the author's surrogate (like the Wanderer in *The Excursion*), providing sympathy for others.

26. "The Moorland Cottage" contains early versions of some of Gaskell's basic character-types: the self-denying daughter, the willful male (Maggie's brother) who is contaminated by exposure to worldly values, the invalid older woman who acts as substitute mother to the heroine. The similarities between "The Moorland Cottage" and George Eliot's *The Mill on the Floss* were commented on by Victorians (including Swinburne), but Eliot claimed not to have read the story. See Gordon Haight, *George Eliot; A Biography* (London: Oxford University Press, 1968), p. 525; Robert A. Colby compares the two works in *Fiction with a Purpose* (Bloomington: Indiana University Press, 1967), pp. 229–230. "Half a Life-time Ago" was first published under the title "Martha Preston." Both it and "The Well of Pen-Morfa," dealing with women thwarted in love who devote themselves to helpless, retarded individuals, owe something to the theme, though not the tone, of Wordsworth's "The Idiot Boy." It is in such devotion as the poor have for their idiot children (which Susan Dixon exhibits for her brother in "Half a Life-time Ago"),

claimed Wordsworth, "that we see the strength, disinterestedness and grandeur of love." Quoted in Mary Moorman, *Wordsworth: The Early Years* (London: Oxford University Press, 1957), p. 386.

27. *Letters*, pp. 68, 70. W. R. Greg, in his review of *Mary Barton*, accused Gaskell of bearing "false witness" against the manufacturers and inculcating the "fatally false idea, . . . viz. that the poor are to look to the rich, and not to themselves, for relief and rescue from their degraded condition and their social miseries." *Edinburgh Review* 180 (April 1849): 426, 419. In Gregg's view, John Barton suffers because he is improvident, ignorant of the laws of political economy. Gaskell, however, stresses that Barton's tragedy proceeds from the very generosity of his nature, his wish to help others and his bafflement when the masters and members of Parliament refuse to consider the misery of the workers. Arnold Kettle has said of Barton, "Apart from Heathcliff he is the nearest approach to a tragic hero which the early Victorian novel permitted itself." "The Early Victorian Social-Problem Novel," in *From Dickens to Hardy*, ed. Boris Ford (Baltimore: Penguin Books, 1958), p. 181. One recalls that Wordsworth, despite his conservatism, maintained in his late years, "I have a good deal of the Chartist in me" (quoted in Moorman, *Wordsworth: The Early Years* p. 228).

28. *Yeast* (London: Dent, 1912), p. 274. Kingsley criticized those who used the Bible as "an opium-dose for keeping beasts of burden patient when they were being overloaded" (quoted in Raven, *Christian Socialism*, p. 14). "I know it is said," another of Gaskell's heroes, Francis Newman, observed in *The Soul*, "that the poor are made more patient by the notion so current among them, that in another life they will get compensation for the hardships which they endure in the present: but this is to buy patience, by propagating delusion" (London, 1877, p. 143; first published 1849).

29. Rosamond is the heroine of a series of Maria Edgeworth's moral tales written for children. As a child of seven, Rosamond foolishly chooses a purple jar that she sees in a chemist's shop over a much-needed pair of shoes. In the course of the tales, she learns to be more prudent. Gaskell was possibly thinking of Rosamond when she created the heroine of *Sylvia's Lovers*: at the beginning of that book, Sylvia chooses a crimson cloak in preference to a more practical grey one.

30. Gaskell's epigraph for *Mary Barton*, taken from Carlyle's essay "Biography," indicates her desire to present something of substance despite the sense of herself as "the Foolishest of existing mortals" with her "Long-ear of a Fictitious Biography." Carlyle, "Biography," in *Works*, Centenary ed., 30 vols. (London: Chapman and Hall, 1898–1901), XXVIII, 49; and see "Corn-Law Rhymes," *Works*, XXVIII, 163. Trollope, on the other hand, bristled at Carlyle's "silly and arrogant" comparison of the novel form to "ass's ears." *An Auto-*

biography, ed. Frederick Page (London: Oxford University Press, 1950), p. 371.

31. Wordsworth, Preface to *Lyrical Ballads,* in *Prose Works,* I, 141 (1850 text). Carlyle's influence was so various that he could be cited by Gaskell in support of cooperation and mutual understanding between masters and workers—Gaskell's invocation for workers to be "bound to their employees by the ties of respect and affection, not by mere money bargains alone" (p. 451) clearly echoes Carlyle's declaration, in *Past and Present,* that "We have profoundly forgotten everywhere that *Cash-Payment* is not the sole relation of human beings" (*Works,* X, 146)—and by Greg, in his review of *Mary Barton,* to argue that since "the necessity of labour is a blessing" (p. 423), workers must maintain their independence from unions or benign legislation, employers or philanthropists, and seek to rise to the top by their own efforts.

32. *Letters* p. 108.

33. Gaskell's affinity with Scott is seen not only in the two authors' use of dialect, their fondness for devoted servants in their novels, and their credulous streak, but more importantly in their fascination with the theme of a protagonist divided between individual (or clan) and national, religious, or civic loyalties. Jem Wilson's bitter sentiment, "God does not judge as hardly as man, that's one comfort for all of us!" (p. 436), which is repeated in *Ruth* and *Sylvia's Lovers,* is an echo of Scott's words in *The Heart of Midlothian:* "God is mair mercifu' to us than we are to each other" (chap. 24). And see George Eliot's *Silas Marner:* "Them above has got a deal tenderer heart nor what I've got" (chap. 16).

34. *Letters,* pp. 225, 223. "Perhaps the earliest general outcry against a novel on grounds of propriety came in 1853 against Mrs. Gaskell's *Ruth,*" according to Kathleen Tillotson in *Novels of the Eighteen-Forties* (London: Oxford University Press, 1961 reprint), p. 58. George Eliot admired the book's domestic descriptions, but deplored Gaskell's "love of sharp contrasts—of 'dramatic' effects." *Letters,* ed. Gordon Haight, 9 vols. (New Haven: Yale University Press, 1954–1978), II, 86. Eliot herself was guilty of such lapses on occasion.

35. W. A. Craik, *Elizabeth Gaskell and the English Provincial Novel* (London: Methuen 1975), p. 51. See, for example, Crabbe's "Ellen Orford" (in *The Borough*) and Wordsworth's "Her Eyes Are Wild." Each poet gave the name Ruth to the title-figure of a poem about an abandoned woman.

36. The leading Unitarian journal, *The Monthly Repository,* defined its purpose with a quotation by Jeremy Bentham that it used as motto for many years: its aim was to teach the individual to learn to trust to himself, "to excite him to place more confidence in his own strength, and less in the infallibility of great names;—to help

him to emancipate his judgment from the shackles of authority" (quoted in Mineka, *The Dissidence of Dissent,* p. 101).

37. Gaskell had already treated the Magdalene–Prodigal Son theme in "Lizzie Leigh" (1850); but where she attributes Lizzie's fall to a desire to see something of the "world" (in the manner of Wordsworth's "Michael"), Ruth is victimized by her very innocence.

38. On his part, Maurice considered *Ruth* to be "as true to human experience as it is to divine morality" (quoted in Hopkins, *Elizabeth Gaskell,* p. 130).

39. *Cranford,* ed. Elizabeth Watson (London: Oxford University Press, 1972), p. 114. All further citations are in the text.

40. Dickens, who published *Cranford* and *North and South* in serial form in his journal *Household Words,* deplored Gaskell's tendency to kill off her main characters. She also poked fun at this habit of hers, insisting to Dickens that a better title than "North and South" (which had been his idea) "would have been 'Death & Variations'. There are 5 deaths, each beautifully suited to the character of the individual" (*Letters,* p. 324). Nina Auerbach has recently paid tribute to the "solidity" and "durability" of Gaskell's dream-community in *Communities of Women: An Idea in Fiction* (Cambridge, Mass.: Harvard University Press, 1978), pp. 90–91.

41. Winifred Gérin emphasizes the importance of wish-fulfillment in Gaskell's works—restoring to life the dead brother and establishing a tight bond between fathers and daughters—which reflects "a great emotional need" in the author's youth (*Elizabeth Gaskell,* pp. 33–38).

42. *The Brontës: Their Lives, Friendships, and Correspondence,* 4 vols., ed. T. J. Wise and J. A. Symington (Oxford: Shakespeare Head Brontë Edition, 1932), IV, 76. Gérin, *Elizabeth Gaskell,* p. 124.

43. "Modern Novelists—Great and Small," *Blackwood's* 77 (May 1855): 558. Margaret Hale's resourcefulness in bearing up under many burdens connects her to Elizabeth Gaskell: the novelist compared herself and her heroine to Rossini's hard-pressed Figaro, "factotum della città" (*Letters,* p. 110). But Margaret's passionate and independent nature owes something to Brontë's Shirley too. After the publication of *Ruth,* Gaskell humorously contrasted herself with Brontë, claiming that "she puts all her naughtiness into her books, and I put all my goodness" (*Letters,* p. 228).

44. *Victorian Cities* (Harmondsworth: Penguin Books, 1968), pp. 89, 100; *Coningsby, Novels and Tales,* Bradenham ed., 12 vols., ed. Philip Guedalla (New York: Knopf, 1927), VIII, 121, 161.

45. Review of *Alton Locke, Edinburgh Review* 189 (Jan. 1851): 1–2; *North and South,* ed. Angus Easson (London: Oxford University Press, 1973), pp. 80, 64, 81. All further citations are in the text.

46. Greg, quoted in Holt, pp. 55–56.

47. *Letters,* p. 321.

48. *The Romantic Novel in England* (Cambridge, Mass.: Harvard University Press, 1972), pp. 22–23.

49. *Letters,* p. 110.

50. This mistrust of self has a Romantic precedent in Coleridge's desire (according to Lockridge, p. 19) not "to know the complete truth about himself." As Coleridge indicated in his notebook, " 'Thought becomes a thing when it acts' on one's full consciousness, and 'therefore I dread to tell my whole & true case,' because to do so would make it 'a substantial reality / I want it to remain a thought in which I may be deceived whole [?wholly].' " (The words in single quotes are Coleridge's.)

51. See Patricia Meyer Spacks, *The Female Imagination* (New York: Knopf, 1975), pp. 91–93: "Suppression as a legitimate form of self-control has long been recommended to women; literary recognition of its dangers as early as Mrs. Gaskell's time is unusual."

52. See John Bayley, *Tolstoy and the Novel* (New York: Viking Press, 1968), pp. 113–117.

53. Gaskell's reaction to "the awkward blot" in George Eliot's life was typical of her tolerance: "Do you know I can't help liking her," she wrote of the author of *Adam Bede,* "—*because* she wrote those books. Yes I do! I *have* tried to be moral, & dislike her & dislike her books— but it won't do" (*Letters,* p. 594).

S I X   George Eliot: The Romantic Legacy

1. For comparisons of Wordsworth and George Eliot see, for example, Robert A. Colby, *Fiction with a Purpose* (Bloomington: Indiana University Press, 1967), pp. 231–234; Robert H. Dunham, "Wordsworthian Themes and Attitudes in George Eliot's Novels" (Ph.D. diss., Stanford, 1971); Humphry House, *All in Due Time* (London: Rupert Hart-Davis, 1955), pp. 109–115; U. C. Knoepflmacher, *George Eliot's Early Novels* (Berkeley: University of California Press, 1968), e.g., pp. 14–24; Thomas Pinney, "George Eliot's Reading of Wordsworth: The Record," *Victorian Newsletter* (Fall 1963), pp. 20–22; Mario Praz, *The Hero in Eclipse in Victorian Fiction,* trans. Angus Davidson (London: Oxford University Press, 1969 reprint), pp. 322–330; Jerome Thale, *The Novels of George Eliot* (New York: Columbia University Press, 1959), e.g., pp. 17–33; Basil Willey *Nineteenth-Century Studies* (Harmondsworth: Penguin, 1964 reprint), pp. 215, 254–256. A more general discussion of Eliot's Romanticism is found in Ted Spivey, "George Eliot: Victorian Romantic and Modern Realist," *Studies in the Literary Imagination* 1 (Oct. 1968): 5–21. Among Eliot's distinguished detractors have been Nietzsche, Yeats, and Edmund Wilson. Calvin Bedient's assault on Eliot in *Architects of the Self* (Berkeley: University of California, 1972) is unfair to the novelist in its insistence that she is anti-Romantic and always on the

side of society and opposed to the rights of the individual, but it is a fair reaction to the icon of George Eliot: for example, "The chief burden of her novels is that human beings are not social, not 'Victorian' enough . . . George Eliot's characteristic subject is the necessary submission of individuals to their own society" (pp. 33–34).

2. Cross, *George Eliot's Life as Related in Her Letters and Journals,* 3 vols., Illustrated Cabinet ed. (Boston, n.d.), I, 11; Haight, *George Eliot: A Biography* (London: Oxford University Press, 1968), p. 23; *The George Eliot Letters,* ed. Gordon Haight, 9 vols. (New Haven: Yale University Press, 1954–78), I, 73, 19; *The Mill on the Floss,* ed. Haight (Boston: Houghton Mifflin Riverside ed., 1961), p. 256. I have used the Cabinet edition for all Eliot novels except in the cases of the excellent Riverside editions of *Adam Bede, The Mill on the Floss,* and *Middlemarch.*

3. *Letters,* III, 168–169, 302; II, 416; V, 387, 417.

4. *Romola,* 2 vols., in *The Works of George Eliot,* 24 vols. (Edinburgh: Blackwood Cabinet ed., 1878–85), II, 370.

5. *Letters,* III, 24. For De Quincey and Mill, see Richard Stang, *The Theory of the Novel in England: 1850–1870* (New York: Columbia University Press, 1959), pp. 4, 9: for example, "It is only the grander passions of poetry, allying themselves with forms more abstract and permanent," that De Quincey found worthy; novels, by contrast, he saw as dependent on a *"canaille* of an audience." In *George Eliot and the Novel of Vocation* (Cambridge, Mass.: Harvard University Press, 1978), pp. 66–71, Alan Mintz links Eliot's sense of calling with her native Protestant background and with the Miltonic conception of the "poetic vocation."

6. Cross, I, 313 ("How I Came to Write Fiction").

7. *Letters,* I, 22 65. "The real premise for this attack upon fiction," declares Ruby Redinger in *George Eliot: The Emergent Self* (New York: Knopf, 1975), p. 85, "was an acknowledgment of its tremendous power, which she had personally felt." See *The Mill on the Floss,* pp. 207–208; and Jean Jacques Rousseau, *Confessions,* trans. J. M. Cohen (Harmondsworth: Penguin, 1953), p. 48.

8. *Lady Blessington's Conversations of Lord Byron,* ed. Ernest Lovell, Jr. (Princeton: Princeton University Press, 1969), pp. 49–50. Elizabeth Barrett Browning touches on this theme (the "man . . . 'marred,' made a Rousseau or a Byron of," very often by having been granted a poetic sensibility) in "A Musical Instrument." See T. A. Trollope, *What I Remember* (London: William Kimber, 1973 reprint) for an account of Anthony Trollope's interchange with Elizabeth Barrett Browning on the subject (pp. 177–179).

9. The remarks on Ruskin are in the "Arts and Belles Lettres" section of the *Westminster Review* 65 (April 1856): 626, 627. The article on von Riehl, which was also written in 1856, is reprinted in *Essays of George Eliot,* ed. Thomas Pinney (New York: Columbia

University Press, 1963), pp. 266–299. Neither von Riehl nor Eliot praises all aspects of peasant life: he notes an obstinacy and "habit of litigation" (*Essays*, p. 278), which she portrays in the miller Tulliver.

10. See (in *Essays*) "Liszt, Wagner, and Weimar" (1855); "Thomas Carlyle" (1855); "The Antigone and Its Moral" (1856), p. 265; "The Morality of Wilhelm Meister" (1855); "German Wit: Heinrich Heine" (1856); "Silly Novels by Lady Novelists" (1856); "Worldliness and Other-Worldliness: The Poet Young" (1857); "Evangelical Teaching: Dr. Cumming" (1855); "Three Novels" (1856). The discussion of genius is on p. 329. Dunham compares Eliot's attack on Young and the conventions of eighteenth-century poetry evident in his work with Wordsworth's similar attack in the Preface to *Lyrical Ballads* ("Wordsworthian Themes in Eliot's Novels," pp. 24–25).

11. *Romola*, II, 235–236. Cf. George Henry Lewes, *Problems in Life and Mind*, quoted in Colby, *Fiction with a Purpose*, p. 294: "The starting point [in cognition] is always Feeling, and Feeling is the final goal and test." For the Romantic preoccupation with music "as a tonal medium for evoking or specifying feeling," rather than as a mimetic art force, see M. H. Abrams, *The Mirror and the Lamp* (New York: Norton 1958 reprint), p. 92.

12. Cross, I, 119–120; Hunt, *The Religion of the Heart* (London, 1853), pp. 31, 60–61. See *Letters*, II, 120, 124–125.

13. Bray, *The Education of the Feelings* (London, 1849, 2nd ed; first pub. 1838), p. viii. See *Letters*, III, 324 (Eliot remembered reading the book in her youth and recommending it to her sister as "very sensible"). Bray's possible influence on *The Mill on the Floss* is considered later in this chapter.

14. *Impressions of Theophrastus Such* (New York, n.d.), p. 121.

15. Cassirer, *The Question of Jean-Jacques Rousseau*, trans. Peter Gay (Bloomington: Indiana University Press, 1963), pp. 83, 36.

16. Rousseau, *Discourse on the Origin and Basis of Inequality among Men*, in *The Essential Rousseau*, trans. Lowell Blair (New York: New American Library, 1974), pp. 150, 166; Cassirer, *The Question*, p. 127. Eliot, *Letters*, I, 162.

17. *Letters*, I, 277; White, quoted in Haight's Preface to *Letters*, I, xv; Cross, I, 378; *Letters*, I, 251–252. For the Victorians' opinion of Rousseau, see Edmund Gosse, "Rousseau in England in the Nineteenth Century," *The Fortnightly Review* 98 (July 1912): 22–38.

18. "The Wisdom of the Child," in *Essays*, pp. 19–20; Rousseau, *Confessions*, p. 490.

19. Rousseau, *Émile*, trans. Barbara Foxley (London: Dent, 1963 reprint), p. 253; Hardy, *The Novels of George Eliot* (London: Athlone Press, 1959), p. 33.

20. See Ellen Moers, *Literary Women* (New York: Doubleday, 1976), pp. 156–157. Rousseau, *La Nouvelle Héloïse*, trans. Judith

McDowell (University Park: The Pennsylvania State University Press, 1968), pp. 172, 82, 163.

21. *Letters*, I, 284; Bray, *The Education of the Feelings*, p. 82.

22. Rousseau, *Confessions*, p. 182; Cassirer, *The Question*, p. 96. The Victorian view is reflected in G. H. Lewes's chapter "The Philosophy of Rousseau" in his *Life of Maximilian Robespierre* (London: 1849), e.g., p. 18.

23. Moers, *Literary Women*, pp. 173–210; Thomson, *George Sand and the Victorians* (London: Macmillan, 1977), pp. 152–184; Colby, *Fiction with a Purpose*, pp. 223–225. Eliot's interest in Chateaubriand is less well documented, but Felix Holt's attack on the author of *René*—"Your dunce who can't do his sums always has a taste for the infinite"—probably reflects a childhood enthusiasm. *Felix Holt*, 2 vols., Cabinet ed., I, 184. Eliot admitted enjoyment of Chateaubriand's *Atala* to Harriet Beecher Stowe (*Letters*, V, 279).

24. Thomson, *George Sand and the Victorians*, pp. 9, 18; Simpson, "George Eliot's Novels," *Home and Foreign Review* 3 (Oct. 1863): 522–549, reprinted in *George Eliot: The Critical Heritage*, ed. David Carroll (New York: Barnes & Noble, 1971), e.g., pp. 241–242. Robert Colby, in *Fiction with a Purpose* (p. 268), considers the influence of Sand's *Jacques* on *Middlemarch*. (And cf. Eliot's reaction to Sand in *Letters* I, 277–278.)

25. "For eloquence and depth of feeling, no man approaches George Sand," Lewes wrote in "The Lady Novelists," *Westminster Review* 58 (July 1852): 133. Eliot, *Letters*, VI, 99.

26. *Lady Blessington's Conversations of Lord Byron*, p. 26; *The Mill on the Floss*, pp. 290–291; Moers, *Literary Women*, p. 176. And see Alexander Welsh, "George Eliot and Romance," *Nineteenth-Century Fiction* 14 (Dec. 1959): 242–243.

27. "Armgart," in *The Legend of Jubal and Other Poems*, Cabinet ed., p. 76.

28. Oskar Walzel, *German Romanticism*, trans. A. E. Lussky (New York: Frederick Ungar, 1965 reprint), p. 74; and see M. H. Abrams, *The Mirror and the Lamp*, pp. 88–94; and René Wellek, "German and English Romanticism," *Confrontations* (Princeton: Princeton University Press, 1965), pp. 3–33.

29. For Schlegel's conception of the novelistic form, see René Wellek, *A History of Modern Criticism: 1750–1950*, vol. II, *The Romantic Age* (New Haven: Yale University Press, 1955), pp. 19–20; but see Arthur O. Lovejoy, "The Meaning of 'Romantic' in Early German Romanticism," *Essays in the History of Ideas* (Baltimore: Johns Hopkins, 1948), p. 198. Heinrich Heine, *The Romantic School*, in *Selected Works*, trans. and ed. Helen Mustard (New York: Random House, 1973), e.g., p. 205.

30. Goethe and Schiller were both more than Romantic, but they were that too. On Schiller's influence see Lovejoy, "Schiller and the

Genesis of German Romanticism," *Essays in the History of Ideas,* pp. 207–227; and on Goethe's place in the "European romantic movement which he, as much as any single writer, helped to create," see Wellek, *Concepts of Criticism* (New Haven: Yale University Press, 1963), p. 163.

31. "Realistic Novels: George Eliot and Anthony Trollope," *Universal Review* (April 1859), p. 217; Simpson, "George Eliot's Novels," in *Critical Heritage,* pp. 245–247; Cross, III, 344; Lewes, *The Story of Goethe's Life* (revised and abridged edition of *Life and Works of Goethe,* Boston, 1873), p. 18; Simcox, quoted in Redinger, *George Eliot: The Emergent Self,* p. 336; Eliot, *Letters,* VI, 89.

32. Cross, I, 375. She was especially fond of *The Maid of Orleans.*

33. Lewes, *The Story of Goethe's Life,* p. 325; Schiller, *Naive and Sentimental Poetry* trans. Julius Elias (New York: Frederick Ungar, 1966), p. 184.

34. G. W. F. Hegel, *The Philosophy of History,* trans. J. Sibree (New York: Dover, 1956), p. 35; Heine, *The Romantic School,* p. 170. More recently, E. L. Stahl has argued that Schiller's heroes are defeated as much by internal weaknesses as by any external cause. *Friedrich Schiller's Drama* (London: Oxford University Press, 1954), e.g., p. 12: "The essential conflict in Schiller's tragedies is the struggle within the hero which the hero's battle against the world elicits but never supplants."

35. *The Spanish Gypsy,* Cabinet ed., p. 162. Schiller's words are translated and quoted in *The Life of Friedrich Schiller,* in Thomas Carlyle, *Works,* Centenary ed., 30 vols. (London: Chapman and Hall, 1898–1901), XXV, 202. For a modern translation see Schiller, *On the Aesthetic Education of Man,* ed. and trans. E. M. Wilkinson and L. A. Willoughby (London: Oxford University Press, 1967), p. 57.

36. Lewes, *The Story of Goethe's Life,* p. 326.

37. Cross, I, 373. Sir Walter Scott's novels provided the other major source of influence in changing Eliot's attitude toward the value of imaginative literature at about this time; but Eliot's earnest sense of the moral possibilities open to the creative imagination derives more from Schiller (it seems to me) than from Scott.

38. Carlyle, *Life of Schiller,* p. 19.

39. *Letter,* III, 318.

40. The phrase is Karl Löwith's in *From Hegel to Nietzsche: The Revolution in Nineteenth-Century Thought,* trans. David Green (Garden City, N.Y.: Doubleday Anchor Books, 1967), pp. 307–309, 331–338. Nevertheless, many great nineteenth-century writers, including Tolstoy, acknowledged debts to Feuerbach.

41. Hegel, *The Philosophy of History,* p. 30. Robert Hartman translates the same phrase as brings "to pass that which the times required" in Hegel, *Reason in History* (New York: Liberal Arts Press, 1953), p. 39. John Sibree and his sister Mary were close friends of Eliot

in her youth. *Daniel Deronda*, 3 vols., in *The Works of George Eliot* henceforth cited as *Works*, 24 vols. (Edinburgh: Blackwood Cabinet ed., 1878–1885), III, 308.

42. *Letters*, II, 153. Feuerbach's rhapsodic mistiness in ideas and phrasing gives him the air of a nineteenth-century guru; Eliot was able to turn into more concrete form in her fiction such a notion as the following, which gives a good idea of Feuerbach's style: *"Feeling is the object of feeling.* Feeling is sympathy; feeling arises only in the love of man to man. Sensations man has in isolation; feelings only in community. Only in sympathy does sensation rise into feeling. Feeling is aesthetic, human sensation; only what is human is the object of feeling. In feeling man is related to his fellow-man as to himself; he is alive to the sorrows, the joys of another as to his own." *The Essence of Christianity*, trans. George Eliot (New York: Harper Torchbooks, 1957), p. 283.

See Friedrich Engels's objection to Feuerbach (quoted in Löwith, *From Hegel to Nietzsche*, p. 308): "He is realistic in form, using man as his point of departure, but he has nothing to say of the world in which this man lives, and so man remains the same abstract man that was the subject of the philosophy of religion." Eliot's connection with August Comte's similarly vague religion of humanity has also un-doubtedly been overrated.

43. Robert Dunham also indicates the impreciseness of speaking of Wordsworthian "influences" on Eliot ("Wordsworthian Themes in Eliot's Novels," pp. 10–11); she would probably have been Words-worthian in temperament had she never heard of him—or indeed had he never lived. The letter to Maria Lewis is in *Letters*, I, 34. Still in her Evangelical phase at this time, however, she would have preferred Wordsworth to have shown "less satisfaction in terrene objects, a more frequent upturning of the soul's eye."

44. *Letters*, III, 382; Willey, *Nineteenth-Century Studies*, p. 215.

45. Cooke, *The Romantic Will* (New Haven: Yale University Press, 1976), e.g., pp. 214–216. One such anxious Victorian was John Stuart Mill, who characterized Wordsworth as "the poet of unpoetical na-tures." *Autobiography*, ed. Jack Stillinger (Boston: Houghton Mifflin, 1969), p. 90.

46. James, "Daniel Deronda: A Conversation," *Partial Portraits* (London, 1888), p. 81. U. C. Knoepflmacher has linked Mary Garth with Wordsworth partly on the basis of the name Eliot had originally selected for her, Mary Dove. See "Fusing Fact and Myth: The New Reality of *Middlemarch*," in *This Particular Web*, ed. Ian Adam (University of Toronto Press, 1975), p. 68. Mary's role in the novel fits the Wordsworthian pattern even without the name.

47. *Letters*, I, 177; VII, 261. She suggested that Harrison look at *The Prelude*, VIII, 608–615, and XI, 393–395: "There is / One great society alone on Earth: / The noble Living and the noble Dead." For

a list of the passages she marked in *The Prelude,* see Pinney, "George Eliot's Reading of Wordsworth" p. 22.

48. *Letters,* III, 111.

49. Cross, I, 369. "For her," Walter Allen suggests in *George Eliot* (New York: Macmillan, 1964), p. 22, "the truly seminal author, as one can see now from her fiction and the temper of her mind, was Scott." In the persona of Theophrastus Such, Eliot observes, "I often smile at my consciousness that certain conservative prepossessions have mingled themselves for me with the influences of our midland scenery, from the tops of the elms down to the buttercups and the little way-side vetches" (*Theophrastus Such,* p. 33).

50. From R. H. Hutton's review in the *Spectator* (July 18, 1863), reprinted in *George Eliot: The Critical Heritage,* p. 199. And see Welsh, "George Eliot and Romance."

51. *Letters,* I, 51–52; *Essays,* p. 169.

52. Redinger, *George Eliot: The Emergent Self, p.* 47. Stowe herself declared, "One of the first living writers of the age, in the novel of 'Romola,' has given in her masterly sketch of the character of Tito the whole history of the conflict of a woman like Lady Byron with a nature like that of her husband." "The True Story of Lady Byron's Life," *Macmillan's Magazine* 20 (Sept. 1869): 388.

53. *Felix Holt,* I, 102; *Letters,* V, 56–57. For Byron's grandniece, see *Letters,* V, 314: "It made me cry to see her young fresh face among the hags and brutally stupid men around her."

54. Sylvia Norman's *Flight of the Skylark: The Development of Shelley's Reputation* (Norman: University of Oklahoma Press, 1954), while containing amusing sketches of the Shelley devotees and detractors, does not go deeply into the nature of Shelley's hold on the Victorian imagination; Roland A. Duerksen's *Shelleyan Ideas in Victorian Literature* (The Hague: Mouton & Co., 1966) is marred by the author's tendency to see those Victorians who shed their youthful sympathies for Shelley as apostates (Disraeli's critique of Shelley's political views in *Venetia,* for example, is seen as a proof of the novelist's own political ambition), but the book contains some suggestive remarks on the similarities of Shelley, Lewes, and Will Ladislaw (pp. 139–149). Lewes's youthful "Percy Bysshe Shelley," which appeared in the *Westiminster Review* 35 (1841): 303–344, was followed by a briefer but equally enthusiastic piece on "Shelley and the Letters of Poets" in the *Westminster Review* 57 (1852): 509: "Of all his contemporaries Shelley seems to us to have been the nearest approach in life and works to the ideal of a poet." And see Edward Bulwer Lytton, *England and the English,* ed. Standish Meacham (University of Chicago Press, 1970; originally pub. 1833), p. 283; Mary Shelley, Preface to Second Collected ed., reprinted in Shelley, *Poetical Works,* ed. Thomas Hutchinson (London: Oxford University Press, 1970 rev. ed.), xxiii; and Browning, Introductory Essay to

Letters of Percy Bysshe Shelley (London, 1852; most of these letters turned out to be forgeries), pp. 7–8, 34–35.

55. *Letters*, II, 126; Lewes, "Percy Bysshe Shelley," p. 317; Cross, III, 345.

56. *Letters*, II, 288; and cf. III, 15: "Sometimes, when I read of the death of some great, sensitive human being, I have a triumph in the sense that they are at rest." Eliot's publisher, John Blackwood, noted apropos of Maggie Tulliver's death, "Providence was kind in removing Maggie. She could not have been happy here" (*Letters*, III, 277). Shelley, "A Defence of Poetry," in *Works*, 10 vols., ed. Roger Ingpen and Walter Peck (London: Ernest Benn, 1930), VII, 137.

57. Shelley, Preface to *The Revolt of Islam*, in *Poetical Works*, p. 32. "Necessity means to him" Carl Woodring declares in *Politics in English Romantic Poetry* (Cambridge, Mass.: Harvard University Press, 1970), p. 256, "what the doctrine of consequences was to mean to George Eliot: since no act can be recovered and every act has numberless consequences, you must in conscience acquire as much knowledge, sympathy, and empathy as you can in order to meliorate the consequences of every act you contemplate." *Prometheus Unbound*, 2.3.40–41; *Daniel Deronda*, II, 371.

58. *Middlemarch*, ed. Gordon Haight (Boston: Houghton Mifflin Riverside ed., 1956), p. 6; Linton, *My Literary Life* (London, 1899), pp. 19, 25.

59. Lewes, "Spinoza," *Fortnightly Review* (1 April 1866), p. 387; "Percy Bysshe Shelley," pp. 307, 320–321; "Hegel's Aesthetics: Philosophy of Art," *British and Foreign Review* 13 (1842): 5–30, reprinted in *Literary Criticism of George Henry Lewes*, ed. Alice Kaminsky (Lincoln: University of Nebraska Press, 1964), p. 47; "Percy Bysshe Shelley," p. 320. For Lewes's relations with the Leigh Hunt circle, see Anna Kitchel, *George Lewes and George Eliot* (New York: John Day, 1933); and see Alice Kaminsky's account of Lewes's Shelley-worship, *George Henry Lewes as Literary Critic* (Syracuse University Press, 1968), pp. 52–57). At one time Lewes planned a full-length biography of Shelley.

60. *Letters*, II, 98; I, 268, 116.

61. Lewes, review of *The Prelude* in *The Leader* (17 Aug. 1850), pp. 496–497, reprinted in *Literary Criticism*, p. 80; review of *Der Romantiker auf dem Throne der Cäsaren, oder Julian der Abtrünnige*, *Edinburgh Review* 88 (July 1848): 95. Lewes's scorn for the "Romanticist" echoes Heine's criticism in *The Romantic School*. For the intellectual similarities between Lewes and Eliot, see Colby, *Fiction with a Purpose*, pp. 288–298; Barbara Smalley considers the possible literary influence of Lewes on Eliot (and on Charlotte Brontë) in her Preface to his novel *Ranthorpe* (Athens: Ohio University Press, 1974), pp. vii–li.

62. *Letters*, IV, 97; Shelley, "A Defence of Poetry," p. 135; Cross,

III, 343. And see *Letters*, VIII, 383. But cf. Jerome Beaty's rejection of Eliot's Romantic claim to have written chapter 81 of *Middlemarch* under "inspiration," when in fact she had carefully planned the scene (Dorothea Brooke's and Rosamond Vincy's tearful confrontation) in advance. *Middlemarch from Notebook to Novel* (Urbana: University of Illinois Press, 1960), pp. 106–107, 122.

63. As the unknown author of the *Scenes of Clerical Life*, Eliot refused to heed Blackwood's advice except in small details. "As an artist," she explained, "I should be utterly powerless if I departed from my own conceptions of life and character. There is nothing to be done with the story, but either to let Dempster and Janet and the rest be as I *see* them, or to renounce it as too painful" (*Letters*, II, 348). And cf. *Letters*, II, 298–299, 335–336, 362: "I only try to exhibit some things as they have been or are, seen through such a medium as my own nature gives me." She did yield to Lewes's perhaps ill-advised suggestions that she conclude *Adam Bede* with the marriage of Adam and Dinah Morris and that she avert the unhappy ending planned for *The Spanish Gypsy*.

64. *Letters*, III, 185, 427. Lewes had disputed the idea of imagination providing what experience has denied in his correspondence with Charlotte Brontë more than a decade earlier.

65. The subtitle of Knoepflmacher's sensitive study *George Eliot's Early Novels: The Limits of Realism* points up the Romantic tendencies in her work. And see Richard Stang's section on Eliot's "Realism with a Difference" in *The Theory of the Novel in England: 1850–1870*, pp. 159–176.

66. *Adam Bede*, ed. John Paterson (Boston: Houghton Mifflin Riverside ed., 1968), p. 34. All further citations are in the text. *Letters*, II, 251; III, 227.

67. See, for example, Mario Praz, *The Hero in Eclipse in Victorian Fiction*, trans. Angus Davidson (London: Oxford University Press, 1969 reprint), p. 322. Eliot received some of the same kind of scorn for her realism that Wordsworth had received from Jeffrey and others. "It is not improving to live for ever," complained one reviewer of *Silas Marner*, "in close contemplation of pigstyes and refuse-heaps. If 'the short and simple annals of the poor' contain nothing pleasanter than what George Eliot can show, it were best to explore them no further." *Dublin University Magazine* 59 (April 1862): 394–401, reprinted in *George Eliot: The Critical Heritage*, p. 192. Ruskin's famous dismissal of the characters in *The Mill on the Floss* as "the sweepings out of a Pentonville omnibus" (in *George Eliot: The Critical Heritage*, p. 167) is ironic in light of Eliot's enthusiasm for Ruskin as a realist: "He is strongly akin to the sublimest part of Wordsworth," she said of the author of *Modern Painters* (*Letters*, II, 422–423).

68. "The Sad Fortunes of the Rev. Amos Barton," *Scenes of*

Clerical Life, 2 vols. in *Works,* I, 66. All further citations are in the text.

69. *Letters,* V, 107, 132, 107; *Middlemarch,* p. 179. All further citations to *Middlemarch* are in the text. This is not at variance with Schiller's celebration of women's dutiful nature or Rousseau's sense of women as subordinate to men.

70. *Letters,* II, 308–309. Speaking of this "conventionally melo-dramatic" scene, Thomas Noble, in *George Eliot's 'Scenes of Clerical Life'* (New Haven: Yale University Press, 1965), p. 144, admits sur-prise that Eliot would have resorted to such a situation, but the scene reveals all too obviously the romantic underpinning of the novelist's realistic format. Her melodramatic instinct allowed Eliot to anticipate the vogue of the "sensation" novel in the 1860s, both in this story and in "The Lifted Veil" (1859). See note 79.

71. The first opera Eliot saw was Donizetti's *La Favorita,* whose protagonist is just such a noble sinner.

72. Knoepflmacher, *George Eliot's Early Novels,* p. 75; *Impressions of Theophrastus Such,* pp. 38–39.

73. Ellen Moers sees in Dinah "a true descendant of Corinne" in her capacity as improvisatrice. (*Literary Women,* pp. 192–193).

74. *Letters,* II, 504.

75. *The Excursion,* 6.651–658. A clue to culpability or untrust-worthiness in an Eliot character (such as Arthur Donnithorne or Mrs. Transome in *Felix Holt*) is their disdain for Wordsworth's poetry. Arthur calls most of the *Lyrical Ballads* "twaddling stuff" (p. 57).

76. See Knoepflmacher, *George Eliot's Early Novels,* pp. 116–127.

77. "The Lifted Veil," in *Works,* vol. containing *Silas Marner,* pp. 284, 278. All further citations are in the text.

78. Rousseau, *Confessions,* pp. 48, 594.

79. Wellek, *Confrontations,* p. 19. "The Lifted Veil" affords proof that Eliot could write in the sensation novel mode in advance of its popularity. The ability to foresee the horrors of the future is used, for example, in Wilkie Collins's *Armadale,* published five years later. For accounts of Eliot's association with the sensation novel, see Colby, *Fiction with a Purpose,* pp. 272–276; Praz, *The Hero in Eclipse in Victorian Fiction* p. 408; and Elaine Showalter, *A Literature of Their Own* (Princeton: Princeton University Press, 1977), p. 171.

80. "Latimer provides a nightmare image of the burden of seeing into other consciousnesses and foreseeing the future as the novelist must do . . . Latimer's dilemma, in its mixture of determinism, solipsism, and hyperaesthesia, corresponds to the perils latent in George Eliot's situation as a novelist." Gillian Beer, "Myth and the Single Consciousness: *Middlemarch* and *The Lifted Veil,*" in *This Particular Web,* p. 101. Knoepflmacher, *George Eliot's Early Novels,* pp. 128–161.

81. *Letters,* III, 41; V, 380.

82. *The Mill on the Floss,* ed. Gordon Haight (Boston: Houghton Mifflin Riverside ed., 1961), p. 35. All further citations are in the text.

83. See *Letters,* VIII, 276: "I should think it quite a chief blessing if that past which lives invisibly, though it has gone away from our outward daily existence, could have some sort of worthy worship in the present. I hardly know what other word to use but *worship;* for there is no such thing as a return, or a making amends for deficiencies."

84. The lack of sympathy shown by the Dodsons to the Tulliver family in its financial misfortune is in marked contrast to the "unworldly" generosity and compassion lavished on Miss Matty in Elizabeth Gaskell's *Cranford.* Although both novelists were concerned with provincial realism, the differing treatment of the same kind of episode shows Gaskell's freedom from Eliot's determinist mentality: the Dodsons cannot act in any other manner than genetics and environment allow, while the Cranford ladies are free to be good-natured if they choose.

85. Bray, *The Education of the Feelings,* pp. 22, 99, 82.

86. That Eliot was a thoroughgoing determinist, whose views were modified to some degree by Feuerbach and Comte, is the position taken by Felicia Bonaparte in *Will and Destiny: Morality and Tragedy in George Eliot's Novels* (New York: New York University Press, 1975); George Levine in "Intelligence as Deception: *The Mill on the Floss,*" *PMLA* 80 (Sept. 1965): 402–409; and Bernard J. Paris in *Experiments in Life: George Eliot's Quest for Values* (Detroit: Wayne State University Press, 1965).

87. E.g., Walter Allen, *George Eliot,* p. 115; Joan Bennett, *George Eliot: Her Mind and Her Art* (Cambridge University Press, 1962 reprint), pp. 120–123; Knoepflmacher, *George Eliot's Early Novels,* p. 207: "Such speeches belong to a thesis-novel. They ought to come from a ventriloquist's puppet and not by the rounded human being whose growth we have observed."

88. From a review of Geraldine Jewsbury's *Constance Herbert, Westminster Review* 64 (July 1855): 288–296, reprinted in *Essays,* pp. 134–135. And cf. Thomas Pinney, "The Authority of the Past in George Eliot's Novels," *Nineteenth-Century Fiction* 21 (Sept. 1966): 131–147.

89. *Letters,* III, 382. In "Brother Jacob," written about this time (1860), Eliot tried to reassert her sense of humor, severely taxed by the writing of *The Mill on the Floss;* but this story of how an intriguing, ambitious confectioner, Edward Freely (né Faux), is thwarted by his giant, retarded brother (Eliot's original title, "The Idiot Brother," suggests that she was thinking of Wordsworth's "The Idiot Boy," with its effortful comic spirits) leaves one with the suspicion that Eliot is using the protagonist's pastry shop as a surrogate for

the corrupting influence of Byronic Romanticism. The first customer to patronize Freely's shop is a wife whose fondness for *Lalla Rookh*, *The Corsair*, and *The Siege of Corinth* has already "given her a distaste for domestic occupations." "Brother Jacob," in *Works*, vol. containing *Silas Marner*, p. 371.

90. Schiller, *Naïve and Sentimental Poetry*, p. 153. "The purpose" of the idyll, Schiller notes, "is invariably only to represent man in a state of innocence, i.e., in a condition of harmony and of peace with himself and his environment" (p. 147). Walter Allen's description of *Silas Marner*—"a fairly-tale saturated in the sense of the actual" (p. 122)—perfectly fits Schiller's definition of the idyll.

91. *Silas Marner*, in *Works*, p. 17. All further citations are in the text.

92. Schiller, *Naïve and Sentimental Poetry*, p. 87; *Essays of George Eliot*, p. 20. The theme of a weaver who is saved by contact with his fellow human beings is the obverse of the theme of Tennyson's "The Lady of Shalott," in which the Byronic-Romantic sense of the artist's necessary alienation is stressed. Also, we see in Marner (as in Tom Tulliver) a qualified rejection on Eliot's part of the Carlyle-Adam Bede work ethic: work in itself can lead to stupefaction if there is no spiritual goal to guide one.

93. Eliot's comparison of the miller Tulliver's fate to that of Oedipus serves, whether consciously intended by Eliot or not, only to underscore the distance between them.

94. *Romola*, 2 vols., in *Works*, I, 436–437. All further citations are in the text.

95. Lerner, *The Truthtellers* (New York: Schocken, 1967), p. 248. Romola thinks of a tale from the *Decameron* to justify her action, but the coincidence of Boccaccio's Gostanza consigning her fate to a drifting boat with Rousseau's similar passive gesture must have struck Eliot as fortuitous: romance and Romanticism unite in a single gesture. *Letters*, IV, 104.

96. Eliot exhibits many affinities with Browning in *Romola*: her subtle depiction of evil in Tito reminds one of Browning's dexterity in creating the Duke in "My Last Duchess"; both Savonarola and the Pope in Browning's *The Ring and the Book* speak for the author's moral purposiveness; the intuitive grasp of reality attained by her Piero di Cosimo (details for whose portrait she derived from Vasari, whom Browning drew on for his Andrea del Sarto and Fra Filippo Lippi) is similar to the powers of perception shown by Browning's artists. Overly idealized though Romola may seem, she is substantially more human than Browning's Pompilia.

97. *Felix Holt*, 2 vols., in *Works*, II, 44. All further citations are in the text.

98. There are many links between Eliot's watchmaker-hero and Kingsley's poet-tailor, gifted workmen who write verse or (in Holt's

case) speak knowledgeably of Chateaubriand and "Ciceronian anti-phrasis" (I, 333). Reviewers of *Adam Bede* had noticed a similarity between Adam and Alton Locke (e.g., the *Saturday Reviewer* who declared that she "had sat at the feet of Mr. Kingsley"; see *George Eliot: The Critical Heritage,* p. 762); and Eliot had perhaps acknowledged the debt when she sent Kingsley a presentation copy of her first novel. In "The Natural History of German Life," she had praised him, along with Wordsworth and Scott, for his democratic-minded art. Like Kingsley in *Alton Locke,* Eliot in *Felix Holt* adapted from Goethe's *Götz von Berlichingen* the scene of the hero who misguidedly becomes the head of an unruly mob, hoping to moderate its passion, and lands in jail as a result.

99. G. S. Venables in the *Edinburgh Review* 124 (Oct. 1866): 435–449, reprinted in *George Eliot: The Critical Heritage,* p. 281. Of Holt, Venables observes that "an artisan who can amuse himself with Ciceronian figures of speech, resembles a workman as a shepherd at the opera or in Sèvres china is like a common farm servant."

100. Quoted in K. A. McKenzie, *Edith Simcox and George Eliot* (London: Oxford University Press, 1961), p. 97.

101. Bennett, *George Eliot: Her Mind and Her Art,* p. 159. Eliot may have been fond of this period, the late 1820s and early 1830s, because her liberal instincts could applaud the reforms to come while her conservative impulse could feel at home in the serenity of the pre-Reform period.

102. There are also links between Mrs. Transome and Lady Mason in Trollope's *Orley Farm* (1862), both of whom suggest figures in the sensation novels of this period in their determination to keep secret from their sons the truth regarding their inheritance and identity.

103. "O May I Join the Choir Invisible" was written in 1867, the year before *The Spanish Gypsy.* In 1869 Eliot wrote "The Legend of Jubal" in which the theme of the artist surviving in his work reaches its climactic expression. *Letters,* IV, 377, 438, 397.

104. *The Spanish Gypsy,* in *Works,* p. 156. All further citations are in the text. These and the following comments are from Eliot's "Notes on 'The Spanish Gypsy,' " printed in Cross, III, 31–37.

105. Among the many notable nineteenth-century operas adapted from Schiller plays are Rossini's *William Tell* (which provided Eliot with inspiration for a crucial scene in *Adam Bede*); Donizetti's *Maria Stuarda,* Verdi's *I Masnadieri* (*The Robbers*), *Giovanna d'Arco, Luisa Miller* (*Kabale and Liebe*), and *Don Carlos;* and Tchaikovsky's *The Maid of Orleans.*

106. K. M. Newton, in "Byronic Egoism and George Eliot's *The Spanish Gypsy,*" *Neophilologus* 57 (Oct. 1973): 388–400, detects in the depiction of Silva a condemnation of Byronic egoism; but this overlooks Silva's more obvious resemblance to one of Schiller's

heroes, such as Max Piccolomini in *Wallenstein*. Silva's choice is not between egoism and duty, but between opposing duties; his dilemma is hence similar to Fedalma's—or to Antigone's, to which Eliot had devoted a significant essay a decade earlier.

107. Jerome Thale, in *The Novels of George Eliot* (New York: Columbia University Press, 1959), p. 78, has suggested that "the character of Dorothea is almost a judgment on the mentality that created Romola," but that "mentality," far from being exorcised, reached its apogee in Daniel Deronda.

108. Haight, Introduction to *Middlemarch*, p. xiv. And see his account of Ladislaw's Romantic affinities in "George Eliot's 'Eminent Failure,' Will Ladislaw," in *This Particular Web*, pp. 22–42.

109. Beaty, *Middlemarch from Notebook to Novel*, p. 24. Rosamond's name possibly derives from Maria Edgeworth's willful child who hankers after a purple jar (see chapter 5, note 29). Whereas Edgeworth's heroine sheds her romantic fancies, Eliot's Rosamond basks in an *Arabian Nights* fantasy world "where everything is given to you and nothing claimed" (p. 257).

110. James's review of *Middlemarch* is reprinted in *The Future of the Novel*, ed. Leon Edel (New York: Vintage, 1956), p. 86; James, *Notebooks*, ed. F. O. Matthiessen and Kenneth Murdock (New York: Oxford University Press, 1961), p. 15.

111. Beaty, *Middlemarch from Notebook to Novel*, pp. 75–76.

112. Cf. Shelley's statement in "A Defence of Poetry": "Man is an instrument over which a series of external and internal impressions are driven, like the alternations of an ever-changing wind over an Aeolian lyre, which move it by their motion to ever-changing melody." The poet seeks (as does the child) to prolong "in its voice and motions the duration of the effect, to prolong also a consciousness of the cause." *Works*, VII, 109–110. U. C. Knoepflmacher, in *Religious Humanism and the Victorian Novel* (Princeton University Press, 1965), pp. 97–98, sees Ladislaw as a Shelleyan figure who, "in the novel's general scheme, . . . is the poet, artist, and radical who stands for 'feeling itself.' " Dorothea's "Hebraism" is needed to complete his "Hellenism."

113. Not only *Childe Harold's Pilgrimage* and Disraeli's *Tancred* are invoked, but also the endings to Kingsley's *Yeast* and *Alton Locke*, both of which concern a heroic voyage in search of values in a foreign land.

114. See William Baker's admirable *George Eliot and Judaism* (Salzburg Studies in English Literature, 1975) for a thorough account of her absorption in Jewish themes and sources. An analogue to *Daniel Deronda* that works in reverse (a Jewish hero is converted to Christianity during a trip to Palestine) is Charlotte Tonna's *Judah's Lion* (1843).

115. *Daniel Deronda*, 3 vols., in *Works*, I, 65. All further citations

are in the text. Klesmer "is unmistakably a Jew" noted David Kaufmann, one of Eliot's most supportive admirers of the novel, in *George Eliot and Judaism*, trans. J. W. Ferrier (Edinburgh, 1877), p. 78; his "unfortunate name . . . is enough for the initiated." According to Baker (*George Eliot and Judaism*, p. 234), Klesmer is Polish-Yiddish for "itinerant musician."

116. "As if all the great poetic criminals were not women!" Gwendolen maintains ironically early in the novel (I, 76).

117. Inheriting his grandfather's Zionist ardor and his father's loving disposition, Deronda, as Bonaparte argues in *Will and Destiny*, p. 76, moves "forward in a predetermined direction." But the Hegelian "World-Historical Individual" is predestined to exert his will in the end.

118. In *Alroy* Disraeli stressed the Romantic-adventurous possibilities in Judaism; Eliot is more concerned with the philosophical-Romantic implications of a faith that subdues even as it arouses: Byronic individualism put to the service of Wordsworthian quiescence.

119. No Eliot novel is so rich in quotations from the Romantic poets—Wordsworth, Coleridge, Keats, Shelley, Goethe, Heine (even Whitman is invoked, for the epigraph to chapter 29, in support of following "who[m]ever speaks to me in the right voice")—and in quotations from the poets dear to the Romantics: Dante, Shakespeare, Milton.

120. *Essays*, p. 385.

121. R. H. Hutton welcomed the idealistic and "religious" tone of *Daniel Deronda*, although he wondered whether the hero's trip to Palestine was "a wild-goose chase." *Spectator* 44 (9 Sept. 1876): 1131–1133. R. E. Francillon declared that Eliot had abandoned the field of realism for that of romance. Francillon shrewdly noted that Deronda is the ultimate expression of Eliot's belief "in the mesmeric effect of personality"; he is "a nineteenth century knight," through whose "eyes, which do not look at common things commonly, we see that romance, the natural history of exceptions and intensities, is as true as reality, and more true than much that seems real." But if Daniel and Mirah belong to the realm of romance, in which anything is possible, Gwendolen is the heroine "of the reality" in the novel, in which all is restricted. *Gentleman's Magazine* 17 (Oct. 1876): 411–427. Both reviews are included in *George Eliot: The Critical Heritage*, pp. 366, 370, 388, 391, 395.

122. Redinger, *George Eliot: The Emergent Self*, p. 473. Mintz, interestingly, sees in Gwendolen the ambitious side of Eliot's sense of "vocation" split off from the messianic side as represented by Deronda (*George Eliot and the Novel of Vocation*, p. 151).

123. *Letter*, VI, 318.

SEVEN   Death and Circuses: Charles Dickens and
the Byroads of Romanticism

1. See, for example, Philip Collins, *Dickens and Education* (London: Macmillan, 1964), chap. 8 ("The Romantic primitivism which finds virtue in the simple life and mind, and suspects vice in educated and urban man, appears strongly in Dickens"; p. 193); Peter Coveney, *The Image of Childhood* (Harmondsworth: Penguin, 1967 rev. ed.), pp. 111–161; Garrett Stewart, *Dickens and the Trials of Imagination* (Cambridge, Mass.: Harvard University Press, 1974); Angus Wilson, *The World of Charles Dickens* (New York: Viking, 1970). Wilson, noting Dickens's "hostility to the excesses of Byronism and Wordsworthianism in *Barnaby Rudge*," adds that "like most Victorian Romantics he fed upon and renounced" his "Romantic predecessors" (p. 148).

2. Walter Bagehot saw Dickens's sentimental excesses in the light of his reaction against "the unfeeling obtuseness" of the Regency period. "Charles Dickens," *National Review* 7 (Oct. 1858): 458–486, reprinted in *Dickens: The Critical Heritage,* ed. Philip Collins (New York: Barnes & Noble, 1971), p. 398. On Dickens's indebtedness to eighteenth-century fiction see Humphry House, *The Dickens World* (London: Oxford University Press, 1960 reprint), chap. 2; and Robert A. Colby, *Fiction with a Purpose* (Bloomington: Indiana University Press, 1967), pp. 125–126. According to George Gissing, in *Charles Dickens* (London, 1898), "It seems never to have occurred to him . . . that novels and fairy tales (or his favourite Arabian Nights) should obey different laws in the matters of incident" (p. 57). Even as mature a novel as *Great Expectations* contains a version (and a parody of that version) of the *Arabian Nights* pattern of a hero aided by genii: Miss Havisham and Abel Magwitch. Both Mario Praz, in *The Hero in Eclipse in Victorian Fiction*, trans. Angus Davidson (London: Oxford University Press, 1969 reprint), pp. 151–162, and Walter Phillips, in *Dickens, Reade, and Collins: Sensation Novelists* (New York: Russell & Russell, 1962 reprint), trace the transition from Gothic novel to Byronic tale to Newgate fiction to sensation novel. R. H. Horne, in 1844, was perhaps the first to point up the unintending sympathy that Dickens occasions for his villains—see the excerpt from *The New Spirit of the Age* reprinted in *Dickens: The Critical Heritage,* pp. 198–202. In *Dickens and Crime* (Bloomington: Indiana University Press, 1968 reprint), Philip Collins offers a useful corrective to the view that Dickens identified with his criminal-protagonists.

3. Collins, *Dickens and Education,* p. 213. In *Pictures from Italy* Dickens briefly mentions the Keats and Shelley graves in Rome, and he quotes from Byron's *Parisina* during his visit to Ferrara. On the links between Dickens and Carlyle, see Collins, *Dickens and Educa-*

tion, p. 216; Louis Cazamian, *The Social Novel in England, 1830–1850*, trans. Martin Fido (London: Routledge & Kegan Paul, 1972), e.g. pp. 80, 83–84, 94–95, 171; Michael Goldberg, *Carlyle and Dickens* (Athens: University of Georgia Press, 1972); William Oddie, *Dickens and Carlyle* (London: Centenary Press 1972).

4. Leavis, *The Great Tradition* (New York: George Stewart, 1948), p. 236. K. J. Fielding offers sensible alternatives to the Romantic readings of *Hard Times* and *Our Mutual Friend* in *Charles Dickens: A Critical Introduction* (Boston: Houghton Mifflin, 1965).

5. In "The Ruffian" (*The Uncommercial Traveller*) Dickens subscribes to Carlyle's position that there exist incorrigible members of the "Devil's Brigade." Dickens regards such characters as Fagin, Bill Sikes, Uriah Heep, and John Jasper as unalterably evil.

6. Charles Kent, review in the *Sun* (13 April 1848), reprinted in *Dickens: The Critical Heritage*, p. 229; Orwell, "Charles Dickens," *A Collection of Essays* (Garden City: Doubleday Anchor Books, 1954), p. 70. Dickens's substitution of domestic for supernatural deities is discussed by J. Hillis Miller in *Charles Dickens: The World of His Novels* (Cambridge, Mass.: Harvard University Press, 1958), e.g., p. 157, and by Alexander Welsh in *The City in Dickens* (Oxford: Clarendon Press, 1971), pt. 3.

7. Richard Ford, *Quarterly Review* 64 (June 1839): 83–102, reprinted in *Dickens: The Critical Heritage*, p. 81; Donald Fanger, *Dostoevsky and Romantic Realism: A Study of Dostoevsky in Relation to Balzac, Dickens, and Gogol* (Cambridge, Mass.: Harvard University Press, 1965), p. 21.

8. *Spectator* review of *Sketches of Boz* (20 Feb. 1836), quoted in John Butt and Kathleen Tillotson, *Dickens at Work* (London: Methuen, 1968 reprint), p. 37; *George Eliot: The Critical Heritage*, ed. David Carroll (New York: Barnes & Noble, 1971), p. 66; excerpt from review in *Metropolitan Magazine* 28 (June 1840): 51–52, reprinted in *Dickens: The Critical Heritage*, p. 93. The discovery "that there is no romance like the romance of real life" was made by Scott, according to Hazlitt in *The Spirit of the Age* (1825), reprinted with *Lectures on the English Poets* (London: Dent, Everyman's Library, 1960 reprint), p. 228. In his first novel, *The Pickwick Papers*, Dickens acknowledged, "there's romance enough at home without going half a mile for it; only people never think of it" (p. 280). All citations, which subsequently appear in abbreviated form (*OT = Oliver Twist*, *OCS = The Old Curiosity Shop*, etc.) in the text, are to the Oxford Illustrated Dickens volumes.

9. "What Crabbe was in poetry, . . . Boz was in prose." "Boz versus Dickens," *Parker's London Magazine* 1 (Feb. 1845): 122–128, reprinted in *Dickens: The Critical Heritage*, p. 169. The reviewer of *The Cricket on the Hearth* for *Chambers's Edinburgh Journal* 5 (17 Jan. 1846): 44–48 saw Dickens as "ambitious of becoming the Words-

worth of prose fiction" (reprinted in *Dickens: The Critical Heritage*, p. 174). Cf. John Forster, *The Life of Charles Dickens*, 2 vols. (London: Dent, Everyman's Library, 1950 reprint), II, 31.

10. On Dickens's "fellow-feeling with his race" see Edwin P. Whipple, *North American Review* 69 (Oct. 1849): 383–407, reprinted in *Dickens: The Critical Heritage*, p. 238. And see Robert Newsom on Dickens's use of a "double perspective which requires us to see things as *at once* 'romantic' and 'familiar.' " *Dickens on the Romantic Side of Familiar Things: Bleak House and the Novel Tradition* (New York: Columbia University Press, 1977), p. 7. Coleridge, *Biographia Literaria*, chap. 14.

11. George Eliot, "The Natural History of German Life," in *Essays*, ed. Thomas Pinney (New York: Columbia University Press, 1963), pp. 271–272; Lewes, *National Magazine and Monthly Critic* 1 (Dec. 1837): 445–449, reprinted in *Dickens: The Critical Heritage*, p. 68; Lewes, "Dickens in Relation to Criticism," *Fortnightly Review* 17 (Feb. 1872): 141–154, reprinted in *The Dickens Critics*, ed. George Ford and Lauriat Lane, Jr. (Ithaca, N.Y.: Cornell University Press, 1961), pp. 61, 69; *Principles of Success in Literature* (1865), excerpted in *Literary Criticism of George Henry Lewes*, ed. Alice Kaminsky (Lincoln: University of Nebraska Press, 1964), p. 7.

12. Quoted by Richard Stang, *The Theory of the Novel in England: 1850–1870* (New York: Columbia University Press, 1959), p. 27.

13. Edwin P. Whipple, "The Genius of Dickens," *Atlantic Monthly* 19 (May 1867): 546–554, reprinted in *Dickens: The Critical Heritage*, p. 478; Stang, *The Theory of the Novel in England, 1850–1870*, p. 27.

14. Epigraph to chap. 41 of *Daniel Deronda*. Albert Guerard's recent claim for Dickens as an antimimetic author, in *The Triumph of the Novel: Dickens, Dostoevsky, Faulkner* (New York: Oxford University Press, 1976), pp. 22–47, curiously revives G. K. Chesterton's view that Dickens only pretended to be a realist: "He denied his own divine originality, and pretended that he had plagiarized from life." *Charles Dickens* (New York: Schocken, 1965 reprint), p. 191. Compare Guerard: "great fiction transcends the quotidian, and is little concerned with banal destinies" (p. 14).

15. See Dickens, *Letters*, ed. Madeline House, Graham Story and Kathleen Tillotson, 4 vols. to date (Oxford: Clarendon, 1965–1977), III, 447. I have used the Nonesuch Dickens edition of the *Letters*, ed. Walter Dexter, 3 vols. (London, 1938) for later correspondence.

16. Forster, *Life of Dickens*, I, 418; Dickens, *Letters*, Pilgrim ed., III, 57. *The Heart of Charles Dickens*, (letters to Angela Burdett-Coutts), ed. Edgar Johnson (New York: Duell, Sloane and Pearce, 1952), p. 133.

17. *Sketches of Young Gentlemen*, reprinted with *Sketches by Boz* (Oxford Illustrated Dickens), pp. 535–537. Dickens noted "Byrons of

the desk and counter," with turned-down shirt collars, on his first trip to America (*American Notes,* chap. 6, "New York").

18. See Fred Kaplan, *Dickens and Mesmerism* (Princeton: Princeton University Press, 1975). Dickens never allowed himself to be mesmerized.

19. Dickens *Letters,* Pilgrim ed., I, 146 (writing to his illustrator, Robert Seymour, who committed suicide after a clash of wills occurred between the young writer and the veteran artist); *Letters,* Nonesuch ed., III, 674; Jeffrey, quoted in *Dickens: The Critical Heritage,* p. 218.

20. *Letters,* Pilgrim ed., II, 155, 186; III, 605.

21. Angus Wilson shrewdly notes that Dickens stylized his childhood when he talked about it, creating "a special poetry about childhood suffering" (*The World of Charles Dickens,* p. 58). Steven Marcus, in *Dickens from Pickwick to Dombey* (New York: Simon and Schuster, 1968 reprint), p. 81, draws attention to the idealized passive figures in Dicken's novels who represent an authentic side of their seemingly strong-willed creator.

22. Forster, *Life of Dickens,* I, 34; II, 194; I, 34.

23. *Letters,* Nonesuch ed., II, 888, 633; *Heart of Charles Dickens,* p. 31; *Letters,* Nonesuch ed., II, 765; quoted in Edgar Johnson, *Charles Dickens: His Tragedy and Triumph,* 2 vols. (New York: Simon and Schuster, 1952), II, 911.

24. Like *Waverley, Barnaby Rudge* was set sixty years in the past. *Romola,* chap. 55.

25. Wilson, *The World of Charles Dickens,* p. 150. Dickens sketches another version of Rousseau's Noble Savage in Hannibal Chollop, the murderous "child of Natur'" whom Martin Chuzzlewit encounters during his journey through America, the land of the incarnate Romantic will. In *The Cricket on the Hearth* (1845), Dickens's theme is that reality, if it is not better than the world of fancy, offers compensatory rewards.

26. Review in *Fraser's Magazine* 42 (Dec. 1850): 698–710, reprinted in *Dickens: The Critical Heritage,* p. 244. Yet Edgar Johnson, noting the "dearth of happy homes and good parents" in the novels, stresses "how relatively seldom [Dickens] portrays what he praises." *Dickens: His Tragedy and Triumph,* II, 685.

27. Both Mario Praz (*The Hero in Eclipse,* p. 127) and Angus Wilson (*The World of Charles Dickens,* pp. 215–216) deplore the Victorianism of *David Copperfield,* sympathizing instead with Steerforth's Romantic "charm." William R. Harvey's "Dickens and the Byronic Hero" is not so much an analysis of as a fan letter to Steerforth: "There are several reasons for our admiration. First, Emily is so insipid that the reader, especially today's reader, does not feel sympathy over her plight; indeed one speculates that her experiences with Steerforth might well have compensated her for the shame that followed." *Nineteenth-Century Fiction* 24 (Dec. 1969): 308–309.

28. Printed in John Butt, "*David Copperfield:* From Manuscript to Print," *Review of English Studies* (July 1950): p. 251.

29. Chesterton, *Charles Dickens*, p. 204; Dickens, *Letters*, Pilgrim ed., III, 576; quoted in Johnson, *Dickens: His Tragedy and Triumph*, I, 452.

30. Brahma Chaudhuri, "Leonard Skimpole in *Bleak House*," *Dickens Studies Newsletter* 5 (1975): 75–78; Dickens, "Leigh Hunt: A Remonstrance," in *Miscellaneous Papers*, vol. XIII of *Works*, Universal ed. (London: Chapman and Hall, 1914); letter of 25 Sept. 1853 to Mrs. Richard Watson, quoted in Doris Langley Moore, *The Late Lord Byron* (New York: Harper & Row, 1977 reprint), p. 500. Dickens wrote his "Remonstrance" at the urging of Thornton Hunt, who was incensed when reviewers of *Bleak House* linked the fictionalized portrait of his father with his own liberal attitudes.

31. K. J. Fielding, "Leigh Hunt and Skimpole: Another Remonstrance," *The Dickensian* (Jan. 1968): 5–9; Leigh Hunt, *Autobiography*, quoted in J. W. T. Ley, *The Dickens Circle* (New York: Dutton, 1918), p. 133; see Dickens, *Letters*, Pilgrim ed., I, 686.

32. See Leslie Marchand, *Byron: A Biography*, 3 vols. (New York: Knopf, 1957), III, 1018–1020, 971–972; Dickens, *Letters*, Nonesuch ed., III, 744. See Moore, *The Late Lord Byron*, chap. 12, on Hunt's ingratitude to Byron.

33. Miller, *Dickens: The World of His Novels*, p. 211.

34. "If you had seen Macready last night—undisguisedly sobbing, and crying on the sofa, as I read," Dickens wrote to his wife after his triumphant reading of *The Chimes* to his London friends, "—you would have felt (as I did) what a thing it is to have Power." *Letters*, Pilgrim ed., IV, 235.

35. He had "no 'city of the mind' against outward ills," as Forster admitted (*Life of Dickens*, II, 200).

36. Collins, *Dickens and Education*, p. 175.

37. *Letters*, Pilgrim ed., II, 172; III, 187.

38. Ibid., II, 181–182. The schoolmaster's speech contains echoes of Kent's speech over the dead Lear.

39. Guerard, *The Triumph of the Novel*, p. 54; cf. Steven Marcus's suggestive section on *The Old Curiosity Shop* ("The Myth of Nell") in *Dickens from Pickwick to Dombey*.

40. See Garrett Stewart's stimulating *Dickens and the Trials of Imagination* for an elaboration of this theme. Stewart's is not so much a reading of Dickens's Romanticism as a Romantic reading of Dickens.

41. "Dickens appreciated the [social] problems through his feelings, and not his reason," as Louis Cazamian recognized in *The Social Novel in England* (p. 123); "and it was through feelings that he sought resolutions."

42. The alliance between Harthouse and Bounderby (the Coketown

industrialist) suggests the union of Mammonism and Dilettantism that Carlyle, in *Past and Present,* saw flourishing to England's misfortune. See Oddie, *Dickens and Carlyle,* p. 59.

43. Both Garrett Stewart and U. C. Knoepflmacher see in *Our Mutual Friend* a resounding affirmation achieved through the power of fantasy. Stewart, *Dickens and the Trials of Imagination,* chap. 6 (Stewart commends Jenny Wren's "escape artistry"); Knoepflmacher, *Laughter and Despair* (Berkeley: University of California Press, 1971), chap. 5. See J. Hillis Miller for a more metaphysical interpretation of the novel ("Dickens' novels are religious in that they demand the regeneration of man and society through contact with something transcending the merely human"; *Dickens: The World of His Novels,* p. 315) and K. J. Fielding, *Dickens: A Critical Introduction,* chap. 13, for a refreshingly commonsensical interpretation.

44. In his comic play "Mr. Nightingale's Diary" (1851), Dickens wrote for himself the part of Gabblewig, a lawyer who disguises himself in rapid succession as a boots, a fashionable gentleman, an elderly invalid, an old woman, and a sexton.

45. Ellen Moers, in *The Dandy: Brummell to Beerbohm* (New York: Viking, 1960), considers Dickens's growing sympathy toward the dandy, abetted by his friendship for Wilkie Collins and other neo-Bohemians. Eugene Wrayburn, with his drone philosophy, emerges as a more sympathetic version of Harold Skimpole (pp. 247–250).

46. "The fascination of repulsion had been upon [Rosa Bud] so long, and now culminated so darkly, that she felt as if [Jasper] had power to bind her by a spell" (*ED,* p. 226). Walter Phillips, in *Dickens, Reade, and Collins: Sensation Novelists,* sees the genesis of the sensation novel's villain in the Byronic villain-hero. Edmund Wilson's famous interpretation of Jasper as Dickens's alter ego, "Dickens: The Two Scrooges," in *The Wound and the Bow* (London: Methuen, 1961 reprint), is brilliantly argued but unconvincing in light of Collins's *Dickens and Crime.*

47. *Letters,* Pilgrim ed., II, 410–411.

EIGHT   George Meredith: A Romantic in Spite of Himself

1. "The Decay of Lying," reprinted in *The Artist as Critic: Critical Writings of Oscar Wilde,* ed. Richard Ellmann (New York: Random House, 1969), p. 298; René Wellek (for Schlegel on the novel's potential), *A History of Modern Criticism,* vol. II, *The Romantic Age* (New Haven: Yale University Press, 1955), pp. 19–20.

2. Dickens, *Letters,* ed. Walter Dexter, 3 vols. (London: Nonesuch Dickens, 1938), II, 773. In later years Meredith was highly critical of Dickens's intellectual defects as a novelist; but some of Meredith's poems were published in *Household Words,* and his early novels

abound in Dickensian echoes. In the letter accompanying the copy of *The Shaving of Shagpat* sent to Charles Kingsley, Meredith declared his fondness for the Arabians ("one of the most marvelous people on Earth—possessing humour and passion beyond any"), although he noted a deficiency in them of the "heroic" and "Romance" spirit: "They represent the mind in a state of childhood, where quick transitions are natural, and lofty aims unknown." Meredith, *Letters,* ed. C. L. Cline, 3 vols. (Oxford: Clarendon Press, 1970), I, 25. It is apparent from the allusions to the *Arabian Nights* in his 1877 lecture on comedy that Meredith was acquainted with a more adult version of the Tales than that read by the young Brontës and Dickens.

3. Trollope, *Letters,* ed. Bradford Booth (London: Oxford University Press, 1951), p. 76 and note; and see Trollope, "An Unprotected Female at the Pyramids," *Tales of All Countries,* 1st and 2nd ser. (London, 1877 reprint), p. 140; Eliot, *Leader* 7 (5 Jan. 1856), reprinted in *George Meredith: The Critical Heritage,* ed. Ioan Williams (New York: Barnes & Noble, 1971), p. 41; S. T. Coleridge, *Collected Letters,* ed. E. L. Griggs, 6 vols. (Oxford: Clarendon Press, 1966–1971), II, 354; J. H. Cardinal Newman, *Apologia pro Vita Sua,* ed. David De-Laura (New York: Norton, 1968), p. 14.

4. Stevenson, "A Gossip on Romance," *Memories and Portraits* (New York, 1887), pp. 262, 255. Stevenson's first published stories were collected in 1882 under the title *New Arabian Nights.* In an excellent study of *The Shaving of Shagpat,* Ian Fletcher sees Meredith mocking his own pretensions as a Shelley-inspired Spasmodic poet, as well as drawing upon Ariosto's exuberant example and Carlyle's earnest warning in *Sartor Resartus.* "The Shaving of Shagpat: Meredith's Comic Apocalypse," in *Meredith Now,* ed. Ian Fletcher (London: Routledge & Kegan Paul, 1971), pp. 34–68.

5. *Letters,* III, 1556. The combination of influences is notable: to the skeptical methodology of Gibbon and Niebuhr, Meredith added the romantic vision of Scott, the comic spirit of Molière, and the philosophical example of Goethe.

6. Meredith referred to Aladdin as "our old well-beloved friend" in the *Westminster Review* 69 (Jan. 1858): 160. *Redgauntlet,* Letter 2; *Middlemarch,* ed. Gordon Haight (Boston: Houghton Mifflin Riverside ed., 1956), p. 257.

7. See Lionel Stevenson, *The Ordeal of George Meredith* (New York: Scribner's, 1953), p. 4; E. M. Ellis, *George Meredith: His Life and Friends in Relation to His Work* (New York: Dodd, Mead, 1920), e.g., pp. 15, 36–37, 48. Such fairy-tale-inspired childhood delusions of grandeur have recently been defended by Bruno Bettelheim in *The Uses of Enchantment* (New York: Knopf, 1976): "Without fantasies to give us hope, we do not have the strength to meet the adversities of life. Childhood is the time when these fantasies need to be

nurtured" (p. 121). For Meredith—as for Dickens and the Brontës—such fantasies of power were especially needed, given his sense of himself as an outsider.

8. Beer, *Meredith: A Change of Masks* (London: Athlone Press, 1970), p. 59; Kiely, *The Romantic Novel in England* (Cambridge, Mass.: Harvard University Press, 1972), p. 21.

9. *The Ordeal of Richard Feverel*, vol. II of *Works*, Memorial ed., 27 vols. (New York: Scribner's, 1909–1911), II, 414. All further citations to the novel appear in the text. Meredith, "Mr. Lytton's Poems," *Works*, XXIII, 104.

10. Scott, "An Essay on Chivalry," in *Miscellaneous Prose Works*, 6 vols. (Edinburgh, 1849), VI, 43, 109–110; Alice Chandler, *A Dream of Order: The Medieval Ideal in Nineteenth-Century English Literature* (Lincoln: University of Nebraska Press, 1970), p. 38.

11. Scott, "An Essay on Romance," in *Misc. Prose Works*, VI, 198. And see John O'Connor's *Amadis de Gaule and Its Influence on Elizabethan Literature* (New Brunswick, N.J.: Rutgers University Press, 1970) for an account of the poem as a Renaissance Courtesy Book. Despite being, like Aladdin, a tailor's son, Evan displays a devotion to the woman he loves that earns him "the epithet of Amadis." *Evan Harrington*, in *Works*, VI, 127.

12. Wellek, "The Concept of Romanticism in Literary History," *Concepts of Criticism* (New Haven: Yale University Press, 1963), p. 131; Edgar Johnson, *Sir Walter Scott: The Great Unknown*, 2 vols. (London: Hamish Hamilton, 1970), I, 57; II, 1244 (Byron called Scott "the Ariosto of the North," *Childe Harold's Pilgrimage*, 4.40); Stendhal, *The Life of Henri Brulard*, trans. Catherine Phillips (New York: Vintage Books, 1955), p. 81; Reynolds, Introduction to her translation of *Orlando Furioso*, 2 vols. (Harmondsworth: Penguin Books, 1975–1977), I, 83.

13. Byron, *Letters and Journals*, ed. Leslie Marchand (Cambridge, Mass.: Harvard University Press, 1973–   ), II, 63; VI, 91, 95, 234.

14. Meredith, *Letters*, II, 715; I, 160–161. See Richard Stang on Meredith's formulation of "Realism with a Difference" in *The Theory of the Novel in England: 1850–1870* (New York: Columbia University Press, 1959), pp. 166–171. *Harry Richmond*, vols. IX and X of *Works*, IX, 318. All further citations to the novel are in the text.

15. *Letters*, I, 523; Walzel, *German Romanticism*, trans. A. E. Lussky (New York: Frederick Ungar, 1965 reprint), pp. 231–232, 236, 238. Lenau was apparently much influenced by Byron (Walzel, p. 159). The *Sturm und Drang* poets glorified "strong, titanic womanhood" (Walzel, p. 79), and even Schiller, despite his endorsement of women's domestic role, created the commanding figure of Johanna (Joan of Arc) in *The Maid of Orleans*. But Schlegel's *Lucinde*, perhaps the most important German Romantic celebration of the new

woman, perpetuates the myth of woman as priestess to the religion of love, with man the object of her adoration. Lucinde's function in the novel is to revitalize and inspire the dejected hero, Julius; she is not, however, deemed capable of an intellectual relationship. The novel has been recently translated by Peter Firchow (Minneapolis: University of Minnesota Press, 1971).

16. See Walzel, *German Romanticism*, pp. 163–184 (on the German Romantic poets' fondness for folk legends); Meredith, *Westminster Review* 67 (April 1857): 618; Walzel, p. 232 (on Richter); and cf. E. V. Brewer, "The Influence of Jean Paul Richter on George Meredith's Conception of the Comic," *Journal of English and German Philology* 29 (1930): 243–255.

17. Meredith, *Westminster Review* 68 (Oct. 1857): 589. See Archibald Strong's comparison of Meredith and Wordsworth in *Three Studies in Shelley and an Essay on Nature in Wordsworth and Meredith* (London: Oxford University Press, 1921), pp. 148–189.

18. In *Keats and the Victorians* (New Haven: Yale University Press, 1944), George Ford considers this less desirable aspect of Keats's influence (e.g., pp. 77, 171). Lionel Stevenson notes, apropos of Meredith's "determination to achieve distinction of phrase" in *Sandra Belloni*, that Swinburne claimed to have seen the novel's original draft "which was then written in 'pure, sweet, Thackerayan English,' " before it was " 'translated' into an artificial idiom." *The Ordeal of George Meredith*, p. 128.

19. E.g., *Letters*, I, 10, on "the laurels that some day or other he means to have," emended to "hopes to have"; 6, "I prepared myself, when I published, to meet with injustice and slight"; 18, "I would have given forth no volume bearing the title of *Poems* without full belief (and such a consciousness may be felt in all humility) that I was a Poet." See Jerome H. Buckley's excellent chapter on "The Spasmodic School" in *The Victorian Temper* (Cambridge, Mass.: Harvard University Press, 1951). The popularizer of the term was possibly Carlyle, who in *On Heroes, Hero-Worship, and the Heroic in History* (1841), characterized Rousseau as "morbid, excitable, spasmodic." *Works*, Centenary ed., 30 vols. (London: Chapman and Hall, 1898–1901), V, 184.

20. *Letters*, II, 918; I, 297, 97. Meredith's appreciation of Byron's humor and "manliness" and his distaste for the postures of "Byronism" are reminiscent of the attitude of another radical Romantic anti-Romantic, Charles Kingsley, whose fictional heroes undergo an anti-Byronic ordeal that anticipates the pattern for Meredith's heroes. Kingsley had high praise for Meredith's 1851 *Poems*, and was in turn praised by Meredith for his "fine manly English tone" (*Letters*, I, 14). Meredith's attack on the "Spasmodism" of the 1850s in *Westminster Review* 68 (Oct. 1857): 585, follows the lines of Kingsley's attack on the "spasmodic, vague, extravagant, effeminate, school of poetry,"

ostensibly inspired by Byron but in fact the offspring of Shelley. See "Thoughts on Shelley and Byron," *Fraser's Magazine* (Nov. 1853), reprinted in *Byron: The Critical Heritage,* ed. Andrew Rutherford (New York: Barnes & Noble, 1970), p. 360.

21. *Letters,* I, 330, 432; "Essay: On the Idea of Comedy and of the Uses of the Comic Spirit," *Works,* XXIII, 43.

22. Karl Kroeber, *Romantic Narrative Art* (Madison: University of Wisconsin Press, 1960), chap. 8.

23. Georg Lukács, *The Historical Novel,* trans. Hannah and Stanley Mitchell (Harmondsworth: Penguin Books, 1969), p. 33. Cf. Ramon Fernandez: "Meredith is the first to have shown that in the order of life a romantic or decadent judgement is always a false judgement . . . He beheaded romanticism." *Messages,* trans. Montgomery Belgion (New York: Harcourt, Brace, 1927), p. 190. Kiely, *The Romantic Novel in England* p. 151.

24. *Letters,* I, 327, 411–412. In *Beauchamp's Career,* Meredith followed Kingsley's example in *Alton Locke* (with the figure of Sandy Mackaye) by providing his hero with a Carlylean mentor. See Lionel Stevenson, "Carlyle and Meredith," in *Carlyle and His Contemporaries: Essays in Honor of Charles Richard Sanders,* ed. John Clubbe (Durham, N.C.: Duke University Press, 1976). Cf. Meredith's friend John Morley on Carlyle's weaknesses, in "Carlyle," *Critical Miscellanies,* vol. I (London, 1871).

25. Kettle, *"Beauchamp's Career,"* in *Meredith Now,* pp. 202, 203–204.

26. E.g., Justin M'Carthy, "Novels with a Purpose," *Westminster Review* 26 (July 1864), reprinted in *Meredith: The Critical Heritage,* p. 127; Juliet Mitchell, *"The Ordeal of Richard Feverel:* A Sentimental Education," in *Meredith Now,* pp. 88–91.

27. See Phyllis Bartlett's discussion of the autobiographical aspects of the novel and of the ironical references to chivalric romance that were largely removed in Meredith's revised version, "Richard Feverel, Knight-Errant," *Bulletin of the New York Public Library* 63 (July 1959): 329–340; and Beer, *Meredith: A Change of Masks,* p. 20. In his 1851 poem "London by Lamplight," Meredith expresses the wish to be the savior of the fallen women he gazes on.

28. "Then truly the System triumphed," Meredith says, without disrespect, of the pure love Richard feels for Lucy (Works, II, 119; and see *Letters,* I, 40), thereby apparently justifying the Rousseauesque premises of Sir Austin's reasoning, but creating a problem in interpretation for subsequent readers of the novel. Richard's love for Lucy (whose name is perhaps meant to suggest Lucy Gray's) is never seen without an egoistic "taint of personality" and possessiveness.

29. *Diana of the Crossways, Works,* XV, 12.

30. Deploring the many imitations of *Jane Eyre* on the literary market, he suggested *Robinson Crusoe* as a more objective first-person

narrative model. *Westminster Review* 67 (April 1857): 613. It is possible, however, that he drew on Charlotte Brontë's unfinished sketch "Emma" for the depiction of the young Harry Richmond, deposited in school as a nobleman's son and then forgotten, with his bills left unpaid, by his father. As in the case of *Vittoria*, Meredith began the novel in the hope of writing a romantic, adventure-filled book that would at last achieve for him some measure of "popularity" (*Letters*, I, 255).

31. *Letters*, I, 453; Lukács p. 35. For the *Bildungsroman* aspect of *Harry Richmond*, see Jerome H. Buckley, *Season of Youth: The Bildungsroman from Dickens to Golding* (Cambridge, Mass.: Harvard University Press, 1974), chap. 3; and Margaret Tarratt, "The Adventures of Harry Richmond—Bildungsroman and Historical Novel," in *Meredith Now*, pp. 165–187. Princess Ottilia's name was perhaps chosen by Meredith in homage to the heroine of Goethe's *Elective Affinities*.

32. Stevenson, "A Gossip on Romance," p. 250.

33. Quoted in Siegfried Sassoon, *Meredith* (Port Washington: Kennikat Press reprint, 1969), p. 110. "One is tempted to say that Harry Richmond is the final wish-fulfillment of Meredith's boyish dreams" of "vast wealth" and "royal descent," says Lionel Stevenson in *The Ordeal of George Meredith*, p. 184. The novel might also have been planned as a parody of the Scott novels involving the Stuart Pretenders.

34. See Beer, *Meredith: A Change of Masks*, p. 68: "The end of the book reasserts the demonic power of fantasy." It is curious how Meredith diverts attention away from the feudal generosity of Squire Beltham: when Janet reads him "the long list of his charities," Harry coldly responds, "He had plenty" (X, 296).

35. *Letters* I, 454.

36. Carlyle, *Sartor Resartus, Works*, I, 153; Kettle, p. 203.

37. *Beauchamp's Career*, vols. XI and XII of *Works*, XI, 31, 310. All further citations are in the text. Chandler, *A Dream of Order*, p. 39.

38. *Letters*, I, 348, 376–377, 443–444.

39. Young, Introduction to the World's Classics ed. of *Beauchamp's Career* (London: Oxford University Press, 1950), p. xiii; Pritchett, *George Meredith and English Comedy* (London: Chatto & Windus, 1970), p. 104.

40. Kettle, p. 190.

41. On the basis of the depictions of women in Meredith's novels before *The Egoist*, Arabella Shore noted: "He has so portrayed them that we can believe him to have, kept to himself, an ideal of something rarer still, of what woman might be, perhaps will be, of what possibly some women even now are." *British Quarterly Review* 69 (April 1879), reprinted in *Meredith: The Critical Heritage*, p. 201.

42. Goode, "*The Egoist:* Anatomy of Striptease?," in *Meredith Now*, p. 222. Diana appears in *Diana of the Crossways* (1885), Nesta in *One of Our Conquerors* (1891), Matey Weyburn and Aminta in *Lord Ormont and His Aminta* (1894), and Carinthia Jane in *The Amazing Marriage* (1895).

Index

Index